ORTHODOX AND WESLEYAN SCRIPTURAL UNDERSTANDING AND PRACTICE

Orthodox and Wesleyan Scriptural Understanding and Practice

edited by

S T Kimbrough, Jr.

ST VLADIMIR'S SEMINARY PRESS
CRESTWOOD, NEW YORK 10707
2005

Library of Congress Cataloging-in-Publication Data

Consultation on Orthodox and Wesleyan Spirituality (2nd : 2000 : Trinity College, Bristol, England)

Orthodox and Wesleyan Scriptural understanding and practice / edited by S T Kimbrough, Jr.

p. cm.

"The essays in this volume are a collection of selected presentations from the Second Consultation on Orthodox and Wesleyan Spirituality held at Trinity College, June 16–20, 2000, in Bristol, UK, and from the Third Consultation convened at the Orthodox Spiritual Academy in Crete, Greece, August 1–7, 2002"—Introd.

Includes bibliographical references.

ISBN-13: 978–0–88141–301–4

ISBN-10: 0–88141–301–1

1. Bible—Hermeneutics—Congresses. 2. Orthodox Eastern Church—Doctrines—Congresses. 3. Wesleyan Church—Doctrines—Congresses. I. Kimbrough, S T, 1936– II. Consultation on Orthodox and Wesleyan Spirituality (3rd : 2002 : Orthodox Spiritual Academy, Crete, Greece) III. Title.

BS476.C593 2005
220.609—dc22

2005032933

ST VLADIMIR'S SEMINARY PRESS
575 Scarsdale Rd., Crestwood, NY 10707
1-800-204-2665
www.svspress.com

ISBN 0–88141–301–1
ISBN 978–088141–301–4

PRINTED IN THE UNITED STATES OF AMERICA

Contents

Abbreviations

BEM	*Baptism, Eucharist, and Ministry*
GOTR	*Greek Orthodox Theological Review*
LCL	Library of Christian Literature
NPNF	*Nicene and Post-Nicene Fathers*
OSL	Order of St. Luke
PG	Patrologia graeca
SVTQ	*Saint Vladimir's Theological Quarterly*

Contributors

The Rev. Dr. Timothy L. Bryan, Faculty Chair, Humanities, Philosophy, Religious Studies, The University of Phoenix (Colorado Campus)

The Rev. Dr. Ted Campbell, President and Professor of Church History, Garrett-Evangelical Theological Seminary, Evanston, Illinois

The Rev. Dr. Kenneth Carveley, Lecturer in Church History, Liturgy, and Cistercian Studies, Director of Studies, The Northern Ordination Course, The College of the Resurrection, Mirfield United Kingdom

The Rev. Dr. James H. Charlesworth, George L. Collord Professor of New Testament Language and Literature, Editor and Director of the Dead Sea Scrolls Project, Princeton Theological Seminary

Dr. Tamara Grdzelidze, Executive Secretary, Faith and Order, World Council of Churches, Geneva, Switzerland

The Rev. Dr. Thomas Hopko, Dean Emeritus, St. Vladimir's Orthodox Theological Seminary, Crestwood, New York

The Rev. Dr. S T Kimbrough, Jr., Associate General Secretary for Mission Evangelism, The General Board of Global Ministries, The United Methodist Church, New York, New York

Dr. Dimitar Popmarinov Kirov, Associate Professor, Orthodox Theological Faculty, University of Veliko Tarnovo, Bulgaria

Dr. Nicholas Lossky, Professor Emeritus at the University of Paris; Professor of Western Church History at Saint Sergius Orthodox Theological Institute in Paris, deacon of the Russian Orthodox Church

The Rev. Dr. John A. McGuckin, Professor of Early Church History at Union Theological Seminary; and Professor of Byzantine Christian Studies at Columbia University

THE REV. DR. GEORGE MULRAIN, President, Conference of the Methodist Church in the Caribbean and the Americas

THE REV. DR. THEODORE STYLIANOPOULOS, Archbishop Iakovos Professor of Orthodox Theology and Professor of New Testament, Holy Cross Greek Orthodox School of Theology, Brookline, Massachusetts

DR. ELIZABETH THEOKRITOFF, independent Orthodox scholar and translator, who has lectured at Holy Cross Orthodox Theological Seminary, Brookline, Massachusetts and the Institute for Orthodox Christian Studies in Cambridge, United Kingdom

DR. PETROS VASSILIADIS, Professor of New Testament, University of Thessaloniki, Thessaloniki, Greece

THE REV. DR. GEOFFREY WAINWRIGHT, Cushman Professor of Theology at The Divinity School, Duke University, Durham, North Carolina

THE REV. DR. MAXINE E. WALKER, Professor of Literature and Director, Wesleyan Center for 21st Century Studies, Point Loma University

THE REV. DR. KAREN B. WESTERFIELD TUCKER, Professor of Worship, Boston University School of Theology, Boston, Massachusetts

DR. GRANT WHITE, Principal of the Institute for Orthodox Christian Studies and a senior member of St. Edmund's College, Cambridge

THE REV. DR. FRANCES YOUNG, Professor Emeritus, formerly Edward Cadbury Professor of Theology in the University of Birmingham, Birmingham, United Kingdom

Introduction

The essays in this volume are a collection of selected presentations from the Second Consultation on Orthodox and Wesleyan Spirituality held at Trinity College, June 16–20, 2000, in Bristol, UK, and from the Third Consultation convened at the Orthodox Spiritual Academy in Crete, Greece, August 1–7, 2002, sponsored by the General Board of Global Ministries of the United Methodist Church and the faculty of St. Vladimir's Orthodox Theological Seminary, Crestwood, New York. They address scriptural authority and interpretation in the Orthodox and Wesleyan traditions and are published here in four sections: (1) Orthodox Scriptural Understanding and Practice, (2) Mutual Learning between Orthodox and Methodists, (3) Wesleyan Scriptural Understanding and Practice, and (4) Liturgy and Scriptural Interpretation. In the last section, there are two chapters on the Feast of the Transfiguration, which are specifically related to the context and date of the Third Consultation. The Feast of Transfiguration in the Orthodox calendar falls on August 6, and its celebration was attended by all participants of the Third Consultation.

Part 1: Orthodox Scriptural Understanding and Practice (Chapters 1–5)

In chapter 1, "Canon and Authority of Scripture: An Orthodox Hermeneutical Perspective," Professor Petros Vassiliadis contends that Orthodox hermeneutical views are difficult to delineate and are more fluid than those of Western Christianity—Roman Catholic, Anglican, and Protestant. Understanding Orthodoxy as "a way of life," he views liturgical practice as a key to any Orthodox interpretation of the Bible. Vassiliadis expands this perspective further when he states, "the Eucharistic dimension is perhaps the only safe criterion in ascertaining the way in which the Orthodox approach any issue pertinent to the Bible. Hence, the Orthodox approach to scripture is primarily ecclesial."

Vassiliadis also addresses questions of Orthodox pneumatology in relationship to canonical authority, as well as an Orthodox Christological perspective, which sees scripture as a coherent whole held together in Christ.

In chapter 2, "Patterns of Biblical Exegesis in the Cappadocian Fathers," Father John A. McGuckin is concerned with the early church's use of scripture, and particularly as expressed in the Cappadocian Fathers. According to his understanding of the scripture principle of *kerygma*, the New Testament writings are not a commentary on the Old Testament. Rather, in the context of the *kairos* of salvation, the Old Testament is a commentary on the New Testament, and Jesus becomes determinative for the church's interpretation of the scriptures. Thus, "the scriptures become a vast trope, an extended metaphor of the experience of God in Christ."

McGuckin then discusses the exegetical procedures of the Cappadocian Fathers: Gregory the Theologian, Basil of Caesarea, and Gregory of Nyssa. In all three he sees, though somewhat differently, an expression of the patristic approach to the Christ Mystery, which, as McGuckin says, "is the overall *skopos* of the biblical text." He underscores the tension between the literal and spiritual senses of scripture. In no way does the author seek a neo-patristic synthesis, the view of the Cappadocians who seek elsewhere the Christ Mystery, which takes place only within the community of salvation and which sees Christian scripture as "an act of faith, not an independent source of it."

Chapter 3, "Holy Scripture, Interpretation, and Spiritual Cognition in St. Simeon the New Theologian" by Father Theodore Stylianopoulos presents St. Simeon's understanding and interpretation of scripture from within his own (St. Simeon's) exegetical writings, relates his interpretive views to contemporary Orthodox scholarship, and addresses the current state of hermeneutics in Orthodoxy today.

Clearly the author sees Symeon's constant, direct, and abundant use of scripture as normative for Orthodox hermeneutics. The primacy of scriptural testimony and the interdependence of scripture and tradition are emphases which are characteristic of Symeon's interpretation. Stylianopoulis stresses two points in particular: (1) he is uncompromising in emphasizing diligence in the study of the scriptures, but the purpose thereof is first and foremost the explication of the gospel and the way of salvation, and (2) he is a constant advocate of hearing and heeding the Word in praxis and in the integration of study and praxis.

Stylianopoulos also discusses the importance of mystical cognition in Symeon's interpretation, i.e., the role of mystical experiences in his biblical interpretation. While the author addresses the vital role of liturgy in Orthodox interpretation of scripture, he acknowledges that the catechetical and doctrinal use of scripture in Symeon's writings and among the Church Fathers continues to be an equally important dimension of Orthodox interpretation of scripture.

Dr. Elizabeth Theokritoff avers in chapter 4 that there is a didactic dimension of liturgy which enables the learning of scripture and its meaning. She examines it from four perspectives: (1) the experience of salvation, (2) the theology of salvation, (3) a typological interpretation of the Old Testament and texts for the Mother of God, and (4) an allegorical interpretation of scripture in the services of Lent. Theokritoff illustrates various ways of interpreting scripture and the diverse levels of meaning found in the scriptural texts. She provides an excellent explication of how scripture is communicated through the various hymns of the Orthodox liturgies.

The eschatological aspect of the didactic dimension of liturgy, as regards scripture, is extremely important. As one celebrates God's saving activity, the learning process is anticipatory. It looks forward to the fulfillment of the church and God's Kingdom and one's own fulfillment in the life of the community of faith.

In the final part of the chapter, Theokritoff illustrates how allegorical interpretation of scripture enlightens one's spiritual journey with Christ and the church, and one's own self-understanding as a follower of Christ.

Professor Dimitar Popmarinov Kirov explores the metaphor of light in chapter 5, "The Mysticism of Light in the Scriptures and in the Orthodox Worship Tradition," as essential to encounter with God and integral to the deepest mystery of Orthodox spiritual practice. The chapter is divided into three sections. In the first, the author explores light in the Old Testament; in the second, light in the New Testament; in the third, the role of light in the Orthodox liturgy.

Light as it appears in the Old and New Testaments culminates in a holistic mystical experience of God, who is light, in the liturgy. The Transfiguration of Christ becomes normative for Christian spiritual experience, and Kirov emphasizes that theophany leads to *theosis*, the goal of all Christian experience. The way of those who seek God is "enlightening, transfiguration, and deification."

Part 2: Mutual Learning between Orthodox and Methodists (Chapters 6–9)

While there have been a number of comparisons of the Wesleyan and Orthodox traditions, Dr. James H. Charlesworth maintains in chapter 6, "Two Similar Paths: Methodism and Greek Orthodoxy," that one of the main resonations of both traditions is that similarly they promote doxological piety more than dogmatic theology.

At the outset of the chapter, Charlesworth traces a series of seven commonalities of Methodism and Orthodoxy. His more profound analysis resides, however, in the treatment of theocentricity, canon and inspiration, theology in hymns and prayers, the way to perfection, and the somatic experience of God. In all of these dimensions of the discussion, Charlesworth sees Methodism and Greek Orthodoxy as placing "prayer and worship above systematic theology." In addition, he views John Wesley's "collegial formula for theological enrichment" ("If thine heart is as my heart . . . Give me thine hand") as unique in Christian history, for it "protects religious freedom and grounds theology in the non-systematic dimension of phenomenology." It is precisely here that the resonation with Orthodoxy is apparent.

In chapter 7, "The Authority of Scriptural Interpretation: An Orthodox Perspective on the Positions of John Wesley and Modern Methodism," Dr. Tamara Grdzelidze sees a primary difference between the Orthodox and modern Methodist perspectives regarding the authority of scriptural interpretation. The Orthodox have a very strong ecclesiological understanding of this matter, while contemporary Methodism demonstrates a rather loose ecclesiology. In her view, John Wesley is less interested in an ecclesiology that is related to the authority and interpretation of scripture.

The author provides a useful summary of contemporary Methodist ecumenical dialogues with Roman Catholics and Orthodox, as well as some ecumenical Anglican dialogues, especially as they relate to scriptural interpretation.

Grdzelidze concludes by raising the question as to whether modern Methodism is moving toward a stronger ecclesiology.

In chapter 8, "God's Word Proclaimed: The Homiletics of Grace and Demand in John Chrysostom and John Wesley," Dr. Frances Young compares these two divines as homeliticians. After numerous illustrations and citations from them, she concludes that both drew the same fundamental message from scripture: "the inseparability of grace and demand."

Young sets both men in their contexts and compares their homiletical styles and message. While the author finds many convergences, she also notes many differences. John Chrysostom preached in a liturgical context, while John Wesley's sermons were often preached to large crowds outdoors. The former's sermons are preserved largely as preached, while the latter's are generally revisions of what was originally preached.

The series of excellent illustrations from the homiletical texts of both men on a variety of themes provide helpful insights, which undergird the emphasis of both homileticians on the inseparability of grace and demand.

Chapter 9, "Lancelot Andrewes: A Bridge between Orthodoxy and the Wesley Brothers in the Realm of Prayer," by Professor Nicholas Lossky focuses on the reality that Lancelot Andrewes, who preceded the Wesleys by a century, but of whom the Wesleys were keenly aware and by whom they were influenced, was deeply rooted in patristics. This was, however, not merely high knowledge of the Early Church Fathers; rather, what Andrewes and the Wesleys share is "the patristic experience of God, deeply rooted in the scriptures and the liturgy of the Church." Lossky understands this to be an ecclesial experience of God with the Church Fathers in Andrewes and in the Wesleys. With illustrations of prayers from Andrewes's *Preces Privatae* and Charles Wesley's hymns, the author shows how close both are to the patristic experience of God, for they "prayed privately in ecclesial, liturgical terms."

In conclusion, Lossky also reveals that the notion of deification, *theosis*, found in Lancelot Andrewes and Charles Wesley, links them to Orthodoxy. The author suggests that it is through the patristic theology of Andrewes that one finds a primary linkage of the Wesleys to Orthodoxy.

Part 3: Wesleyan Scriptural Understanding and Practice (Chapters 10–15)

In chapter 10, Ted Campbell outlines the struggle that Methodists throughout their two-hundred-plus-year history have faced, either to reject or accept the value of "Tradition" or "tradition" as relates to the interpretation of scripture and the life of faith. While he shows that John Wesley seems to have departed from the Reformation understanding of scripture as its own best interpreter, and that Wesley seems to allow that what we would identify as "tradition" can in fact be normative for interpreting the meaning of the Bible, Methodists of the succeeding two centuries tended to follow the doctrine of the sufficiency of scripture; that is, "scripture interpreted by scripture."

Since Vatican II, however, as indicated by the broad acceptance of what has been called "the Wesleyan Quadrilateral" (scripture, tradition, experience, and reason), there has been a shift toward a general acceptance of tradition as a viable interpreter of scripture. Thus, Methodism in recent years has tended to return to John Wesley's openness to tradition. Campbell illustrates this in a number of ways; for example, the first inclusion of the Nicene-Constantinopolitan Creed in a Methodist hymnal in 1964, the 1972 United Methodist statement "Our Theological Task," and the role of Methodist theologian Albert Outler in ecumenical dialogue.

In chapter 11, "Charles Wesley's Lyrical Commentary on the Holy Scriptures," S T Kimbrough, Jr. emphasizes that no discussion of Wesleyan interpretation of scripture and its authority can be complete without an examination of Charles Wesley's two-volume commentary on the Bible, *Short Hymns on Select Passages of the Holy Scriptures* (1762), which was written completely in poetical verse and which he refused to let his brother, John, edit. Wesley moves from Genesis to the Book of Revelation, focusing on a central idea, word, phrase, or theme of a biblical passage, the citation of which generally precedes each hymn or poem.

Kimbrough surveys the background of Charles Wesley's scriptural interpretation. While there is in Charles Wesley's writings a tension between a biblical literalism, and a more open-ended interpretation of scripture, he writes:

> The word in the bare literal sense,
> Tho' heard ten thousand times, and read,
> Can never of itself dispense
> The saving power which wakes the dead.

He understands that it is Christ who unseals the sacred book, a view clearly concurrent with Orthodoxy.

There follows a study of Charles Wesley's use of scriptural language, biblical languages, and his own translations of scripture, and an analysis of a series of theological concepts which are seminal to the Wesleyan and Orthodox traditions: the Holy Trinity (including a theology of the Mystery), the church ("His mystical body and One!"), universalism, holiness, perfection, and love.

This is a foundational study for future analyses of the congruencies and differences in scriptural interpretation among the Early Church Fathers and contemporary Orthodoxy and Methodism.

Chapter 12, "The Visitation of the Word," by Dr. Kenneth Carveley, involves what the author calls an "experiential trilogy" of the visitation of the Word drawn from his encounters with Orthodoxy and his own Methodist background. The trilogy consists of "the scent of truth," "a heart strangely warmed," and an encounter of Mary's engagement with the angel, which Carveley titles "on a wing and a prayer."

The author makes a strong case for *lectio divina* as mediating Christ's presence in Orthodoxy and Methodism. He then draws interesting parallels between the symbolic-iconographic use of the text of scripture in Orthodoxy and John Wesley's "scripture sense and scripture phrase," and the way in which Christ speaks through these dimensions of both traditions.

Dr. George Mulrain speaks in chapter 13, "The Impact of the Psalms on Worship within Methodism," as one who has grown up and had an extended ministry in the Methodism of the Caribbean, which has strong ties to British Methodism. He begins his study of psalmody in Caribbean Methodism with a brief analysis of the importance of psalmody in the Wesley tradition, paying tribute to the Anglican tradition from which it comes. Acknowledging the importance of the Book of Common Prayer psalter and the metrical psalmody of Thomas Sternhold, Mulrain describes the interest of John and Charles Wesley in both the liturgical and private use of the psalms.

While American Methodists rejected the form of the psalter prepared by John Wesley for use in America, and tended to read the psalms rather than sing or chant them, the Methodists of the Caribbean were inclined to retain psalm chanting in their worship. In recent times, however, there has been a decline in this practice.

Mulrain points out the importance of the use of the full spectrum of the psalter in worship, for it encourages congregations to bring the breadth of human experience, including rage and violence, as an offering to God in worship. He avers, "Chanting the complete psalm is to be preferred to singing individual verses, because in so doing, we are more likely to receive the total picture of our relationship with God." This is at the heart of his plea for the restoration of psalm singing or chanting in Methodist worship.

In chapter 14, "At Home in the Body of Scripture," Dr. Maxine Walker provides an interesting analysis of the metaphor of "home" as a means of mirroring the perceptions of a contemporary Orthodox woman, Frederica Mathewes-Green, and the eighteenth-century mother of John and Charles Wesley, Susanna Wesley. Walker's analysis of the metaphor is divided into three sections: (1) "home is the incarnate God in whom we live and move and have our being," (2) "home is a lens for reading and interpreting," and (3) "home is being in communion."

In the case of both women, Walker shows how from different perspectives, Mathewes-Green being essentially visually oriented, and Wesley being essentially verbally oriented, the goal of their spirituality is basically the same—*theosis.* All discernment of God's scripture and revelation leads to *theosis.* Mathewes-Green perceives this revelation through the visual world and ethos of Orthodoxy, and Wesley through the verbal world of a wide open spectrum of readings "in ancient and modern philosophy, ethics, natural religion, and poetry." Walker enriches her enlightening study of the "home" metaphor with a wide range of illustrations from home, family life, and the Orthodox and Wesleyan tradition.

Dr. Timothy Bryan focuses on "The Use of Scripture in the Lives of Early Methodist Preachers" in chapter 15. His primary interest is in the Anglican priest and Methodist apologist John William Fletcher and his scriptural interpretation, which illumines his understanding of the Christian doctrine of perfection.

After an introduction to Fletcher, Bryan explains how Bible reading, contemplation, and prayer shaped the life and ministry of this man of God, whom John Wesley saw as his successor to lead the Methodist movement.

Bryan refers particularly to the following works of Fletcher to illustrate and glean various aspects of his biblical interpretation: *An Equal Check to Antinomianism and Pharisaism, The Last Check to Antinomianism, Portrait of Saint Paul,* and *Scripture Scales.* Perhaps one of the unique qualities of his scriptural interpretation was his ability "to draw together apparently disparate passages and conflicting doctrines" as "an act of piety and a revelation of the whole truth." A hallmark of this approach to Christian faith and life was Fletcher's view of "strength in the Scriptures and Christ."

Part 4: Liturgy and Scriptural Interpretation (Chapters 16–20)

Chapter 16, "The Poet as Expositor in the Golden Age of Byzantine Hymnography and in the Experience of the Church" by Dr. Elizabeth Theokritoff, discusses the role of liturgical poetry in the interpretation of scripture. She does so by drawing on the hymnic literature of three outstanding Orthodox hymnographers—Romanos the Melodist (ca. 560), John of Damascus (ca. 665–749), and Kosmos of Maiouma (ca. 675–752)—and Methodism's most outstanding hymnographer, Charles Wesley (1707–1788). Theokritoff's averment that "hymnography is the primary way in which the tradition of scriptural interpretation is passed on, since it is readily accessible to every churchgoer in a way systematic commentaries are not," holds true for both the Orthodox and Wesleyan traditions.

The author draws on the hymnography of the three Orthodox hymn writers mentioned above by examining various *kantakia*, the canon of the Baptism of Christ, canons on the Transfiguration, and the Easter canon of John Damascene. Where appropriate, she interjects commonalities and differences with Charles Wesley's interpretation of scripture, particularly in reference to texts treated by both the Orthodox hymnographers and Wesley. While the hymnographers of both traditions often explicate the universal meaning of a text, Wesley tends to emphasize the personal and moral implications. Characteristic of both traditions, however, is that the "one thing hymns teach us about reading scripture . . . is to be alert to the resonances of every word."

In chapter 17, according to Grant Sperry White, "The Recovery of the Great Eucharistic Prayer in the Wesleyan Tradition" marks a significant change liturgically, theologically, and ecumenically for Methodists or people in the Wesleyan tradition. The prayer to which he refers is "the ecumenically popular West Syrian tradition of Eucharistic prayer," which includes an extended narrative of thanksgiving focused on salvation history and climaxing in the gift of the Holy Spirit after Christ's resurrection.

The author traces the history in the Methodist connection of the development of the inclusion of this prayer, noting that British Methodism in recent times has included a version somewhat different from The United Methodist Church of North America. Both restore, however, the *epeklesis*, a prayer for the invocation of the Holy Spirit, the spirit of which has been implicit in Methodism but which now has been made liturgically explicit.

Linked with the recovery of the great Eucharist prayer is also a recovery of a biblical and patristic spirituality, which can be lived out anew when this prayer is offered. In the recovery, Sperry White also sees the opening of an immediate point of contact—namely, ascetic theology and practice—between Wesleyan and Orthodox Christians. It gives the former as well "the opportunity to live into Eucharistic ecclesiology" and to see themselves as *ecclesia* rather than *ecclesiola*.

Along with an example of how one United Methodist congregation is living into and living out this recovered prayer, the author provides an appendix of the complete text of the United Methodist "Great Thanksgiving" from "A Service of Word and Table" found in *The United Methodist Hymnal* of 1989.

In chapter 18, "The Liturgical Functioning of Orthodox Troparia and Wesleyan Hymns," Karen B. Westerfield Tucker addresses the commonalities and dissimilarities of liturgical singing in Orthodoxy and Methodism. Interestingly, both traditions develop musically from simplicity to complexity, from monodic to polyphonic singing.

Through numerous helpful examples of Orthodox *troparia* and Wesleyan hymns the author discusses the differences and similarities of singing in the two traditions. As striking as the common use of metaphors, images, and biblical language is in the *troparia* and hymns, perhaps even more striking are the shared hermeneutical principles emphasized by Westerfield Tucker. For example, "both read the story of the old covenant through the lens of the new," which often leads to typological interpretation of events and persons in the Old Testament.

Liturgically, the Orthodox and Wesleyan traditions realize the dialogical aspect of prayer and praise through singing, which enables the faith community's encounter with God.

Father Thomas Hopko provides a thorough description and anaysis of "The Transfiguration Liturgy in the Orthodox Church" in chapter 19. He also includes the preparatory liturgy of the Prefeast of Transfiguration, which invites the faithful to participate in the feast. It announces also both "the theological content" and significance of the coming event.

The prescribed biblical texts for both the Prefeast and the Transfiguration (for matins and the divine liturgy) are noted in detail. Not only are the specific texts indicated, but the scriptural allusions in the hymns are carefully cited.

Throughout the discussion, the author points out the differences between the Slavonic and the Byzantine liturgies of the Transfiguration.

In the concluding sections of the chapter, Father Hopko addresses specific themes of the Transfiguration liturgy: "God's glory in the face of Christ," "Light from light," "Transformation of Adam and all creation," "Jesus Christ, God, and man," "Moses and Elijah," "Transfiguration and crucifixion," "Blessing of the grapes and first fruits" (in the Byzantine liturgy only).

In chapter 20, "The Transfiguration of Jesus in Wesleyan Exegesis and Application," Geoffrey Wainwright brings together for the first time a summary of the interpretations of John and Charles Wesley of the biblical passages relating to the Transfiguration. Before launching into these interpretations, however, Wainwright draws a contrast between the Orthodox understanding of the Transfiguration as an explicit Trinitarian mystery and the Wesleyan understanding, which has a much stronger Christological focus, sociological purpose, and eschatological reach.

The primary source of John Wesley's biblical exegesis of the Transfiguration comes from his *Explanatory Notes upon the New Testament.* The "Wesleyan Application" of which Wainwright speaks is found in a series of hymns by Charles Wesley which are primarily from three sources: *Short Hymns on Select Passages of the Holy Scriptures* (1762), *Hymns and Sacred Poems* (1740), and hitherto unpublished poems (see the citation of *The Unpublished Poetry of Charles Wesley* in footnote 12 of this chapter).

The Christocentric emphasis of John Wesley's interpretation of the Transfiguration is applied by Charles Wesley in poetical language which seeks "to recognize and promote the inclusion of believers into the history of salvation, which the scriptures narrate and announce," according to Wainwright. Hence, the poems emphasize that the resurrected life can be anticipated in the present, we may rise now as new creatures, one may be transfigured in selfless humility. These realities are made possible by an encounter with the transfigured and risen Christ, who is "met in prayer and meditation on the scriptures." In the Wesleyan tradition, one encounters him in evangelical preaching, the "mysteries" of the sacraments (baptism and Holy Communion), forgiveness, and healing.

At the conclusion of the chapter, Wainwright ventures a suggestion as to what the discovery of the Transfiguration could mean for Methodists, some of whom now celebrate a "Transfiguration Sunday" on the Sunday immediately preceding Lent.

S T Kimbrough, Jr.
Editor

PART 1

Orthodox Scriptural Understanding and Practice

1

Canon and Authority of Scripture: An Orthodox Hermeneutical Perspective

Petros Vassiliadis

Preliminary Remarks

To address any issue, "from an Orthodox perspective," is an extremely difficult task. On what ground and from what sources can one really establish an Orthodox perspective? The Roman Catholics have Vatican II to draw from; the Orthodox do not. The Lutherans have the Augsburg Confession; the Orthodox do not. The only authoritative so-called "sources" the Orthodox possess are in fact common to the rest of the Christians: the Bible and the Tradition. How can one establish a distinctly Orthodox perspective on a basis which is common to non-Orthodox as well? In addition, the breadth and extent of these so-called "sources" is nowadays strongly debated, at least within the scholarly community, and sometimes they are even differently interpreted.

Another issue which makes an "Orthodox perspective" problematic is that Orthodoxy always appears as something exotic, an interesting "eastern communitarian phenomenon" *vis-à-vis* the "Western" individualistic mentality, provoking the curiosity and enriching the knowledge of Western believers and theologians. According to an eminent Orthodox theologian this role has been played too much up to now.[1] Most serious interpreters of Orthodoxy define it as referring to the wholeness of the people of God who share the right conviction (or the *doxa* = right opinion) concerning the event of God's salvation in Christ and his Church, and the right expression (*orthopraxia*) of this faith.[2] Everyone is, therefore, invited by Orthodoxy to transcend confessions and inflexible institutions without necessarily denying them. Orthodoxy is not to be identified only with us Orthodox in the historical sense and with all our limitations and shortcomings,[3] especially the scholarly ones. The term was originally given to the Church as a whole over against the heretics, who, of their own choice, split from the main body of the Church. The term is, thus, exclusive for all those who willingly fall away from the historical stream of life of the One Church, but it is inclusive for those who profess their spiritual belonging to that stream.[4] Orthodoxy, in other words, has ecclesial rather than confessional or even historical connotations. And it is from this angle that I propose to tackle the subject.

What I am going to present in this chapter as "personal reflection for further discussion" with non-Orthodox biblical scholars is the way Orthodox theology in a broad sense addresses specific questions pertinent to the canon—and by extension the authority—of the Bible (why a canon, what canon, and how, etc.); namely the whole issue of the Bible within the given religious system, the Eastern Orthodox Church. After all, the canon is an issue closely related to the way the Bible is viewed and considered in the Church, as all Holy Writings are viewed and considered in any given religious system.

Despite all I said above as the necessary preliminary remarks, the Orthodox have issued from time to time official doctrinal statements concerning the Bible, which under certain theological conditions can lend authority to the Orthodox perspective of the canon and authority of the Bible. These are the canons of certain local synods (Laodicea, Carthage, etc.) and of some Fathers (Athanasios, Basil, Gregory of Nazianzos, Amphilochios of Iconion), whose canonical status became universal (ecumenical) through the decisions of the famous Penthekti (Quinisext) Council in Troullo (691–692 C.E.). But all of these canons leave the issue of the number of the canonical books of the Old Testament (and to an extent some of the New Testament too [e.g., Apocalypse]) unsettled.[5] It may not be an exaggeration to state that the undivided Church has not solved the issue of, and therefore has not imposed upon her members, a canon of the Bible.

The whole problem was brought in a more rigid and authoritarian way to the attention of the Orthodox only after the tension between the Roman Catholic Church and the Protestants. After the model of the Western "confessions," a number of *omologiai* (Confessions of the Orthodox Faith) from the 17th century onwards (Cyril, Mitrophanis, Mogila, Dositheos, etc.)[6] started to come out, including statements concerning the canon of the Bible. With no problem in the content of the New Testament canon, these statements differ from both Catholic and Protestant canons only in the Old Testament. But these statements, all coming from the period of their indirect engagement with the polemics between Catholics and Protestants, are no longer considered as representing the Orthodox tradition.[7] In addition, some of them incline toward the wider canon of the Old Testament (49 books), whereas others seem to support a smaller canon (39 books), depending on their Catholic or Protestant source, or the "enemy" they wished to combat in those days.

In short, the Orthodox—having to respond to the burning issue of their fellow Christians in the West—seem to have settled on and accepted as canonical:

(a) With regard to the New Testament—together with the Catholics and the Protestants—the 27 books of the New Testament in their usual order. It is to be noted, however, that the Apocalypse still enjoys a special status, having yet to enter into liturgical usage. The only remaining problem is the text the various *autocephali* Churches use in their liturgical services. The Greek-speaking ones use the so-called Patriarchal text, a Greek edition similar to the *textus receptus*, prepared by a synodical committee in 1904, whereas the Slavic Churches use the Old Slavonic translation. The Romanian Orthodox Church uses an old Romanian translation. Only the so-called diaspora (better Western Orthodox) and the new missionary (Asian and African) Churches, plus the autonomous Finnish Orthodox Church, use modern translations, based on the critical text. It is a hopeful sign that with the modern interconfessional development in the Bible Societies movement, and the ecumenical cooperation with

Catholics and Protestants, most Orthodox Churches are in the process of new common-language translations. On a university and scholarly level, of course, the vast majority uses the critical editions, despite their shortcomings.[8]

(b) With regard to the Old Testament—together with the Catholics, the Protestants and the Jews—for sure the 38 books of the *Tanakh* (the Hebrew Scriptures), separating Ezra and Nehemiah and making a total of 39. The only difference from all of the above is that the official version in the Orthodox Church is not the Hebrew original, called the Masoretic text, but the Septuaginta. In addition to those—together with the Catholics—the Orthodox Church, following the tradition of the Early Church, has added 10 more books in the canon, which are called *Anagignoskomena* (i.e., "readable, worthy of reading"). As in the Catholic Church, these are neither of secondary authority (i.e., Deuterocanonical, a term invented in the sixteenth century by Sixtus of Siena) nor Apocrypha (i.e., non canonical, as in the Protestant Churches), a term which in the ancient Christian tradition was given to other books (the Book of Jubilees, the Assumption of Moses, the Martyrdom of Isaiah, etc.) whose authority was rejected by the Church. Those are the books the Protestants normally call Pseudepigrapha. Some Orthodox scholars, under the influence of modern scholarship and terminology, apply to them alternately the term (wrongly in my view) Deuterocanonical. In view, however, of their wide use in the liturgy, their authority can hardly be differentiated from the so-called canonical books of the Bible. It is also to be noted that the Orthodox *Anagignoskomena* do not exactly coincide with the Deuterocanonical books (only seven) of the Catholic Bible.

In short, (a) with regard to the text, the Orthodox accept the authenticity (some like *Oikonomos ex Oikonomon* even their inspiration![9]) of the Greek translation of the Septuaginta. (b) With regard to the number of the *Anagignoskomena*, these are the Catholic Deuterocanonical, plus Maccabees 3 and Esdras, and dividing Baruch from the Epistle of Jeremiah. There are some additional texts that are normally taken up in the Orthodox Bibles and are either accorded some value (like the Prayer of Manasses and Psalm 151) or added as appendices (like Maccabees 4 in the Greek version alone, or the Deuterocanonical Esdras 2 in the Slavonic version alone). (c) With regard to the sequence, as well as the naming, of the 49 books, these are as follows: Genesis, Exodus, Leviticus, Numbers, Deuteronomy (= Pentateuch), Joshua, Judges, Ruth, *Vasileion* (Regnorum) 1 and 2 (= 1 and 2 Samuel), *Vasileion* (Regnorum) 3 and 4 (= 1 and 2 Kings), *Paralipomenon* 1 and 2 (1 and 2 Chronicles), *Esdras* 1 (= Deuterocanonical), 2 *Esdras* and *Nehemiah* (= the canonical Esra), Esther (together with the Deuterocanonical additions), Judith (= Deuterocanonical), Tobit (= Deuterocanonical), (some editions [e.g., the 1928 Bratsiotis edition] follow the order cod. B and A; i.e., Tobit, Judith, Esther), Maccabees 1 and 2 (= Deuterocanonical) and 3, Psalms (in some editions plus Psalm 151 and the 9 Odes and the Prayer of Manasses), Job (in some editions after the Song of Songs), Proverbs, Ecclesiastes, Song of Songs, Wisdom of Solomon (= Deuterocanonical), Wisdom of Siracides (= Deuterocanonical), 12 Minor Prophets (starting with Hosea and ending with Malachi), Isaiah, Jeremiah, Baruch (= Deuterocanonical), Lamentations, Epistle of Jeremiah (= Deuterocanonical), Ezekiel, Daniel (together with the Deuterocanonical additions; i.e., Susana, the Prayer of Azariah and the Songs of the Three Youths, and the story of Bel and the Dragon), and

Maccabees 4 (as an appendix in the Greek versions only, whereas the Slavonic version, probably under Western influence, contains also the 2 Deuterocanonical Esdras).

What has so far been presented is the "canon" of the Bible according to the accepted, and blessed by Orthodox ecclesiastical authorities, editions of the Bible. There is neither conciliar nor official canonical or doctrinal authority attached to it as yet. Not to mention, of course, that with the so-called Oriental Orthodox Church the problem of the canon is still more complex even for the New Testament, ranging from a shorter canon to a much wider one (37 books in the Ethiopian Church). It was for this reason that in the agenda of the forthcoming Holy and Great Synod of the Orthodox Church the canon of the Bible was originally added for a final settlement. But such an event is not expected in the foreseeable future, unless a truly ecumenical Synod can ever take place. Until that time, when the entire Church of God can definitively decide about her criteria and her canonical documents, if any, the Orthodox perspective in dealing with all issues pertinent to the Bible, especially its authority, has to bear in consideration the following parameters.

1. The Liturgical Background

The essence of Orthodoxy, *vis-à-vis* Western Christianity in its entirety (i.e., Catholic, Anglican, and Protestant), is beyond any theological statements or affirmations. I would dare say it is a way of life; hence the importance of its liturgical tradition. It is exactly for this reason that the Orthodox have placed the Liturgy on such a prominent place in their theology. "The Church, according to a historic statement by the late G. Florovsky, is first of all a worshipping community. Worship comes first, doctrine and discipline second. The *lex orandi* has a privileged priority in the life of the Christian Church. The *lex credendi* depends on the devotional experience and vision of the Church."[10] Any doctrinal statement, therefore, concerning the Bible—and more specifically the canon and authority of the Bible—should come only as the natural consequence of the liturgical (i.e., eucharistic) communion experience of the Christian community, of the Church.

Post-modernity has challenged the priority of texts over experience, a syndrome still dominant in modern scholarship. It has even challenged the priority of theology over ecclesiology. I would even dare state that it has challenged the priority of faith over the communion experience of the Kingdom of God. The dogma, imposed after the Enlightenment and the Reformation over all scholarly theological outlook, that the basis of our Christian faith can be extracted only from a certain historical and critically defined *depositum fidei*, most notably from the Bible (to which usually Tradition was added), can no longer be sustained; more careful attention is now paid, and more serious reference is now given to, the eucharistic communion experience that has been responsible for and produced this *depositum fidei.*[11]

Recent scholarship is moving away from the old affirmation that the Christian community was originally initiated as a "faith community." More and more scholars are now inclined to believe that it started as a communion fellowship gathered at certain times around a Table in order to foreshadow the Kingdom of God. Of course this eucharistic Table was not "lived"—at least by all—as a Mystery cult, but as a foretaste of the coming Kingdom of God, a proleptic manifestation within the tragic realities of history of an authentic life of communion, unity, justice and equality, with no practical differentiation (soteriological and beyond) between Jews and Gentiles, slaves and free people, men and women (cf. Gal. 3.28). This was, after all, the profound meaning of the Johannine term *aionios zoe* (eternal life), or the Pauline phrase *kaine ktisis* (new creation), or even St. Ignatius's controversial expression *pharmakon athanasias* (medicine of immortality). In short, more and more scholars incline to think that it was the ritual (social, liturgical, even eucharistic worship) that gave rise to story (Gospel and other "historical" accounts, etc.), rather than the other way round.[12]

In saying all of this, I do not by any means suggest a return to a pre-critical approach to the Bible, although I do not hide my discontent with modernism, if not for anything else at least because it has over-rationalized everything from social and public life to scholarship, from emotion to imagination, seeking to over-control and to limit the irrational, the aesthetic and perhaps even the sacred. In its search to rationalize and historicize everything, modernism has transformed not only what we know and how we know it, but also how we understand ourselves. Hence the desire of a wide range of intellectuals (not limited to scholars or even theologians) for wholeness, for community, for *Gemeinschaft*, for an antidote to the fragmentation and sterility of an overly technocratic society, and at the end of the road for post-modernism.[13]

Having said all of this, it is important to reaffirm what sociologists of knowledge very often point out, that modernism, counter (alternative) modernism, post-modernism, and even demodernism are always simultaneous processes. Otherwise post-modernism can easily end up as and evaporate in a neo-traditionalism, and in the end neglect or even negate the great achievements of the Enlightenment and the ensuing scholarly critical "paradigm." The rationalistic sterility of modern life has turned to the quest for something new, something radical, which nevertheless is not always new but very often old recycled: neo-romanticism, neo-mysticism, naturalism, etc. In fact, all these neo-isms share a great deal in common with the early 18th century reactions to the modernist revolution, which Orthodox biblical scholarship should unequivocally reject.[14]

2. The Concept of Tradition

In the Orthodox Church, closely connected to the liturgical background in dealing with the Bible is the concept of tradition. Tradition (in Greek, *paradosis*), according to modern sociological definition, is the entire set of historical facts, beliefs, experiences, social and religious practices, and even philosophical doctrines or aesthetic conceptions which form an entity transmitted from one generation to another either orally or in a written and even in an artistic form. Thus, tradition constitutes a fundamental element for the existence, coherence, and advancement of human culture in any given context.

In the wider religious sphere—taking into consideration that culture is in some way connected with cult—tradition has to do more or less with the religious practices; that is, with the liturgy of a given religious system, rather than with the religious beliefs that theoretically express or presuppose these practices, without, of course, excluding them.

In Christianity, paradoxically, tradition was for quite an extensive period of time confined to the oral form of Christian faith, or more precisely to the non-biblical part of it, both written in later Christian literature or transmitted in various ways from one generation to another. Thus, tradition has come to be determined by the post-Reformation and post-Trentine dialectic opposition to the Bible, which has taken the over-simplified form: Bible and/or (even versus) Tradition. Only recently, from the beginning of the ecumenical era, has tradition acquired a new wider sense and understanding, which nevertheless has always been the authentic understanding in the ancient Church. Tradition no longer has a fragmented meaning connected to only one segment of Christian faith; it refers to the whole of Christian faith: not only to Christian doctrine but also to worship.[15]

It is not a coincidence that the two main references in the New Testament of the term in the sense of "receiving" (in Greek, *parelavon*) and "transmitting" (in Greek, *paredoka*), as recorded by St. Paul in his first epistle to the Corinthians (chs. 11 and 15), cover both the *kerygma* (doctrine in the wider sense) and the Eucharist (the heart of Christian worship).

Thus, the importance of tradition in Christianity underlines a sense of a living continuity with the Church of ancient times, of the apostolic period. Behind it lies the same determination that kept the unity of the two testaments against the Gnostic (Marcion) attempt to reject the Old Testament tradition in this sense is not viewed as something in addition to, or over against, the Bible. Scripture and Tradition are not treated as two different things, two distinct sources of the Christian faith. Scripture exists within Tradition, which although it gives a unique pre-eminence to the Bible, it also includes further developments—of course in the form of clarification and explication, not of addition—of the apostolic faith.[16]

Of course, at first glance the very concept of tradition seems to be a contradiction, since the Holy Spirit who guides the Church to all truth (Jn. 16.13) cannot be limited by traditional values only, for the "*pneuma* blows wherever he [or she] wishes" (Jn. 3.8). If we take the trinitarian and eschatological principles of Christian faith seriously into account, the Church as a *koinonia* proleptically manifesting the glory of the coming Kingdom of God (i.e., as a movement forward, toward the eschaton, a movement of continuous renewal), then she can hardly be conditioned by what has been set in the past, with the exception, of course, of the living continuity and of the communion with all humanity—in fact with all the created world—both in space and in time. The consequences of such an affirmation for reconsidering and reassessing the concept of the canon and authority of the Bible are inescapable.[17]

Thus, tradition can hardly be considered as a static entity; it is rather a dynamic reality. It is not a dead acceptance of the past but a living experience of the Holy Spirit in the present. In other words, it is a relational principle, completely incompatible with all kinds of individualism and with the absolute and strict sense of objectivism. In G. Florovsky's words, "Tradition is the witness of the Spirit; the Spirit's unceasing revelation and preaching of the Good News . . . It is not only a protective, conservative principle, but primarily the principle of growth and renewal."[18]

3. The Eucharistic Criterion

It is not an exaggeration, therefore, to state that the liturgical—more precisely the eucharistic—dimension is perhaps the only safe criterion in ascertaining the way in which the Orthodox approach any issue pertinent to the Bible: the way they read the Bible; the way they know, receive, and interpret the Bible; the way they are inspired and nourished by the Bible. Those who regularly attend the Eucharist according to the Eastern Orthodox Rite realize—some perhaps are astonished or even shocked by the fact—that in the Orthodox Divine Liturgy, the Bible normally is not read but sung, as if the Bible readings were designed not so much in order that the faithful understand and appropriate the word of God, but as if they were designed to glorify an event or a person.[19] The event is the eschatological Kingdom, and the person the center of that Kingdom, Christ. Perhaps this is the reason why the Orthodox, while always traditionally in favour of translating the Bible into a language people can understand (cf. the dispute in the Photian period between Rome and Constantinople over the use in the Church's mission to Moravia of the Cyrillic script; i.e., a language beyond the "sacred" three: Hebrew, Greek, Latin), they are most reluctant in introducing common-language translations of the Bible readings in their Divine Liturgy. For in the Orthodox Divine Liturgy, it is not only Jesus Christ in his first coming who speaks through Scripture; it is also the word of the glorified Lord in his second coming which is supposed to be proclaimed. Personally, I have challenged quite recently the view (widely accepted among Orthodox systematic theologians) that the entire eucharistic liturgy (i.e., both the "Mystery of the Word," or "Liturgy of the Catechumens," and the "Eucharistic Mystery," or "Liturgy of the Faithful") is eschatologically oriented, arguing for the evangelistic character of the Bible readings, as well as of the entire "Mystery of the Word."

Any particular issue, therefore, like the canon and authority of the Bible, cannot be detached from the framework of the ecclesial eucharistic community. Without denying the legitimacy of its autonomous status within world literature, the historical process of development of the individual books, their historical collection, as well as the authority attached at a quite late stage to the Bible as a closed composition (canon), but also the famous patristic—even conciliar (ecumenical)—statements, the Orthodox have always believed that the Bible acquires its full meaning and authority only within this ecclesial eucharistic community.

All of the functions within the life of the Church pertinent to expressing the faith, determining the truth, and authoritatively preserving it are related to the eucharistic identity of the Church, and therefore are the responsibility of the eucharistic community as a whole. Even synodality, the ultimate criterion of the truth, is mutually inter-related with the Eucharist. In 1848 the Patriarchs of the East turned down the invitation of Pope Pius IX to participate in Vatican I by saying, "after all, in our tradition neither patriarchs nor synods have ever been able to introduce new elements, because what safeguards our faith is the very body of the Church, i.e. the people themselves." Thus, they consciously underlined that the ultimate authority of the Church lies neither in doctrinal *magisteria* nor in any clerical (even conciliar) structure, but in the entire people of God. The only limitation is that this "communal" *magisterium*, the "many" in the Church's life, cannot function in isolation from the "one" who is imaging Christ; that is, the one presiding in love over the local (bishop), regional (*protos* or primate), or universal Church (Pope or Patriarch). And this "one" is the only visible expression of the Church.

All that has been said so far, being the result of the "eucharistic ecclesiology," is neither an "excessive generality" nor a kind of "liturgicalism" or "eucharisticism," a quasi-hermeneutical key to solve all questions.[20] It is rather a conscious shift of the center of gravity from a verbal or written authority to a communal and eschatological one.

4. The Ecclesial Perspective

The Orthodox perspective, therefore, in dealing with the Bible is first and foremost ecclesial. The "eucharistic and trinitarian" approach to all aspects of theology is the approach most widely used by Orthodox in recent times. Eucharistic theology gives pre-eminence to the local communities and—believe it or not—to the contextual character of Christian life. Trinitarian theology, on the other hand, points to the fact that God is in God's own self a life of communion and that God's involvement in history aims at drawing humanity and creation in general into this communion with God's very life. The implications of these affirmations for the proper way of dealing with the Bible are extremely important: the Bible is not read primarily in order to appropriate theological truths or doctrinal convictions, or to follow moral commands and social or ethical norms, but in order to experience the life of communion that exists in God. And historically this was the way the Bible was approached by certain groups in the Orthodox tradition (monastics, ascetics, nyptic women and men, etc.): as a means for personal spiritual edification; as a companion to achieve holistic personal growth, to reach *theosis* (deification); in other words to share the communion that exists in God. This tradition of *lectio divina* is, of course, by no means distinctive of the Orthodox East; it belongs to the entire Christian tradition.[21] All these mean that the traditional (Orthodox?) attitude to the reading of Scripture is personal. The faithful consider the Bible as God's personal letter sent specifically to each person.

Having said all of this, I must make clear that the hermeneutic developed quite recently and based on the model of the charismatic saint—namely, that only the illumined (and glorified through the ascetic life according to the Eastern tradition) person can authentically understand the word of God—is a hermeneutic that goes to a rather unacceptable extreme.

Nevertheless, the words of Scripture, while addressed to us human beings personally, are at the same time addressed to us as members of a community. Book and ecclesial community, or Bible and Church, are not to be separated. In the West, the authority of the Bible was imposed or rediscovered (as it is the case in the Protestant and Roman Catholic traditions respectively) in order to counterbalance the excesses of their hierarchical leadership, the authority of the institutional Church. In the East this task—not always without problems, I must confess—was entrusted to the charismatic, the spiritual, the *starets*. In the West, where more emphasis was given to the historical dimension of the Church, this solution was inevitable; in the East, where Orthodox theology has developed a more eschatological understanding of the Church, it is the people, the members of the eucharistic communities, that are the guardians of the faith. To relate again to the above-mentioned charismatic hermeneutic, the charismatic claims must be tested by the communal tradition and the life of the Church as the final criterion. Experience of God belongs to the whole Church and not only to an elite group, which would smack of Gnosticism.[22]

It is these considerations, among others, that make us believe that a dynamic encounter of the East with the West will not only enrich both approaches to the Bible; it will also enhance and broaden the different understandings of catholicity.

This interdependence of Church and Bible is evident in at least two ways.

(1) First, Christians *receive* Scripture through and in the Church. The Church told them what Scripture was. In the first three centuries of Christian history, a lengthy process of testing was needed in order to distinguish between those books which were authentically "canonical" Scripture, bearing authoritative witness to the Church's self-understanding, and above all to Christ's person and message; and those which were "apocryphal," useful perhaps for teaching, but not a normative source of doctrine. Thus, it was the Church (in her ecclesial rather than institutional form) that had decided which books would form the canon of the New Testament. A book is part of Holy Scripture not because of any particular theory about its date and authorship, but because the Church had treated it as canonical; it is debatable whether that treatment was juridical (i.e., through a proper conciliar process) or experiential (i.e., "eucharistic" in the above-mentioned sense).

(2) Secondly, Christians also interpret the Bible through and in the Church. If it was the Church that told them what Scripture was, equally it was the Church that told them how Scripture was to be understood. Going deep into the history of the liturgical life of the Church, one immediately realizes that the Bible might be read personally, but not by isolated individuals. It was read by members of a family, the family of the One, Holy, Catholic, and Apostolic Church. It was read in communion with all of the other members of the Body of Christ in all parts of the world and in all generations of time. Orthodox Christianity believes that God does indeed speak directly to the heart of each person during the Scripture readings, but all need guidance, a point of reference. And this point of reference is the ecclesial community, the Church.[23]

Because Scripture is the word of God expressed in human language, there is of course a place for honest critical inquiry in dealing with the Bible. The Orthodox Church has never officially rejected critical inquiry of the Bible, although in the past—and this is our common history with Western Christianity—the interpretation of certain passages was determined by the *regula fidei*.[24] In theory, she makes full use of biblical commentaries and of the findings of modern research. In her attempt to grasp the deeper meaning of the word of God, she even makes use of a wide range of methodologies. In her struggle to make it relevant to the world, it is quite legitimate to even accept the contextual approach to the Bible. Taking for granted that "every text has a context," which is not merely something external to the text that simply modifies it, but constitutes an integral part of it, Orthodoxy is in fact even prepared to accept a kind of "hermeneutics of suspicion": certain biblical sayings, clearly influenced by the cultural and social environment of the time of their production (e.g., those referring to women, slavery, etc.), can be legitimately valued according to, and measured over against, the ultimate reality of the Gospel, the inauguration of the Kingdom "on earth as it is in heaven" (Mt 6.10).[25] Even an "inclusive language" can be legitimated, as long as it does not disaffirm the fundamentals of the Christian faith. Of course, any idea of rewriting the Bible cannot (and will not) be accepted. These suggestions are the inevitable consequences of placing the authority of the Bible over the eucharistic community, exactly as the concept of "canon within the canon" was developed by honest Protestant scholars (most notably in the case of Käsemann and others) in an attempt to set up an ultimate criterion to match with Christian doctrine. It is important to note at this point that the Orthodox Church in her long tradition has never allowed any doctrinal statement not clearly rooted in the Bible.

In short, all critical suggestions in the biblical field are legitimate and can easily be expressed and even proposed for adoption to the Christian community. However, all individual opinions, whether coming from members within the Christian communities or from any expert outside of them, are to be finally submitted to the Church; not in the form of a juridical or scholarly *magisterium*, but always in view of the eschatological character of the Church as a glimpse and foretaste of the coming Kingdom. In other words, in the Orthodox Church objectivity and the individual interest are always placed at the service of the community and of the ultimate reality of God's Kingdom. It is of fundamental importance that the Orthodox approach the Bible, as the inspired word of God, always in a spirit of obedience, with a sense of wonder and an attitude of listening, but never as a closed (canonical?) issue; hence the clear-cut distinction between the word of God and the Bible, made of course by all Christians, but more strongly underlined by Orthodox.

5. The Hermeneutical Concept of *Theoria*: Pneumatology

The way the Orthodox interpret the Bible is related to the perennial issue of hermeneutics and the important and peculiar concept of *theoria*, or *theoptia*, a concept that goes back, according to most Orthodox scholars, to the early Christian community.[26] The words of Jesus recorded in the Gospel tradition—whether authentic or not—while very similar both in form and sometimes in content with those of contemporary rabbis, were in fact very different in their profound perspective, at least with regard to the authority of Scripture. To the contemporary Judaism, the supreme authority of every single word of the Bible was unquestionable. There could be no question of its inspiration or authenticity. This hermeneutical idea is clearly expressed in the tractate *Sanhedrin* of the Babylonian Talmud: "He who says 'The Torah is not from God' or even if he says 'The whole Torah is from God with the exception of this or that verse which not God but Moses spoke from his own mouth' shall be rooted up" (99a).

The historical Jesus, on the other hand, did not hesitate to reinterpret the Scriptures critically in a very radical way. It was not only that he regarded the whole Bible in the light of the two great commandments (love of God and love of neighbor), or that he established in the six antitheses of the Sermon on the Mount a new Law; one can even argue that Jesus's messianic interpretation of Scripture—namely, the fulfillment of the prophecies in his mission—was not novel, since similar messianic interpretations have been found in the Dead Sea Scrolls. What is novel and pioneering is Jesus's revolutionary proclamation, and the early Church's assured conviction, that the reign of God was at hand; in fact, it was inaugurated in Jesus's own work. And this was also the main feature of the early Christian hermeneutics: namely its christocentric character.

The question which arises is whether Jesus (and his Church thereafter) undermined the authority of the existing Scripture at that time by replacing it with another authority contained in certain written documents. At the beginning of the second century, the answer was certainly no. Bishop Ignatius of Antioch, although he knew some of the New Testament books—certainly 1 Corinthians and other Pauline letters, probably John and possibly the Synoptic Gospels, at least some of them—never appealed to them; nor did he make extensive use of the Old Testament. His only authority was Jesus Christ and his saving work and the faith that comes through him (*emoi ta archeia Christos*: to me the "charters" are Jesus Christ).[27]

This new understanding of scriptural authority, which began to show up in the New Testament writings, was the result of the early Christian pneumatology. The doctrine, of course, of the Holy Spirit in the New Testament and the early Fathers cannot be easily reduced to a system of concepts; actually, this systematization did not happen until the 4th century. However, with this doctrine, Christianity opened up new dimensions in the understanding of the mystery of the divine revelation. Of course, this new pneumatological perspective in patristic theology did not replace the normative christocentric one. This new development was in fact a radical reinterpretation of Christology through pneumatology. By placing the Holy Spirit on an equal status in the trinitarian dogma with the Father and the Son, the Christian theology of the early undivided Church broke the chains of dependence on the past authorities. The conciliar declaration of the divinity of the Holy Spirit was undoubtedly one of the most radical considerations of the mystery of deity—to my view certainly of equal importance with the dogmatic definition of the *homoousion* of the *Logos* to the Father.

It is a commonplace that the first Christian method of interpreting the Old Testament, used by the New Testament writers, was generally that of typology. However, this method's real meaning and profound significance have been lost or at least concealed by the conflict, which arose a hundred years or so later, between the exegetical schools of Alexandria and Antioch. The typological method, apart from the affirmation of the historical reality of the biblical revelation—a concept which was lacking from the allegorical method—was in fact based on the presupposition that the authority of the Law and the Prophets was somehow limited; for the entire Old Testament looks beyond itself for its interpretation. It was along those lines that the famous Antiochean principle of *theoria* was later developed by some ecclesiastical writers. This term was especially used in Eastern hermeneutical tradition for a sense of scripture higher or deeper than the literal or historical meaning, based, of course, firmly on the latter. Its meaning, however, was not exhausted simply by that; it had some further very significant connotation. Acknowledging that in the Church every Christian, and the saint in particular, possesses under the guidance of the Holy Spirit the privilege and the opportunity of seeing (*theorein*) and experiencing the truth, later

Byzantine theologians developed (or presupposed) a concept of revelation substantially different from that held in the West, especially in high scholasticism under the influence of Aristotle. Because the concept of *theologia* in Cappadocian and Antiochean thinking was inseparable from *theoria* (i.e., contemplation), theology could not be—as it was at least in high scholasticism—a rational deduction from "revealed" premises; that is, from Scripture or from the statements of an ecclesiastical *magisterium.* Rather, it was a vision experienced by the faithful, whose authenticity was, of course, to be checked against the witness of Scripture and Tradition. The true theologian, in later Byzantine thinking, was to a considerable extent the one who saw and experienced the content of theology, and this experience was considered to belong not to the intellect alone (the intellect, of course, is not excluded from its perception), but to the "eyes of the Spirit," which place the whole human being—intellect, emotions and even senses—in contact with the divine existence.[28] According to J. Meyendorff, "this was the initial content of the debate between Gregory Palamas and Barlaam the Calabrian, which started the theological controversies of the fourteenth century (1337–1340)."[29]

Defining revelation, therefore, as a living truth, accessible to a human experience of God's presence in his Church without the absolute limitations of certain scriptural documents, and in later ecclesiastical theology even of conciliar definitions, the Orthodox pneumatology in some sense seems to reject the idea of any canonical authority. According to an ancient Byzantine hymn from the feast of Pentecost, still used in the Orthodox liturgy, "the Holy Spirit is the source of all donations" (*panta horigei to pneuma to hagion*).

6. The Christological Perspective

In addition to the ecclesial perspective in dealing with the Bible, and despite the hermeneutics of *theoria* and the pneumatological novelty in Orthodoxy, the christological perspective is also affirmed in the Orthodox Church. In a joint statement by the Orthodox and the Anglicans, issued in a conference held in Moscow (1976), it was rightly stated that "the Scriptures constitute a coherent whole." Its wholeness and coherence lies in the person of Christ. He is the unifying thread that runs through the entirety of the Bible from the first sentence to the last. It is Jesus who meets his people on every page. "In him all things hold together" (Col. 1.17). Without neglecting the analytical approach, breaking up each book into what are seen as its original sources, the Orthodox traditionally used to pay greater attention to the way in which these primary units had come to be joined together. The unity of Scripture, as well as its diversity, is equally affirmed; its all-embracing end, as well as its scattered beginnings, is taken into consideration. But in general, the Orthodox prefer, for the most part, a "synthetic" style of hermeneutics, seeing the Bible as an integrated whole, with Christ everywhere as the bond of union.[30] This christocentrism, however, has never developed into a christomonism, which led Christian mission early in the twentieth century to a kind of "christocentric universalism." As I underlined above, in the Orthodox Church, with few exceptions, Christology was always interpreted through pneumatology. This "trinitarian" understanding of the divine reality was what actually prevented the Church from intolerant behavior, allowing her to embrace the entire *oikoumene* as the one household of life.

This christological, and therefore incarnational, perspective in dealing with Scripture—in other words, in reading, understanding, interpreting, and of course determining the extent of the Bible—has given rise within the Orthodox world to the legitimacy of a pictorial presentation of the Bible, and at the same time to a witnessing to the gospel through icons. Such a witness to the gospel through icons, especially those of the Byzantine art and technique, has been found exceptionally efficient and effective for the dissemination of the profound meaning of the Christian message, by stressing its transfigurative and eschatological dimensions. For in the Orthodox Church, icons are not only the "book of the illiterate," but also a "window to the heavens." What the icons actually express is not a dematerialization, but a transfiguration of the world. For in the icons, the material and cosmic elements, which surround the holy figures (divine and holy alike), are also shown transformed and flooded by grace. The Byzantine icon in particular reveals how matter, in fact the whole of creation, human beings and nature alike, can be transformed: not just to the original harmony and beauty they possessed before the Fall, but to a much greater glory they will acquire in the *eschaton*. Although depicting worldly schemes, icons are not concerned with the world we live in, but foreshadow the world to come. As in the Eucharist, so also in the icons; the same interaction of past, present, and future is manifest, and the same anticipation by this world of the world to come is present.[31]

Concluding Remarks

If any conclusion is to be drawn from the above short and sketchy reflection on canon and authority of the Bible based on a broad understanding of Orthodox theology, this is in fact a questioning of the ultimate authority given to the concept of canon in the West. By certainly relativizing the authority of the canon as an issue of cardinal importance and of binding significance for the life of the Church, I do not claim to have offered the final solution to the problem. My views, deliberately emphasizing the peculiarities of my tradition, are to be synthesized both with the ecclesiological views widely held among Catholics, which underline a more centralized authority, and with the evangelical ones that have shifted the emphasis from an ecclesial to an individual (or better, personal) appropriation of salvation.

Endnotes

[1]J. Zizioulas, *Being as Communion: Studies in Personhood and the Church* (Crestwood, NY: St. Vladimir's Seminary Press, 1985), 26.

[2]More in my "Orthodoxy and Ecumenism," *Eucharist and Witness: Orthodox Perspectives on the Unity and Mission of the Church* (Geneva, MA: WCC/Holy Cruss, 1998), 7–28, especially 9ff.

[3]N. Nissiotis, "Interpreting Orthodoxy," *Ecumenical Review* 14 (1961): 1–27.

[4]Ibid., 26: "We should never forget that this term is given to the One, (Holy, Catholic and) Apostolic Church as a whole over against the heretics who, of their own choice, split from the main body of the

Church. The term is exclusive for all those, who willingly fall away from the historical stream of life of the One Church but it is inclusive for those who profess their spiritual belonging to that stream."

[5]Here is an overview of the entire issue in all Greek Orthodox introductions to the New and Old Testaments. Old introductions: K. Kontogonis, *Bible* (Athens, 1859); Sp. Papageorgious, *Old Testament* (Alexandria, 1910); B. Antoniadis, *Old Testament,* (Constantinople, 1936); P. Bratsiotis, *Old Testament* (Athens, 1937, [2]1975); B. Antoniadis, *New Testament* (Athens, 1937); B. Ioanndis, *New Testament* (Athens, 1960). More recent introductions: M. Siotis, *New Testament I* (Athens, 1971); Savas Agourdis, *New Testament* (Athens: Grigoris, 1971); Ioannis Karavidopoulos, *New Testament* (Thessaloniki: Pournaras, 1983, [2]2000); I. Panagopoulos, *New Testament* (Athens, 1994); D. Doikos, *Old Testament* (Thessaloniki, 1980); A. Hastoupis, *Old Testament* (Athens, 1981). A general view of Old Testament studies in Greece in English can be found in B. Vellas, "Old Testament Studies in Modern Greek Orthodox Theology," *Theologia* 13 (1941–48): 330–39.

[6]On all these see I. Karmiris, *Orthodox Ecclesiology* (Athens, 1971).

[7]Georges V. Florovsky, *Bible, Church, Tradition: An Eastern Orthodox View* (Belmont: Nordland, 1972; also in Greek translation idem., *The Body of the Living Christ: An Orthodox Interpretation of the Church* (Thessaloniki: Pournaras, [2]1981), 15.

[8]On the issue of the translation of the Bible in Orthodoxy, see my *Biblical Hermeneutical Studies* (Thessaloniki: Pournaras, 1988), 143ff.

[9]Oikonomos's views have been expounded in his work *On the LXX Interpreters (Hermeneutai) of the Old Testament Books Four* (Athens, 1844–49).

[10]G. Florovsky, "The Elements of Liturgy," in G. Patelos, ed., *The Orthodox Church in the Ecumenical Movement* (Geneva: WCC, 1978), 172–82, see 172; cf. also my "Orthodoxy and Ecumenism" (cf. above footnote 2), 9.

[11]More on these in my "The Eucharistic Perspective of the Church's Mission," *Eucharist and Witness,* 49–66.

[12]More on this view in my "Paul's *theologia crucis* as an Intermediate Stage of the Trajectory from Q to Mark," in L. Padovese, ed., *Atti del VI Simposio Di Tarso Su S. Paolo Apostolo* (Rome: Ateneo Antoniano, 2002), 43–52; also in H. Koester, ed., "Story and Ritual in Greece, Rome and Early Christianity," www.pbs.org/wgbh/pages/frontline/shows/religion/symposium/story.html.

[13]The phenomenon of post-modernity and its bearing upon biblical studies and especially upon the mission of the Orthodox Church is being examined in my recent book *Postmodernity and the Church: The Challenge of Orthodoxy* (Athens: Akritas, 2002).

[14]Cf. Jimmy D. G. Dunn's most recent book, *Jesus Remembered,* vol. 1 of Christianity in the Making (Grand Rapids: Erdmans, 2003), 92ff. Also in my "The Universal Claims of Orthodoxy and the Particularity of Its Witness in a Pluralistic World," to be published in the forthcoming *Festschrift* for Archbishop Christodoulos.

[15]J. Breck, *Scripture in Tradition: The Bible and Its Interpretation in the Orthodox Church* (Crestwood, NY: St. Vladimir's Seminary Press, 2001), has recently reshaped this Bible-Church relationship into a Bible-in-Tradition one; for a critical assessment of his approach, see Theodore Stylianopoulos's review in *SVTQ.* Most contemporary Orthodox speak of the indissoluble unity of Bible and Tradition (cf. N. Nissiotis, "The Unity of Scripture and Tradition," *GOTR* 11 [1965–66]: 183–208).

[16]More in my "Tradition," *Dictionaire Oecumenique de la Missiologie: 100 Mots pour la Mission* (Paris/Genèv: Cerf/Labor et Fides, 2001), ad loc. Cf. also my "*Orthodoxie und kontextuelle Theologie,*" *Oekumenische Rundschau* 42 (1992): 119–25; Kallistos Ware, "Tradition," in N. Lossky et al., eds., *Dictionary of the Ecumenical Movement,* Geneva [3]2003, ad loc.; G. Florovsky, "The Function of Tradition in the Ancient Church," *GOTR* 9 (1963): 181–200.

[17]Cf. my "Orthodoxy" (cf. above footnote 2), 7–28.

[18]G. Florovsky, "Sobornost: The Catholicity of the Church," in E. L. Maschall, ed., *The Church of God* (London: SPCK 1934), 64ff.

[19]Cf. also D. Staniloae, "*La Lecture de la Bible dans l'Eglise Orthodoxe,*" *Contacts* 30, no. 104 (1978): 349–53.

[20]Cf. Theodore Stylianopoulos, *The New Testament: An Orthodox Perspective,* vol. 1 (Boston: Holy Cross, 1997), 63, note 35, where he warns some Orthodox theologians against some inconsistent and excessive hermeneutical statements.

[21]A balanced approach to this tradition is a book written by the Orthodox of the New Skete, titled *In the Spirit of Happiness* (Boston: Little, Brown and Co., 1999).

[22]Theodore Stylianopoulos has convincingly critiqued the biblical hermeneutic based on the model of the charismatic saint, so widespread among conservative Orthodox, in his *The New Testament*, 175ff.

[23]Of course, we are not talking here about the "intended" or "objective" meaning of certain biblical passages—if objectivity can be achieved—but their ultimate authority.

[24]Savas Agouridis, "The *regula fidei* as Hermeneutical Principle Past and Present," in Prosper Grech et al., eds., *L' Interpretazione della Bibbia nella Chiesa: Atti del Simposio promosso dalla Congregazione per la Dottrina della Fede* (Citta del Vaticana: Libreria editrice vaticana, 2001), 225–31; also in more detail (in Greek) in his *The Hermeneutics of the Holy Scriptures* (Athens: Artos Zoes, [1]1979, [2]2000).

[25]Cf. my pupils' recent scholarly works: D. Passakos, *Eucharist and Mission: Sociological Presuppositions of the Pauline Theology* (Athens, 1997); idem, "Eucharist in First Corinthians: A Sociological Study," *Revue Biblique* 104 (1997): 192–210; E. Kasselouri, "The Hermeneutics of Suspicion and the Epistles to Thessalonians," in the *Proceedings of the IX Conference of Orthodox Biblical Scholars: The Apostle Paul's Two Epistles to Thessalonians: Literary, Historical, Hermeneutical and Theological Problems* (Thessaloniki, 2000): 209–23; also her "Der Begriff der Tradition und die Frauenordination: Ein orthodoxer Ansatz," *Ökumenische Rundschau* 51 (2001): 167–77; M. Goutzioudis, *The Epistle to the Hebrews in Ancient Ecclesiastical Tradition and in Modern Biblical Scholarship* (Thessaloniki, 2000).

[26]Cf. J. Breck, *The Power of the Word* (Crestwood, NY: St. Vladimir's Seminary Press, 1986).

[27]More on this (in Greek) in B. Stoyannos, *Christomatheia: The Christocentric Hermeneutical Principle in St. Ignatius the God-Bearer's Epistles* (Thessaloniki, 1976).

[28]J. Meyendorff, *Byzantine Theology: Historical Trends and Doctrinal Themes* (New York: Fordham, 1974), 5ff.

[29]Ibid., 9.

[30]Kallistos Ware, "How to Read the Bible," *The Orthodox Study Bible* (Nashville: Nelson, 1992), 762–70.

[31]Cf. my "The Reading of the Bible from the Orthodox Church Perspective," *Ecumenical Review* 51 (1999): 25–30.

2

Patterns of Biblical Exegesis in the Cappadocian Fathers: Basil the Great, Gregory the Theologian, and Gregory of Nyssa

John A. McGuckin

Introduction

In this lecture, I would like to consider some fundamental principles involved in the early Church's use of the scriptures, and to demonstrate their continuity in some of the classical Greek Fathers. I begin my remarks with a brief consideration of the kerygmatic proclamation of the apostolic period, and then move on to consider some exegetical patterns among the Cappadocians. Much modern comment on the patristic approach to biblical interpretation has been obsessed with fixing them as Antiochenes or Alexandrians, a scholarly categorization that derives from the fifties of the previous century. It is abundantly clear, however, even from a cursory reading, that the great fourth-century exegetes do not follow these rules of being literalists or allegorists that we impose on them.[1] The strong Antiochene-Alexandrian divide has meant that much patristic scholarship has begun its consideration of Greek exegesis from the starting point of hermeneutical method rather than of exegetical principle, which was what most concerned the Fathers as theologians. An important case in point is the Cappadocian exegetes who are simultaneously, and unrepentantly, Alexandrians and Antiochenes, and who each advance deep considerations on what constitutes the authentic Christian use of the scriptures.

The Scripture Principle of the Early *Kerygma*

In a recent essay on the role of scripture in the origins of the Church, Jacques Gillet argued that the New Testament writings "do not aspire to oppose the Christian experience to that of Israel, to erect in the face of the Hebrew scriptures a new and concurrent corpus. The writings of the New Testament did not appear right alongside those of Israel but in their wake and at their end. They are at bottom a reading of, and commentary on, the Jewish scriptures."[2] This seems to me to state the process of origins correctly but radically to miss the point (the "at bottom" aspect) that peculiarly distinguishes the Christian scriptures and their fundamental charism. They are not commentary on the scriptures of Israel,[3] however much they may derive their focus (even at times their apparent genre) from that task. They are fundamentally and coherently commentaries on the significance of Jesus and are the confessions of the community's faith in the centrality of his person and, from that basis of Christocentric confession, only then an explanation (*Hermeneusis*) of how this surprising message finds its validation in key instances of the old story of Israel's covenant life with God. In other words, the Old Testament becomes the commentary on the New, since chronological priority has little significance in the eschatological priority of the *kairos* of salvation. This principle of soteriological order (*taxis*) is a distinctive mark of how the apostolic and patristic writers approach exegesis.

The Christian genre of scriptural commentary, as such, and it is an interesting thing to reflect on, is the invention of the Gnostics, making its first appearance with Heracleon and being appropriated for the wider Church by the Alexandrian theologians. Many of the important Fathers, and some whom we will consider in this paper, resisted the very notion of a biblical commentary in the sense of following the narrative line of a determinative text. Their understanding of biblical exegesis remained that of the more ancient period, a more discontinuous, confessional, and event-centered typology of the Christ-event.

Jesus determined the pattern of his Church's approach to the scriptures,[4] and this is reflected in typical sayings and provocative exegeses such as his message to the disciples:[5] "Blessed are your eyes because they see, your ears because they hear. I tell you solemnly, many prophets and holy men longed to see what you see, and never saw it; to hear what you hear, and never heard it" (Mt. 13:16–17). The only exegetical sign he allowed for the correct interpretation of the complex nexus of symbols comprising the saving message was the ambivalence of the "Sign of Jonah."[6] The Church is built upon the rock of confession. And that confession was elicited by the simple (and yet so complex) question that cascaded through the list of Israel's prophets to reach the climacteric "Who do you say that I am?" (Mt. 16:13–18). Once the principle has been established that Christ is the key to the entire covenantal relationship of the world to its God, all else is simply a matter of unraveling. John's Gospel puts it in a series of dramatic hermeneutical challenges, which are still provocative to those who wish to dismiss them as mere anachronisms: "Your father Abraham rejoiced to think that he would see my day. He saw it and was glad" (Jn. 8:56). Or: "If you had really believed in Moses you would have believed me, because it was me that Moses was writing about" (Jn. 5:46). The earliest disciples summed up this whole "scriptural principle," which they learned from Jesus, in that luminous narrative of the journey to Emmaus: "Then he said to them, 'Oh how foolish you are. How slow to believe the full message of the prophets. Was it not ordained that the Christ should suffer and so enter his glory?' Then starting with Moses and going through all the prophets, he explained to them the passages throughout the scriptures that were about himself" (Lk. 24:25–27). Every time this has been exegeted to me in the course of my education (several times over the years), I have been struck by the common refrain added by the commentator: "And what a pity it is that we are not given the list of those texts." And yet we are. This is exactly what the Gospels and Epistles set out to do. Moreover, it was a custom that continued powerfully on to form the first structures of patristic exegesis. The whole process of Christocentric typology derives from this activity, as can be seen in that profoundly typological analysis of Passover that survives in Melito of Sardis's *Peri Pascha*.[7] It is an approach that was preserved by Cyprian of Carthage in the ancient book of *Christological Testimonia*,[8] which he used for his hasty construction of sermons after his conversion from paganism and his more or less immediate elevation as presbyter and bishop. This is the scripture principle that governs exegesis in the age before biblical commentary, the first apostolic age of the Church. The Christocentric focus is not meant as an explanation of how every scriptural passage has a Jesus reference, although soon the Fathers will set out to argue that case as, for example, in the great cosmic Logos theology of Origen of Alexandria. It is more precisely an understanding that certain key passages which are Christological types explain the authoritative Jesus-event, which in turn explains the re-establishment of communion with God, the covenantal foundation of the Church as the elect community, the sole principle which explains the existence of the covenant literature that typologically anticipated the Church. It is this architecture, I think, which is brought to a clear focus (though not originated by Paul) in the Pauline expression of the *kerygma*.[9] He claims it was the traditional *kerygma* of the Church (traditional already by the fifties of the first century). He states the case most dramatically: "I taught you what I myself had been taught, namely that Christ died for our sins in accordance with the scriptures; that he was buried, and that he was raised to life on the third day, in accordance with the scriptures" (1 Cor. 15:3–4).

In his phrase *Katà tàs Graphàs*, Paul does not intend to interpret the entire biblical story per se. He is interested only in the elucidation of the Jesus salvation-event, through the medium of biblical history understood as the prelude[10] to that eschatological event. This is why for Paul, and the other apostolic authors and most of the Fathers following them, certain elements of the story are lifted out and other aspects not so conducive to his kerygmatic purpose are left "in the shade." It is the classical Christian scripture-principle of the interplay of shadow and reality, type and antitype. The scripture thus becomes a vast trope, an extended metaphor of the experience of God in Christ. To make it more than this (as, for example, to presume that all of scripture is strictly speaking a normative text)[11] is an application of biblicism unsupported by the Apostolic Tradition. The Christological mystery is thus the heart of the scriptural ethos (the *Tendenz* of the text). Paul reads scripture simply "*In Lumine Christi*."[12] Only in this light is scripture itself a Mysterion, as it elucidates the *Mysterium Christi*, with the interpreter mystically guided by the Spirit into the directing "Mind of Christ."[13] In this process (the dynamic of the apostolic preaching of the Jesus *kerygma* through the interpretation of the scriptures), Paul and his patristic followers are fundamentally at one. Theodore Mopsuestia, who has often been wrongly interpreted as a theologian who is very interested in the historical literal meaning of his texts, expressed the kerygmatic principle most clearly (perhaps too bleakly) when he protested not only against the excessive allegorization of texts, but even against the ready typological interpretation of the Old Testament. Messianic interpretations of traditional passages, such as the majority of instances in the Book of Psalms,[14] are drastically cut back on the basis of his theory that the Old Testament can be interpreted through history, but the New Testament, as an eschatological mystery, cannot be interpreted by history; it must itself interpret history and can be coherently interpreted only by reference to the eschatological mystery the consummation of the ages which Christ will initiate at the *parousia.* If the Old Testament is historical and open to historical interpretation, the New Testament is, strictly speaking, historically transcendent. Although it begins in history, it looks to a future the Old Covenant does not envisage. For Theodore, the New can explain the Old, therefore, but the Old cannot comprehend the New.

Exegetical Procedures in the Cappadocian Fathers

Let us turn to look at how this architecture of the scripture principle is appropriated by the Cappadocian Fathers. The term Cappadocian Fathers is a collective name given to the main defenders of the Nicene faith in the generation after St. Athanasius. They were a close circle of Cappadocian landowners, either related as family or by close kin ties, and have traditionally been numbered as "the Three": Basil of Caesarea, his brother Gregory of Nyssa, and their friend Gregory the Theologian, or Gregory of Nazianzus. For accuracy's sake, we ought to add another theologian to their midst (Amphilokius of Ikonium, Gregory Nazianzen's cousin) and also a fifth, a Cappadocian "mother" (Macrina, the elder sister of Basil and Gregory of Nyssa).[15] The three usual figures are, however, the most significant thinkers, and the central character of all their work was the progressive clarification of the Christology of the *Homoousion*[16] and the divinity of the Holy Spirit, and how this could be harmonized with Christian monotheism. Gregory Nazianzen was frequently the one who pressed most insistently for a clear expression of the *Homoousion* of the Son and the Spirit, thus being the chief architect for the classical doctrine of Trinity.[17] The two Gregorys lived to see their theology vindicated at the Ecumenical Council of Constantinople in 381, where Gregory Nazianzen briefly presided. All three use the scriptures extensively in their work.[18] Here it will be possible only to take a few instances as examples of their commonality in exegetical *skopos* (the governing proclivity of their vision), and also of their significant differences in hermeneutical method.

Gregory the Theologian

One of the most extraordinary things about Gregory the Theologian, considering that he was the one said by Jerome to have been his "teacher of biblical interpretation,"[19] is that he never composed a single biblical commentary. And yet he struck Jerome as the most insightful commentator of his generation. We have extant almost every homily that Gregory ever delivered. There is not a question here of loss of materials,[20] simply that the theologian saw scriptural commentary functioning in a way very different than his great intellectual mentor Origen, or those other Fathers who produced extensive commentary on the biblical canon. There is only one passage, Oration 37,[21] where he actually takes a text (Mt. 19:1–12) and follows through its implications consistently, and that was a most special occasion when the Emperor Theodosius had taken control of his eastern capital and was considering an amendment to the Roman law over marriage legislation that was increasingly out of harmony between West and East. Consulting with Gregory, the unworldly and celibate bishop, as to how the varieties of Church laws could be brought into harmony (one canonical system which absolutely forbade divorce and remarriage and accordingly had altered civil Roman law; and the other which allowed it), Theodosius received the extraordinary response that the Eastern civil (and thus canonical) law ought to be relaxed so that it afforded women the same rights to divorce as men. What an unexpected exegesis that must have been, when Theodosius surely was intending to bring the Eastern Church in line with the West as part of his overall religious policy. To explain his decision (a *judicatum* that has since become the standard Orthodox canonical approach to marriage legislation), Gregory knew he needed to approach the text as a lawyer and explain its meaning closely. But here, of all texts, surely the meaning is already clear and apparent. Jesus tells the Pharisees that "What God has joined together Man must not separate," and then that "Whoever divorces his wife (I speak not of fornication) and marries another, is guilty of adultery." Most exegeses of this passage that I have seen certainly argue that the meaning is abundantly clear: Jesus wishes to make the marriage legislation of his day more rigorous, and the Church (at least in the West) followed him correctly in doing just that.[22]

Gregory, who has been spending over a year and a half in Constantinople preaching to hostile crowds the Nicene faith of the co-equal divinity of Jesus and the consubstantiality of the Spirit of God, and getting stones thrown at him in his pulpit for his pains, is not at all so sure that the common idea of the meaning of the text is what the biblical mystery is all about. If that were so, why are the Arians (among the most careful biblical theologians and proof-texters of that century) so thoroughly misguided on every important point as far as Gregory is concerned? Or why is it that true faith in the deity of the Spirit (his other major theological concern) simply cannot be demonstrated by biblical concordancing? To answer his fundamental question on how one interprets the *Mysterium Christi* through the scriptural text, Gregory takes his listeners (who presume the meaning is already clear) through the text and makes them listen again with fresh ears. Gregory refuses to resolve the matter to proof verses, a similar rule he has established in breaking out of the Arian doctrinal impasse. Following classical Hellenistic principles of literary interpretation,[23] Gregory insists that the proper way to interpret the text is to lay out the wider contextual meaning: the *skopos*, or the clear *Tendenz* of the passage in relation to the overall character of the thought and personality of the speaker. If it is a law, then we should consider the nature and character of the Law Giver. To understand Jesus's rules, therefore, we must first understand and know Jesus. What is the character (*ethos*) of Christ's law then? What would everyone agree about it? Gregory says that this answer clarifies everything else. Christ's law is philanthropic and inclusively merciful. Christ is like the fisherman who goes out with a wide dragnet to bring all manner of fish into his boat. He is generously inclusive of all those fish, "or rather human beings, who are swimming in the turbulent and sorrowful waters of this life."[24] Throughout his earthly life, Christ consistently manifested this compassionate approach to humans. It ought, therefore, to be the guiding premise that leads us to consider the specific question about marriage; but before extrapolating on that, Gregory takes the occasion to show how it relates to theological positions on the Arian question too, for many Arian exegetes have taken the sufferings and limitations of Jesus to be evidence that the Word cannot possibly be co-equal to the eternal deity.[25] Gregory answers that such a conclusion denigrates true theology and mistakes his compassionate economy for revelations about theology. It is the standard answer he gave throughout the *Theological Orations*, that Arian exegetical attacks on the Nicene position make the fundamental error of mistaking *economia* for *theologia*.[26] In regard to the question about marriage, here we have quintessentially the same problem: those who do not know the difference between economy and theology are not able to function as interpreters of the Mystery. The marriage text is fundamentally a question about *economia*: how God deals with the imposition of law over his creatures and through law leads them to salvation.

As the starting point in the biblical text, Gregory takes the pharisaic question to Jesus about the legitimate reasons for divorce,[27] a question he regards as a "tempting" of Jesus, since it is impertinent to ask the maker of marriage, the creative generator of all humankind, such paltry, narrowly focused questions.[28] In return, Christ demonstrates his cosmic sense of the implications of the *economia* by giving them the answer, which is a question in return: "Do you not see how God made them in the beginning as male and female?" Only in the context of this kind of cosmic *economia* can one rightly approach the question in hand, Gregory implies. But when he does turn to the issue, his is no theoretical generality. He comes into the precise issue with sharp focus and a finely honed agenda. Why, he asks, does Roman law punish the female adulteress with severe penalties, but a man who commits adultery has no penalty under the law? The answer, Gregory says, is that the law was obviously made by men. "I do not accept this law. I cannot approve this custom," he concludes. It is a legislation that is unjustly hard on women and children, who suffer from it while men are released with impunity. Such a law cannot reflect the God who is equitably even-handed to all.[29] What possible justification could be brought for this uneven treatment of women in a Christian context of legislation? Gregory raises some of the arguments he has heard advanced. Is woman not the cause of the fall? Well, he replies, Eve sinned, but Adam did no better, and have such thinkers not considered that Christ redeemed both Adam and Eve since those days, so how can such texts apply as paradigms of Christian behavior? Is not Christ honored primarily as a male who is one coming "from the seed of David"? Certainly, Gregory says, this is a title of Christ, but it celebrates his ancestry purely from his mother's side. In contrast to all of these weak biblical paradigms, he says, one ought to consider the apostolic revelation that the husband in a marriage ought to reverence his wife as he would reverence Christ himself. It is the woman alone, not the man, who is the icon of the Word of God in this case.[30]

Yet if the latter is a strong biblical paradigm, he continues, suggesting the marriage bond is "of the kingdom," it seems to suggest that second marriage is not permissible in the Church (an ancient prohibition of the early Church's canon law that had been relaxed in later centuries in accordance with the prevailing Roman civil law). And if second marriages are not legitimate, what does this say about third marriages, which were also tolerated by secular law? Having set out his context, Gregory then gives his *judicatum.* First marriages are "according to the law"; that is, they reflect the exact intent of Christ's law of reverence for the icon. Second marriages are not exactly in accordance with Christ's law, though they do correspond to secular law, but they are not to be forbidden in the Church because they are "according to indulgence"; that is, they are permitted to Christians on account of an economy of mercy, so that their weaknesses will not close them off from grace. Christ's word of law, as Gregory implies, is seriously meant as the right way, and so marriage ought to be a unique lifelong event, but when it does not happen this way and the marriage bond is broken, the overarching principle of Christ's law also has to be invoked; that is, the compassion which is the motivation for all of his legislations and commandments, a compassion that seeks to rescue and save the mass of humankind. This is why the economy of indulgence in the second marriage does not contradict the first law of single marriages, but refines it in the event of a lapse according to the deeper "intentionality" of the legislator. As to third marriages, Gregory does not forbid them either but advises they should be subject to some kind of penalty. If the first marriage is "legal," and the second "indulgential," the third is "transgressive." Anything beyond this, he says, is "swinish."[31] It is interesting to see Gregory's psychological character as a compassionate and carefully observant man (celibate ascetic though he was) so abundantly evidenced in that one area of society where so much joy and yet so much misery is evidenced in human affairs: intimate domestic relations. His concern is dominated by two equally marked principles: a remedy for an unjust and unequal treatment of women under the law, and a desire to inform Church law with compassionate realism and take the stated laws of Christ beyond their fundamentalist significance to their ultimate goal; that is, the mercifully economic salvation of men and women who are, as he says, "swimming in a turbulent sea of grief." This is perhaps enough on his one and only explicit commentary on scripture to show what a brilliant and careful exegete Gregory was. It would be misleading, however, to think that because this was his only explicit commentary, scripture is not constitutive of Gregory's thought. It is the substrate of everything he writes. His biblical citations would flood the margins of any critical edition of his works. His normal approach, however, especially when he is writing his most intimate texts, his poetry, and his accounts of Church life involving his family and his pro-Nicene friends (especially Basil), the times when he is least apologetically activated, is to describe himself and his communion in terms clearly drawn from biblical stories. He takes the stories and fits them into the patterns he sees evidenced in his own life and in the lives of others whom God has raised up in his generation for the defence of Christ's Church. So his mother, Nonna, is really Hannah. He is the child of Hannah, a new Samuel given to the old priest (his aged bishop father). Or his father, Gregory the Elder, is really Abraham[32] coming from a far country (he was a pagan convert), whereas his mother is Sarah (a Christian by birth) and herself gives birth to a new Isaac, the child of promise.[33] Like Paul,[34] Gregory receives revelatory intimations in dreams and visions of the night,[35] he is caught up to see things others have not seen, and on the basis of that vision, his own claim to apostolic authority is founded. One might take all this as incredibly self-referential, but such a critique can miss the fundamental claim inherent in such extended biblical typology: that here in Gregory is a theologian who claims to know the true mystery of the scripture and to teach it with apostolic authority in the midst of a generation that seems to have lost its way. His teaching is the *Homoousion* of the *Logos* and the Spirit of God, a doctrine of the Trinity for which he himself is largely responsible and for which he invents words and terms not hitherto known in the Church's tradition. In his fifth *Theological Oration*,[36] he even claims this inspiration given to him is new revelation for a New Age, in which apostolic authority had been seen once again operating in him. This is something more than merely self-referential. It seems to me a logical development of how the inspired interpreter who is given the *Mysterium* of the scripture in the mystical communion with Christ (as Paul was thereby commissioned as apostle) is seen by Gregory as the only one who can rightly explicate the *skopos* of the texts to the Church.[37] As scripture is itself a Christ-Mystery,[38] so too must the interpreter, to have the authority of Christ in explaining the *logia*, be in communion with the Christ. This is quintessentially the patristic appropriation of the apostolic doctrine of the scripture principle. Gregory spells out what the conditions of that communion are in his first two *Theological Orations*:[39] a lifelong fidelity that purifies the mind and heart, so that the Spirit of Christ will rest within it. The mind's purification involves deep intellectual training across many years, and that of the heart involves constant asceticism. Christ does the rest by indwelling the temple once purified and illuminating it with his inspiring Spirit. Gregory has nothing but scorn for bishops and theologians (we should understand that today as primarily referring to those who interpret the scriptures in the churches) who have not had this threefold initiation: of the mind, the heart, and the soul. He describes them as pilots who ignorantly steer the ship onto the rocks.

Basil of Caesarea

It has been said for a long time that Basil is another example of those who did not leave an explicit biblical commentary behind.[40] That may need to be revised. In antiquity, he was associated with a *Commentary on the Prophet Isaiah*,[41] but since the time of Erasmus, it has been customary to deny his authorship. A new critical study by Nikolai Lipatov has recently defended the Basilian ascription, at the same time issuing the first English translation of the work.[42] Basil's most famous and best exegetical works, however, are the *Commentary on the Psalms*,[43] and the *Nine Homilies on the Hexaemeron*,[44] the Genesis account (Gen. 1:1–26) of the making of the world and its living creatures. In his apologetical works *Against Eunomius*, directed against the neo-Arians, and also in his beautiful *Treatise on the Holy Spirit*,[45] directed against the opponents of the Trinity, he also shows a typical patristic style of using the biblical text in defence of his theology. Our remarks here shall largely relate to the *Hexaemeron* and the *Treatise on the Holy Spirit*.[46]

Basil clearly knew Origen's work and often uses it quietly and unostentatiously,[47] well aware how the Nicene movement, whose Western allies he so much wanted to win over to the Syrian Nicene party,[48] held Origen accountable for the suspicion attached to the word *Homoousion* in the Eastern Church.[49] Gregory of Nazianzus claimed[50] that both he and Basil had prepared the *Philokalia of Origen* while he was staying with Basil in his Pontic monastery during the winter of 361–362. That collation of major (and non-controversial) texts of Origen focuses largely on exegetical principles.[51] The evidence from Basil's own pen suggests that it was largely a work of Gregory's, which, typically, he associated with Basil for the sake of friendship and honour. Basil's own approach to the scriptures is much more that of the "simple man," albeit in his case a simplicity that is crafted with consummate rhetorical skill to make it appear simple.[52] The classical example is his *Hexaemeron Homilies*. He delivered these as a priest of the Caesarean Church in Lent some time between 365 and 370. His audience was largely comprised of skilled labourers who came to church for morning and evening lectures.[53] Basil takes his listeners through the creation account in a way that is poetically moving as well as scientifically impressive. He is pulling out all the stops, sharing the latest scientific and biological knowledge of the era with his audience, in a studied "simplicity." Time after time, he makes the connection between the craftsmen and workers standing listening and the beauty of the creation as a mirror of the character of God the Worker, who crafted it personally;[54] a thought, Basil suggests, which is far more exciting than the other standard workers' pleasure, and obsession, of betting on the horses. His regular comparisons of the providential plan which God demonstrates in the animals with what he expects from humans is one of the chief substructures of his commentary. A camel is an unforgiving and stupid beast that harbors resentment for a long time until it spies its opportunity and returns a bite for the hurt it received days before. Those who nurture feuds are basing their familial pride on the emulation of a camel.[55] The shark was given sharp teeth so that it could swallow prey whole, prey which would otherwise have been carried off by ocean currents. It reminds Basil of human sharks, those who swallow up the small fry in business deals.[56] The kaleidoscopically self-disguising octopus reminds him of politicians who change color with equal ease.[57] The series reaches its climacteric in a small but telling point about the undistinguished sea anemone that knows how to cling to the rocks when the weather turns rough. "If God," he says, "has not forgotten even the sea polyp in his providence, how could you ever think he does not care for you?"[58] I raise these few examples in order to contextualize properly what has often been lifted wholesale out of Basil and thus misinterpreted. It relates to his statement at the end of the series of lectures on the *Hexaemeron* when he appears to attack allegorism as a biblical method. He says:

> I know the laws of allegory, though less by myself than from the works of others. There are those truly who do not admit the common sense of the scriptures, for whom water is not water, but some other nature, who see in a plant, a fish, what their fancy wishes, who change the nature of reptiles and of wild birds to suit their allegories, like the interpreters of dreams who explain visions in sleep to make them serve their own ends. For me grass is grass. I take all in the literal sense. [Like Paul] I am not ashamed of the Gospel.[59]

Now, in context this is not an attack on allegorical method as such, but on excessive allegorization of details such that the moral import of the text's overarching *skopos* loses itself in a welter of secondary details. Like his audience of craftsmen workers, Basil knows that the teleology is the fundamentally important thing. If a table does not have sturdy and equal legs, it hardly matters how well it has been carved. He delivers these remarks right at the end of his discourses, as if he were apologizing for the "plainness" of his series of lectures on providence within cosmology. These are graceful but highly rhetorical remarks that have been taken far too literally by subsequent commentators. What he means to convey by them is essentially the same as Gregory Nazianzen's earlier ideas on the intentionality of scripture (the "Mind of Christ"), which the preacher is called upon to deliver sacramentally to the audience. Those interpreters who do not conform their minds to the intentionality of scripture, Basil says, are "corrupters of the truth." Their attitude is given away predominantly in the fact that they "will not conform their reasoning to Holy Scripture, but distort the sense of the Holy Scriptures to fit their own will."[60] This is why he has faith in the "common sense" of the scriptures, in contrast with the varieties of cleverness found in Hellenism. The "utterances of the Spirit" have a certain innate simplicity about them, an honest inartifice, which is characteristic of the truth. Basil compares it to the beauty of chaste women in contrast to the adornment of the harlot.[61] His implication is that scripture needs to come to the hearer with the simplicity that makes one capable of recognizing the master architecture of the Spirit of God, the constant character of simplicity of holiness. This is why, for me, the culminative reflection of all the *Hexaemeron* stories comes in the last of them, when he asks the question that must have been agitating his audience for a week: when would he ever get to the making of humanity? Here he reveals the *skopos* of his own work as biblical theologian: that the audience might engage in a task even more difficult than the explanation of the creation which he has been attempting, and that was the explication of their own hearts: "In truth the most difficult of all sciences is the knowledge of one's own self, but even the scrutiny of heaven and earth is not as useful as the attentive study of our own being, for teaching us to know God."[62]

All of Basil's remarks about common sense for the common man have been very well targeted in this set of homilies addressed to the workers of Caesarea. But it is going too far to conclude that Basil is interested only in moral applications of the scriptural text for his hearers. His theology in the *Hexaemeron* travels much farther than that. His ending devolves from his remarks on the creation of the mystery, which is humanity: "Let us make man in our own image and likeness," the text says.[63] Basil's conclusion is that if even Man is like God, how can the Arians dare to say the Son is unlike the Father?

The understanding of the transformative *skopos* of the scripture is given more explicit treatment in his great essay on the divinity of the Holy Spirit, a product of his mature episcopal preaching. Basil, as bishop of the metropolitan Church, had introduced a doxology into common prayers that replaced the customary "Glory to the Father, through the Son, in the Holy Spirit" with a version that was in harmony with the Western practice: "Glory to the Father, and to the Son, and to the Holy Spirit." The controversy that this raised against him was answered in this famous treatise, which lays down the neo-Nicene doctrine of the Trinity. Reflecting particularly on the function and office of the Holy Spirit, Basil has several occasions to explicate the scripture principle. Here, and it needs to be remembered how he is being attacked as an "innovationist" for his co-equal doxology of the Three, Basil admits he has no explicit biblical support. This, however, is not the same as having no support in the Apostolic Tradition, because the sense of the scripture (included in the Apostolic Tradition) is not reducible to its literal grammar. Even if the alternative doxology is biblically instanced (Glory to the Father through the Son), he can still claim a truer biblical inspiration for clarifying its intent with non-biblical phrases, and thus re-expressing it. This is the apostolic "freedom of the sons of God" that he invokes in words borrowed from Paul: "We acknowledge that the word of truth has, in many places, made use of these expressions [that is, the doxology "through the Son"] but we absolutely deny that the freedom of the Spirit is in bondage to the pettiness of Hellenism." By this he means that a fundamentalist literalism is not customary in the Church, only in the academy, and when imported into the Church (he has in mind the neo-Arians famed for their semantic exactitude and logical-positivist reductionism), it often "masks a deep seated hostility to true religion."[64] For Basil, the confession that Son and Spirit are divine hypostases co-equal in glory to the Father is not explicitly stated in scripture, but is the entire force, or intentionality, of the scriptural *kerygma* he is called on to preach. This *skopos* of the scripture, however, is itself an insight into the heart of the Spirit-inspired scriptures, and as such, it is precisely a gift of the Spirit, who first presented those scriptures for the edification of the Church. Without the gift of the Spirit, the intentionality of the scriptures remains closed like a sealed book. Basil describes it in a famous passage, which I abbreviate here:

> Our passions have alienated us from close friendship with God. Only when a man has been purified and returned to his natural beauty, when the Image of the King has, as it were, been cleaned and restored to its pristine form, only then is it possible to draw near to the Paraclete.... Souls in which the Spirit dwells are illuminated by the Spirit, and themselves become spiritual so that they can even send out grace to others.[65]

It is the gift of the Spirit alone, which makes theology comprehensible, and only to those who have been purified in heart.[66] Basil is reminding his hearers subtextually of the words of Jesus: "Blessed are the pure of heart, for they shall see God" (Mt. 5:8). For Basil, those who do not have the gift can neither see God, nor speak accurately about him, even if they were to cite chapter and verse, even if they were to be world-renowned experts in semantics. For him, and for the Fathers in general, all is a closed book if the mystery of scripture is not given as a charism within the context of the governing dynamic of the Spirit, which vivifies the Church. In this context, he speaks of the common practice of the Spirit to foreshadow realities that would become apparent only to the eyes of later disciples. The biblical type is a darkened projection,[67] like a dim slide; a paradox of revelation not by illumination, but by revelatory obscurity. It is a sign of something that will be more brilliantly demonstrated in later times and as such is comprehensible only to those who have the gift of the Spirit and can see retrospectively. This is nothing new. Origen[68] and Athanasius[69] had given a classical expression of it. But Basil's genius lies in the illuminative rhetorical detail, and he gives a basic explanation of why so much typology lies in, and maps out, the Old Testament. It is God's intention, he says, "by types, to train the eyes of the heart, so that the transition to the 'wisdom hidden in the mystery' (1 Tim. 4.7) will be made easier."[70] This is quintessentially the patristic approach to the Christ-Mystery, which is the overall *skopos* of the biblical text, a charism of the Spirit, which is not given outside the economy of sanctification. This is why, of course, his brilliant and complicated defense of the co-equal deity of the three hypostases is built around a confession of where Basil got it all from, if not from explicit biblical verses. It derives, he says, from the simple creed he was asked to recite at his baptism, when, being sanctified by the Spirit, he first understood that the threefold immersion, following the biblical command to baptize in the name of the Father "and" of the Son "and" of the Holy Spirit,[71] contained all of the divine theology he now was confessing in his doxology to the Father "and" to the Son "and" to the Holy Spirit.[72] This is that "unwritten tradition" Basil speaks about, the sacred *paradosis*, which contains the scripture within it, and also the principles of its interpretation, since it derives from God even prior to the revelatory text itself and is the very economy of salvation, the modality of the divine presence active in the world.

Gregory of Nyssa

The youngest of the Cappadocian triad shows the most interest in Origenian biblical theory.[73] The influences of Gregory Nazianzen, whom he always admired greatly because of his rhetorical brilliance, and his own brother Basil, whose work he explicitly continued after his premature demise,[74] can explain this. Immediately after Basil's death, Gregory was most active in continuing his brother's stress on a straightforward literal approach for the common sense of the narrative. The more he developed as an independent agent, and eventually as an internationally recognized theological authority in the Church of the age of Theodosius, the more he came under the wider philosophical culture of Gregory Nazianzen and the Origenians. Gregory often writes about how he understands the principles of biblical interpretation.[75] In his earlier works, *On the Hexaemeron* and *On the Making of Man*, which are designed as continuations of Basil's *Hexaemeron Homilies*, he follows the literal sense faithfully. In his later writings, such as the *Life of Moses* and the *Commentary on the Song of Songs*, he more or less tells the reader that it is the spiritual sense that now interests him almost exclusively. In this he demonstrates an important principle, which he lifts to the highest prominence in his own theological work: *epektasis*, the idea that souls are designed for communion with God, and it is this endless progression (*prokope*) into the divine mystery (a bounded infinity) that mirrors, for a limited creature, the eternity of God, who calls his own creature into communion with the Uncreated. In short, Gregory explicitly theorizes on what most of the other patristic exegetes understand implicitly: the quality and depth of biblical interpretation and kerygmatic proclamation depends on the advancement of the individual in the endless progression of the Mystery as experienced. Our point on the ascending curve of the mystery of *prokope* is determinative of our insight. This is essentially the same idea Gregory Nazianzen insists upon in his first *Theological Oration*,[76] but with Gregory of Nyssa, it is given a larger Origenian context and has come to be of more especial interest in the latter decades of the 20th century, when relativism in the analytical standpoint (the disappearance of the objective commentator) came to dominate much of so-called post-modern hermeneutical theory. In Gregory, however, the subtlety of his position in calling into question the commentator's relative standpoint does not open him to relativity on the issue of the truth of the Apostolic Tradition. He can be both highly fluid in terms of his acknowledgment of the tentativeness of interpretation and most certain of his adherence to the living tradition of truth. The coherence is provided by his understanding of the entirety of the biblical message as a soteriological economy. Each instance of the biblical message, both as a received grace for the individual and as a preached *kerygma* for the community, can be variously approached, according to the individual's degree of understanding and communion with the divine, but it is constantly gauged and assessed by the common character of the experience of the Church's union with God—an experience that can be recognized in past ages,[77] but also most particularly in the present *kairos*—the communion with God enjoyed by the saints, who thus become important arbiters of correct exegesis. This complex theory aligns what we might call a "patristic principle"[78] alongside the "scripture principle"; the two together are an important fourth-century reappropriation of Apostolic Tradition, and still today constitute a fundamental basis of Orthodox approaches to the scriptures and to the practice of theology generally.[79]

If a commentator finds points of conflict in individual cases of scripture, whether it is a defective reading or a difficulty in the coherence of the individual text, Gregory says[80] the commentator's basic task is to be able to recognize the single clear trajectory of the economy and, by so recognizing the macro-coherence of the idea of salvation, be able to resolve the individual difficulty by contextualizing one's response properly within the universal scheme. Exegesis thus works as an act of faith in the coherence and philanthropy of God as revealed in Christ. This is his notion of *akolouthia*, the proper order of things,[81] and the characteristics revealed in that harmonious unfolding of experience in the Church's passage through history. He expresses this notion so many times[82] that it becomes a distinguishing characteristic of his thought and gives to both his theology and his exegesis (though the two are, of course, ultimately the same) a profound cosmic dimension. The idea has been illustrated already in an important study by Jean Daniélou.[83] It will be enough to point out here that the idea of the scriptures as a soteriological journey, a veritable pilgrimage to the promised land of restored communion with God, through the story of Israel, to the supreme locus of the incarnation of the Word, and on to the eschatological hope of infinite potentiality in the divine communion is not so much an exterior criterion of interpretation laid arbitrarily over the biblical records as much as it is a patristic form of explaining why there is any scripture at all. In other words, the canon of scripture did not pre-exist the Church, even though many of the texts that constituted it were prior to the Church. The very recognition that there is a canon of scripture, a body of revelation that moves coherently "from glory to glory,"[84] is fundamentally an act of faith in the economy of Christ's salvation as appropriated in the experience of the Church. It is this which gives the lie to the many recent attempts (generally posited on admirable ecumenical motives) to posit a common understanding of scripture between the Church and Judaism. The Old Testament and the Hebrew scriptures are far from being the same thing, as anyone who has studied for even a few days in the different contexts of university, seminary, yeshiva, and parish could tell within minutes, and it does no service to the relations between different communities of faith to pretend otherwise.

A Brief Conclusion

There are many profundities communicated in the reading of great souls who are themselves engrossed in the Word of God. This is not the place to try to package them as a neo-patristic synthesis, but it may be appropriate to attempt some reflective summary, beyond stating what has been said several times already that the Fathers see scripture fundamentally as a Christ-Mystery which can be fully elucidated only within the community of salvation, by those who have been initiated by the Spirit and who can see the coherence of the larger mystery of salvation of which scripture is but a part. University-level study of scripture has, more or less, constructed itself in direct opposition to those principles: an understandable, albeit a curious, thing, and one that is worth more reflection in theological circles than it has hitherto received. If I had to offer a useful summation beyond this, I would probably say that my reading of the Cappadocians tells me that Christian scripture is an act of faith, not an independent source of it, although, of course, the acts of the faith of the community can also elicit faith through the ages, and scripture demonstrably has this power, although it ultimately serves to admit to that community of salvation to which it refers and in which it finds its authentic and dynamic proclamation. Scripture is, then, not a historically conditioned corpus of texts to which we bring objective interpretative skills. Scripture, in the patristic understanding, is already a commitment, an enrollment into a community shaped by shared experiences, hopes, and values. The message of the Cappadocians seems to me not only to be in profound harmony with the springs of Apostolic Tradition, but also to offer to contemporary Christian exegetes vital ways forward. Orthodox theologians, who have, through many generations, tried to keep alive the holistic approaches of the patristic interpreters, have much to learn in the present era about the veritable explosion of hermeneutics that has taken place in the West over the preceding two centuries. Orthodox theology may also have much to teach, for in the West our generation has seen the great biblical interest of the Reformation era dwindle away, in many important instances, into a hermeneutical abandonment of the very notion of sacred canon, even a widespread abandonment of the basic belief that there is a tradition of truth which the scripture upholds, and teaches, with confidence, coherence, and great joy. Without that fundamental confidence, we cannot appropriate the apostolic spirit that is essential for a true "community of interpretation," that spirit which animated Paul's assured words, "I taught you what I myself had been taught."

Endnotes

[1]For an excellent contemporary overview, see T. G. Stylianopoulos, *The New Testament: An Orthodox Perspective,* vol. 1, *Scripture, Tradition, Hermeneutics* (Brookline, MA: Holy Cross Press, 1997), esp. ch. 4, 101–122.

[2]J. Guillet, SJ, "The Role of the Bible in the Birth of the Church," in P. M. Blowers, ed., *The Bible in Greek Christian Antiquity* (Notre Dame: University of Notre Dame Press, 1997), 35.

[3]Unless we are so to redefine the meaning of commentary that it becomes neologistic. I take "commentary" to mean a literature that "follows after" (the plot, or the higher meaning) another authoritative corpus of literature. The Christian writings set out to convey the Jesus story, and in the process, they claim

the Hebrew scriptures as supportive authorities for their *kerygma*. It is the Old Testament which thus becomes the commentary on the New in the particular way the evangelists write.

[4]I do not wish to become involved here in the complex and important discussion of how this can be demonstrated except by the manner in which Jesus is "written" by the church to have interpreted scripture in this way. I can make it clear, though, that I do not share the presupposition of much late twentieth-century biblical theology that Jesus's disciples were theological geniuses of a high order, in contrast to the Master himself. I entirely share the same presupposition as the early Christian writers that Jesus, as a biblically rooted rabbi, spent much time on the discussion of the significance of the scriptures as the fundamental core training of his followers. The presumption that, of all that was transmitted from Jesus to the disciples, the pattern of biblical exegesis would have been constitutive seems to me to be a historically defensible one, and one that can be borne out in a multitude of specific case studies.

[5]The context is their confused complaint about the obscurity of the parables (Mt. 13:10f).

[6]"It is an evil and faithless generation that asks for a sign. The only sign it will be given is the sign of Jonah. And leaving them standing there he walked away" (Mt. 16:4).

[7]From the mid-second century.

[8]The Ad Quirinum. It is preserved as a writing of Cyprian's (it is much older than he) and was thereby saved for posterity as one of a typical genre of *Testimonia* books that were the very first manuals for Christian bishops of the second century, destined to give way before the rise of patristic biblical commentary in the later third century. The principle of *Testimonia* can be seen, for example, in the initial verses of Mark's Gospel. Mark is clearly using a *Testimonia* source here (for he gets his citations wrong).

[9]The main instances of the apostolic *kerygma* can be discerned in the structures presented in Acts 2:14–39; 3:13–26; 4:10–12; 5:30–32; 10:36–43; and also in the Pauline letters: Gal. 1:3–4; 3:1, 4; 6:1; Thess. 1:10; 1 Cor. 15:1–7; Rom. 1:1–4; 2:16; 8:34; 10:8–9.

[10]The "foreshadowing": the shadow cast, which by its presence announces the imminent arrival of the person. The choice of term is instructive, for Paul and for his patristic heirs. Shadows do not illuminate; they adumbrate.

[11]In the sense that fundamental norms can be literally extrapolated from any part of the biblical corpus, a position sometimes associated with sections of evangelical Protestantism. Orthodoxy understands the normativity of scripture not literalistically in this sense, but in the extended metaphorical sense of the manner in which *paradosis* (the kerygmatic tradition and experience of the risen Christ in the Church) conveys the authentic Christ-experience across generations of believers. Cf. J. A. McGuckin, "Eschaton and Kerygma: The Future of the Past in the Present Kairos (The Concept of Living Tradition in Orthodox Theology)," *St. Vladimir's Theological Quarterly* 42, nos. 3–4 (Winter 1998): 225–271; see also G. Florovsky, *Bible, Church, Tradition: An Eastern Orthodox View*, Revelation and Interpretation (Belmont, MA: Nordland Publishing, 1972), 17–36.

[12]Rom. 16:25–26; 2 Cor. 3:6; 4:6.

[13]1 Cor. 2:1–16; Jn. 16:13.

[14]Theodore allows only four messianic instances at all in the Psalms (Pss. 2, 8, 44/45 and 109/110).

[15]Macrina was Gregory's teacher and was instrumental in Basil's conversion to asceticism. She was a leading force in the female ascetic movement in Cappadocia, probably under the influence of Eustathius of Sebaste (which may account for the manner in which Basil relegates her to silence). Eustathius was Basil's first mentor, who inducted him into the ascetical life and encouraged him to be involved synodically (as a deacon) in the anti-Arian struggle. Eustathius was a leading *Homoousian* theologian, and later in his life, he progressively resisted the idea of the ascription of divinity to the Holy Spirit as conveyed by the extension of the *Homoousion* to the Spirit of God too. This (and other personal issues) led to an increasing tension between Eustathius and Basil, and finally to a complete rupture when Basil declared for the *Homoousion* of the *Logos*, and the hypostatic deity of the Spirit of God. If Macrina continued her allegiance to Eustathius as a spiritual mentor (she had preceded Basil in the ascetical life), familial honour made it impossible for Basil to criticise her explicitly, but he did abandon her to a total silence (a *damnatio memoriae*), unlike his younger brother, Gregory Nyssa, who recounts how significantly she had mediated Basil's Christian sensibility.

[16]The adherence to the doctrine of the Council of Nicaea 325.

[17]Cf. J. A. McGuckin, "Perceiving Light from Light in Light: The Trinitarian Theology of St. Gregory the Theologian," *Greek Orthodox Theological Review* 39 (1994): 7–32.

[18]For a wider context, see J. Bernardi, *La Prédication des Pères Cappadociens* (Montpellier: Publications de la Faculté des Lettres et Sciences humaines de l'Université de Montpellier, 1968), vol. 30, part 2.

[19]*De Viris Illustribus* 117; Eph. 50. 1; In Isaiam 3.

[20]Although the twelfth-century Gregorian commentator Elias of Crete does claim that Gregory wrote a *History of Ezekiel the Prophet.* If so, it is lost. Cf. F. W. Norris, "Gregory Nazianzen: Constructing and Constructed by Scripture," in P. M. Blowers, ed., *The Bible in Greek Christian Antiquity* (Notre Dame: University of Notre Dame Press, 1997), 149–62, esp. 149.

[21]A fuller consideration of the text in its larger contextual situation in the life of Gregory may be found in J. A. McGuckin, *St. Gregory of Nazianzus: An Intellectual Biography* (Crestwood, NY: St. Vladimir's Seminary Press, 2001), ch. 6.

[22]Cf. H. Crouzel, *L'église primitive face au divorce du 1ère au Vième siècle* (Paris: Beauchesne, 1971). Crouzel marshals his evidence well but fundamentally misrepresents the case when he tries to argue also that this was the same tradition throughout the Eastern Church. His exegesis of Gregory Nazianzen is so misguided, in my opinion, that I can find no explanation for it.

[23]Of an Aristotelian type that the *Ethos* (a thing's teleological dynamic) encapsulates the essence, the *Ousia.*

[24]Orat. 37.1. PG 36, 284. Alluding in a subtle and deliberate way not to the parable of the dragnet (Mt. 13:47–50) but to the story of Peter's call to be a fisher of men (Lk. 5:1–11).

[25]Orat. 37.4. PG 36, 285–88.

[26]The Eastern Church finds this a common issue in its dialogue with Western Christianity. Things in the Western churches which are sometimes variously seen to be "constitutive aspects" of the Christian faith (the Petrine principle, the Augustinian doctrine of grace, the *filioque*, the requirement to be "born again" and so on) are often seen from the East to be *theologoumena* elevated so high that they have taken on pseudo-creedal status.

[27]Mt. 19:1–9; cf. also Mt. 5:32.

[28]Orat. 37.5. PG 36, 288.

[29]Orat. 37.6. PG 36, 289.

[30]Orat. 37.7. PG 36, 292.

[31]Orat. 37.8. PG 36, 292.

[32]Orat. 1.7. PG 35, 400. Orat. 8.4. PG 35, 793.

[33]Carmen De Rebus Suis 2.1.1. vv. 424–31. PG 37, 1001–1002.

[34]2 Cor. 12:1–4.

[35]Carmen De Rebus Suis 2.1.1. vv. 194–204 (PG 37, 985–986); and vv. 452–456 (PG 37, 1003–4). Cf. J. A. McGuckin, *St. Gregory of Nazianzus: An Intellectual Biography*, 62–70.

[36]Orat. 41.

[37]It is very similar to Origen's own theory of inspiration as taught in his doctrine of the true High Priest. Cf. J. A. McGuckin, "Origen's Doctrine of the Priesthood," *Clergy Review* 70 (1985): 277–86; ibid., no. 9 (September 1985): 318–325; (synopsis in *Theology Digest* 33, no. 3 [1986]).

[38]For a fuller patristic analysis of the theme, see J. A. McGuckin, "Moses and the Mystery of Christ in Cyril of Alexandria's Exegesis," *Coptic Church Review* 21, no. 1 (Spring–Summer 2000): 24–32; and 21, no. 2 (2000): 98–114. German version in Tübingen *Theologische Quartalschrift* 4 (1998): 272–286.

[39]Orats. 37–38. See ET and the fine commentary in F. W. Norris, *Faith Gives Fullness to Reasoning: The Five Theological Orations of Gregory Nazianzen* (Leiden: E. J. Brill, 1991).

[40]Cf. M. Simonetti, *Biblical Interpretation in the Early Church* (Edinburgh: T and T Clark, 1994), 64–67.

[41]It shows heavy dependence on the commentary on the same book by Eusebius of Caesarea.

[42]N. Lipatov, tr., *St. Basil the Great: Commentary on the Prophet Isaiah*, Texts and Studies in the History of Theology, vol. 7 (Mandelbachtal-Cambridge: Editions Cicero, 2001). The same scholar's defense of the Basilian authorship of the *Commentary* appeared under the same imprint, titled *The Commentary on the Prophet Isaiah Attributed to St. Basil the Great: A Quest for the Author.*

[43]It is based upon the Psalm commentary of Eusebius of Caesarea, and also that of Origen. In Basil's work, 18 Psalms are involved. Modern scholarship accepts 13 as genuine: 1, 7, 14, 28–29, 32–33, 44–45, 48, 59, 61 and 114 in the LXX numbering (PG 29, 209–494). Here he takes the Psalter as a general guide for living and is like the Antiochene theologians in restricting the Christological reading of the psalms (only Ps. 44 is so interpreted).

[44]PG 29, 3–208. ET by B. Jackson, *St. Basil: Letters and Select Works*, Nicene and Post Nicene Fathers of the Church, vol. 8, reprint (Grand Rapids: Eerdmans, 1989), 51–107. (Henceforth cited as "Jackson: *Basil*," followed by page numbers.)

[45]Jackson: *Basil*, 1–50.

[46]For a fuller treatment, see M. Girardi, *Basilio di Cesarea interprete della scrittura: lessico, principi, ermeneutici, prassi* (Bari: Edipuglia, 1988).

[47]The beginning of his comments on the words "In the beginning" is a deliberate contrast to those of Origen, who goes to extraordinary allegorical lengths in interpreting the Genesis story. Commentators who have seen in this an explicit Origenian attack have often failed to note that Basil is, at the same time, emulating Origen's words on the phrase "In the beginning," which form the magnificent opening remarks of the latter's commentary on John.

[48]Never with much effect, because Basil was attached to the party of Meletius of Antioch, whom Athanasius and the West had denounced.

[49]Origen had defended the divine eternity of the Son of God but had also ridiculed those who held to the notion that God could be a "substance." His own context of meaning was provided by his anti-Monarchianist theology, but this ridiculing of the term *homoousios* was taken up by leading Origenian Arians of the fourth century, such as Eusebius of Caesarea and Eusebius of Nicomedia, and the posthumous association had blackened Origen's reputation in many quarters.

[50]Gregory of Nazianzus, Ep. 115. Cf. J. A. McGuckin, *St. Gregory of Nazianzus: An Intellectual Biography*, 102–104.

[51]Reflecting *De Principiis*, 4.1–3.

[52]In *Hexaemeron Homily* 3.8 (Jackson: *Basil*, 70–71), he speaks of the theory that the waters above and below the firmament (Gen. 1:7) refer to angelic beings as "dreams and old women's tales." It was a speculation of Origen.

[53]*Hexaemeron Homily* 3.1. Jackson: *Basil*, 64–65.

[54]See, for example, *Hexaemeron Homily* 4.1. "Can we, whom the Lord calls to the contemplation of his own works, ever tire of looking at them, or be slow to hear the words of the Holy Spirit? Shall we not rather stand around the vast and varied workshop of divine creation and, carried back in mind to the times of old, shall we not view all the order of creation?" Cf. Jackson: *Basil*, 72.

[55]*Hexaemeron Homily* 8.1. Jackson: *Basil*, 95.

[56]*Hexaemeron Homily* 7.3. Jackson: *Basil*, 91.

[57]*Hexaemeron Homily* 7.3. Jackson: *Basil*, 92.

[58]*Hexaemeron Homily* 7.5. Jackson: *Basil*, 93.

[59]*Hexaemeron Homily* 9.1. Jackson: *Basil*, 101. The last citation is Rom. 1:16, where Paul is talking about how only faith leads to faith, and how scripture designates this as the path of the upright man to life (Hab. 2:4). He says more or less the same a little farther on: "Why should I prefer foolish wisdom to the oracles of the Holy Spirit? Shall I not rather exalt Him who, not wishing to fill our heads with these vanities, has regulated all the Economy of Scripture with a view to the edification and the perfecting of our souls? Those who give themselves up to the distorted meaning of allegory seem to me not to have understood this, and have tried to give Scripture a majesty of their own invention. It is to believe themselves wiser than the Holy Spirit, and to bring forth their own ideas under a pretense of exegesis. Let us hear scripture as it has been written" (*Hexaemeron Homily* 9.1. Jackson: *Basil*, 102 [translation modernized]).

[60]He has in mind the Hellenistic philosophers who argued for the pre-existence of matter and denied the absolute power of the divine creator (*Hexaemeron Homily* 2.2. Jackson: *Basil*, 59).

[61]*Hexaemeron Homily* 3.8. Jackson: *Basil*, 70.

[62]*Hexaemeron Homily* 9.6. Jackson: *Basil*, 106.

[63]Gen. 1:26.

[64]*On the Holy Spirit* 2.4. Jackson: *Basil*, 3.

[65]*On the Holy Spirit* 9.23. Jackson: *Basil*, 15 (translation emended).

[66]"Those that trample on worldly things and rise above them are witnessed as being worthy of the gift of the Holy Spirit. The world cannot receive God. Only the saints can contemplate him through purity of heart" (*On the Holy Spirit* 22.53. Jackson: *Basil*, 34).

[67]"This is, as it were, in a shadow and a type. The nature of the divine is very frequently represented by the rough and shadowy outlines (*skiagraphia*) of the types. The type is an imitative anticipation of the

future" (*On the Holy Spirit* 14.31. Jackson: *Basil*, 19).

[68]*Commentary on Ps. 1.* It was a text given prominence in Gregory and Basil's compilation of the *Philokalia of Origen* (ibid., ch. 2, 1–5). Cf. G. Lewis, tr., *The Philocalia of Origen* (Edinburgh: T and T Clark, 1911), 30–34.

[69]*De Incarnatione* 57.1–3: "[1]. But for the searching or the Scriptures and true knowledge of them, an honourable life is needed, and a pure soul, and that virtue which is according to Christ; so that the intellect guiding its path by it, may be able to attain what it desires, and to comprehend it, in so far as it is accessible to human nature to learn concerning the Word of God. [2]. For without a pure mind and a modelling of the life after the saints, a man could not possibly comprehend the words of the saints. [3]. For just as, if a man wished to see the light of the sun, he would at any rate wipe and brighten his eye, purifying himself in some sort like what he desires, so that the eye, thus becoming light, may see the light of the sun; or as, if a man would see a city or country, he at any rate comes to the place to see it; thus he that would comprehend the mind of those who speak of God must needs begin by washing and cleansing his soul, by his manner of living, and approach the saints themselves by imitating their works; so that, associated with them in the conduct of a common life, he may understand also what has been revealed to them by God."

[70]*On the Holy Spirit* 14.33.

[71]Mt. 28:19.

[72]*On the Holy Spirit* 10.25–26. Jackson: *Basil*, 16–17.

[73]See A. Meredith, *Gregory of Nyssa* (London: Routledge, 1999); Monique Alexandre, "*La théorie de l'exégèse dans le De Hominis Opificio et l'In Hexaemeron*," in M. Harl, ed., *Écriture et Culture Philosophique dans la Pensée et Grégoire de Nysse* (Leiden: E. J. Brill, 1971), 87–110.

[74]Especially in his own continuation of the *Hexaemeron* and in his *Against Eunomius.*

[75]See his *On Virginity, Treatise on the Psalm Inscriptions, On the Soul and Resurrection, Against Eunomius, Catechetical Discourse, Life of Moses* and the *Prologue to the Song of Songs*, where (in the latter) he makes his own exposition of the *De Principiis* of Origen (Book 4), which had been edited by Gregory Nazianzen in his *Philokalia.* Monique Alexandre gives a brief analysis of this list in her study ("*La théorie de l'exégèse dans le De Hominis Opificio et l'In Hexaemeron*," 87–88).

[76]Orat. 37.

[77]Hence the point of his *Life of Moses* and also his determination to provide a Christian explanation of a notoriously difficult text in his *Homilies on Ecclesiastes.*

[78]The concept that the saints who enjoy clearer communion with God have a sharper insight into biblical truth. See J. A. McGuckin, "Origen's Doctrine of the Priesthood," *Clergy Review* 70, no. 8 (August 1985), 277–86; ibid., no. 9 (September 1985): 318–25; idem. "The Vision of God in St. Gregory Nazianzen," *Studia Patristica* 32, E. A. Livingstone, ed. (Leuven: Peeters, 1996), 145–152.

[79]For a fuller discussion, see J. A. McGuckin, "Eschaton and Kerygma: The Future of the Past in the Present Kairos [The Concept of Living Tradition in Orthodox Theology]," *SVTQ* 42, nos. 3–4 (1998): 225–71.

[80]See, for example, the prologues of his early works *On the Hexaemeron* and *On the Making of Man.*

[81]It had long been established as the principle for recognizing a corrupt text. Origen summarizes the list of signs that designate when the "material" reading of a scriptural passage cannot be accepted (historical impossibility, apparent immorality, its general lack of fit with the tone of the text and so on). See J. A. McGuckin, "Origen as Literary Critic in the Alexandrian Tradition," in L. Perrone, ed., *Origenianum Octavum* (Leuven: Peeters, 2002). Gregory more or less follows him in his *Prologue to the Homilies on the Song of Songs.* For both Origen and Gregory, this *akolouthia* is far more than a grammatical principle, but is rather the "theological grammar" of the whole divine dispensation for the world. The patristic implication is that without this deeper grammatical understanding (or syntax of meaning) one cannot even begin to interpret the text.

[82]It can be seen especially in the *Homilies on the Beatitudes* and the *Psalm Inscriptions* but is prevalent in most of his mature work.

[83]J. Daniélou, "*Akolouthia chez Grégoire de Nysse*," *Revue des Sciences religieuses* 27 (1953): 219–249. Monique Alexandre ("*La théorie de l'exégèse dans le De Hominis Opificio et l'In Hexaemeron*," 95–96) illustrates the treatment of a similar exegetical idea in Philo's *Creation of the World* (chs. 28–29, 64–67, and 131).

[84]One of Gregory's key texts: cf. 2 Cor. 3:18.

3

Holy Scripture, Interpretation, and Spiritual Cognition in St. Simeon the New Theologian

Theodore Stylianopoulos

In reaction to the disintegrating aspects of modern biblical studies prevalent in academic circles, as is well known, a number of scholars have called for a corrective shift toward greater attention to the canonical authority, unity, theology, and spirituality of the Bible.[1] In particular, a small but increasing number of scholars has looked to the patristic tradition for both inspiration and direction in the recovery of Holy Scripture as the word of God integrally connected to the Church, tradition, doctrine, liturgy, prayer, and spiritual life.[2] In this paper, I aim to reflect on the Orthodox side of this hermeneutical discussion with chief reference to a single Church Father, St. Symeon the New Theologian (949–1022). In doing so, my purpose is threefold: (1) to present St. Symeon's understanding of scripture and its interpretation by means of a close reading of his works;[3] (2) to engage the discussion of St. Symeon's views with the hermeneutical positions of contemporary Orthodox biblical scholars and theologians; and (3) in the process, to offer some comments on the status of the hermeneutical question in Orthodoxy today.

The Nature and Function of Scripture

St. Symeon lived and worked in the context of the life of the Great Church of Constantinople, where he served and taught as monk and abbot, attracting devoted adherents as well as unrelenting enemies.[4] An heir to the monastic, liturgical, dogmatic, and ecclesiastical tradition of Eastern Christianity, he fully shared the classical patristic view of the unquestioned authority, unity, and primacy of scripture as divine revelation. For him, the Bible was not merely an ancient record of the oracles of God but the living voice of God heralding the way of salvation to each generation. For example, in an extensive admonition to negligent monks on the appropriate conduct of monastic life, he writes, among other things:

> Do you not tremble, O man, when you hear God day by day saying to you through the whole of sacred Scripture, "Let no evil talk come out of your mouths" (Eph. 4:29) . . . Have you not heard that God is Judge . . . What does He say? "He who looks at a woman lustfully has already committed adultery with her in his heart" (Mt. 5:28).[5]

In the same discourse, he refers to the Bible as the "divinely inspired Scriptures" and "the word of God," invoking the biblical metaphors of the "two-edged sword" (Heb. 4:12) and "burning fire" (Jer. 20:9).[6] Because the scriptures clearly reveal the will of God and provide unfailing guidance toward salvation, they are to be studied with utmost diligence and to be obeyed with absolute care:

> We need great soberness, great zeal, much searching of the divine Scriptures. The Savior has [said]: "Search the Scriptures" (Jn. 5:39). Search them and hold fast to what they say with great exactitude and faith, in order that you may know God's will clearly from the divine Scriptures and be able infallibly (ἀπταίστως) to distinguish good from evil (Heb. 5:14) . . . Nothing is so conducive for saving us as the following of the divine precepts of the Savior.[7]

St. Symeon nowhere takes up the question of the nature or function of the Bible as separate topics for discussion. His many references to and innumerable citations from scripture in terms either of phraseology or entire passages amply demonstrate his exalted view of the Bible as divinely inspired, absolutely authoritative, infallible,[8] and in full harmony with the whole stream of tradition in all its forms—dogmatic, liturgical, monastic, catechetical, devotional, and ecclesiastical. For him, truly, it can be said that scripture is known as "Scripture *in* Tradition," according to the catchy expression of John Breck's new volume.[9]

However, the intriguing hermeneutical element resident in St. Symeon's extraordinary witness in the religious world of his time is precisely his reliance on and use of scripture to critique the prevailing view and practice of the operative religious tradition by clerics, monks, theologians, state officials, and lay people alike. To put it concisely, St. Symeon's bold and prophetic call for radical renewal within the Byzantine Church, a highly controversial position that led to his condemnation and lengthy exile at the hands of the ecclesiastical authorities, had to do with nothing less than aspects of the truth of the gospel seemingly swallowed up and forgotten in an ocean of traditional religious formalism unable to bear the words of an evangelical voice.

St. Symeon's biblical position may be defined in terms of two major points. The first point has to do with his constant, direct, and abundant use of scripture. Virtually not a single page of his writings can be found without references to the Bible, whether by allusion or explicit use of biblical phraseology or even collections of scriptural citations. This feature of his writings is by no means insignificant. Canon 19 of the Quinisext Council (691) had already decreed that biblical interpreters had to adhere to the fixed interpretations of the Church Fathers and not follow their own minds in their work.[10] Because of the enormous influence of the earlier great Doctors of the Church, as well as the understandable fear of heresy, it was a time in Byzantium marked by the development of chains of patristic interpretations on biblical passages (ἀνθολόγια). This tendency toward traditionalism eventually led to a deep reservation about the private reading of the Bible in the Orthodox Church, especially after the Reformation, a tendency not unknown even today. However, in St. Symeon, as is the case with the Church Fathers of the fourth century, such as St. Basil and St. John Chrysostom, we find not only a direct and abundant use of scripture, but also explicit directions to others to "search the scriptures" according to the words of the Lord (Jn. 5:39).[11] Here is an author whose mind and writings are saturated with the language, teachings, and spiritual sensibilities of the biblical witness.

The second point pertains to St. Symeon's theological conviction that the divine revelation contained in the scriptures is the decisive criterion of truth for faith and life. In other words, the scriptures for him provide the conscious theological grounding of his message and spirituality. He writes:

> Nothing whatever is more profitable for the soul which has chosen to study God's law day and night than searching the divine scriptures. The meaning of the Holy Spirit's grace is hidden in them. It fills a man's spiritual perception with every pleasure, lifts it entirely from earthly things and the lowliness of what is visible, and makes it both angelic in form and a sharer in the angels' very life.[12]

Elsewhere he speaks of the nourishment of the heart with the living bread of the word, the wine of the knowledge of God, and the divine grace of the Spirit to be discovered in the Bible.[13]

St. Symeon is, of course, cognizant of the lives and teachings of the Church Fathers who preceded him. From time to time, he cites examples from their lives, and on rare occasions, he also quotes from their writings. He claims that his message is in harmony with both the scriptures as well as the Fathers. He also assumes and is certainly governed by the dogmatic trinitarian tradition as he expounds on the mystery of God in the Bible. Nevertheless, as far as direct focus and reliance for truth and guidance in life is concerned, nothing can compare with his concentration on the primacy of the testimony of scripture. He not only incessantly seeks to build his case almost exclusively on biblical texts, but also repeats an authoritative refrain that he gives "no advice beyond that which is in the commandments of God and the divine Scriptures."[14] "Everything I have said is true, is in accordance with the divine and God-inspired Scriptures . . . Believe, follow the Holy Scriptures, and do whatever they tell you, and you will find everything without exception to be as it is written."[15] His functional appeal to the Church Fathers pales in comparison with the invocation of the authority of scripture as the ground of truth. For example, in a lengthy discourse on the conscious gift of the Spirit and the new creation in Christ, he gives a single, brief citation from St. Basil the Great, while the whole of his exposition is replete with biblical texts. As he concludes, he exhorts:

> Believe first of all that these things are true and in accordance with the Holy Scriptures and, by studying the latter thoroughly, know that here, already, the seal of the Holy Spirit is given to those who believe. And, having believed, pursue it so that you may obtain. . . . Run, fight, pursue, seek, knock, ask, and incline toward nothing else until you have obtained it . . . until you hear: "Well done, good and faithful servant; you have been faithful over a little, I will set you over much" (Mt. 25:21); until you have become children of the light and of the day.[16]

Thus we come to the first major hermeneutical question in Orthodox theology—the relationship between scripture and tradition. What is more correct to say hermeneutically, "Scripture *in* Tradition" with John Breck, or "Scripture *and* Tradition," which is the more usual formulation? Of course, both propositions could be reasonably argued. In fact, there are instances, as in the case of St. Symeon, in which for the sake of the truth of the gospel one could even speak of "Scripture *versus* Tradition," instances in which the actual life of the Church may have departed from a full understanding and actualization of the good news. Without getting lost in semantics, the issue concerns the interdependence of scripture and tradition. A balanced discussion of the issue is partly dependent on the definition of terms. Since scripture is already largely defined by virtue of its canonization, which inevitably distinguishes (not separates) it from tradition, the more problematic term is tradition—small "t" or capital "T," and how would one exactly specify the contents of these symbols? It is clear that there was no argument between St. Symeon and his opponents about the divine character and formal authority of the Bible. But there was sharp disagreement between them on matters pertaining to the very essence of the received tradition—what St. Symeon viewed as the apostolic faith and life. In this connection, the whole witness of St. Symeon constituted a crucial *biblical* critique of the ongoing stream of tradition as apparently understood and lived by the majority of that era. It could be argued that the matters in contention involved Tradition with a capital "T" insofar as they included the understanding of the gospel, the believer's relationship to Christ and the Spirit, the perception of the sacraments, the role of the priesthood and monasticism, as well as the practice of the evangelical virtues.[17]

This is not the place for a more detailed discussion of the hermeneutical relationship between scripture and tradition, or for an extensive analysis of John Breck's thesis about "Scripture in Tradition." Elsewhere, I have expressed my views on the organic continuity and mutual interdependence between the Bible and tradition.[18] Suffice it here to say that, in general and abstract terms, the interplay between sacred texts and ongoing religious traditions marks parallel dynamics in all religions, including Christianity, Judaism, and Islam. Even within the diversity of Christian communities, no community reads the Bible except as "Scripture in Tradition"—namely, the tradition by which each community defines itself. As far as Orthodox theology is concerned, the canonization of the scriptures and the massive authority attributed to the Bible by the Church Fathers, including St. Symeon the New Theologian, require what is often forgotten: that the full voice of the biblical witness must be kept alive, guide, and, when necessary, even critique the life of the Church. In the words of Thomas Hopko, "Everything in the Church is judged by the Bible. Nothing in the Church may contradict it. Everything in the Church must be biblical."[19]

Accordingly, Orthodox hermeneutics must seek a proper balance in the explication of the organic unity and interdependence of the Bible and tradition. Just as it is critical that the Bible is not severed from tradition, so also it is vital that the overwhelming influence of developing tradition does not overshadow the biblical witness, as in the case of St. Symeon's era. The fact that Holy Scripture is born from the womb of tradition by no means legitimizes an uncritical control of tradition over scripture because, then, the canonization of scripture as a standard of truth would be meaningless. My brief constructive critique of John Breck's thesis is that it allows too great an opening for an imbalance between scripture and tradition, favoring the latter to the diminishment of the biblical witness. Indeed, a reader misses in Fr. John's otherwise elegant and substantial scholarship a significant biblical critique of any aspects of contemporary Orthodox theology and practice,[20] which in some respects may not be dissimilar to what St. Symeon encountered in his time. It is appropriate for Fr. John to demonstrate how Orthodox Mariology, Christology, and spirituality stand in harmonious coherence with the scriptures. It is also equally appropriate that an Orthodox hermeneutical position allow critical biblical light to be shed on such matters as the proclamation of the gospel in the Church, the understanding of hierarchy, the vision and practice of ministry, the centrality of Christ and the Spirit in daily life, and the formalism of worship and piety toward the kind of renewal the New Theologian vigorously advocated. To focus on "Scripture in Tradition" without equal emphasis on scripture's authority to speak "to" and challenge tradition risks the danger of tradition co-opting and silencing the prophetic and evangelical voice of scripture so powerfully heralded by the New Theologian.

The Study and Interpretation of Scripture

The use of scripture and appeals to biblical texts unavoidably raise questions about method, hermeneutical presuppositions, and the soundness of exegetical results, whether implicitly or explicitly. Orthodox theologians and biblical scholars have long discussed these matters, especially in the light of the fact that modern biblical criticism is acknowledged to be largely a western development, intertwined with problematic presuppositions of the Enlightenment, despite some of its precedents in Christian antiquity among Alexandrian and Antiochene scholars. Although virtually all Orthodox, biblical scholars affirm the use of critical historical studies of the Bible, and biblical departments in Orthodox universities and seminaries confirm the fact, deep uncertainties remain about the extent of interaction with the style and methodologies of international biblical scholarship. Rare among us is the Orthodox biblical scholar who has not felt at one time or another what John Breck honestly discloses in his preface—a failure to minister to our students' needs by giving lectures as "exercises in [historical and literary] analysis" rather that as "a living and life-giving witness" to the word of God.[21] The hermeneutical task of defining a distinct Orthodox approach to biblical studies—especially concerning the relationship of historical studies and Christian doctrine, modern methodologies and the patristic exegetical heritage, biblical interpretation and liturgy, as well as academic scholarship and spirituality—remains an open-ended issue in Orthodox theological scholarship.[22]

In his works, St. Symeon makes no explicit comments on formal matters of interpretation. On occasion he will offer allegorizing explications of texts. For example, for him Christ's words "I was hungry and you gave me no food" (Mt. 25:35) meant not material food as much as spiritual food for those who desperately need it and by which Christ is truly fed.[23] Less frequently he refers to traditional typological interpretations, such as to the seven days of creation as a type of seven ages to come and the garden of Paradise as a sign of the eternal kingdom.[24] However, apart from these rare examples, St. Symeon largely counts on the plain meaning of texts as they stand grammatically and syntactically, with various degrees of attention to context, much as most homilists and some theologians do even today. He takes for granted the unity of scripture to the extent that he can freely quote and combine texts from any book of the Bible.

Although he is aware that the meaning of a text can be forced and twisted,[25] he nevertheless assumes that the plain voice of scripture can be heard by all who resolve to engage it with care and are willing to listen to, accept, and apply its message.

However, a striking and paradoxical aspect of his use of scripture is, on the one hand, his incessant admonitions to study it diligently and, on the other, his repeated warnings not to meddle in vain disputations. His own work indicates that prior to and especially after his first mystical experience, St. Symeon engaged in direct and concentrated study of Bible.[26] As an inspired interpreter and teacher, according to his own claims, he thoroughly studied the scriptures, collecting and memorizing texts for particular purposes, and producing an impressive corpus of biblical teachings—particularly on his favorite topic of the new creation, indeed the resurrection of the soul, as a present reality, and the new baptism by the Holy Spirit, through the indwelling of Christ and the Spirit.[27] Nor was he hesitant to engage in theological disputes on such subjects as the Holy Trinity, predestination, and the question of whether the glorified saints had knowledge of one another in the afterlife,[28] all essentially based on the Bible. Although he regarded these questions as meddling, they had nevertheless to be addressed by correct teaching. In principle and by necessity, St. Symeon did not therefore reject scholarly study as such. Yet his views were governed by a clear vision of what for him defined appropriate study of scripture, a vision whose elements are instructive for biblical scholars in every age.

The first major element in his hermeneutical vision is an unremitting attention to the central purpose of biblical study—namely, the explication of the good news of Christ and the way of salvation. In his *First Ethical Discourse*, commenting on his own task inspired and illuminated by the Spirit, St. Symeon explains at length that his purpose is threefold: to clarify the mystery of the new creation in Christ; to manifest Christ's love in this manner; and to have all of his readers share in the promised blessing of being brothers and sisters to Christ, a blessing by grace equal to the apostles.[29] In the same context of the discussion about not inquiring into matters pertaining to life after death, he continues:

> Let us be persuaded by the Master who says: "search the scriptures" (Jn. 5:39). Search, that is, and not meddle! Search the Scriptures and do not busy yourselves with disputes which lie outside the sacred writings [i.e., direct knowledge of mysteries beyond death]. Search the Scriptures so that you may learn about faith, and hope, and love. . . . Why should we busy ourselves with matters which are beyond us, in particular when in truth we fail to see things which lie at our very feet?[30]

He nevertheless takes on the task of answering at length the meddling question and shows that indeed the glorified saints enjoy mutual conscious knowledge in heaven.

For St. Symeon, meddling questions and vain disputes were those that detracted from the central purpose of biblical study, which is simultaneously both theocentric and soteriological—to attain to the knowledge of and personal participation in the mystery of God as testified by scripture. The "treasure" to be found in the biblical texts is the living Christ by the power of the Spirit. Through the scriptures, God speaks to those who sit in darkness that they may see the great light that shines in the present just as much as in the days of the apostles.[31] The pastoral ministry of "tending the sheep" is to teach the faithful "to have untroubled, sincere, and unhesitating faith in Me [Christ], to love Me with all their soul and all their mind, just as I have loved them . . . Teach them the communion that comes by their doing and fulfilling the commandments."[32] The scriptures present many precepts, various ways and many works of righteous persons, but there is really one and the same path for all, one goal and destination, one city to be reached—the holy Zion, the kingdom of heaven, the place where believers reign with Christ—and that realm is the realm of the holy and undivided trinity of faith, hope, and love, already shared by believers and summed up in Christ, who is addressed as "Holy Love."[33] Why study the Bible? St. Symeon's answer is clear and direct:

> Take heed how you listen! Christ our God says, "Search the Scriptures" (Jn. 5:39). Why does He say this? First, that we may be taught the way that leads to salvation. Second, that by practicing the commandments we may walk without turning aside, and attain to the salvation of our souls (2 Pt. 1:9). What, then, is our salvation? Jesus Christ . . . the good news of great joy . . . Christ the Lord (Lk. 2:10f.).[34]

The second major element in St. Symeon's vision of sound biblical study is an unyielding emphasis on *praxis*—the scriptures must be not merely heard but also obeyed, not merely read but applied, not only studied but actualized by embracing and living the precepts they teach and command. It is in this regard that the Saint makes innumerable references to his own experience, not as one who had formal training as a scholar, but as one who practiced what he discovered in the Bible. The main thing is "to walk in the light of the divine Scriptures and go in the way of God's commandments."[35] In his *First Theological Discourse*, he excoriates the "modern theologians" of his time who analyze spiritual mysteries only to be admired at banquets and to make a name for themselves. Reliance must be placed not on mere words, but on Christian life and conduct. Without true repentance and following the footsteps of Christ, the Holy Spirit does not open one's mind to the mysteries of scripture. To conduct analysis without a sense of awe is brash insolence; to teach the things of the Spirit without the Spirit is presumptive pride; to speak of the things of God without spiritual illumination is to theologize on the basis of pseudo-knowledge (1 Tim. 6:20). Even if one were to pass through all the degrees of philosophy, the spiritual treasure cannot be won without the evangelical precepts of faith, repentance, confession of sins, humility and the like.[36]

St. Symeon's emphasis on the necessary integration of biblical study and spiritual life is most explicit in *Catechetical Discourse* 24. Here he draws a clear hermeneutical differentiation between "spiritual knowledge" (πνευματικὴ γνῶσις) and ordinary intellectual knowledge, what he calls "secular (or worldly) and pagan knowledge" (κοσμικὴ καὶ ἑλληνικὴ γνῶσις), as applicable to biblical study. His case for a spiritual reading of the Bible may be summed up as follows.[37] True spiritual knowledge is enshrined in "the Gospel of Christ and in the other divine Scriptures," likened to a treasure chest containing God's commandments and unutterable blessings that sparkle like pearls of light and life. Ordinary secular learning can master the scriptures to the extent that the chest can be carried on the erudite scholar's shoulders. One can memorize all the scriptures and freely quote them. Nevertheless, the chest remains closed to those who have not practiced the commandments. No human wisdom can open the chest. "Nor is it by Scripture that the contents of Scripture become clear," because spiritual knowledge has to do not with the letter of scripture (that is, mere conceptual knowledge of its contents), but with the Spirit who actualizes the mystical reality of the new creation signified by those teachings. Only Christ himself by the power of the Spirit is able to unlock the treasure, which is none other than the personal and conscious revelation of the Lord himself to those who love him and keep his commandments, just as he promised in Jn. 14:21. Let no one then be deceived, because spiritual knowledge can be acquired in no other way than through the conscious indwelling of Christ and by participation in all of his blessings, such as perfect love of God and neighbor, mortification of the earthly members (Col. 3:5), freedom from the oppression of the devil, renewal by the Spirit, adoption as sons, and endowment with the mind of Christ (1 Cor. 2:16). The hermeneutical key is thus not "leaning on the mere study of the Scriptures," but the "uncovering of the eyes of our minds" in those who are "born from above" (Jn. 3:3) and are transformed by the Spirit. Otherwise, for those who are "despisers and negligent," despite great learning, the Holy Scriptures remain a sealed book. "The mystical and divine glory and power hidden in them" cannot be disclosed to those beset by lack of repentance and spiritual blindness in terms of life and conduct.

What implications can be drawn from St. Symeon's hermeneutical vision? On the one hand, as a zealous prophetic and evangelical voice, his is an uncompromising position. The distinction between the two kinds of knowledge is virtually absolute with no allowance for gray. The intense focus on the saving message of scripture, as well as on Christian praxis, is such that the Saint attributes little or no value to learning and analysis apart from a committed and fervent Christian life. Perhaps his monastic background inclined him to devaluate scholarly preoccupation, just as equally all worldly endeavors, despite the fact that he himself was an educated man, a skillful writer, and not reluctant to engage in controversy over meddling questions. Nor does he consider the possibility that two equally faithful students of the Bible could honestly disagree on a matter either of contextual exegesis or application of a biblical teaching to new circumstances in the Church's life. Such questions do not arise in the scope of his thought. In this regard, his uncompromising position on "spiritual" and "secular" knowledge can function only as a corrective rather than an absolute standard. The diversity and development of the Christian tradition, including internal theological disputes, gives ample evidence of a far more complex hermeneutical interaction between faith and culture, spiritual and secular knowledge. The Alexandrian and Antiochene Fathers in their use of the Hellenic heritage for the explication of the gospel serve as powerful examples of the necessity of theological scholarship's conversation with the intellectual currents and methodologies of any given epoch.

On the other hand, as a corrective, St. Symeon's hermeneutical perspective, rooted in scripture itself and the classic patristic tradition, is highly instructive for exegetical and theological study. First, it reminds us that the Bible is not "like any other book," but a sacred text of the Church whose subject matter is the mystery of the living God in loving engagement with men and women transformed by the encounter. The mystery of God cannot be exhausted by formal studies, whether historical, literary, or theological, as if the Bible were either a collection of ancient human wisdom or a deposit of theological propositions. Secondly, the essential purpose of biblical interpretation is not to solve or dissolve the mystery of God as much as it is to keep the mystery alive before the Church and the world.[38] But to do so, biblical study must be true to the central message of the scriptures and to the content of the spiritual realities they proclaim—the good news of redemption from sin and death, the risen Christ, the gift of the Spirit, the new creation, the liberation of life, the hope of the coming kingdom. And thirdly, Christian interpreters cannot be but just that—Christian, interpreting the Bible as the Christian Bible. In other words, the explication of the revelation of the mystery of God in Christ and the power of the Holy Spirit cannot be apart from the response of faith and obedience leading to the renewal of life within the body that we call Church. Formal studies are valuable in illuminating historical events, concepts, and institutions. But in the end, genuine knowledge of God and fit proclamation of it come by way of personal engagement. "For it is not a matter of solving [the] mystery, but of participating in it."[39]

Interpretation and Mystical Cognition

In this last section of my paper, my intent is not to give an account of St. Symeon's mystical experiences,[40] but to probe further the hermeneutical function of mystical cognition, following up the above discussion about the spiritual and worldly knowledge of the scriptures. In particular, I want to consider the charismatic authority claimed by St. Symeon as an interpreter of scripture, the contextual elements of mystical cognition, as well as the implications of these matters for Orthodox heremeneutics.

A striking aspect of St. Symeon's spirituality is his incessant claim of his own direct experience of the living God in the manner of the prophets, the apostles, as well as the preceding saints, a claim that infuriated many of his contemporaries to no small degree. St. Symeon compared his case to Christ himself, who did works of the Spirit but was rejected by those who thus "blasphemed against the Spirit."[41] He writes:

> I perform my ministry to the Spirit . . . it is not I who speak great and extraordinary things to your charity, but the Spirit of God . . . We minister to you the oracles of God . . . He who fails to believe him who speaks through the Spirit commits a sin and blasphemes against the Spirit (Mk. 3:29).[42]

Moreover, he saw himself as part of a living tradition of charismatic saints stretching across the centuries "joined together in the bond of the Spirit . . . a golden chain . . . in faith, love and good works . . . a single chain that cannot be easily be broken."[43] St. Symeon believed himself to be a living link of this tradition by virtue of his connection with his own now-deceased spiritual elder, whom he regarded as a glorified saint and who had blessed him similar to the way Elijah had blessed Elishah.[44]

On the basis apparently of St. Symeon's testimony, the late Fr. John Romanides of blessed memory staunchly advocated an exclusive theological and exegetical hermeneutic centered on the paradigm of the charismatic saint,[45] a position of considerable appeal to many, not least because of the traditional veneration accorded to saints in the Orthodox Church. According to Romanides, the prophets, apostles, and saints, who enjoyed the mystery of divine contemplation and deification (θεωρία and θέωσις), are the unerring prototypes of theological and exegetical study. Not speculative theologians and exegetes who deal merely with words and concepts, but only those who have reached a stage of divine illumination, if not full divine union, can correctly speak of things pertaining to God, sharing the "same species of knowledge" as did the prophets and the apostles. It was widely known that Romanides had little regard for the entire enterprise of theological and biblical scholarship, whether Orthodox or not, operative beyond his own exclusive hermeneutical perspective. To quote him in connection with biblical studies:

> For the Fathers authority is not only the Bible, but the Bible plus those glorified, to wit the Prophets, Apostles and Saints. The Bible as a book is not in itself either inspired or infallible.
>
> It becomes inspired and infallible within the communion of Saints who have the experience of divine glory described in, but not conveyed by, the Bible. To those outside of the living tradition of θεωρία the Bible is a Book which does not unlock its mysteries.[46]

There are several reasons why Romanides' absolute hermeneutical position cannot be supported by the witness of the New Theologian without significant qualifications. To question St. Symeon's understanding of the inspiration, truth, and authority of the canonical scriptures is to fly in the face of every page he has written. As has been noted above, the Saint's chief reliance in demonstrating his teachings is on the biblical texts themselves, to which he continuously appeals and invites his readers to ponder. All are exhorted to study the scriptures, all can approach its mysteries, all have the capacity to achieve contemplation of its spiritual realities, unless they refuse to learn, because the ability is given to all by God.[47] St. Symeon himself and the saints he invokes are existential examples of what the canonical scriptures authoritatively proclaim. When he writes, "we present to you the truth from divine scripture and from experience itself to show you the royal way,"[48] he implies not that he has added something to the truth of scripture, but only that he has embodied it in life and conduct. The primary authority is found in the canonical scriptures themselves.

In parallel fashion, St. Symeon provides a startling qualification of his own authority with respect both to his hearers and readers and to the Bible. In his great apologia, where he makes some of the highest claims to authority, he nevertheless presents his teaching as his "opinion," open to the judgment of his interlocutors. For his part, he writes what he *thinks* is the truth (Ἔγω μὲν οὖν οὕτως οἴομαι τὴν ἀλήθειαν ἔχειν). For their part, they must see and test what he says (ὑμεῖς δὲ ἴδετε καὶ δοκιμάσετε τὰ λεγόμενα παρ' ἱμῶν).[49] He sought to persuade those who presumably had yet shared neither his mystical experiences, nor his spiritual knowledge of the Bible. On what basis are they to see and test his words? Two principles are indicated in the same context. One is the common creation of human beings in the image of God, which for the Saint means the endowment of human reason as a gift of God.[50] The other is the primary authority of the Bible "as we establish and assert all things from the Holy Scriptures themselves and clearly demonstrate them."[51] With regard to those who pervert the teachings of the apostles, it is "from the very divine Scriptures themselves [that] we collect that which strengthens and corrects their thinking and that of their followers."[52]

The above references show that St. Symeon in his direct appeals to scripture, as well as his arduous efforts to persuade his readers through reasonable argument open to all, was largely an heir of the classic patristic tradition which relied on the plain meaning and the principle of the clarity of scripture. Church Fathers such as St. Athanasius, St. Basil, St. Gregory the Theologian, and St. John Chrysostom[53] attributed massive authority to the literal meaning of the Bible for secure instruction, understandable by all serious readers, concerning God's will and the way of salvation. For them—granted the inseparable unity of faith, life, and study—the plain meaning of scripture was to be derived by contextual and grammatical exegesis, not by reference to any esoteric methods or appeals to elite groups. In the face of exegetical diversity and controversy, of which there was no lack in Christian antiquity, the normative interpretation of the Bible took place through open theological debates and the Ecumenical Councils representing the whole witness of the Church. Only the Gnostics claimed elite groups, special revelations, secret teachings, and esoteric approaches unknown to the wider Christian community. While we highly value the apostles and saints as witnesses and guides to Christian faith and life, we cannot follow a narrow hermeneutic that converges on the charismatic figure as an exclusive authority seemingly raised above the Bible, above the Councils, and above the Church. Such a position would undercut the Church's ongoing direct access to the Bible, as well as the Church's right to test charismatic claims. Just as St. Symeon challenged his readers to test his words by reference to scripture and the wider tradition, the apostolic advice must remain operative: "Do not believe every spirit, but test the spirits" (1 Jn. 4:1).

However, the question about the spiritual reading of scripture remains. What is behind St. Symeon's unending emphasis on spiritual knowledge and spiritual perception of scripture? I believe the answer lies in his understanding of mystical cognition, as well as the context and ways it manifests itself, and frankly, the answer may be simpler than many think. In *Catechetical Discourse* 35, a stirring review of his life in the form of a prayerful thanksgiving to Christ, he relates how he first longed to find the way of salvation, the forgiveness of his sins, and a spiritual guide. And although he formally knew and could read from the scriptures about the gift of the Spirit and other blessings of the new creation, he essentially knew nothing at all and "remained insensitive to all" (ἀναισθήτως πρὸς πάντα διεκείμην).[54] He thought that the words of scripture applied to others in the past or in the world to come, not to the present life. And then, in his spiritual struggles, like St. Paul, he was granted a dramatic vision of Christ as Light, which at first he did not fully understand. He subsequently lapsed into slackness and worse sins. However, clinging to his spiritual father in repentance and obedience, he finally withdrew altogether from the affairs and pleasures of the world, and once again, but gradually, experienced various levels of transformation up to an experience of heaven.[55] Then he realized that the King and Creator himself dwelt within him as he, even in sleep, was able to conquer an accustomed sexual fantasy of the devil. It was in such ways of struggle and growth that he continued to comprehend the source of his previous spiritual deadness, the veil of insensitivity (κάλυμμα ἀναισθησίας, cf. 2 Cor. 3:14ff.); namely, the power of sin and evil passions, which Christ dissolved bit by bit just as the sun dissolves a thick mist.[56] The Saint's soul was cleansed and his mind's eyes were opened to the singular truth of his life's message: that the living God himself as testified by scripture "appears clearly and is consciously known (ἐμφανῶς δείκνυται καὶ γνωρίζεται πάνυ γνωστῶς) and even speaks as a friend "face to face" (Ex. 33:11) to those who love and sincerely seek him.[57] This is the great truth, the burning love, and the intoxicating joy, to which St. Symeon and the past saints testify, in whom the Spirit dwells and Christ lives and moves:

> He becomes in them all the things about which you hear in the divine Scriptures concerning the kingdom of heaven—a pearl, a mustard seed, leaven, water, fire, bread, drink of life . . . a lamp, bed, marriage bed, wedding chamber, bridegroom, friend, brother, and father . . . the terms are without number![58]

In sum, the above are the contextual terms in which the New Theologian describes his personal conversion and the mystical cognition derived from it. He uses a rich array of words, such as θεθρία (contemplation), αἴσθησις (perception), πεῖρα (experience), ὅρασις (vision), ἔλλαμψις (flashing, illumination), ἄνωθεν γέννησις (new birth, cf. Jn. 3:3), ἀνάστασις ψυχῆς (resurrection of soul), καινὴ κτίσις (new creation), and many others. He writes, "These, then, are the divine mysteries of Christians. This is the hidden power of our faith (ἡ ἐγκεκρυμμένη τῆς πίστεως ἡμῶν δύναμις) which unbelievers, or those who believe with difficulty, or rather believe in part, do not see nor are able at all to see."[59] He repeats the same theme in diverse ways and images, but the grand message remains the same. One might compare his case with that of the Evangelist John, who expounds the same message about Christ in various contexts, language, and images as Jesus meets with Nicodemus, the Samaritan woman, the paralytic, the man born blind, and the crowds. The same powerful message resounds again and again in all of St. Symeon's writings.

It is not our place either to analyze or to evaluate the nature *per se* of St. Symeon's mystical experience. However, it becomes quite clear that the mystical cognition deriving from it is neither a specific exegetical method, nor some esoteric interpretation of the Bible. Rather, it has to do with the receptivity of faith, a spiritual sensibility of soul, an awareness of God's transforming presence, a sense of freedom and renewal, accompanied by an enormous awe and wonder, as well as the conviction that the above "mysteries" (μυστήρια) of which the Bible speaks are facts and realities, not mere words and concepts. Again, one may compare the case, as St. Symeon often does, with Jesus's message to those who "seeing they do not see, and hearing they do not hear" (Mt. 13:13).[60] The incomprehensibility of Jesus's message about the kingdom lay essentially not in the lack of clarity or mental understanding of the stories and parables as heard by hearers, but in their lack of openness of heart to the immediate, powerful reality of the kingdom breaking into people's lives just as Jesus spoke and acted! No faith was stirred and no light came on—nothing clicked! Similarly, St. Symeon's whole point is that the scriptures speak quite clearly about the gospel, Christ, the Spirit, the new creation, and so on, but the "majority"[61] of his contemporaries refused truly to listen and believe, to repent and be forgiven, to be cleansed and illuminated, in order to experience firsthand the marvel of these mysteries of the Bible open to all. Naturally, such transforming experiences would rearrange one's priorities, including scholarship, and enliven one's sensitivities to the centrality of Christ and the gospel within the whole story of salvation and the life of the Church. Nevertheless, this powerful witness of the New Theologian diminishes neither the authority of the Bible, nor the discipline of serious study, nor the responsibility to communicate with others on the basis of reasonable discourse through responsible scholarship. What it does emphasize is that theological and biblical study must be accompanied by a serious life of faith and practice, and also the task of putting priorities aright.

What implications can be drawn from the preceding discussion concerning contemporary Orthodox hermeneutics? As has been noted, most Orthodox theologians and biblical scholars have given public approval of international biblical scholarship. Yet, clearly, a great deal of unease has been expressed about the spiritual dryness, even theological emptiness, of biblical scholarship by an increasing number of theologians and scholars from all Christian traditions. Much of this is due to the radicalism of revisionist biblical scholars, such as those involved in the Jesus Seminar, with little commitment to the authority of the Bible, the proclamation of the gospel, and the good estate of the Church. But dissatisfaction also arises from the perceived lack of sufficient spiritual and theological fruits derived from biblical scholarship in an age thirsting for spirituality. Even attempts to popularize the fruits of biblical scholarship, with rare exceptions, seem to breathe the same scholarly spirit and to fall short of the desired impact. To be fair, it must also be said that the works of systematic theologians have not been any more successful in ministering to the pastoral and spiritual needs of God's people.

In my humble judgment, the chief challenge in biblical hermeneutics lies not in speculative theories of knowledge, whether philosophical, literary, or sociological, but rather in the task of how to balance appropriately scholarship, normative theological teaching, and devotional or spiritual reading of the Bible. On these matters I have expressed myself more fully elsewhere.[62] Here I merely rehearse a summary of my position, asking the indulgence of my readers. I am convinced that biblical study, and all study of the Christian tradition as well, such as in patristics and liturgics, involves three interrelated moves—historical, evaluative, and applicatory. In biblical study, the historical part is properly called "exegesis," a word whose etymology defines the very task: to bring out of the biblical texts of whatever is there, not to import into them what is not there ("eisegesis"). The task is accomplished best by contextual and grammatical interpretation with due attention to authorial purpose, coherence, and emphasis, as well as language, literary forms, and types. The Antiochene and Cappadocian Fathers relied on this method especially during the great christological and trinitarian controversies focused on largely on biblical texts and based on the cogency of contextual interpretation. We call it a historical task today simply because of the historical consciousness developed in recent centuries. A task requiring training, honest historical research becomes the foundation of Christian biblical and theological scholarship, involving both sympathy for the subject matter and mutual accountability on the part of those engaged in it. Certainly, the wealth of biblical knowledge available in lexica, commentaries, and many good books on biblical theology attest to the value of historical exegesis over many years.

The second move, involving evaluation of the exegetical results, is far more problematic because the weight of judgment is transferred from the scope of the biblical authors to that of the reader. An exegetical scholar may produce the most eloquent and accurate account of the Prophet Ezekiel's or St. Paul's life and thought in the context of their respective social and religious worlds. However, what aspects of those accounts a reader accepts as authoritative, valuable, and even normative for his or her life (as well as how and why he or she accepts them as such) depends on the reader's own faith, willingness, worldview, context of life, and assumed presuppositions. It is at this level that most of us part company, including scholars who may either share or diverge in perspectives, depending on our background, intellectual experience, and personal courage. At this level, which is properly the philosophically and theologically evaluative level, chaos prevails in contemporary Christian scholarship precisely because of group and individual preferences. And yet, Holy Scripture and the classic Christian tradition itself give testimony of the possibility of convergences for those committed both to biblical and ecclesial authority. As far as Orthodox theologians and biblical scholars are concerned, the plumb line is the doctrinal teaching of the Church derived not from a *magisterium* rooted in a single person, but from the life of the whole Church expressed through councils to be received by the whole people of God. This stricture does not necessarily stifle creativity and the present work of the Spirit because, as new situations arise, Orthodox Christians have the responsibility of thinking through issues in both prayerful and cogent ways, always mindful of the doctrinal sense of the Church derived from scripture, tradition, and the ongoing inspiration of the Holy Spirit.

The third move, which is what most readers of the Bible do without much reflection to the first and second, is application of the biblical text to their personal lives, their Church, and the world. Here the primary operative element is the life of faith, prayer, and obedience to the evangelical precepts—just as St. Symeon the New Theologian insisted. To disclose his personal presence and blessings, God requires neither biblical nor doctrinal erudition, but a longing and trusting heart willing to seek him out and to serve him. At this level of spiritual reading of the Bible, some Orthodox scholars have narrowed the window of effective applicability to, or put primary weight on, either notions of entire devotional patterns[63] or the context of the liturgical use of scripture.[64] It is not that these emphases are insignificant in the Orthodox tradition. However, to present them as the truly definitive Orthodox approach to the decisive apprehension of the biblical message is to ignore the large role of the catechetical and doctrinal use of scripture among the Church Fathers, including St. Symeon. It seems one-sided to accentuate either the moments of devotional study or an abstract Eucharistic vision as the most crucial elements of Orthodox hermeneutics. St. Symeon himself was highly aware of what his fellow monastics chanted and heard from the Bible in liturgical services, yet was highly dissatisfied about their spiritual knowledge of biblical teachings because of their slackness of spirit with regard to both worship and scripture. His accents were on the whole horizon of living faith centered on Christ, particularly a deep love for him, a consequent unfailing observance of Christ's precepts, as well as prayerfulness as essential elements of the spiritual comprehension of scripture's message open to all, scholar or not.

Nevertheless, whether explicitly or implicitly, the works of St. Symeon, as does the rich biblical heritage of the Church Fathers as a whole, presuppose all three moves in biblical study—the exegetical, the doctrinal, and the contemplative. What is required is the appropriate balance between them in terms of purpose, place, and audience. None of these elements should be missing in any endeavor, whether in an exegetical paper, a theological treatise, or a parish educational group. Yet the appropriate emphasis must be dictated by context. The perfect paradigm, of course, is the ideal interpreter as one integrated person—scholar, theologian, and saint.

Endnotes

[1]A sampling might include Richard John Neuhaus, ed., *Biblical Interpretation in Crisis: The Ratzinger Conference on Bible and Church* (Grand Rapids: Eerdmans, 1989); Carl E. Braaten and Robert W. Jenson, eds., *Reclaiming the Bible for the Church* (Grand Rapids: Eerdmans, 1995); Brevard S. Childs, *Biblical Theology of the Old and New Testaments* (Minneapolis: Fortress, 1992); Gordon D. Fee, *Gospel and Spirit: Issues in New Testament Hermeneutics* (Peabody: Hendrickson, 1991); M. Robert Mulholland Jr., *Shaped by the Word: The Power of Scripture in Spiritual Formation* (Nashville: Upper Room, 1985); Joseph A. Fitzmeyer, SJ, *Scripture, the Soul of Theology* (New York: Paulist, 1994); Donald G. Bloesch, *Holy Scripture: Revelation, Inspiration and Interpretation* (Downers Grove, IL: InterVarsity, 1994); and T. F. Torrance, *Reality and Evangelical Theology: The Realism of Christian Revelation* (Downers Grove, IL: InterVarsity, 1982, 1999).

[2]The most notable example is the enormous project, led by Thomas C. Oden, to gather the harvest of the entire patristic exegetical tradition in the series Ancient Christian Commentary on Scripture, covering both the Old and New Testaments and presently being published by InterVarsity. See also Christopher A. Hall, *Reading Scripture with the Church Fathers* (Downers Grove, IL: InterVarsity, 1998); Kenneth Tanner and Christopher A. Hall, *Ancient and Postmodern Christianity: Paleo-Orthodoxy in the 21st Century, Essays in Honor of Thomas C. Oden* (Downers Grove, IL: InterVarsity, 2002); Andrew Louth, *Discerning the Mystery: An Essay on the Nature of Theology* (Oxford: Clarendon, 1983); Theodore Stylianopoulos, *The New Testament: An Orthodox Perspective,* vol. 1, *Scripture, Tradition, Hermeneutics* (Brookline, MA: Holy Cross Press, 1997); and John Breck, *The Power of the Word in the Worshiping Church* (Crestwood, NY: St. Vladimir's Seminary Press, 1986); and most recently John Breck, *Scripture in Tradition: The Bible and Its Interpretation in the Orthodox Church* (Crestwood, NY: St. Vladimir's Seminary Press, 2001).

[3]These have appeared in English translation as follows: C. J. deCatanzaro, *Symeon the New Theologian: The Discourses* (New York: Paulist, 1980); Paul McGuckin, *Symeon the New Theologian: The Practical and Theological Chapters and the Three Theological Discourses* (Kalamazoo, MI: Cistercian, 1982); and Alexander Golitzin, *St. Symeon the New Theologian on the Mystical Life: The Ethical Discourses,* vol. 1, *The Church and the Last Things* (Crestwood, NY: St. Vladimir's Seminary Press, 1995), and Alexander Golitzin, *St. Symeon the New Theologian on the Mystical Life: The Ethical Discourses,* vol. 2, *On Virtue and Christian Life* (Crestwood, NY: St. Vladimir's Seminary Press, 1996). Whenever deemed necessary, the original Greek has been consulted. For this paper, I have chosen not to engage St. Symeon's extensive poetical hymns, preferring to work with his expository works.

[4]For a review of his life and thought, see Alexander Golitzin, *St. Symeon the New Theologian on the Mystical Life: The Ethical Discourses,* vol. 3, *Life, Times and Theology* (Crestwood, NY: St. Vladimir's Seminary Press, 1997).

[5]*Catechetical Discourse* 3.6/deCatanzaro, 66, lines 226–234 (always the same lines in *Sources Chrétiennes*).

[6]Ibid., 3.8, 67–68, lines 270–71 and 294–296.

[7]Ibid., 67, lines 279–289.

[8]I have found only a single instance where St. Symeon exercises a mild critique of scripture but quickly backs away when he writes, "The divine Scriptures indicate that there are three places where the mind likes to dwell. I would say myself that there are really two such places—not that I want to teach the contrary to Scripture, God forbid—but I do not count the middle position between the first and the last" (*The Practical and Theological Chapters* 1.78; see McGuckin, 55). This is an obscure passage, which may signify the

carnal, virtuous, and spiritual levels of human existence according to McGuckin, or perhaps "psychic" (ψυχικὸς) for "virtuous," to match Pauline terminology (1 Cor. 2:14).

[9]The full title is cited above, n. 2.

[10]H. R. Percival, ed., *The Seven Ecumenical Councils*, in *The Nicene and Post-Nicene Fathers*, vol. 14 (Grand Rapids: Eerdmans, 1991), 374–375.

[11]A key biblical passage quoted by St. Syrneon in many places, e.g., *Catechetical Discourse* 3.8/deCatanzaro, 67, and *Catechetical Discourse* 28.1/deCatanzaro, 295, as well as *First Ethical Discourse* 12.12.12/Golitzin, vol. 1, 63.

[12]*Twelfth Ethical Discourse*/Golitzin, vol. 2, 155.

[13]*Thirteenth Ethical Discourse*/Golitzin, vol. 2, 164.

[14]*Catechetical Discourse* 12.8/deCatanzaro, 179, lines 243–244.

[15]*Third Ethical Discourse*/Golitzin, vol. 1, 129–130.

[16]*Fifth Ethical Discourse*/Golitzin, vol. 2, 61.

[17]St. Symeon in many places fulminates against those who oppose his teaching concerning the reality of the apostolic life, the new creation, the indwelling of Christ and the Spirit, indeed the second baptism of the Spirit for repentant adults in every generation. He refers to his opponents' position as "blasphemy against the Holy Spirit" and "the worst of all heresies" because it undermines the incarnation, Christ's saving work, the gift of the Spirit, as well as the authority of the Bible. See, for example, *Catechetical Discourse* 29/deCatanzaro, 308–17. Then, at least in one instance, he backs away from the radical charge of heresy, calling it rather "impiety" (ἀσέβειά ἐστι μᾶλλον ἤ αἵρεσις, *Catechetical Discourse* 32.2/deCatanzaro, 336, lines 47–48). However, to question the reality of Christ's work in the way St. Symeon perceives it to be questioned by his opponents is to question the truth of the gospel, and that certainly belongs to the realm of heresy, unless one holds to a merely abstract or legal understanding of dogma.

[18]Stylianopoulos, *The New Testament*, 47–61 and 207–214. See n. 2 above for the full title.

[19]Thomas Hopko, *The Bible in the Orthodox Church*, 66–67.

[20]Apart from occasional expressions of regret about ignorance of the scriptures in our times evident among Orthodox Christians.

[21]Breck, *Scripture in Tradition*, x–xi.

[22]For a review of these issues in Orthodox scholarship, and for a bibliography, see Stylianopoulos, *The New Testament*, 71–77 and 162–185.

[23]*Catechetical Discourse* 9.2/deCatanzaro, 151, lines 36–49. In *Ethical Discourse* 1.6/Golitzin, vol. 1, 43, he builds a long allegorical interpretation on the image of Christ's body—hands, shoulders, breast, belly, thighs, legs, and feet—as representing various virtues given to Christians to function as the body of Christ. Elsewhere in the same discourse (1.1.1/Golitzin, 61), the oxen and fatted calves mentioned in the Parable of the Banquet (Mt. 24:4–6) mean nothing else than "the virgin's Son, the calf who is 'fatted' with divinity"; and, again in 1.1.2/Golitzin, 67, "the thick darkness under his feet" (Ps. 18:9) is "the flesh of the Lord," whose shoelaces John the Baptist was unworthy to untie.

[24]*Ethical Discourse* 1.1/Golitzin, vol. 1, 24.

[25]In one instance, he writes, "We do not arrive at this meaning through forced reasoning" (*Ethical Discourse* 1.6/Golitzin, vol. 1, 48). See also n. 8 above for St. Symeon's mild disagreement with a scriptural teaching.

[26]See, for example, *Catechetical Discourse* 35.3/deCatanzaro, 360–361, and *Catechetical Discourse* 34.9–10/deCatanzaro, 354–355, where he speaks about his "labor and toil" to "dig and excavate" the treasure to be found in Holy Scripture.

[27]Apart from his ever-present focus on the new creation, see, for example, his biblical expositions on the pastoral ministry, which he views primarily as a teaching ministry (*Ethical Discourse* 1.1/Golitzin, vol. 2, 139–53), and his homiletical pieces on the texts of Eph. 5:16 and 1 Cor. 15:47 in Golitzin, vol. 2, 155ff. and 163ff. respectively.

[28]See especially *The Three Theological Discourses*/McGuckin, 107–40, and *Ethical Discourses* 1 and 2/Golitzin, vol. 1, 50–75 and 83ff.

[29]*Ethical Discourse* 1.1 O/Golitzin, vol. 1, 57–58.

[30]Ibid., 1.12/Golitzin, vol. 1, 63–64.

[31]*Catechetical Discourse* 34.12/deCatanzaro, 357.

[32]*Eleventh Ethical Discourse*/Golitzin, vol. 2, 147.

[33]The eloquent and stirring message in St. Symeon's *First Catechetical Discourse*/deCatanzaro, 41–46, "On Charity."

[34]*Catechetical Discourse* 28.1/deCatanzaro, 295.

[35]*Catechetical Discourse* 29.2/deCatanzaro, 311.

[36]See *First Theological Discourse*/McGuckin, especially 107–113 and 116–117.

[37]See deCatanzaro, 261–66.

[38]I owe the phraseology and the idea to Andrew Louth, *Discerning the Mystery: An Essay on the Nature of Theology* (Oxford: Clarendon, 1983), 69–71.

[39]Ibid., 69.

[40]For an insightful piece on this subject, see James Price, "Mystical Transformation of Consciousness in St. Symeon," *Diakonia* 19, nos. 1–3 (1984–85): 6–16.

[41]See especially *Catechetical Discourses* 32 and 34.

[42]*Catechetical Discourse* 34.5/deCatanzaro, 350–51 and lines 129, 133–134, 141–142, and 154–156.

[43]*Practical and Theological Chapters* 3.4/McGuckin, 73.

[44]See especially *Catechetical Discourse* 16.2/deCatanzaro, 200, lines 67–78. In 6.7/deCatanzaro, 126 and lines 265–67, he writes, "Just as a father freely gives his son a share [of his estate], so he bestowed on me his unworthy servant, freely, without effort on my part, the Holy Spirit."

[45]John Romanides, "Critical Examination of the Applications of Theology," *Procés-Verbaux du deuxième Congrés de Théologie Orthodoxe tenu à Athènes 1976*, ed. by Savas C. Agouridis (Athens, 1978), 413–441.

[46]Ibid., 432.

[47]See *Catechetical Discourses* 15.2/deCatanzaro, 194, line 58; 24.5/deCatanzaro, 265, lines 172–74; and 32.5/deCatanzaro, 338, lines 110–115.

[48]*Catechetical Discourse* 34.6/deCatanzaro, 352, and lines 174–176.

[49]Ibid., 34.9/deCatanzaro, 354, lines 245–248.

[50]See *Catechetical Discourse* 35.1/deCatanzaro, 359, lines 11–12; and the *Third Theological Discourse*/McGuckin, 126–128.

[51]Ibid., lines 255–257.

[52]Ibid., lines 263–265.

[53]A valuable recent review of their theology, biblical orientation, and hermeneutical perspective is by Christiopher A. Hall, *Reading Scripture with the Church Fathers*, 56–101.

[54]35.3/deCatanzaro, 360, line 50.

[55]35.6/deCatanzaro, 361, lines 129–39, where up to eight or nine steps of spiritual transformation may be counted.

[56]35.7–8/deCatanzaro, 363–65, lines 140–154, 179–181, and 190.

[57]35.9/deCatanzaro, 365, especially lines 205ff.

[58]35.9–10/deCatanzaro, 365–66, especially lines 205ff. and 225ff.

[59]*Catechetical Discourse* 13.5/deCatanzaro, 184, lines 124–127.

[60]*Catechetical Discourse* 32.1/deCatanzaro, 336, line 29.

[61]Although he addresses himself to all who would listen, St. Symeon concedes, at least at one point, that the many cannot reach his radical vision: "While I agree myself that many things are impossible for the majority, I am saying this in particular for those of my order [i.e., the monks] who are lazy and do not choose to despise the world" (*Fourth Ethical Discourse*/Golitzin, 38).

[62]Stylianopoulos, *The New Testament*, especially chapters 6 and 7.

[63]For example, John Breck in *Scripture in Tradition*, chapter 4, titled "In Quest of an Orthodox *Lectio Divina*," 67–86, including notions of "*sensus plenior*." Compare a more cautious approach to contemplative reading of the Bible by Bradley Nassif, "Antiochene θεωρία in St. John Chrysostom's Exegesis," in *Ancient and Postmodern Christianity: Essays in Honor of Thomas C. Oden*, eds., Kenneth Tanner and Christopher A. Hall (Downers Grove, IL: InterVarsity, 2002), 48–67, where the author concedes that "under the rubric of θεωρία Chrysostom occasionally lapses into incredulous allegorical interpretations" (53).

[64]See Σάββας 'Αγουρίδης, *'Ερμηνευτική τῶν ἱερῶν κειμένων* (ΑΡΤΟΣ ΖΩΗΣ, ΑΘΗΝΑ, 2000), 79–95. See also the emphasis on the "Eucharistic vision" by Petros Vassiliadis, in *Lex Orandi: Μελέτες λειτουργικής θεολογίας* (Thessaloniki, 1994); *Eucharist and Witness: Orthodox Perspectives on the Unity and Mission of the Church* (Geneva: WCC, 1998); and his article "Holiness in the Perspective of Eucharistic Ecclesiology" in *Orthodox and Wesleyan Spirituality*, ed., S T Kimbrough, Jr. (Crestwood, NY: St. Vladimir's Seminary Press, 2002), 101–16. So also John Breck in *The Power of the Word in the Worshiping Church* (Crestwood, NY: St.Vladimir's Seminary Press, 1986).

4

Praying the Scriptures in Orthodox Worship

Elizabeth Theokritoff

Scripture has a fundamental place in Christian worship and in Christian spiritual life. This can be taken for granted, in principle at least. But I would want to go farther and say that worship is scripture's natural habitat. When we encounter scripture in the context of worship and the prayer of the Church, this lays the basis for our approach to scripture in our private reading and study.

What is it that we learn in worship? We encounter what Canon A. M. Allchin has characterized as "a very traditional way of handling the Bible" as "a book which has not just one meaning but many." We learn "a way of seeing things [in which] past, present and future can come together, and reading and experience can interact."[1] He is actually speaking of an example from Welsh Methodism. I am going to give examples from the services of the Orthodox Church, which have acquired over the centuries a great wealth of liturgical texts which are a mosaic of scriptural allusions and quotations. The texts build on the way the New Testament uses the Old Testament, revealing an integrated pattern of God's mighty acts extending from creation to the life of the Church, within which we encounter him today. This is the way the Church introduces us to the scriptures as both "the sacred book of the world" and the language of our own prayer, the expression of our own spiritual journey, the revelation which gives shape to our own experience of God.[2]

We shall look at some detailed examples under four headings:

1. How scripture speaks of our experience of salvation, taking examples from Holy Week and Easter.

2. How scripture speaks to us of the theology of salvation, drawing on Christmas services.

Then I want to look more specifically at two ways of reading scripture and how the Church guides us in applying them:

3. A typological interpretation of the Old Testament, as exemplified in texts for the Mother of God.

4. An allegorical use of scripture, which we encounter primarily in the Lenten services.[3]

1. How Scripture Speaks of Our Experience of Salvation

For anyone who has attended Orthodox Holy Week and Easter services during the past sixteen centuries, the first impression is likely to be that they are intensely historical. They take us day by day—at times, hour by hour—through the gospel accounts of the final days leading up to Christ's death and resurrection. But the subsequent impression may be that perhaps they are not so historical after all—or not in the way we first thought. Certainly, they follow the scriptural account in sequence—more or less. But a deeper acquaintance with the services makes it clear that despite the overlay of colorful "historical" detail, one thing this time of the Church's year is not is a reenactment of historical events. It is precisely what it has been from earliest times: a celebration of Christ our Passover, our passage from death to life. For this reason, the Paschal period is also the celebration of the eschatological reality that we begin to experience as members of the Church.

The events which stand at the threshold of Holy Week, the raising of Lazarus and Christ's entry into Jerusalem, bring us face to face with eschatological reality in the form of the general resurrection. This is clear in the gospel account of the raising of Lazarus: Martha is thinking in terms of her brother's resurrection on the last day, only to discover that this reality is standing in front of her in the person of him who is the Resurrection and the Life (Jn. 11:24). And the same emphasis is clear in the celebration of the feast. Lazarus Saturday and Palm Sunday share a *troparion*—a theme hymn for the feast—which begins, precisely, with "The general resurrection": "Giving assurance of the general resurrection before Thy Passion, Thou hast raised Lazarus from the dead, O Christ God." Christ gives assurance of the general resurrection by raising Lazarus, and as a result, the children greet him as victor over death. Palm Sunday is unusual in having a second *troparion*, and this is a text which reminds us that we ourselves have experienced the presence of the Resurrection and the Life: "Buried with Thee in baptism, Christ our God, we have been granted immortal life by Thy Resurrection." For many centuries, this celebration of man's regeneration (cf. Mt. 19:28) was one of the main annual occasions to bestow the washing of regeneration (Tit. 3:5). This connection reminds us that "walking in newness of life" as baptized Christians is not simply a metaphor for ethical conduct, but means quite literally what it says; we walk in the new life, the life of the resurrection.

The raising of Lazarus is not an isolated sign that the eschatological reality is being inaugurated. A text at Matins on Palm Sunday makes this clear:

> Before Thy voluntary Passion, Christ our God, Thou has given to all men an assurance of the general resurrection; for at Bethany *Thou hast raised* ... *Lazarus who was four days dead*, and as Giver of Light, O Savior, *Thou hast made the blind to see* (Lauds 4).[4]

What has healing the blind got to do with the general resurrection? To start with, the writer has noticed that Matthew places the healing of the blind men immediately before the entry into Jerusalem (Mt. 20:29–34). Now, this is an incident which shows Christ as the one who restores sight to the blind, fulfilling the messianic prophecy of Is. 61:1 (LXX). Martha was shown in action that he is the Resurrection and the Life; this is our first "assurance" in the above verse. And John the Baptist was told that "the blind see" (Lk. 7:22); this was the answer to his question as to whether Christ is "the one who is to come."

This is precisely what we are celebrating at the Entry into Jerusalem: Christ as "the one who is to come." We celebrate Jesus's entry into Jerusalem on an ass as the coming of the Lord, and hence, by extension, we celebrate his presence on earth as the coming of the Lord. For this reason, the cosmic significance of the event is prominent in several texts.[5] This, indeed, is the message conveyed already by the use of Pss. 117/8:26–7: "Blessed is he that comes in the name of the Lord. The Lord is God and has appeared unto us." But Palm Sunday is not the main occasion on which we encounter this text. In fact, it is entirely probable that long before the Church established a feast day for the gospel incident in which Christ is acclaimed with these words, the acclamation itself was enshrined in the Eucharist, as the people's response at communion.[6] The Eucharist is our primary encounter with the One "who comes and will come again," as we sing on Palm Sunday. Our reception of the Lord in Holy Communion is the first fruits of an eschatological reality yet to be fulfilled; it is "the heavenly bread and the cup of life."

At Christ's entry into Jerusalem, the identity of the visible event with the coming of the Lord is further reinforced by a visual image: this is an occasion when we see Christ seated. This is just the sort of detail in the gospels that the liturgical texts take up and reveal as profoundly symbolic. To see Christ as man "seated"—even on a donkey—is to recall where he is "seated" according to his divine nature. As we sing in the words of the great sixth-century poet St. Romanos, Christ is "seated in heaven upon a throne, and on earth upon a foal"; he receives "the praise of angels and the songs of the children" (*Kontakion*). It may not be immediately apparent that this is actually referring to a specific revelation of God in the Old Testament. But it is in fact taking up a connection which, again, is found in the Divine Liturgy, where the Old Testament and New Testament texts are juxtaposed so that we have the heavenly powers crying out, "Holy holy, holy Lord of Sabaoth; heaven and earth are full of Thy glory" (cf. Is. 6:3). "Hosanna in the highest: blessed is He that comes in the name of the Lord" (cf. Mt. 21:9). Jesus on his foal is none other than "He who once Isaiah saw" (Is. 6; Lauds 3). The *kanon* at Matins therefore proclaims, "The Lord of Hosts is come. Let all earth stand in reverence before his face" (Hab. 2:20; *Kanon* 8.3).

One more eschatological connection should be mentioned: the events celebrated on Palm Sunday concern Jerusalem. The feast as we have it today grew up in Jerusalem. All of this can be seen only as pointing forward to the new Jerusalem of the prophets, third Isaiah in particular.[7] Alike in the gospel accounts and during Holy Week in the early Christian era, Jerusalem is a focus for the gathering of peoples. The contribution of the liturgical texts is to link this with the gathering in of God's people, which is prominent in Isaiah's eschatological vision, and found also in Zephaniah, the other "Rejoice, daughter of Zion" prophecy read at the feast (cf. Zeph. 3:18, LXX: "I will gather together your broken ones"). Thus the *kanon* at Matins proclaims:

> Zion, holy mountain of God [cf. Ps. 2.6], and Jerusalem, lift up thine eyes round about and behold thy children, gathered in thee. For lo, they have come from afar [Is. 60:4] to worship thy King (*Kanon* 5.2).

It is a pure Isaianic image of the renewed eschatological Jerusalem. We shall meet it again in the Easter services. And furthermore, we meet it at every Eucharist, which is the *synaxis*, the gathering of the Church.

We begin Holy Week, then, with the proclamation of the general resurrection, the greeting of Christ, who comes to inaugurate this reality, and the reminder that we join in greeting him by virtue of our baptism. And we continue with this theme of greeting Christ, for the first three days of Holy Week are dominated by the image of Christ the Bridegroom. The "*troparion* of the Bridegroom" at the beginning of Matins of Holy Monday, Tuesday, and Wednesday (and the *exapostilarion* on the same theme at the end) have impressed themselves on people's minds to such an extent that these services are known as "services of the Bridegroom." It is worth looking at the *troparion* in some detail; it is a good example of the way in which scriptural passages are combined and interpreted in the light of each other. We see that the *troparion* is compounded of at least four scriptural passages, all concerned with watchfulness in preparation for the end.

> Behold, the Bridegroom comes at midnight [Mt. 25:1–13, ten virgins]; and blessed is the servant whom He shall find watching [Mt. 24:45ff.], but unworthy is he whom He shall find in slothfulness. Beware then, O my soul, and be not overcome by sleep, lest thou be given over to death [cf. Mt. 22:13, the man with no wedding garment] and shut out of the kingdom [ten virgins again]. But return to soberness [cf. 1 Thess. 5:6, "Awake and be sober"; also 1 Pet. 5:8].

And almost all of these themes appear in more succinct form in Rev. 16:15, "Lo, I am coming like a thief! Blessed is he who is awake, keeping his garments."

The sense of this text is undoubtedly eschatological. It marks the period of most intense eschatological expectation in the entire year, when we hear in concentrated form all of Christ's teaching about the end contained in Mt. 21–24. But it is equally clear that this *troparion* has a baptismal sense. It is in baptism that we encounter Christ; it is in baptism that we enter into his passion and resurrection, in which is "the judgment of this world" (cf. Jn. 12:31, which we hear at Matins on Holy Wednesday). The baptismal reference is clearer in the other "Bridegroom" text, the *exapostilarion*, which speaks explicitly of the wedding garment:

> I see Thy bridal chamber adorned, and I have no wedding garment that I may enter. Make the vesture of my soul to shine.

This is the baptismal robe, which gives entry to the eucharistic banquet, and ultimately, if kept shining white, to the fullness of the eschatological banquet in the Kingdom. But "returning to soberness" in the *troparion* equally has much to do with "keeping one's [baptismal] garment"; we know from Cyril of Jerusalem that 1 Pet. 5:8ff., "Awake and be sober," was read on Easter Monday in the presence of the newly baptized.[8] There is not actually much point in trying to disentangle baptismal and eschatological themes, since the one meeting with the Bridegegroom is an image of the other. As St. Gregory the Theologian told his catechumens, "The lamps which you will kindle [after baptism] are a sacrament of the illumination there with which we shall meet the bridegroom, shining and virgin souls."[9]

The baptismal framework of Holy Week is very clear in the Paschal services themselves. The Vespers leading into the first Easter Liturgy, now celebrated on Holy Saturday morning, is dominated by a long series of readings which has changed little since this vesperal Liturgy was the great annual baptismal service in Jerusalem. The primary focus of the fifteen Old Testament readings here is, on the one hand, the Passover—the movement from death to life, from slavery to the promised land—and, on the other, the eschatological vision of the prophets (i.e., the content of that life into which we have passed).[10] Two readings are marked out by the addition of sung refrains. One of these is the Red Sea crossing, regarded from an early date as a prefiguration of salvation through baptism, of our personal experience of the Exodus. The other is the Song of the Three Children, the supreme type of deliverance from death by the power and presence of the Lord.

The same emphasis appears on Easter night. St. John Chrysostom once welcomed the newly baptized on Easter night with the words, "Now you have been received as citizens of the heavenly Jerusalem,"[11] and again, we can say that the experience of celebrating the "Christ, our Passover," has not changed much since. We can illustrate this from the Easter *kanon* of St. John of Damascus, which actually accounts for most of the hymnographic material proper to Easter.

St. John of Damascus makes it very clear at the outset what we are celebrating: "The day of Resurrection." (NB the deliberate ambiguity: he does not say, in the manner habitual to liturgical texts, "Today Christ is risen." The day of Christ's rising is equally the dawning of the great eschatological Day.) It is the "Passover of the Lord," who has caused us to pass over from death to life and from earth to heaven (*Kanon* 1; *Eirmos*). We have passed through baptism into Christ's death: "Yesterday I was buried with Thee, O Christ . . . I was crucified with Thee yesterday" (*Kanon* 3.2). And now we find ourselves in the new Jerusalem of Isaiah, the new Jerusalem of the Book of Revelation. This difficult and often disturbing book (which, incidentally, is nowhere read liturgically in the Orthodox Church) becomes more approachable when we realize how much of its apocalyptic vision we are already experiencing in the Church.

In this new Jeruaslem, then, we "drink a new drink." Our experience of him who "makes all things new" is expressed constantly in the language of the Paschal services, as also in the liturgical order; the entire week of Easter is called the "Week of Renewal." And since our Passover in Christ is an antitype of the Exodus, this "new drink" is not one brought forth miraculously from the barren rock" (*Kanon* 3.e). It is the cup which Christ promises to drink new with his disciples in the Kingdom (Mt. 26:29), but as it is also a "fount of incorruption welling up from the tomb of Christ." We are probably not wide of the mark if we also see in it the "water of life flowing from the throne of God and of the Lamb" (Rev. 21:1).

It is towards the end of the *kanon* that we see images of the Church and Kingdom most clearly. We are invited to "partake of the new fruit of the vine, of divine gladness, in the high day of the Resurrection and the Kingdom of Christ" (*Kanon* 8.1), the great eschatological day again. If the Eucharist is the banquet of the Kingdom, the Church gathered for the Eucharist is the new Zion, which is called upon to "Lift up [her] eyes all around, and see [her] children, like lights divinely radiant, from the west and from the north and from the sea and from the east" (*Kanon* 8.2). The "radiant children" are at once the baptized "shining like lights in the world" (Phil. 2:15),[12] and the righteous "shining like the sun in the kingdom of their father" (Mt. 13:43)—the properties of both are symbolized by the candles held by worshippers on Easter night.

The Easter *kanon* ends, however, with an abrupt reminder that our experience of realized eschatology in the Church is only the first fruits of a reality yet to be fulfilled:

> O Christ, great and most holy Passover; O Wisdom and Word and Power of God, grant us to partake of Thee more perfectly [or "more directly"] in the day of Thy Kingdom, which knows no evening (*Kanon* 9.2).

This illustrates nicely the principle of scriptural interpretation expressed succinctly by St. Maximus the Confessor: "The things of the Old Testament are the shadow. Those of the New Testament are the image. The truth is the state of things to come."[13] And it equally illustrates the tension inherent in the experience of salvation that we enjoy so far.

2. How Scripture Speaks to Us of the Theology of Salvation

Let us turn now to the theology of salvation. How does scripture speak to us of the nature of Christ and its soteriological significance? We shall find some answers in the Christmas services.

If we were to choose one Old Testament verse to sum up the essence of the feast of the Nativity, it could well be argued that this should not be "Unto us a Child is born" but "From the womb before the morning star have I begotten Thee"(Ps. 109/110:3, LXX). This verse is used at the Little Entrance in the Divine Liturgy on Christmas Day and holds a prominent place at the feast, as does a New Testament text with a similar point, Heb. 1:3: "being the brightness of His glory and the express image of His person." The feast has never lost its pointedly anti-Arian character. It is these texts, which focus on Christ as the *divine* Son, "begotten of the Father before all ages," that define the backdrop against which we look at all the details in the gospel accounts relating to his birth on earth as man. In the words of St. Romanos's *kontakion* for the feast, we see "a young Child, the pre-eternal God."

In this perspective, all the ordinary, human circumstances of Christ's birth become extraordinary paradoxes: "He who holds the reins of the undefiled powers [cf. Ps. 79:2] is laid in a manger of dumb beasts," and so on.[14]

And these paradoxes are not the object of wonder only, but of awe, even fear. This is especially true of texts for the forefeast (the feast proper begins at Vespers on Christmas Eve);[15] in fact, it is built into the structure of the forefeast of Christmas because the liturgical structure of the days leading up to Christmas is modeled closely on Holy Week. Thus the final *stikheron* at the Hours on Christmas Eve ("Today is born of the Virgin He who holds the whole creation in the palm of His hand" [9th Hour, 3]) echoes the well-known corresponding *stikheron* on Holy Friday, which speaks of the terrible paradoxes of the crucifixion: "Today He who hung the earth upon the waters is hung upon a cross." A very important point is being made here, and it is that of Phil. 2:7: when Christ "empties himself, taking the form of a servant," he is embarking upon a course which leads inexorably to the cross. This is how the Church prepares us for the celebration of the Nativity.[16]

At the feast itself, there is no less contrast between Christ's divine and human states, but another model for his act of self-emptying becomes prominent alongside that of Phil. 2. This is the model of 2 Cor. 8:9: "though he was rich, yet for your sake he became poor, so that by his poverty you might become rich." Here we have a pattern, which can be characterized as salvation by reciprocal process. According to this pattern, Christ's condescension is not only awe-inspiring; it is transforming:

> *Obedient* to the decree of Caesar, Thou wast enrolled among his *servants* . . . and hast *set us free* who were servants of the enemy and of sin. Wholly *sharing in our poverty*, Thou hast *made our clay godlike* through Thy union and participation in it (1 *Kanon* 5.1).

Christ enters into our condition in order to raise us to his condition; the "wealth" of Christ is commonly glossed as his divinity.

These patterns for envisaging Christ's saving work are closely related to another pattern very prominent at Christmas (and also at the Annunciation): salvation by recapitulation. In another striking image of the transformation effected by Christ's birth, St. Romanos writes, "Bethlehem has opened Eden . . . Come, let us take possession of the things of paradise within the cave" (*Kontakion*). Why has Bethlehem opened Eden? Because it contains the second Adam. And the second Adam's self-emptying, laying aside the wealth of his divine status, is the saving reversal of the error of the first Adam, who considered "being like God" precisely a "thing to be grasped." When Christ saves by taking on what is proper to us, this is to say that he saves as second Adam, with all that this implies. The whole idea of recapitulation, the way that the incarnate Christ untangles the knot into which Adam had tied himself, receives considerable elaboration at the Christmas services.

In the Christmas texts, the central point of contrast between the old and the new Adams is couched in the terms already mentioned: the Word empties himself, and in accepting him, humanity rejects its earlier attempt to grasp "likeness to God" for itself (cf. 2 *Kanon* 8.1). But of course the Fall story is not concerned only—or even primarily—with wanting to be like God, but rather with obedience; we are back with Phil. 2. Listen to how the first hymn for the feast proper—at Vespers on Christmas Eve—characterizes "the present mystery":

> The middle wall of partition has been destroyed; the *flaming sword turns back*, the *cherubim withdraw from the tree of life*, and I *partake of the Paradise of delight from which I was cast out through disobedience.* Why am I now returning to Paradise? Again, because the express Image of the Father [2 Cor. 4:4], the *Imprint of His eternity* [NB characteristic use of Heb. 1:3 to sum up who the Son is] *takes the form of a servant* [Phil. 2:7], and without undergoing change He comes forth from a Mother who knew not wedlock. For what He was, He has remained, true God: and what He was not, He has taken upon Himself, becoming man through love for mankind.

We have already been reminded what is implied in "taking the form of a servant": being obedient even unto death. There is also a visual counterpart to this at the

Christmas services. It is often remarked that in the icon of the Nativity, the black mouth of the cave in which Christ lies resembles a tomb, and the swaddled baby looks like a corpse. So at the beginning of the Christmas services, we are reminded by the hymn just cited that the movement of salvation that we are seeing is that described in Phil. 2:5–11, and when the icon of the feast is brought out later in the service, we can see this movement summed up before our eyes.

Moving on to some other aspects of recapitulation: still in Vespers, the serpent discovers that its plans have gone horribly wrong when it sees

> *the woman whom once he deceived become the Mother of the Creator.* O, the depth of the riches and wisdom and knowledge of God! She who brought death to all flesh, the instrument of sin, has through the Mother of God become the first-fruits of salvation for the whole world. For a child is born of her [cf. 1 Tim. 2:15], the all-perfect God. And by His birth He seals her virginity, undoing the cords of sin by His swaddling clothes. Through becoming an infant, He heals Eve's pangs in travail (Compline, *Stikhera* 4).

The source of death has become the source of life because a child is born of her, the all-perfect God, because that aspect of human existence, which was overshadowed by the curse ("in sorrow shalt thou bring forth children"), becomes the way blessing comes into the world. Note the interpretation of 1 Tim. 2:15 implied here: woman is saved by the birth of the child (cf. "Through becoming an infant, he heals Eve's pangs in travail").

The most unequivocal sign of the undoing of the curse is to be found in the Nativity gospels themselves, and the liturgical texts highlight this. "Peace on earth," the angels sing, "and goodwill [or good pleasure] among men." Where do we see this "goodwill"? We see God's good pleasure "among" Mary and Joseph and the shepherds and whoever else is standing around the manger. The Virgin has overthrown the curse of Eve because she has become the Mother of the Father's good pleasure (Matins, Lauds 3). The meaning of God's goodwill is absolutely concrete and personal.

We may end this section with a supreme example of the "Christology of salvation," of salvation through the incarnation:

> O Christ our Defender, *Thou hast put to shame the adversary of man, using as a lure Thine ineffable Incarnation.* Taking man's form, Thou hast now bestowed on him the joy of becoming godlike: for it was in hope of this that of old we fell from on high into the dark depths of the earth (*Kanon* 7.2).

Again, this text (by St. John of Damascus) takes up the serpent's false promise of deification. The enemy used the lure of divinity, so Christ used the lure of humanity, of his flesh. We have to understand the underlying image here: it is the very graphic one of Christ descending to Hades and being swallowed up by the devouring monster (death), causing it to vomit up everyone else it had devoured. (This image is most often found in texts for the Resurrection and is vividly presented in the sermon attributed to St. John Chrysostom, which is read on Easter night.) Where does this idea come from? It is a faithful reflection of the Lord's words to Job: "You shall draw out the dragon ["Leviathan"] with a fishook" (Job 40:25).[17] The function of Christ's humanity here is to act as bait on the fishhook. It all fits together beautifully, but not everyone nowadays finds this sort of imagery easy to relate to. In case you prefer the same thing without the imagery, here it is on Christmas Eve (9th Hour) and at Annunciation, and on Holy Friday (6th Hour): "He himself likewise partook of the same nature, that through death He might destroy him who has the power of death, that is, the devil, and deliver all those who . . . were subject to lifelong bondage" (Heb. 2:14–15). Here we have precisely the same pattern of salvation, lacking only the colorful details.

3. Typological Reading of Scripture

In the examples already given, we have seen various ways of interpreting scripture reflecting various levels of meaning to be found in the scriptural text. And we have seen that one very important level of meaning is the typological: Adam is a type of Christ, and so on. This is the prime way in which the Church reads the Old Testament as a book about Christ. It should be noted that unlike moral allegory, which we shall talk about at the end, typology has to do with events which point forward to other events or realities. The typological event may or may not be historical in the modern sense; it does not matter. The point is that what God's people regarded as their own history is seen in the Church as foreshadowing a future reality: God's acts in the past speak of the mystery hidden from ages and generations. We shall therefore give a few examples of typology from feasts of the Mother of God, since these are concerned with nothing other than this mystery. The Annunciation, the principle feast of the Virgin, can be considered the supreme feast of the Incarnation: "today . . . the mystery from all ages is revealed," as we sing in the *troparion.* The other great feasts of the Mother of God—her birth, entrance into the temple, and falling asleep—celebrate events which are not recorded in the canonical New Testament at all, so the very shape and theological substance of these feasts is taken from the Old Testament, from Old Testament types which point forward to the Incarnation. As the Angel says to Mary in a dialogue hymn for the Annunciation, "It is thou who are prefigured by the dark sayings of the prophets and the symbols of the Law" (*Kanon* 5.2).

Since the incarnation is a mystery and therefore beyond the grasp of our reason, it is not surprising to find that images and symbols often serve better than mere systematic formulations in initiating us into its meaning. This is not a notion we are very used to today, so it is easy to fall into the assumption that imagery is decorative and devotional. We may feel that calling the Virgin "Gate of heaven" or "Tree of glorious fruit" is pious and beautiful, but really an optional extra to the faith of the church, or, at worst, a distraction from it. But the liturgical texts introduce us to a way of speaking in scriptural images which is sober and theologically quite precise. It does not take us off into a flight of pious fancy; it enables us to tap into the "symbols of the Law" with all their wealth of meaning.

"Symbols of the Law" basically means "of the Pentateuch." The symbols most directly connected with the incarnation *per se*, and therefore with the Mother of God, are those which concern the tabernacle or temple and their contents. We see the germ of this typology already in the New Testament: Christ speaks of the temple of his body

(Jn. 2:21); the veil of the temple is rent at his death (Mt. 27:51). The Word has now "tabernacled" among us (Jn. 1:14), so that we, who are his body, are the temple of God (1 Cor. 3:16; 2 Cor. 6:16). The tabernacle, the temple, and especially the Ark of the Covenant can all be seen as images, symbols, *mysteries* of the presence of the God who, unlike the gods of Israel's neighbors, is not localized and has no tangible image. We can perhaps say even that they represent a longing for the fulfillment of that presence. "Will God indeed dwell on the earth?" asks Solomon, a little wistfully, at the dedication of the temple (3/1 Kgs. 8; 27). The Church gives him his answer by reading Heb. 9:1–7, concerning the organization and contents of the tabernacle, at the feast of the Virgin's Entry into the temple.[18] The whole point of this feast is that she fulfills the meaning of the temple: "The living temple of the holy glory of Christ is offered in the temple of the Law" (Lord, I Have Cried, 3). She is to be brought up in the tabernacle, in the place of propitiation, in order to become the "tabernacle"—the dwelling place of him who was begotten of the Father before all ages, for the salvation of our souls (cf. Vespers, Lity. 1). As she is led into the temple at the age of three, the hymns keep hailing her as a "three-year-old heifer"[19] (e.g., 2 *Kanon* 5.5). Why a heifer? We are not being taken into the barnyard; we are being taken to the very beginning of the "symbols of the Law." "But Abram said, 'O Lord God, how am I to know that I shall possess [this land]?' He said to him, 'Bring Me a heifer three years old' " (Gen. 15:7ff.); so the heifer is sacrificed, and this is the Lord's covenant with Abram, the seal of the promise concerning his descendants and the land they will inhabit, one of the prototypes of the Church. The three-year-old Mary, then, is being prepared to be the starting point for the fulfillment of this whole process of God's covenant with his people.[20]

Returning to the temple image: the two Old Testament readings proper to the feast of the Entry concern precisely Solomon's dedication of the temple (though not including the remark about "Will God dwell with men?" [3/1 Kgs. 7:51; 8:1, 3–7, 9–11], and the Lord's instructions to Moses about setting up the tabernacle (Ex. 40:1–5, 9–10, 16, 34–35). The third reading concerns Ezekiel's vision of the temple gate, which is to remain closed (Ezek. 43:27–44:4), a classic type of the Mother of God and a hardy perennial at her feasts.[21] All three readings end with the glory of the Lord filling the house of the Lord; or, according to Exodus, "the cloud overshadowed the Tabernacle, and the glory of the Lord filled the Tabernacle." This sign of the Lord's true presence is fulfilled at his incarnation when the power of the Most High overshadows the Virgin, so that she is manifested as "the king's daughter all glorious within" (Ps. 44/45:14), to quote another Old Testament passage regularly used at feasts of the Mother of God.[22]

The Ex. 40 reading is notable because it is part of the lengthy narration alluded to in Heb. 8:5, in which the Lord gives Moses several chapters' worth of minute instructions as to how the tabernacle is to be constructed. This passage is of great importance for the typological understanding of scripture, because God says, "See that you make everything *according to the pattern that was shown to you on the mountain*" (Ex. 25:40; Heb. 8:5). As the author of Hebrews explains, these things are "a copy and shadow of the heavenly sanctuary"; that is, the Old Testament is not the prototype, but a copy of a reality yet to be fulfilled. How is it fulfilled? On two levels, one might say, in two stages. Firstly, the Old Testament type is fulfilled in historical reality. This is why Heb. 9:1–7 is read for feasts of the Mother of God: all the objects concerned with the temple, the tabernacle, and the Ark of the Covenant are types of the Mother who bore God incarnate. There is a particular emphasis on the "container" symbols, for obvious reasons: God is "contained" in her womb. That is what the Incarnation necessarily implies. She is the "tabernacle" because the Word of God has "tabernacled among us."

But the fulfillment of types does not stop with the Lord literally present in the antitype of the temple. Look, for instance, at the way Old Testament typology is used in the Akathistos Hymn, which is one of the masterpieces of Byzantine poetry and the centerpiece of a service which is extremely popular, especially in the Greek tradition.[23] The hymn (stanza 21) speaks of her as "Lamp of the living Light" (cf. the lampstand of Heb. 9:2); she is also the "Laver washing clean the conscience" and "Cup wherein is mixed the wine of mighty joy." The "laver" belongs to the blueprint for the tabernacle (cf. Ex. 30:18), but here it also points forward to baptism, our entry into the life of Christ's body, the Church. The "cup," on the other hand, takes us to another Old Testament passage read at feasts of the Mother of God: "Wisdom has built her house . . . she has mixed her wine" (Prov. 9:1–2). This reading refers at once to the living "house" of the Divine Wisdom incarnate, and to the eucharistic banquet, and ultimately eschatological, which he (or she, if one continues the Wisdom metaphor) offers. The fulfillment of Old Testament types in the Mother of God *takes us forward* to the life of the Church and of the Kingdom.

The Hebrews reading for the Mother of God stops at 9:7, which is still referring to the old covenant. But the argument of the passage, as we know, is that the true High Priest enters the archetypal, heavenly sanctuary not made with hands. So is the Church taking those first verses out of context? No, she is simply underlining how it is that the Lord has become the antitype and fulfillment of the high priest, by entering in the first instance into the sanctuary not made with hands but created by himself, the sanctuary which is his mother. This is how he is able to enter the heavenly sanctuary as our High Priest.

4. Allegorical Use of Scripture

Our life of prayer and worship has two aspects. We have talked so far about the universal aspect—the celebration of God and his works. We celebrate the great span of God's work of mercy in creation and salvation. The examples we looked at first, which show how we appropriate salvation through incorporation into the body of Christ, are also universal because they speak of the way we are all called to appropriate the Kingdom which is to come. But then there is clearly also a personal, subjective aspect of prayer and worship: where do I stand in relation to God in my present spiritual state?

How do we draw on scripture for this personal aspect of prayer and worship? We are frequently told, when reading scripture, to apply it to ourselves, but it is obvious that the primary sense of a large amount of scripture is not about us at all in any direct sense. This is equally true of many texts which provide moral examples, whether positive or negative; if I refrain from murder, fornication, and the worship of golden calves, does this mean that a whole area of humankind's turbulent relationship with the Lord has no relevance for my own spiritual life? Not if you read a text such as the *Great Kanon of St. Andrew of Crete,* in which we see a whole array of scriptural passages allegorized in such a way as to throw light on my own spiritual life.

As used liturgically, allegory is primarily a way of making the connection between the scriptures and my own inner state. Now, since the festal and sacramental services have an objective and universal character, instances of allegory here can be counted on the fingers of one hand. Allegory belongs to the weekday and particularly the Lenten services, which focus much more on our own spiritual state.

The *Great Kanon* holds a special place in the Orthodox Lenten services. It is a poem of great length, written by a seventh-century Bishop of Crete, and is sung in installments on the first four days of Lent and in full in the fifth week. The subject of the *kanon* is sin and repentance: it is my sin and my repentance, but it is equally the entire history of man's relationship with his Creator.

Towards the end of the *kanon,* St. Andrew says:

> I have put before thee, O my soul, Moses' account of the creation of the world, and after that *all* the recognised Scriptures that tell the story of the righteous and the wicked (Ode 9).

And he is not exaggerating much. But the process of presenting these examples to his soul is not as straightforward as it sounds. Some of St. Andrew's "examples" are classic spiritual allegory; for example, the "two wives" for whom Jacob labored so long and hard (Gen. 29ff.) are to be understood as action, which has many children, and knowledge in contemplation, neither of which will succeed without toil (Ode 4).[24] This is a way of making an instructive moral point which has precious little to do with the literal meaning of the text. But other examples are more subtle:

> O my soul, the hand of Moses shall be our assurance, proving that God can cleanse a life full of leprosy and make it white as snow [Ex. 4:6–8]. So do not despair of thyself, though thou are leprous (Ode 6).

One of the most notable features of the Church's use of allegories for our spiritual state is the frequency with which the images chosen have to do with sickness and health. In the previous ode, St. Andrew does something very similar with the New Testament:

> O my soul, do as the woman who was bowed to the ground. Fall at the feet of Jesus, that He may make thee straight again: and thou shalt walk upright upon the paths of the Lord (Ode 5).

In these instances, the connection is not all arbitrary; it reflects a profound sense that sin is not primarily the transgression of a rule which incurs punishment, but a departure from a state of wholeness, from psychosomatic well-being. And this is its own punishment; it is a self-inflicted wound.

It is clear that in all of these cases, we are not dealing with a primary meaning of the scriptural text. But it is also clear that there is fundamentally nothing artificial in applying these texts to my own soul. The story of humankind's apostasy and return is my story: "I have torn the first garment that the Creator wove for me in the beginning, and now I lie naked" (Ode 2). This identity comes across very clearly if we look at the scriptural content of the Lenten period as a whole. The theme of the first two weeks is the Fall and fasting, followed by the Prodigal Son, the Publican and Pharisee, the Good Samaritan, and the Rich Man and Lazarus.[25] A quick glance at the way these themes are used will illustrate how the allegory serves to make the connection between the story of all mankind and my own spiritual sickness. "In my wretchedness I have cast off the robe woven by God," laments Adam on the eve of Lent (Cheesefare, Vespers); and again, "I was stripped naked, and now I am in want." So Adam is like the Prodigal Son: he has forsaken his proper dress and his proper place, and hence he is "in want." And when we come to the week of the Prodigal, we are shown the causes of this in our own behavior:

> *Throwing off from my unruly mind the bridle of the Father,* I have lived with *bestial thoughts of sin,* and in my misery like the prodigal I have *wasted all my life. Forsaking the food that gives strength to man's heart,* I have *fed upon the pleasure* that gives passing satisfaction (3rd Week, Sunday Vespers).[26]

And again, "In my unreason I have become like the dumb beasts, and have *stripped myself of all divine grace*" (3rd Week, Wednesday Vespers).

So we have the recurring themes of hunger, want, nakedness; these are the recurrent symptoms of our condition. We notice that the "diagnosis" uses typical ascetic terminology—the reference to the debilitating effects of indiscipline and evil thoughts (*logismoi*). This means that in linking our own state to the scriptural stories, the hymnographers are drawing on a highly developed science of the human condition.

The allegorical interpretation of the Rich Man and Lazarus, in the final week of Lent, fits into the same pattern. It is an allegory by no means unrelated to the primary sense of the story. By showing the insensitivity characteristic of the Rich Man, I make my own mind, my *nous,* the faculty with which I am meant to apprehend God, into a Lazarus, "lying before the gate of repentance, starved of every good thing and sick with carelessness" (6th Week, Wednesday Vespers). This identification of my innermost self with the beggar Lazarus, neglected in mortal sickness by the Rich Man, who is also myself, leads into an identification with the other Lazarus, and so forward into Holy Week:

> Bringing together contemplation and action, let us hasten to address a petition to Christ: *that by His dread authority He will bring to life our mind, dead and buried like another Lazarus,* to offer Him palms of righteousness and to cry: Blessed are You that come (6th Week, Thursday Matins).

In other words, my sickness is described in terms which point to its remedy.

Turning finally to the parable of the Samaritan, we have a somewhat different sort of allegory: a story whose primary point is ethical and is applied to Christ (with the help of a pun in Greek: Christ comes to our aid not *ek Samareias* but *ek Marias*). But it is a theological allegory with a personal point; the focus is on Christ's saving work *in my own life.* It is thus the ideal vehicle for making the connection between our own spiritual state and the salvation offered by Christ. Again, according to this parable, we find ourselves naked, destitute, and wounded:

> Departing from Thy divine commandments as from Jerusalem, and going down to the passions of Jericho, I was led astray by the false glory of the cares of this life. *I fell among the thieves of my own thoughts; they stripped me of the robe of sonship that was mine by grace*, and now I lie wounded, as though without the breath of life . . . But Thou, O Lord . . . hast of Thine own will poured out blood and water from Thy side for my salvation, and as with oil Thou hast anointed me (5th Week, Friday Vespers).

All of this, of course, is preparing us for Holy Week; and it is in that context that we might see these images, and above all the central, baptismal image of the "robe of sonship." The frequent use of the allegory as part of the personal focus of Lent is in no way giving scripture an individual slant unrelated to the life of the Church. Rather, it is showing us how to find our own place in the "sacred book of the world." It is showing us how scripture speaks of the many forms of our nakedness, Adam's nakedness, as well as revealing how we are clothed with the first robe restored at baptism. And it is showing us how scripture makes us confront our own hunger, while at the same time inviting us to the banquet of the Kingdom.

Endnotes

[1]*Resurrection's Children* (Norwich: Canterbury, 1998), 2–3.

[2]The Greek theologian Panayiotis Nellas has captured the essence of the Orthodox experience of scripture in the following passage: "It is well known that for the Orthodox tradition the line from Adam to Christ defines the truth of history, the deeper content and goal of the historical process. Thus the Holy Scriptures from Genesis to the Apocalypse constitute for the Church the sacred book of the world, precisely because they contain the central stages of this deeper historical process.

"To this deep river, which leads from the Beginning to the End, the faithful of every age bring whatever concerns them and their world, so that by baptising these things in it, by identifying them with the current of this river, they may transfer them from the ephemeral—from the 'flux of time'—to the permanent; from the narrow limits of daily life or life in a particular age to that which has its being in Christ and so contains the eternal and infinite. This transposition—the *Great Kanon* calls it *diavasis*, 'passing over'—constitutes the kernel of repentance and is one of the central aims of reading the Scriptures and praying" (P. Nellas, *Deification in Christ*, tr. N. Russell (Crestwood, NY: St. Vladimir's Seminary Press, 1987), 170.

[3]I am well aware that even to use terms such as typology and allegory is to enter a minefield. The intention here, however, is not to enter into the complexities of scriptural interpretation and how it is to be classified, but to indicate the extent to which the liturgical texts clearly do use scriptures in different ways for different purposes.

[4]Holy Week and Lenten texts are taken from Mother Mary and Kallistos Ware, *The Lenten Triodion* (London: Faber and Faber, 1978). The translation may occasionally be adapted.

[5]Cf. texts from Matins: "Christ, *He who comes manifestly as our God, shall come* and shall not tarry, from the mountain overshadowed by the forest, born of a Maiden who hath not known man . . . Let the mountains and all the hills break forth into great rejoicing at the mercy of God, and let the trees of the forest clap their hands" (Is. 49:13, 55:12; *Kanon*. 4.e.1).

[6]Cf. Liturgy of St. James; *Apostolic Constitutions* (8.13) has "Hosanna to the Son of David. Blessed . . ."

[7]The hymn just quoted begins, "Rejoice, O Jerusalem, and all ye that love Zion, keep feast" (cf. Is. 66:10). Passages such as this are readily associated with the prophecy of Zechariah quoted in the gospels: "Tell the daughter of Zion, 'Behold your king is coming' " (Zech. 9:9).

[8]Cf. Inscription to Catechetical Oration XIX (Mystag. I), PG 33:1065–6.

[9]Or. 40, *On Holy Baptism*, 46, PG 36.

[10]Only three of the readings are concerned specifically with the resurrection *per se*, and these are later additions: (7) Zeph. 3:8–15; (8) 3/1 Kgs. 17:8–24; (12) 2/4 Kgs. 4:8–37. The Book of Jonah, cited by Christ himself as the "sign" of his death and resurrection, is a different case and belongs to the earliest stratum of readings.

[11]*On Pascha*, 5, PG 52:771.

[12]Cf. the use of this passage by St. Gregory the Theologian in an exhortation to appropriate behavior after baptism; Or. 40, *On Holy Baptism*, 37, PG 36:412C.

[13]*Scholia* on Dionysius, *On the Church Hierachy*, PG 4:137.

[14]The text in full reads, "Christ our God, whom the Father begat from the womb before the morning star, has come, made flesh; and He who holds the reins of the undefiled powers [cf. Ps. 79:2] is laid in a manger of dumb beasts. He who looses the tangled cords of sin [Prov. 5:22] is wrapped in swaddling rags" (1 Kanon 6.1; texts for fixed feasts from *The Festal Menaion*, tr. Mother Mary and Kallistos Ware [London: Faber and Faber, 1969]. Translations may be adapted.)

[15]E.g., the hymn at the Hours on Christmas Eve, which begins an account of the incarnation with the portentous words of Isaiah: "Hearken, O heaven, and give ear, O earth [Is. 1:2]. Let the foundations be shaken [Ps. 81:5], and let trembling lay hold upon the nethermost parts of the world" (6th Hour, 2).

[16]This passage of Philippians (Phil. 2:5–11) is not read at the Nativity. But it is read for the Birth of the Mother of God, the event which can be seen as the beginning of the final preparation for the Incarnation.

[17]Cf. Gregory of Nyssa, *On the Three-day Period of the Resurrection* (W. Jaeger, *Gregorii Nysseni Opera* IX, 281), who says explicitly that in this text, Christ announces in advance what will take place through him.

[18]The same reading is used at lesser feasts of the Mother of God.

[19]These passages have been bowdlerized in *The Festal Menaion*, which substitutes "sacrificial victim."

[20]Elsewhere, she is "the immaculate heifer who has conceived the divine calf" (2 *Kanon* 5.3); cf. the parable of the Prodigal Son. She is a sacrifice preparing the way for greater sacrifice.

[21]To be precise, this is a type which illuminates the Christological significance of Mary's virginity. The gate is to remain shut because the Lord, the God of Israel, has entered by it. Once we accept this incident as a type of the Virgin, then, when we proclaim her "ever-virgin," we are confessing that it was indeed "the Lord, the God of Israel," who entered her womb to be conceived as a baby; that is why her womb will "remain shut."

[22]At the feast of the Entry, this verse occurs in the antiphons at the Divine Liturgy in Greek usage.

[23]It is also, incidentally, a text whose Christological focus is very clear, as we see, for example, in the penultimate stanza:

We all sing in honour of thy Son, O Mother of God, and praise thee as a living temple. For the Lord who holds all things in His hand made His dwelling in thy womb; He hallowed and glorified thee, teaching all to cry to thee:

Rejoice, Tabernacle of God the Word.
Rejoice, greater Holy of Holies.
Rejoice, Ark made golden by the Spirit. (stanza 23)

[24]Cf. also: "Ah, how I have emulated Lamech, the murderer of old, slaying my soul as if it were a man, and my mind as if it were a young man. With sensual longings have I killed my body, as Cain . . . killed his brother" (Ode 2). "O my soul, thou has become like Hagar the Egyptian, thy free choice has been enslaved, and thou hast borne as thy child a new Ishmael, stubborn willfulness" (Ode 3b).

[25]These themes remain clearly evident in the hymnography, although they are no longer the themes of the Sunday gospel readings. In the case of the Prodigal and the Publican, the gospels are now read on Sundays preparatory to Lent.

[26]Cf. 3rd Week, Wednesday Vespers: "In prodigality I have squandered my patrimony; I have become destitute and gone to live in the land of evil citizens. In my unreason I have become like the dumb beasts, and have stripped myself of all divine grace."

5

The Mysticism of Light in the Scriptures and in the Orthodox Worship Tradition

Dimitar Popmarinov Kirov

The mystical experience is a result of the endeavor of the human being to get near to God, to participate in his life. The human soul is attracted by the wish to touch God's absolute nature. In the essence of religious mysticism is the struggle to overcome the phenomenal side of the natural being,[1] to break the wall of the naturally determined world. One aspect of this religious experience is the appearance of light in the world and the attempt to reach its fundamental and mystical essence. In the Orthodox tradition, light itself and the symbolism of light play a magnificent role. It can be found everywhere: in the readings of the scripture, in the worship, in the interior of the temple, in the architecture. But the most important place where light should be, according to the Orthodox mystical tradition, is in the heart of the person, the place where good and evil are at war, where the battle for the human soul takes place. That is the deepest mystery of the Orthodox spiritual practice.

Light and the Old Testament

The first phenomenon which appeared after creation (Genesis 1:3–5) is light. In the creation story, there is no explanation of this light. The main idea is that the light has being but the darkness does not.[2] As a direct act of God, it has an ontological source. It is the product of God's words of creation: "Let there be light" (Genesis 1:3). After it comes God's affirmation that light is good. Light became a perfect tool in God's hands for further development and the sustaining of life. So light in the Old Testament tradition is a sign of God's creative power. Naturally, light is always related to the fire. Fire, in the context of the religions, usually signifies *theophania.* As phenomena of the material world, light and fire both have fundamental places in the universe. In the Bible, one of the most striking places where both of them are found is in the encounter between Moses and God (Exodus 3:2). God reveals himself in fire (Exodus 19:18; Leviticus 9:24). Fire is a tool of God's activity in the world (Judges 6:21; 2 Kings 1:10, 12; Job). At the center of all light is presupposed the existence of fire. In this sense, light can be accepted as primal evidence of God's self-revealing activity. It radiates from

God towards the created world and touches every being. It is the "manifestation of divine operation in a world which apart from it is darkness and chaos."[3]

Usually the light, coming from God, is accepted as supernatural light, which is different from natural light But at the same time, in the Bible there is no distinction between natural and supernatural light. The same can be said of the natural and supernatural worlds. This understanding lies deeply at the heart of the Orthodox vision of the world. The division of natural and supernatural is an invention of the rational mind, mostly developed by scholasticism.[4]

As it is evident from the Old Testament, God's light in the universe is not related to the sun or the moon or the stars; light is created by God before them. In this sense, light is not accepted as something which should be worshipped. Created by God, light has a metaphysical source. So God's light is not the same as the light coming from the luminaries. But God's light may be seen as a source of light in the material world. Later on, in the time of Isaiah (60:19), one finds a clear distinction between the light given by God and the light of the sun. Nevertheless, practically, it is not easy to distinguish in the Bible between the metaphorical and the direct use of light.

The opposite of light is darkness (Isaiah 45:6–7). Yet both can be comprehended as part of God's mystery. God, who is light, at the same time resides in divine darkness. The darkness is metaphysical also. All the things which are created are in this darkness. They become evident only when God reveals them through the light. The early Church's theology, in the words of St. Gregory of Nyssa, interprets this darkness as the impossibility of man to penetrate the mystery of God's being. He wrote, "Therefore, Moses, when he grew in the knowledge, confessed that he sees God in darkness"; that is, then he understood that "God in His essence is above every knowledge and achievement."[5] So the divine darkness is the weakness of the human mind to comprehend God's essence and God's creative power. Light in this sense is the intelligible knowledge revealed by God about himself and about the created world. From this perspective, everything originally is kept in darkness. God's mind is where everything which is created is darkness to God's creatures. Only through the divine light do these things become visible in the world. In this sense, light enlivens everything. Hence, light, as revelation, has a superior value (Ecclesiastes 2:13) over the darkness.

In the Bible, light and life are interrelated. Moreover, light is in the essence of life. Without light, there is no life. Light is a manifestation of the nature of God. Light is definitely needed by human beings in order to live. In themselves, they do not have light. They shine only through God's light: "Let the light of your face shine on us!" (Psalms 4:6; 31:16). In this sense, in the Old Testament there is a foretaste of the idea of deification of human beings. Originally, the destiny of Adam was to grow and become as close as possible to God. He was created a little lower than the angels.[6] Human beings are crowned with "glory and honor" (Psalm 8:5). Thus, their purpose is to shine as brightly as possible.

Light is a divine gift which brings us closer to God. In this closeness, humankind finds the spring of life, its abundance, real life. God allows the chosen people to draw near. They become the friends of God (Exodus 33:11). The best example is Moses. He enters into the cloud, into the divine darkness, in order to receive the law. He draws much closer to God than others, and he communicates with God. Other people are forbidden to enter into the divine cloud. They know that God is there, but they look from the outside. Moses enters and touches the divine. And this is possible only because God allows it. Others are not ready for such revelation. This is the greatest God-human encounter in the Old Testament. Through light, God imparts knowledge, which means hope. God gives the direction, the way. When one follows his way, he or she encounters God personally. So in seeking God and following his commandments, Israel receives more and more revelation. Through people, God communicates with the chosen nation. Step by step, God reveals to them that the final aim is not only personal salvation, but the salvation of the nation, the collective salvation of Israel, the salvation of all creation.

This is one of the reasons why the Israel of the Old Testament did not recognize Jesus as Messiah. In the people's understanding of that time, the most important thing was the good of the nation. The high priest Caiaphas declared, "It is expedient for us, that one man should die for the people, and that the whole nation perish not" (John 11:50; 18:14). The nation is more important than a person. The Jews believed this because they trusted what they received from Moses. With time, their misunderstanding became a metamorphosis of Jewish thought. They were not able to see that God was warning them not to turn light into darkness. Isaiah angrily spoke to those who preferred the pleasures of the kingdoms of this world, "Woe unto them . . . that put darkness for light, and light for darkness" (Isaiah 5:20). And when Jesus was born as the Messiah, they did not recognize him. They did not see him as light, as the Son of God dwelling in human form, being simultaneously God and man. They could not recognize him, because Jesus's life, teaching, and way of life were completely different from their expectations of a Messiah.

This led them astray from the true revelation. Their real desire became the temptation of the world. People needed the kingdom of Israel on earth, here and now. In the face of the high officials, they wanted earthly power, which would be given to them through the Messiah. Therefore, knowing what people were wanting in a Messiah, the devil tried to tempt Jesus with all the kingdoms of the world (Matthew 4:9; Luke 4:5–7). Therefore the inability of encountering Christ is a sign that Israel lost its vision of God's light as truth, lost the desire to meet God himself, to desire him, to be illumined by his light, to yearn for the total being of God.

Jewish religious expectations at the time of Jesus Christ were largely ideological, one sided, and anticipated political achievements. People were expecting the kingdom of this world, not the heavenly kingdom. Nevertheless, the light of the truth remained. And it remained not in the doctrines of the rabbis and the priests. It remained in the hearts of the common people. They felt the sanctity, the real light in the person of Jesus Christ, and they became his followers. The great majority of people was very weak; they easily changed their minds from "Hosanna" (Matthew 21:9, 15; Mark 11:9–10; John 12:13) to "crucify him" (Luke 23:21; John 19:6, 15). The high officials easily manipulated the people. But the main point is that the people had the right feelings in their hearts. Therefore, it was possible in their hearts to penetrate God's light. After the resurrection, when they faced the truth, many among them became the first members of the Church. They repented and believed in Jesus Christ.

Light and the New Testament

In the New Testament, light is directly identified with God. According to the Prologue of the Gospel of John, the Word is God, and God is the Word. In the Word, there is Light, the only real Light from which all life in creation begins. There is a parallel between the light of the creation story and the light of God, which dwells in Jesus Christ. The Revelation of John is a continuation of the revelation that relates light and life (Psalm 36:9). In Revelation, God "communes with and furnishes him directly with the experience of his presence."[7] So light as a peculiarity of God is common for the three persons of the Godhead. In the world, it is revealed mostly from *Logos*, the second person of the Trinity. In this sense, light is an expression of the creative activity of God. When it is present in men, it enlightens them, brings insights and understanding, illumines the darkness.[8]

If God is light (1 John 1:7), then that light has a permanent quality. Therefore, it is related to the eternity of God. Insofar as man is created in the image and likeness of God, the light has its place in human beings, as does eternity (Ecclesiastes 3:11). However, human beings must allow the light to shine in them, or through them. It is given to every person, for God's light is light for all people (John 1:4). God's light is truth, grace, and knowledge. It is the source of real life, "The true light, which enlightens everyone, was coming into the world" (John 1:9).

Following John's vision of God's light, it is quite important to see the relation between light and belief. Faith in Jesus Christ is the true Light, because he "is not one of many lights in the world. He is the Light of the world itself who enlightens all men and women who sit in lands of darkness and in the shadow of death. He is Life itself, confined to no one culture tradition or nation."[9] Those who do not believe do not have light in themselves. They may accept the light or reject it. This relates to the question of the free will of human beings. They freely choose light or darkness. Those who believe dwell in the light and know the truth.

At the same time, light has in itself many other qualities of God's grace. It is a manifestation of God's simplicity. Physical light is evidence of God's grace. The diverse qualities of light radiate from the person of Jesus Christ, in whom resides all of creation. He unites the whole creation with God. Through the incarnation of the *Logos*-Light, God imparts mystical knowledge to the people. The incarnation mystically transports human beings into the very life of God. Of course, this does not mean disappearing in God.

One of the most amazing and mystical places in the gospels is the story of Jesus Christ's transfiguration. It can never be described or explained in a rational way. Therefore "many scholars, past and present, have treated the transfiguration story with suspicion, regarding it either as a misplaced resurrection story or as a legendary product of later Christian piety."[10] But for the devoted believing person, as a historical event, in its deeper meaning, it is at the same time a meeting point between the temporal world and eternity, or, better said, an invasion of eternity into the world, simultaneously revelation and *theophania*.

The actual meaning of the Greek word *metemorphothe* is "to be transformed," "to change one's form,"[11] or "to change in another kind."[12] This metamorphosis has its roots in the Old Testament. The appearance of Moses and Elijah signifies not only the fulfillment of the Old Testament in the person of Christ, but also God's presence in him, that he is God altogether. There are three evidences of this: (1) the light which radiates from Jesus, (2) the appearance of Moses and Elijah, and (3) God's voice coming from the cloud. Here the appearance of Moses is important. In the Old Testament, Moses prefigures Jesus Christ (Deuteronomy 18:15, 19). Like Christ, Moses in a way is transfigured when he draws closer to God to speak with him face to face (Exodus 34:27–35). The people could not see him, because his face was shining. In order to speak with them, the face of God was veiled (34:35).[13]

People who have real mystical experience with God are transfigured only to some extent (e.g., in the Old Testament, as quoted above; also 2 Corinthians 3; Revelation 1:13ff., and also in the apocryphal literature, such as Enoch). It is important also to observe that during such an experience, not only the bodies of the people who are in close relation with God, but also their clothes, their garments, become radiant with light. This means that they also in some way are transfigured. In this sense, for the Orthodox tradition, they become holy. Thus, it is possible to speak of the transfiguration of matter, of its being made holy. The Orthodox believer sees such a process in the life of the saints, their holy relics, and the miracle-working icons. G. B. Caird, a writer from the Congregational Church, expresses the Orthodox understanding very well: "the intense devotions of saint and mystic are often accompanied by physical transformation and luminous glow (further partial parallels are supplied by the accounts of the changed appearance of writers, artists, composers, and scientists, when the creative inspiration is upon them)."[14]

The light from the burning bush and the light from Mount Tabor have the same essence. This reveals the undivided unity of the two testaments and of God's revelation. This means that they are following the same purpose—delivering human beings from sin and enabling their purification, transfiguration, and salvation. In the Old Testament, the fire was burning the bush without consuming it. God does the same with us. In each of us, he lights the light, through the gift of the Holy Spirit, according to the measure of each of us. But he remains invisible, inaccessible: "He communicates Himself to us, gives Himself to us in His infinite love, through the divine energies, which radiate from the three persons of the Trinity. Christ's body, a human body like ours, appears on Tabor penetrated by the grace of the divine light. He is the reflection of the beauty of the Father. He makes the uncreated light, the gift of the Spirit, to shine on the world."[15]

Light in itself is a mode of the revelation, showing its unchangeable essence. In this sense, God's light, as a mode of the revelation, shines through space and time, through history, and is not determined by it. Coming from eternity, it enters the world and becomes a historical, real event. The incarnation is the meeting point of human beings and God's grace, the mystical encounter between humankind and the spiritual world.

From the founding of the Church until now, light as a mystical phenomenon has had a very great part in the life of Christians. So light as an expression of God's grace in the spiritual and material world has received the highest expression in Orthodox hesychasm. Many books and articles have been written about it; therefore I will mention only some main ideas. As is well known, the center of this mystical experience is in seeing the uncreated light. As St. Gregory Palamas understands, it is one of the forms of God's manifestation in the world. "It is uncreated as all God's energies, and at the same time it is in His innermost and inaccessible essence."[16] This is the light which comes from God. This light has no material essence but has been seen by physical eyes. As Bishop Kallistos writes, "Although non-physical, the divine light can be seen by a man through his physical eyes, provided that his senses have been transformed by divine grace."[17]

There are some conditions under which this light may be seen and experienced. *First*, one must be prepared. This means that the said persons should be purified through ascetic life; that is to say, to have matured to such a spiritual level that the spirit and the body are open to receive this uncreated light. *Second*, this high religious experience is possible only through the grace of the Holy Spirit. It should be observed again that it is not the simple sense of physical sight which receives this perception, but the eyes, which are transformed by the Spirit in order to perceive such light. In the mystical act of seeing the divine, the division of the body, soul, and spirit is overcome. A process of the reintegration and deification of the whole human nature begins. *Third*, at the moment of encounter, the body, soul, and spirit begin to see the divine objects simultaneously. The divine light penetrates the whole human being, starting from the spirit, going through the soul and body, and finishing with related objects around it. This is the mystical experience described by many Orthodox saints. Two examples follow.

The *first* is from the life of one of the Bulgarian saints, Theodosity of Tarnovo. He was a disciple of one of the greatest hesychasts, St. Gregory from Sinai, who went into the monastery of Paroria, on the border between Bulgaria and Bysantium. His disciple, St. Evtimiy of Tarnovo, the last Bulgarian Patriach of the second Bulgarian kingdom,[18] relates that once he saw him during a very deep prayer become like a column of fire. He was shining.[19]

On another day, St. Theodosity foretold with tears that he would be the last Bulgarian Patriach and that the Turks would capture the country. Here is quite obviously the close relation between ascetic ecstasy[20] and light, between light and knowledge. Being closer to Jesus Christ, one shines through his light. This light is the same divine light which is natural to his divinity. It does not change in time and space, but it is received by people only when they are purified and ready to accept it. This is the process of the transfiguration of every person who follows him, a process which leads to deification in God.

It should be mentioned also that the light, which has been seen by the saints, is the same light which the disciples of Christ saw during the transfiguration. It is the divine light existing in God; it is the natural brightness of Christ's divinity.[21] So this is the divinity to which every person is called.

For those to whom is given the possibility to participate in this mystical experience comes the obligation to stay at this level of mature spirituality. Otherwise there may be unfortunate consequences. This is the case with the *second* example. It comes from the famous story about the conversation between Nikolay Motovilov and St. Seraphim of Sarov. This story is very popular among Orthodox believers predominantly in the Slavonic countries. It is well known that St. Seraphim satisfies the wish of Motovilov to experience the presence of the Holy Spirit. Motovilov relates:

> Then Father Seraphim took me firmly by the shoulders and said: "My son, we are both at this moment in the Spirit of God. Why don't you look at me?"
>
> "I cannot look, Father," I replied, "because your eyes are flashing like lightning. Your face has become brighter than the sun, and it hurts my eyes to look at you."
>
> "Don't be afraid," he said. "At this very moment you yourself have become as bright as I am. You yourself are now in the fullness of the Spirit of God; otherwise you would not be able to see me as you do."
>
> Then bending his head towards me, he whispered softly in my ear: "Thank the Lord God for His infinite goodness toward us . . . But why, my son, do you not look me in the eyes? Just look, and don't be afraid; the Lord is with us."
>
> After these words I glanced at his face, and there came over me an even greater reverent awe. Imagine in the center of the sun, the dazzling light of its midday rays, the face of a man talking to you. You see the movement of his lips and the changing expression of his eyes, you hear his voice, you feel someone holding your shoulders, yet you do not see his hands, you do not even see yourself or his body, but only a blinding light spreading far around for several yards and lighting up with its brilliance the sow-blanket which covers the forest glade and the snow-flakes which continue to fall unceasingly . . .
>
> "What do you feel?" Father Seraphim asked me.
>
> "An immeasurable well-being," I said.
>
> "But what sort of well-being? How exactly do you feel well?"
>
> "I feel such a calm," I answered, "such peace in my soul that no words can express it."[22]

These cases are almost identical with the biblical passages mentioned above, both of Moses and the transfiguration of Christ. Motovilov sees St. Seraphim's shining face as the face of Moses. People cannot look at the face of Moses. The same may be said of Motovilov. The face of the saint is like the sun. Motovilov is afraid to look at Father Seraphim's face. Light radiating from his face penetrates everything, the very being of the person. Motovilov cannot see even his own body. It is important to note, however, that this spiritual experience is possible only because of the permission of St. Seraphim. It is not due to the merit of Motovilov; "otherwise you would not be able to see me as you do," says the saint. This "whole passage is of extraordinary importance for understanding the Orthodox doctrine of deification and union with God. It shows how the Orthodox idea of sanctification includes the body: it is not Seraphim's (or Motovilov's) soul only, but the whole body which is transfigured by the grace of God."[23]

This story has a second part, which is not often noted as an example, but its meaning is a good lesson for anyone who desires to meet God without being prepared. Motovilov did not have the ascetic training of fighting with the evil powers, with thoughts, with his evil will. He was not purified. He was not spiritually mature and became proud that he had such an experience with the Holy Spirit. He taught that his personal experience with the Holy Spirit is enough to keep evil from him. This was the greatest fault of Motovilov. As St. Seraphim foretold, he was possessed for almost thirty years by an evil spirit. When one has the light, one must keep it. Otherwise, it becomes darkness. So those who desire to meet God must be prepared for the encounter.

The transfiguration includes the whole being of the person. It starts from the lowest levels of the body, soul, and spirit. In this pilgrimage toward purification and enlightenment, these three strata of the human being start to act in one direction, in harmony. They do not contradict one another; rather, they begin to overcome opposite desires, of which St. Paul speaks: "For the good that I would, I do not: but the evil which I would not, that I do . . . O wretched man that I am!" (Romans 7:19, 24). So the light of the Holy Spirit penetrates every fiber of human beings and enlightens them. In this sense, they are in the process of change, of transformation, a process of full transfiguration. This is what one of the greatest hesychasts, St. Gregory Palamas, confirms: the eyes see this light "after having been transformed by the Spirit. For in the age to be this same body will endure forever, gazing upon the divine light."[24]

Finally, the process of transfiguration initiates a process of deification (*theosis*). The way of those who seek God passes through enlightening, transfiguration, and deification. It should be noted that these three processes transpire simultaneously. The result is sanctity—a sign of the growth of a person in God; of the re-creation of one's integrity; of approaching the condition of the human being who has not fallen, a status which abolishes the dualism of body and spirit; of the material and the spiritual; of the heavenly and the earthly. It is a foretaste of the kingdom of God here on earth. As St. Paul describes it, our Lord Jesus Christ "shall change our vile body, that it may be fashioned like unto his glorious body" (Philippians 3:21). The only condition is to be baptized, to be members of Christ's Church. "After our baptism, we are able to transform ourselves, this becomes possible. We do not always accomplish this, because we remain free to accept or to reject God's gifts—this is the case of the buried talent, which (alas!) bears no fruit. But if we accept to cooperate[25] with God, if we allow His grace to act in us, we are able to transfigure and sanctify ourselves; that is, we can become saints. Illumined in baptism, nourished by the sacrament of the Eucharist, daily we draw closer to God, in order at the end of time to become *partakers of the divine nature*" (2 Peter 1:4).[26]

Light and the Liturgy

Light has a significant role in the created world, in human life and all its dimensions, in people's everyday lives. But most of all, Orthodox tradition is represented in Orthodox worship, which follows the liturgical year.

> The liturgical year is in the harmony with the seasonal cycle, according to the order of nature. Our feasts are inserted into the created world and give it all its meaning. This is no accident, for God has sent His Son into this world and thus bodily linked to the cosmos. Each feast is an encounter between heaven and earth, between the Creator and His creature. The heavens are rent (Is 64:1), and God descends towards us,

> dwells in created matter and infuses it with His Light. The expectation of the coming of the Lord takes place in winter, in darkness: the birth of Christ comes as the solstice, "*the Sun of Righteousness*": "*The people who sat in darkness have seen a great light ...*" (Is 9:2; Mt 4:16). Our hope increases as we prepare for *Pascha*, during Great Lent; the resurrection of Christ coincides with the renewal and awakening of nature. At Pentecost, the Holy Spirit illumines the world and everything is enlivened. Nature is in its full glory. At the height of summer, Christ, our true light, the uncreated Sun, appears transfigured on the mountain.[27]

The old world before Christ was in the situation of the lost sheep. There was no hope. Pagan religion could not satisfy the spiritual needs of the people. Highly educated people from the high classes lived in spiritual desperation; ordinary people did not trust their gods anymore. In this dark situation, the pagan world was experiencing that salvation from the absurdity of human existence would come from the East, that it would be a great Light from the East. Svetonii writes that people from Judah will conquer the world. In the whole world there was an eschatological tension of messianic expectations. The same feelings were common in Judah. At one moment, the expectations of the pagan world and of the people of God coincided.[28]

This eschatological tension and these messianic expectations are well preserved in the heritage of Orthodox worship and hymnology. For the new faith, the uncertainty, the hesitations, is already gone. The heavenly Child is born on earth. He unites heaven and earth. He unites the chosen people and the pagan world. He abolishes the dualism between the peoples of the earth. The truth becomes one, because his light is shining all over the world. Mystically, the world becomes one in Christ, the God-Child. And this is the great mystery, the great wisdom. So at the feast of his birth, the Church sings:

> Your Nativity, O Christ our God,
> has shown to the world the light of wisdom!
> For by it, those who worshipped the stars
> were taught by a star to adore you,
> the Sun of Righteousness,
> and to know you, the Orient from on high.
> O Lord, glory to you![29]

Taking part in this celebration, one mystically breaks the walls of space and time and enjoys the moment of the uniting of heaven and earth. The light from the star which guided the Magi now shines in the very being of believers, of the partakers in this mystery, in worship and gives them more than rational knowledge. The Son of God, who dwells in eternity, through the incarnation and birth enters the time and space of history. Through him, human beings enter eternity. This is one of the main truths which this feast of the Nativity conveys. God enters humankind, and humankind may enter God (*theosis*).

The birth of Christ is the central focus in the history of salvation. Jesus lived in the world as a man. God in him was not visible to others. When he started to reveal his divinity, it was visible only to those who had eyes to see and ears to hear (Mark

8:18). The New Testament declares that Christ is the true Light, "*the light of the world*" (John 9:5). This means that the whole of God's energies are concentrated in the world. God's energies are God's uncreated light, which shines through the whole universe, through every creature.

Resurrection is the final and total victory over death. Therefore, this is the greatest joy on earth. This is why Orthodoxy venerates this event as "Feast of feasts." St. Gregory of Nazianzus describes it thus: "It is the feast of feasts, the holiday of holidays, which surpasses not only human feasts, but even feasts of Christ, as the light of the sun is brighter than that of the stars. It is the day of resurrection and the beginning of true life."[30] Resurrection is a sign that a radical change has transpired—death is defeated. Resurrection is accompanied by light, the concentration of God's energies, concentrated in the person of the resurrected Jesus. Therefore during Pascha, light has a central place in worship. It is simultaneously a reality and a symbol of the victory of life over death. At the same time, it is important to notice that the victory of Jesus Christ is not only God's victory over death. It is a common victory, the victory of God and humankind together. This is the highest point of *synergia*. Therefore, it is also a human victory; it is a victory for everyone. In the humanity of Jesus, we are in him and he is in us. Therefore, it is our victory also. And we can feel this victory more and more as our lives are in accordance with his teaching, if we are in his light, if we become one blood and one body with him.

This is why Orthodoxy uses all of its imagination to express this event in its worship. During the paschal service, people are standing in the church with lighted candles in their hands as a symbol of God's light, which shines in their hearts also. The candles are burning and people are singing the Paschal Canon.

> Ode 1, Hirmos:
>
> This is the day of resurrection.
> Let us be illumined, O people.
> Pascha, the Pascha of the Lord.
> For from death to life
> and from earth to heaven
> has Christ our God led us,
> as we sing the song of victory.
> Refrain: *Christ is risen from the dead.*
>
> Troparion:
>
> Let us purify our senses
> and we shall see Christ
> shining in the unapproachable light
> of His resurrection.
> We shall clearly hear Him say:
> Rejoice, as we sing the song of victory.

The temple is full of light, people greet each other, "Christ is risen!" And answer, "Indeed, he is risen!" The text of the *troparion* confirms that the light is everywhere, that the whole universe is celebrating, but most of all that the light is in the hearts of the people.

Ode 3:

Now all is filled with light;
heaven and earth and the lower regions.
Let all creation celebrate the rising of Christ.
In Him we are established.

In the same ode, in the *hipakoe*, tone 4, angels are saying:

Why do you seek among the dead as a man
The One Who is everlasting light?
Behold the clothes in the grave.

The Lord is risen.
He has slain death, as He is the Son of God,
Saving the race of men.

The light from the feast is spread all over the world. Therefore, salvation is proclaimed to everybody. Ode 7 *troparion* says:

This is the bright and saving night,
Sacred and supremely festal.
It heralds the radiant day of the resurrection
On which the timeless light
Shone forth bodily from the tomb for all.

There are many other places in the Paschal Canon which show what a great place and meaning the light has in the feast of Pascha. It could be said that light includes all of its dimensions: from spiritual to material, from divine to human. So it is the divine energy of God which radiates to and through all creatures, bringing life and neglecting death. Orthodox worship gives another important meaning of the light in the feast of the Holy Spirit and the founding of the Church. This event is very well expressed in Orthodox iconography. In the icon of Pentecost, "The descent of the Holy Spirit upon the apostles is considered like a cosmic event. All creation is penetrated by the luminous rays, the divine energies which God communicates."[31] In this event, we could find something which reminds us of the Old Testament *theophania* of God in fire, the relation between fire and light. This connection is quite well expressed in the Holy Liturgy. The spoon by which the faithful receive communion is called a "pair of tongs" (NRSV), the tool through which the lips of the prophet Isaiah are cleansed. In this sense, the holy people speak about the Eucharist as "receiving, eating of fire."[32] This is a mystical receiving of God in oneself through the deified human nature of Jesus Christ. In the event of Pentecost, when the Church was founded, the common activity of the Holy Trinity is quite obvious. God the Father sends the Holy Spirit and the Son in order through the Church to prepare the transfiguration of the world. This is expressed immediately after the descent of the Holy Spirit upon the apostles. At once they realized everything which happened before, which is happening now.

Divine grace opened their eyes and enlightened all their being in order to understand everything. At this moment, the vale of the old person from their eyes fell down, and baptized by the Holy Spirit, they became new persons, transformed people. Under the grace of the Spirit, they could bridge time and space, to go deep and catch the meaning of events and things in their essence, in the past and in the future. Spiritually, they were able to overcome the diversities and the divisions of the world. They could contemplate its archetypes and grasp their meaning. A sign of it is the moment when they started to talk in different tongues. From the time of the tower of Babylon, the differentiation of the tongues was a sign of separation and alienation between people. Now it is going through a process of uniting. This is very well expressed in the *stichera* of the vespers of the feast, tone 8:

> The tongues, ones confused because of
> The audacity of the builders,
> Are now filled with the wisdom
> Of the glorious knowledge of God.
> Once the Lord condemned the impious for their sin;
> Today Christ illumines the sinners.
> Once the tongues were divided in punishment;
> But now their harmony is restored
> For the salvation of our souls.

In order to receive the Holy Spirit, the light of its fire must be ignited within oneself. Only then will the light, which comes from this fire, transfigure the person. Then he or she will be a real partaker in the life of the Trinity, as the *sticheron* of the feast says:

> We have seen the true Light!
> We have received the heavenly Spirit!
> We have found the true faith
> Worshipping the undivided Trinity
> Who have saved us![33]

Jesus Christ enlightened human nature in its fullness with his resurrection. With the descent of the Holy Spirit upon the apostles and the Church, this light is dispensed to everyone who desires to be enlightened, living the life of the Church. It is an opportunity for everyone to exercise free will, if one desires to have the light within. This possibility of choice is expressed most of all in the feast of the Transfiguration. Jesus Christ is transfigured before his disciples. He showed them and everyone who he is. It is now up to all to express their own desire: do they desire to follow the way of transfiguration and transformation, of becoming one of the disciples of Christ, of becoming like one of those on Mount Tabor, of choosing the way of sanctity, of choosing the divine light, or only the reflection of this light? In order to choose the right way, the Church prays through the *troparion* of the feast, tone 7:

> You were transfigured on the mount,
> O Christ God,

Revealing your glory to your disciples
As far as they could bear it.
Let your everlasting light
Shine upon us sinners!

Through the prayers of the Theotokos,
O giver of light,
Glory to You.

The *kontakion*, tone 7, says:

On the mount where you transfigured,
and your disciples, O Christ God, beheld your glory,
As far as nature would allow,
So when they see you crucified
They will understand that your suffering is voluntary
and proclaim to the world
That you are truly the Father's refulgent light.

* * *

Light is a reality and as a symbol is present everywhere in the Holy Scriptures. It shows the power of God and divine love through the created world. Through it, human beings live spiritually and physically. The uncreated light as energy of the Trinity gives life and sanctifies the universe and all humankind. From the founding of the Church, light has a very important place in its life. By receiving the mystical, uncreated light of God through the Church's sacraments, everyone has the possibility to become a partaker in the divine life of God, to be deified.

Endnotes

[1]P. Minin, *Drevno Tsarkovnata Mistika* [The Old Church Mysticism], in Bulgarian (Veliko Tarnovo: Praxis, 1999), 8.

[2]Nikolay Shivarov, "Satvorenieto" [The Creation], in *Sbornik po bogoslovie* (Sofia: Nov Chovek, 2000), 18.

[3]Otto A. Piper, "Light and Darkness," *Interpreter's Dictionary of the Bible* (Nashville: Abingdon, 1962), 3:130, col. 2.

[4]Usually, supernatural is defined as "reality which lies beyond the natural world." G. R. Evans, *The Supernatural*, in *A New Dictionary of Christian Theology*, ninth edition (London, 1996), 557, col. 1: in order to be opposed to the pantheistic identification between God and the world.

In the first chapters of Genesis, Adam is in direct relationship with God. The "natural" world became such after the sin of Adam. He disobeyed God and created distance between his descendants and God. With the sin of Adam, the order ordained by God in the world was destroyed (Romans 8:20). Thus the world became "natural" because it departed from God, and the part of the creation which did not fall remained, as identified later on by the theologians, as supernatural.

In the Bible, there is no such division. For the Old Testament person, the world is one. Adam and people after him are in direct contact with God. Before the fall, Adam directly communicates with God. This does not mean that Adam and God are in a pantheistic relationship. On the contrary, they are different persons. Adam lives in close unity, but not in identity, with God. God allows Adam to know him. The reproach of God towards Job and his friends, who were wanting to know God's ways (Job 40–41), is not because God rejects the possibility that people may know him, but because the distance is not bridgeable. People "have no real conciousness of the impossibility of a man to reach the deepness of God's providence," of God's way (Assist. Dimitar Popmarinov, "Prakticheskata bibleyska madrost v St. Zavet / stradanieto I silata na viyarata" [Practical, Biblical Wisdom in the Old Testament / The Suffering and Strength of Faith], in the periodical *Duxovna Kultura* [Sofia: Sinodalno Izdatelstvo, 1993], 6). The only possibility for the creatures is to come near to God and to participate in his life through the light of his energies. But they can never pass the ontological abyss between them and God. No one creature can participate in God's essence. God's transcendence is absolute. And the conciseness of this reality keeps the Bible and the Orthodox doctrine of *theosis* from pantheistic understanding. It is possible to give many examples of the feeling of this distance: Psalm 104:2; 119:105, 135.

[5]P. Minin, *Drevno Tsarkovnata Mistika*, 36.

[6]In this long note, I dare to give you a hypothetical and therefore subjective vision of the way of the world, perceived in my Orthodox feelings. These are only some insights.

According to the Orthodox tradition, committing sin means to alienate oneself from God, from his light, to choose the darkness. Tracing the way of humankind after the fall, one can say that there is a drifting away from God. It is possible to trace several main stages of this development up to now.

First, in the time immediately after the fall, humankind is still not so far from God. There is still in the human mind the knowledge from paradise—knowledge is not yet dispersed, not extroverted. Human beings still are not dividing the reality of object and subject; they comprehend the reality in its totality, in its fullness. But these possibilities are becoming weaker. Departing from God, humans lose the possibility to be in real contact with God. Knowledge becomes weaker and partial, fragmented. More and more, humans become dependent on nature.

The *second* stage is mythology. People, losing the clear face of God, start to identify God with creatures and with nature. Yet in mythology, a great part of this prehistoric knowledge still can be found, this sense of close relations between man and God. But God is seen mostly in nature, in the cosmos, in the universe, in the elements of the creation. People start to depersonalize God and to personalize nature, to identify its separate elements as gods. But primitive knowledge is still alive in oral tradition.

The *third* stage is the *racio*. It is the moment when alphabets, writing, and philosophy appear. The world is no longer in the hearts of the people. It is externalized. Precepts succumb to rational thought, and the inner powers of the soul are suppressed. Thus the process of alienation goes farther. It becomes alienation not only from God, but also among human beings (the story of the tower of Babel). During the time of oral tradition, people have personal encounters; they meet face to face; all of their senses participate in receiving and exchanging knowledge. After the appearance of the written word, people are separated, alienated once more. One person is no longer oriented to the other person. Letters appear as a mean of communication between people.

The *fourth* stage is technology. Technology changes humankind. Now God is too far away and becomes an abstract idea, an idol in the rational human mind. God is no longer the real God of the Bible. People largely hope to be saved by technology. In the electronic age, people do not need each other as before. People simultaneously are very close and very far from each other. Externally they are very close, but internally they are very far apart. Technology replaces other human beings. Our neighbor is no longer a human being, but a computer. The world becomes virtual. Reality is changed. For the new generation, the virtual world sometimes is more real than the world outside of the computer. Alienation is total. In this process, people are alienated not only from God, but from one another. With globalization, people manufacture their own slavery.

Finally, in believing in technology, people adore themselves. Thus, this process would seem irreversible.

Despite this decline, there were people, a remnant, who kept the true vision and loved God. They lived with God and God's commandments. They were the holy people Israel.

[7]Georgius I. Mantzaridis, *The Deification of Man* (Crestwood, NY: St. Vladimir's Seminary Press, 1984), 115.

[8]John Marsh, *The Gospel of Saint John* (Singapore: Penguin, 1968), 104.

[9]Thomas Hopko, "Orthodoxy in Post-Modern Pluralism Societies," *The Ecumenical Review* 51, no. 4 (1999): 369.

[10]G. B. Caird, *The Gospel of Saint Luke* (Singapore: Penguin, 1983), 132.

[11]D. E. Nineham, *The Gospel of Saint Mark* (Singapore: Penguin, 1983), 234.

[12]*Starogratsko-Bulgarski Rechnik* [Greek-Bulgarian Dictionary] (Sofia, 1992).

[13]The vale is a symbol of the abyss, which exists between human beings and God. It is the ontological barrier which does not allow creatures to annihilate God's essence.

[14]G. B. Caird, *The Gospel of Saint Luke*, 132.

[15]Catherine Aslanof, ed., *The Incarnate God*, 2 vols., Eng. trans., Paul Meyendorff (Crestwood, NY: St. Vladimir's Seminary Press, 1995), 1:36–37.

[16]P. Minin, *Drevno Tsarkovnata Mistika*, 89.

[17]Kallistos Ware, *The Orthodox Way* (Crestwood, NY: St. Vladimir's Seminary Press, 1998), 127.

[18]St. Ephtimiy, Patriarch of Tarnovo, lived in a difficult and tragic period of Orthodoxy. At that time, almost the whole of the Eastern Orthodox world had been conquered by the Turks and Islam (the middle of the 14th and the beginning of 15th centuries).

[19]*Zhitiya na svetiite* [Life of the Saints], in Bulgarian (Sofia: Sinodalno izdatelstvo, 1974), 592.

[20]*Ekstasis* usually is understood as a state of being outside or beyond oneself, being united with God (L. Thunberg, *The Vision of St Maxsimus the Confessor* [Crestwood, NY: St. Vladimir's Seminary Press, 1985], 107).

[21]Georgius I. Mantzaridis, *The Deification of Man*, 100.

[22]Timothy Ware, *The Orthodox Church* (Baltimore: Penguin, 1969), 131–132.

[23]Ibid., 132.

[24]*Answer to Akindinos* 3.2.3, *Works* 3, 162. Quote from G. I. Manzaridis, *The Deification of Man*, 100.

[25]Gr. *Synergia*; i.e., to unite our will with God's will, voluntarily to submit our to God's will and to cooperate with God for our salvation.

[26]Catherine Aslanof, ed., *The Incarnate God*, 1:173.

[27]Ibid, 1:11.

[28]Emanuil Svetlov, *Na Pororge Novogo Zaveta* [At the Threshold of the New Testament] (Bruxelles: Zhizn s Bogom, 1983), 563.

[29]Troparion, tone 4. Catherine Aslanof, ed., *The Incarnate God*, 1:147. All additional liturgical texts which are not explicitly mentioned are taken from this book.

[30]Ibid., 2:147.

[31]Quoted from Paul N. Harrichak, *The Divine Liturgy of the Great Church* (Reston, VA: Holy Trinity Orthodox Church, 1983), 109.

[32]Paul Evdokimov, *The Art of the Icon* (Redondo Beach, CA: Oakwood Publications, 1990), 123.

[33]Quoted from Paul N. Harrichak, *The Divine Liturgy of the Great Church*, 109.

PART 2

Mutual Learning between Orthodox and Methodists

6

Two Similar Spiritual Paths: Methodism and Greek Orthodoxy

James H. Charlesworth

Introduction

Since the time of John Wesley (1703–1791),[1] Greek Orthodox priests and Methodist ministers have tended to ignore each other; sometimes they have disdained the other.[2] A comparison of these two "paths" probably should refer to Greek Orthodoxy and Methodism, but as a Methodist minister and a New Testament scholar who teaches in a Presbyterian seminary, I am better prepared to talk about Methodism and Greek Christianity.[3]

In the present essay, I do not intend to compare and contrast these two forms of Christianity. Much can be said about how they are different. I shall leave a discussion of differences for other scholars. In this essay, I will share what has become obvious to me having worked for over thirty years with his eminence Archbishop Damianos and the Holy Council of St. Catherine's Monastery, having studied and worshiped with monks on Mt. Athos, having lived in Methodist parsonages as the son of the Rev. Dr. Arthur Charlesworth, the son of the Rev. Dr. Thomas Charlesworth, and having served the Methodist Church and its successor the United Methodist Church officially since 1963.[4] These varied experiences convince me that Methodism and the Greek Church, in many ways, are fundamentally similar, especially since neither seeks to establish a set dogmatic or systematic theology. They are two similar paths developed by inspired men (and women) in the attempt to be faithful to God through his Son, Jesus Christ, especially through praying and singing (or chanting) hymns or psalms. Later, I shall explain and emphasize this major point of my essay: that these twin paths, Methodism and Greek Orthodoxy, similarly promote doxological piety more than dogmatic theology.

At the outset, I think it wise to explain why a comparison of these two paths is fruitful and why a shared appreciation should evolve naturally. First, I think many of us see a growing ecumenical movement towards a global Christianity. Thus, we may bridge the chasm between Eastern and Western cultures that widened beginning in the twelfth century, especially in the universities, and through the growing influence of Thomas Aquinas (c. 1225–1274).[5] In the West, especially after the Renaissance and Reformation, theologians tended to disparage mysticism and tradition. They sought to be systematic and analytical, choosing to focus on logic to establish theological truths. John Wesley broke with this emphasis, and his mysticism and love of early traditions, most of them shared by the Eastern Church, align early Methodism with the Greek Orthodox. In his *Explanatory Notes upon the New Testament*, Wesley pointed out that the proper means of interpreting the Bible was to perceive "the mysteries and insights of revelation" that are given "to the eyes of faith." He was not using the Bible to establish "literal propositions to philosophers and critics."[6]

Second, a comparison of these two paths is promising, since the Wesleys and the members of the Greek church perceived themselves to be in direct continuity with the early churches, especially those in Athens, Corinth, Philippi, and Thessalonica. John Wesley, who "regarded himself as a sort of bishop,"[7] although not elevated to that rank within the Anglican church, appealed to the apostolic origin of deacons, presbyters, and bishops; this position was especially stressed by Wesley during the Conference of 1745.[8]

Third, the Methodist and the Greek Orthodox revere the pope but deny papal supremacy and are dismayed by the claim of papal infallibility (especially infallible *ex cathedra* pontifications). Fourth, Methodism and Greek Orthodoxy share many emphases; for example, they reject the concept of clerical celibacy.[9] Fifth, perhaps only a minor point, the size of Methodism in the USA and in Greece may bring out further similarities, since both number about 9 million members.[10]

Sixth, I am convinced of the promise of a deeper relationship among Methodists and the Greek Orthodox, because of developments in my area of specialization. In the past, New Testament scholars pointed to the different backgrounds of Jesus and of Greek Orthodoxy. For example, a specialist on Greek Orthodoxy, Kallistos Ware of Pembroke College in the University of Oxford and Bishop of Diokleia, simply reported, "Whereas Christ himself came from a rural background, Greek Christianity was from the start predominantly urban."[11] Thus, many have assumed that Jesus came from a rural context but Greek Orthodoxy developed within an urban culture. This contrast is no longer valid. Jesus grew up near Sepphoris, which was being built as the capital of Galilee when he was a young man. In *Jesus and Archaeology*, scholars and archaeologists stress, in differing ways, why Jesus lived near and was influenced by urban centers, especially those built in Lower Galilee by Herod Antipas, namely Sepphoris and Tiberias. Galilee was not simply a rural farming culture.[12] Therefore, the geographical spawning grounds of Jesus and Greek Orthodoxy are more similar than supposed.

Seventh, in fasting, the Methodists and the Greek Orthodox have another commonality that is a foundation for building bridges of understanding. Methodists today should follow or appreciate John Wesley's habit of fasting "not to eat for a period prescribed," so as to purify the body and soul and become more sensitive to the needs and concerns of others.[13] Wesley usually fasted all day on Friday.[14] He judged fasting had sadly been "almost universally neglected by the Methodists,"[15] even though there were in his time days set aside for a "national fast."[16]

Of course, fasting has been practiced for centuries in the Greek Orthodox church. St. Symeon the New Theologian exhorted his readers to "observe the great Lenten fast by eating every third day (not counting Saturdays and Sundays)."[17] Nikitas Stithatos expressed the following thought: "Bodily desires and the impulses of the flesh are checked by self-control, fasting and spiritual struggle."[18] St. Gregory of Sinai advised that those "engaged in spiritual warfare regain their original state by practicing two commandments—obedience and fasting."[19] Fasting must be accompanied by prayer; hence, St. Gregory Palamas's words are on target: "If you do not cut off the inner flow of evil thoughts by means of prayer and humility, but fight against them merely with the weapons of fasting and bodily hardship, you will labour in vain."[20]

Finally, I deem it singularly important to focus on Methodism and Greek Christianity, since the New Testament documents were composed in Greek, since I teach them in advanced Greek classes, and since John Wesley emphasized the importance of the Greek of the New Testament. In fact, Wesley frequently used Greek expressions in his sermons, journals, and letters.[21] I am also convinced that Wesley and the Greek church are united by a penchant for mysticism and hymnic celebration; this shared characteristic distinguishes them from Latin Christianity—and its offshoots—since it is more practical and legally focused.

Theocentricity

Both Methodism and Greek Orthodoxy endeavor to be theocentric and to experience the one-and-only Creator. In his sermon on "The Unity of the Divine Being," John Wesley affirmed that God is "one, eternal, omnipresent," "all-perfect," "omnipotent," omniscient, and holy being, and "above all is his mercy." Wesley also believed that the early Jews and first Christians believed, as he did, that God "alone is a pure Spirit."[22] This awesome Being is known through the life and teachings of the Son and experienced as present in the Holy Spirit. Both paths condemn tritheism and doceticism, but each suffers from practioners who commit these two perennial heresies.

A sociologist would hear a similar chant in Methodist and Greek Orthodox services, since both chant *kyrie eleison*. Both stress that dogma is not found primarily in long systematic treatises written by scholars; it is to be found in chants and hymns led by priests and ministers. For both paths, theology is not something executed in a study by an erudite scholar; theology evolves from experience that is shaped by prayers to and meditations upon the Creator. As Vladimir Lossky has stated, "theology and mysticism support and complete each other. . . . Mysticism is . . . the perfecting and crown of all theology."[23] While the Greeks live this insight, John and Charles Wesley would seem to affirm it.

For both ways, God is both knowable and unknowable. God cannot be fully known by humans. Gregory of Palamas stressed this distinction by pointing out the concepts of essence and energy. The radical otherness and transcendence of God is the divine essence; God's essence is impossible for humans to know. What they can apprehend is God's immanence or his energies. As Basil of Caesarea stated, "We know our God from his energies, but we do not claim that we can draw near to his essence. For his energies come down to us, but his essence remains unapproachable."[24]

These thoughts by great thinkers in the Orthodox tradition are echoed by Charles Wesley in his 1749 hymn titled "Thou Hidden Source of Calm Repose." The unknowableness of God explodes in Charles Wesley's "Come, O Thou Traveler Unknown."

This hymn was composed in 1742 and is an exegetical reflection on Gen. 32:24–32, the account of Jacob's wrestling with the Unknown One who would not reveal his name:

Come, O thou Traveler unknown,
whom still I hold, but cannot see!
My company before is gone,
And I am left alone with thee,
With thee all night I mean to stay,
and wrestle till the break of day.

Even though God is far off and transcendent—"O thou Traveler unknown"—the Wesleyan tradition, like the Orthodox church, celebrates God's presence. Thus, in Charles Wesley's "Ye Servants of God," penned in 1744 and based on Rev. 7:9–12, we hear the words, "God ruleth on high, almighty to save, / And still he is nigh, his presence we have."[25] Perhaps the stress on the presence of the incarnate Lord is best known to Methodists, and others, in Charles Wesley's "Love Divine, All Loves Excelling," composed in 1747: "Love divine, all loves excelling, / Joy of heaven, to earth come down."

While worshiping with Greek Orthodox monks, I have experienced an affirmation of the purpose of worship that is defined by The United Methodist Church. Note these words in *The United Methodist Book of Worship*: "Our worship in both its diversity and its unity is an encounter with the living God through the risen Christ in the power of the Holy Spirit."[26] In worship, we Methodists, in harmony with Greek Christians, seek to transcend worldly concerns in order to experience here on earth the presence of the one and only Awesome One.

John Wesley, the Canon, and Inspiration

Most of what I have found written on the Wesleys and what has been claimed about the relation of Methodism to the Greek church seems to stress that the Wesleys worked with a closed canon, or a collection of books that are found, for example, in the New Revised Standard Version. This is misleading. The Wesley's father, Samuel, as well as John and Charles, appreciated many of the books that are now considered, wrongly, extra-canonical and inferior to the canonical masterpieces. Samuel taught young ministers, including John and Charles, to imitate the morality found in the *Testaments of the Twelve Patriarchs.* This masterpiece is part of the Old Testament Pseudepigrapha.[27] John, Charles, and other Methodists had easy access to it, since by 1722 the second edition of J. A. Fabricius's *Codex pseudepigraphus Veteris Testamenti* was available.

The Wesleys had a special fondness for the so-called Old Testament Apocrypha, basing hymns and sermons, for example, on the *Wisdom of Solomon.* There are reasons to conclude that John Wesley had memorized portions of *Sirach.* These points are known, since I drew attention to them in "The Wesleys and the Canon: An Unperceived Openness."[28] This research discloses that for the Wesleys, God's Word is not confined to the canon as known in the NRSV.

At this point I wish to mention some contradictory conclusions found in recent scholarship. For example, Scott J. Jones offers two mutually contradictory conclusions.

In his *John Wesley's Conception and Use of Scripture*, he contends that "Wesley clearly stands with the larger Protestant tradition in rejecting the Apocrypha as part of the Bible" (p. 59).[29] Later, in the same book, he contends that "Wesley occasionally treats the Apocrypha as Scripture" (p. 143). These two statements are antithetical. Which of these statements is accurate, or is either accurate?

My reading of John Wesley makes me reluctant to systematize his thoughts. Sometimes he suggests that the Apocrypha is not as authoritative as the Bible. The best example is in his *Popery Calmly Considered*, in which he claims, unequivocally, that "We dare not receive them as part of the Holy Scriptures."[30] Wesley bases his categorical rejection of the Apocrypha on two observations: "none of these books were received as such by the Jewish Church" and neither were they accepted "by the ancient Christian Church."

Here John Wesley errs in both instances. The Jews during the time of Jesus were not a "church," and they did not use the concepts of canonical or apocryphal. Moreover, many Jews clearly deemed some of the books considered later "extra-canonical" as equal, and sometimes superior, to the works later placed in a closed canon. The leaders of the early Christian church, including Tertulian and Origen, considered many of the so-called extra-canonical works inspired. As John Wesley himself knew, Jude quotes from *1 Enoch* as prophecy (using the Aorist).

At other times, John Wesley clearly is deeply moved by the apocryphal books and does use them as if they are full of God's Word. Thus, Scott Jones's second statement is more accurate. John Wesley did not use the works in the Apocrypha as if there was a clear distinction between their status and that of the so-called canonical books. He had an openness to the apocryphal works; it is this openness which is harmonious with, indeed consistent with, his theological appeal to a variety of theological positions. Both are grounds for a fundamental relation with Greek Orthodoxy. Along with the members of the Greek church, Wesley believed that God had revealed the divine self in the Canon and also in books on the fringes of the Canon.

Theology Is Couched in Hymns of Praise and Petition

I come now to my major point. The Wesleys and the Greek Orthodox recognize that the purest theology is one that is found in praise. Praise grounds faith in a somatic connection with the Creator that has been expressed and felt through the centuries, beginning with David, who probably composed some words found in the Psalter.

Surely on Mt. Athos and in St. Catherine's Monastery at the foot of Jebel Musa, I have felt the presence of God and a kinship spirit. I have no doubt that monks in both sacred locations would agree with John Wesley when he summarized the Wesleyan approach to dogma with words derived from Jehu's greeting to Jehonadab (2 Kings 10:15), "If thine heart is as my heart . . . Give me thine hand."[31] Dogma and doctrine must begin in the heart. They must culminate as the fruit of the lips, as the Qumran Community stated about a century before the birth of Jesus.

By the principle of reducing theological differences to the thoughts of the heart, John Wesley avoids the Charybdis of a latitudinarianism that extends into meaninglessness and faithlessness and the Scylla of a dogma that stifles freedom and deadens creativity. He also opens the windows to glance back at the time when all Christians were united under one universal governing body, allowing fresh air to enter into a room full of Christians who have been stifled by too many debates that have led nowhere.

The obvious criticism could be that Wesley's principle—"If thine heart is as my heart . . . Give me thine hand"[32]—is so vacuous as to allow terrorists to claim that they are submitting to the will of Allah and that they have a right to destroy civilians in a foreign country. Wesley's principle will not sanction such nonsense. It is founded upon and presupposes a core *theologicum* that is interrogative:

> Is thy heart right with God? . . .
>
> Is God the centre of thy soul? The sum of all thy desires? . . .
>
> Art thou employed in doing, "not thy own will, but the will of Him that sent thee?"—of Him that sent thee down to sojourn here awhile, to spend a few days in a strange land, till, having finished the work he hath given thee to do, thou return to thy Father's house? . . .
>
> Is thy heart right toward thy neighbour? . . .
>
> Do you "love your enemies?" Is your soul full of good-will, of tender affection, toward them?[33]

These interrogatives are followed by four exhortations centered upon John Wesley and by implication to all Christians and even others: First, to love him as a fellow citizen of the New Jerusalem. Second, to commend God "in all thy prayers" to "speedily correct" what is amiss and wanting in Wesley. Third, to "provoke me to love and to good works." Fourth, "love me not in word only, but in deed and in truth."[34] Wesley's *paraenesis* is directed towards a "catholic spirit"; Wesley envisions a global ethic that transcends and permits divergent theologies and means of worship. After all, to sail the ship of Christianity forward with a cognitive articulation of theology or means of worship strands it fatefully on the sandbar of human fallibility, *humanum est errare et nescire*, which Wesley translates idiomatically: "To be ignorant of many things, and to mistake in some, is the necessary condition of humanity."[35] Wesley concludes that "a man of a catholic spirit is one who . . . gives his hand to all whose hearts are right with his heart. . . ."[36]

Still lacking, however, seems to be any coherent core to John Wesley's theology. Is there one? Thomas A. Langford pointed out that the Wesleyan tradition is not primarily theological but that it is, nonetheless, theological, representing not one tradition but "the intersection of multiple influences: Anglicanism, Protestantism, Roman Catholicism, early Christianity." For Langford, "the nucleus of the Wesleyan tradition" is found in certain themes:

> Around this point—the grace of God in Jesus Christ—several attendant commitments form a tight nexus: biblical witness to Jesus Christ, vital experience of God in Christ as Savior and Sanctifier, commitment to human freedom and ethical discipleship, and the shaping of church life around missional responsibility.[37]

Today, the need is to move ahead, hand-in-hand, with all who are seeking to be faithful to God. As a hymn jointly published in 1746 by the Wesleys states: "Father, on

Thee whoever call, / Confess Thy promise is for all."[38] This thought demands theocentricity that does not undermine trinitarianism. Langford has rightly placed emphasis on the nexus of the Wesleyan tradition: the grace of God offered freely for all to experience.[39]

Some forms of Christianity focus on an intellectual and dogmatic explanation of Christian faith. One can mention especially Roman Catholicism and Presbyterianism. These traditions are admirable, and the intellectual dimension of Christian thought is essentially important. In my opinion, however, dogma can tend to cloud the human view of the Eternal. With Methodists and the Greek Orthodox, I tend to believe that the New Testament and the early ecumenical councils defined doctrine sufficiently. The need for a system of church dogmatics was replaced by John Wesley's statement that we should be concerned with the direction of our hearts so we can join hands together, even when we are as different as Jehu and Jehonadab.

Wesley's choice of characters for his theological theme needs clarification. Jehu became king of Israel and was ruthless. He killed Ahab's relatives. His words caused Jezebel to be cast out of her tower. He kept the golden calves that had been used by Jeroboam at Bethel and at Dan. He was impetuous; his wild driving of a chariot was proverbial. Jehonadab, in contrast, was a Rechabite, one who lived according to a strict religious code. Sometime during the time of Jesus, or later, a Jew in the *History of the Rechabites* quoted Rechab's exhortation:

> Hear, O sons of Rechab and daughters of your father, and remove your clothes from your body, and do not drink a carafe of wine, and do not eat bread from the fire, and do not drink liquor and honey until the Lord hears your petition.[40]

How different were Jehu and Jehonadab! One was a ruthless ruler, the other an ascetic. Yet each related to what was in the heart; each ignored their vast differences. Hence, Wesley can state,

> I dare not, therefore, presume to impose my mode of worship on any other. I believe it is truly primitive and apostolical: But my belief is no rule for another. I ask not, therefore, of him with whom I would unite in love, Are you of my Church? of my congregation?[41]

In these words I hear a confession and a commitment that unite the Methodists and the Greek Orthodox. They echo the pellucid theological truth articulated by Paul: Τῇ ἐλευθερίᾳ οὖν, ᾗ Χριστὸς ἡμᾶς ἠλευθέρωσε[42]—"toward freedom Christ has freed us." These are my favorite words in Paul's letters. Indeed, Christ means freedom. It is this freedom to be close to our Creator that unites each of us, first with our Father in heaven and then with each other here on earth in a purified koinonia.

A good portion of John Wesley's genius was revealed, in my opinion, when he insisted on the collegial formula for theological enrichment. Indeed, his approach is unique in the history of Christianity.[43] This collegial formula allowed for freedom in pulpits and in discussion, affirmed religious toleration, and made allowance for doctrinal pluralism. Indeed, the pioneers in Methodist theology—John and Charles Wesley, Jacob Albright, and William Otterbein—had only a minimal interest in dogma.[44] What is to be central is not a book or a set of books on dogmatics. What is affirmed is another paradigm: the living experience and witness of our contemporary pastors, teachers, professors, and people with whom we share our communal life.

This emphasis on a collegial formula galvanizes me to Methodism, as I disdain limiting theology to a set of concretized and systematic dogmas. Indeed, the "absence of a single official theological system"[45] is the heart of Methodist polity and theology, and it affirms both the freedom of thought for the individual and the guidance today and tomorrow of the Holy Spirit. This collegial formula protects religious freedom and grounds theology in the non-systematic dimension of phenomenology. I also have experienced a similar aversion to too much dogmatics in Greek Orthodoxy—and such becomes clear when I remember the years with Abba Sophronios of St. Catherine's Monastery.[46] Obviously, prayer is superior to any intellectual effort in Greek Christianity, or as St. Gregory of Sinai stated, "For stillness means the shedding of all thoughts for a time, even those which are divine and engendered by the Spirit."[47] This thought demands careful reflection which moves thought towards meditation and prayer.

Prayer and liturgy are thus fundamental in Christian living and being—and that includes thinking. Both the Methodist way and the Greek Orthodox way articulate theology not through massive tomes but within praise and celebration.

Charles Wesley's hymns fostered a heart-to-heart relation of the creature to the Creator. He encapsulated in his hymnic creations the truth contained in his brother's formula; that is, the heart of Methodist thought—not dogma—is placing a heart near to another heart, so that potential antagonists may give each other their hand. This unity leads to an expression that has resounded in my mind for decades and explains why I am committed to Methodism. Prayer and praise are *cor ad cor loquitur*. That is the purest form of theology—when the heart becomes silent beyond language and before its Creator.

Having worshiped with Greek Orthodox priests (for two weeks on Mt. Athos and for decades in St. Catherine's Monastery in the Sinai in a church built by the orders of Justinian in the sixth century), I have often pondered the longevity and continuity of Greek in the Greek Orthodox liturgy. On the one hand, I observed the parochialism in the teaching I received in Duke Divinity School when a revered professor mentioned that with Erasmus Greek had been rediscovered and with Zwingli the New Testament was habitually quoted in Greek. The naiveté of such teaching became exposed to me; it was uninformed of worldwide Christianity. The members of the Greek church did not need Erasmus to "rediscover" Greek. It continued as a living language in text and worship. On the other hand, I observed how liturgy and the melodious repetition of *kyrie eleison* and other well-known exhortations and celebrations like *basileiou tou theou* resonated off ancient pillars and walls. I perceived something special: for the Greek Orthodox, liturgy is theology. Praise replaced dogma.

This way of doing theology and striving to live advanced spiritual lives has always been my *viaticum* in this complex *via*. It is in praise that I feel uplifted and released from human constraints. The continuity of lament and praise continues from the earliest biblical books, through the so-called intertestamental literature and the New Testament books, to overflow into the earliest patristic texts, and especially into the *Odes of Solomon*, the earliest Christian hymnbook. Both Methodists and Greek Orthodox know that prayer and praise are the hallmarks of the *homo religiosus* and that language was given to the human so that in prayer *cor ad cor loquitur*. The tradition is wide and extensive. My scan is surely selective: The psalms are so well-known that it would be otiose to do more than draw attention to them and to the fact that they contain traditions that seem to date from the tenth to the fourth centuries BCE. The collection of rules found in the quintessential Qumran composition called the *Rule of the Community*, composed near the end of the second century BCE, ends with a hymn of praise:

> As the day and night enter I will enter into the covenant of God,
> and as evening and morning depart I will recite his statutes. . . .
> I will praise him with the offering of the utterance of my lips in the row of men,
> and before I lift my hand to enjoy the delights of the world's produce. . . .
> A light (comes) into my heart from his (God's) wondrous mysteries. . . .
> Blessed are you, my God, who opens for knowledge the heart of your servant. . . .
> (1QS 10.10–11.16)[48]

This prayer in the *Rule of the Community* adumbrates both Greek Orthodox and Methodist affirmations of prayer. They seem harmonious with Evagrios the Solitary's words on prayer, especially the following: "35. Undistracted prayer is the highest intellection of he intellect. 36. Prayer is the ascent of the intellect to God."[49]

The Stoic Epictetus knew that "If we had sense we ought to do nothing else, in public and in private, than praise and bless God and render him due thanks" (*Discourses* I, xvi.25). The author of the *Odes of Solomon*, sometime around AD 100, affirmed his dependence on God:

> As the sun is the joy to them who seek its daybreak,
> So is my joy the Lord;
>
> Because He is my Sun,
> And His rays have lifted me up;
> And His light has dismissed all darkness from his face. (Ode 15:1–2)[50]

John Owen (1616–1683) summarized his life with this prayer: "Teach me, Lord, to pray as I ought and to live as I ought to pray."

These emphases on the paradigmatic and fundamental importance of praise in the life of the *homo religiosus* are echoed in *The United Methodist Book of Worship* (p. 54):

> It is right, and a good and joyful thing,
> always and everywhere to give thanks to you,
> Father Almighty (*almighty God*), creator of heaven and earth.

In his "Thoughts on the Power of Music," John Wesley emphasized the vast difference between ancient Greek music and the music of his day. The latter undermined the power of music because it was all harmony and no melody: "Our composers do not aim at moving the passions, but at quite another thing; at varying and contrasting the notes a thousand different ways." For Wesley, "modern music has no connexion with common sense, any more than with the passions." He preferred, clearly, the ancient Greek music: "It is all melody, and no harmony." He opined that there is "no more reason to doubt of the power of Timotheus's music, than that of Alexander's arms." Music is to be melodious and to stir the passions. Music has the power "to transport, as it were, the mind out of itself." He called on his contemporaries to produce music that raised "various passions," as did "the ancient Greek musicians."[51]

The exegesis of Wesley's dictum seems to be that, while harmony focuses on the relation of notes in a sequence, melody is directed at humans and their life-defining passions. With these perspicacious insights, Wesley grounds the heart of music somatically—after all, the body's heartbeat resonates with the rhythm of music—and builds the pillars for a bridge that connects Methodism with Greek Orthodoxy. The foundation of this bridge is wide indeed, since music has a universal symbolic power. As Hans Küng states, "the art of music is the most spiritual of all symbols for that 'mystical sanctuary of our religion,' the divine itself."[52]

It is in singing or chanting that my thoughts and being ascend and I experience a oneness with the One. That is indeed another aspect that I think unites the Methodists and Greek Orthodox. Why is this so? It is because for both ways, the stress is placed on the immanence of God. In Charles Wesley's hymns and in the architecture of Greek Orthodox churches, the same point is central; it is the experience of the One who became incarnate in space and time. The incarnation remains definitive. With other Methodists, and many Orthodox scholars, I affirm that human "understanding of biblical truth depends upon the Spirit's 'inward testimony' in the hearts of faithful believers in the community of faith."[53] I would add, and emphasize, that this inward testimony needs to be guided, or at least informed, by the advances supplied by experts in biblical philology, historiography, archaeology, and theology. My caveat seems fundamental and is supported by the Methodist position that Christian doctrines developed from scripture must "take due account of scientific and empirical knowledge."[54]

The Way to Perfection

John Wesley's position on "perfection" is a significant issue that needs discussion, especially when it becomes clear how John and Charles differed on some of the major questions related to perfection.[55] One cannot simply review the Wesley hymns in search of insights on "perfection." While some of Charles Wesley's hymns were written as theological reflections, those which shaped the worship life of Methodists generally had more of a doxological impact. John Wesley, who did not always have editorial control over his brother's hymns, warned that some of them might contain expressions that inadvertently "partly express, partly imply" impossible theological ideas.[56]

Methodists are distinguished among Protestants and are often chided by others for the claim that they are going on to perfection. When a bishop asks me if I am going on to perfection, I answer "Yes, by the grace of God." When other Christians laugh at me for attempting to go on to perfection, I often ask, or at least wonder, where they wish to be headed.

This way to perfection is embodied in Charles Wesley's "Love Divine, All Loves Excelling," especially in the final verse:

Finish, then, thy new creation;
    Pure and spot-less let us be.
Let us see thy great salvation
    Perfectly re-stored in thee;
Changed from glory into glory,
    Till in heaven we take our place,
Till we cast our crowns before thee,
    Lost in wonder, love and praise.

Notice, especially, the stress on perfection in Charles Wesley's "Short Hymn on Matt. 20:22":

They all *must* first Thy sufferings share,
    Ambitious of their calling's prize,
And every day Thy burdens bear,
    And thus to late perfection rise.[57]

The Greek Orthodox also strive, with God's help, to move toward perfection. The Elder Paisios of Mt. Athos shared his conviction that Christians "ought to love afflictions and not try to get rid of them; afflictions are necessary means leading to our perfection."[58]

About a century before the birth of Jesus, a Jew shared an insight that takes Wesley's thought back at least 1700 years. In the Qumran collection of rules, the *Rule of the Community*, we find the following thought:

> For my way (belongs to) Adam. The human cannot establish his righteousness; for to God (alone) belongs the judgment and from him is the perfection of the Way." (1QS 11.10–11)[59]

This thought is strikingly similar to the theology typical of the Wesleys. Note, for example, the words of Charles Wesley in his "Let Us Plead for Faith Alone," composed in 1740: "God it is who justifies, / Only faith the grace applies." In his poem or hymn titled "The Promise of Sanctification," Charles Wesley offered these words on perfection:

That I thy mercy may proclaim,
    That all mankind thy truth may see,
Hallow thy great and glorious name,
    And perfect holiness in me. . . .

Now let me gain perfection's height!
    Now let me into nothing fall!
Be less than nothing in my sight,
    And feel that Christ is all in all![60]

What did John Wesley mean by "perfection"? He thought that Christian perfection is "the humble, gentle, patient love of God, and our neighbour, ruling our tempers, words, and actions." Wesley apprehended "the scriptural term perfection" to mean that Christians are "to love God with all their heart, and to serve him with all their strength."[61] Two of the key biblical texts that he stressed are "the words of God and not of man"[62] are Phil. 3:12, "Not that . . . I am already perfect (τετελείωμαι)," and Heb. 6:1, "Let us go on unto perfection (τελειότητα)."[63] In contrast to his brother Charles, who contended that perfection occurred at death, John Wesley speculated that perfection was "generally" obtained at death but that it can occur "maybe ten, twenty, or forty years before."[64] Seeking to discern how many years this occurred after justification, Wesley, quoting Horace, pondered *Pretium quotus arroget annus?* ("What number of years sanction lives?") Wesley's use of the interrogative here is most appealing to me.

John Wesley warned that "Christian perfection" does not mean that one is exempt from "ignorance, or mistake, or infirmities, or temptations." Christian perfection, rather, is synonymous with holiness,[65] or in his own words, "perfection is another name for universal holiness: Inward and outward righteousness: Holiness of life, arising from holiness of heart."[66] One who has attained perfection still needs to "grow in grace; and daily to advance in the knowledge and love of God his Saviour."[67]

Perfection is possible because of prevenient grace. In *The Book of Discipline of the United Methodist Church*, we find a definition of prevenient grace:

> Out of our heritage we gratefully reaffirm belief in "prevenient grace," the divine love that anticipates all our conscious impulses and persuades the heart toward faith. But grace signifies also God's accepting and pardoning love: the active cause of our justification, by which we are made new creatures in Christ. (p. 76)

This thought is biblical, and perfection is synonymous with holiness, as John Wesley pointed out. The author of 1 Peter exhorted his readers, quoting Lev. 20:7, "set your hope fully upon the grace [*cavrin*] that is coming to you" and so "be holy [ἅγιοι] yourselves in all conduct" (1 Pet. 1:13–15).

The goal of perfection is well known in Greek Orthodoxy. For example, John Climacus (c. 570–c. 649), the anchorite who became Abbot of Sinai, focused his *Ladder of Paradise* on the ideal of Christian perfection.[68] At the top of the ladder, the enlightened spiritual person encounters God. John Climacus intended his work for monastics, especially cenobites. Note these excerpts form his *Ladder of Paradise*:[69]

> Indeed everyone should struggle to raise his clay, so to speak, to a place on the throne of God. (Step 26; p. 248)

> The chaste man is not someone with a body undefiled but rather a person whose members are in complete subjection to the soul, for a man is great who is free of passion even when touched, though greater still is the man unhurt by all he has looked on. (Step 15; p. 172)

> I do not think anyone should be classed as a saint until he has made holy his body, if indeed that is possible. (Step 15; p. 178)

> To have mastered one's body is to have taken command of nature, which is surely to have risen above it. And the man who has done this is not much lower than the angels, if even that. (Step 15; p. 181)

> . . . and physical love can be a paradigm of the longing for God. (Step 26; p. 236)

> I long to know how Jacob saw you fixed above the ladder (cf. Gen. 28:12). That climb, how was it? Tell me, for I long to know. (Step 30; p. 289)

On Hesychasm—to be discussed next—John Climacus advised, "The life of stillness, especially when practiced by solitaries, must be guided by conscience and common sense" (Step 27; p. 270).

Both John Climacus and the Wesleys emphasized that religion depends on spiritual experience of the Divine.[70] This occurs for many today in private prayer and meditation as well as in common worship, especially in raising voices together to the One who is at the same time present and elusive. Both members of the United Methodist Church and the Greek Orthodox Church share these goals and perspectives. Surely, here is ground upon which to build a strong relation of appreciation.

The Somatic Experience of the Divine

Related to reflections on perfection are the somatic dimensions of spirituality. I am convinced there is a clear and fundamental relationship between Hesychasm and John Wesley's mysticism. The Greek Orthodox movement called Hesychasm seeks to produce divine silence (*hesuchia*) in the human heart. What is Hesychasm? Perhaps the best definition is supplied by Nikitas Stithatos, who wrote the following:

> Stillness is an undisturbed state of the intellect, the calm of a free and joyful soul, the tranquil unwavering stability of the heart in God, the contemplation of light, the knowledge of the mysteries of God, consciousness of wisdom by virtue of a pure mind, the abyss of divine intellections, the rapture of the intellect, intercourse with God, and unsleeping watchfulness, spiritual prayer, untroubled repose in the midst of great hardship and, finally, solidarity and union with God.[71]

Those who practice Hesychasm seek to recite prayer, especially the *Cardiake Proseuche* (Ἰησοῦ εὐχή) or "Jesus Prayer," developed by the Greeks, so as to obtain silence. The Jesus Prayer is the very heart of Orthodox prayer: "Lord Jesus Christ, Son of God, have mercy on me, a sinner."[72]

By reciting the Jesus Prayer and being silent in meditation, the heart may be at rest and begin to perceive the divine light. John Climacus experienced faith, hope, and love; note his words: "To me they appear, one as a ray, one as light, and one as a disk, and all as a single radiance and a single splendor" (Step 30; p. 286). The Greek church places much emphasis on obtaining a vision of divine light. Symeon the New Theologian (949–1022) believed that the divine light was not a physical or material light. It was the uncreated glory of God himself. Nikephoros taught Hesychasm on Mt. Athos in the thirteenth century, as did Gregory in St. Catherine's Monastery in the fourteenth century.[73]

When Barlaam of Calabria (1290–259) attacked the Hesychasts, Gregory Palamas (1296–1359) of Mt. Athos defended them, especially in his "In Defence of Those Who Devoutly Practise a Life of Stillness"[74] and in other works.[75] Palamas appealed to the distinction between divine essence and divine energy; note his words:

> Because both the divine essence and the divine energy are everywhere inseparably present, God's energy is accessible also to us creatures; . . . Therefore God's grace and energy are accessible to each one of us, since it is divided indivisibly. But since God's essence is in every way indivisible, how could it be accessible to any created being?[76]

Thus, the divine essence is beyond human comprehension, but the divine energies are made available to the saints by God himself. Palamas stressed that the body participates in this apprehension of divine energies. In the attempt to become advanced spiritually, with the help of God, one becomes quiet and inwardly still so as to receive and experience "the uncreated light and grace of Christ's Transfiguration."[77] According to Kallistos Ware, in the "opinion of many, the hesychastic and Philokalic element constitutes the most dynamic aspect of contemporary Orthodox life."[78]

John Wesley must have known about hesychastic theology, since the *Philokalia*, which revived this teaching, was published in 1782.[79] He shared not only the patristic hermeneutic of *theōria*—the vision of God's presence in biblical history[80] —but also Palamas's holistic view of human nature. After all, he could explain the presence of the Divinity by reporting, "I felt my heart strangely warmed."[81] Quite unusual in the history of Roman Catholicism and Protestant Christianity (not to mention the Coptic and Syriac anchorites), which too often has esteemed those who disparage the body and teach that the body is the source of sin, is a prayer by John Wesley. In it, he offers God his body: "I give thee my body: May I glorify thee with it, and preserve it holy, fit for thee, O God, to dwell in."[82]

Palamas's point that the human can apprehend the divine energies seems reflected in John Wesley's sermons.[83] Note in particular Wesley's following comment: "Is thy faith ενεργεμενη δι' αγαπης, *filled with the energy of love?*"[84] Is it not singularly important that Wesley chose to express himself in Greek? I know of no place in which John Wesley cites Palamas, but he seems to share his thought.

Also, like Palamas and other Hesychasts, John Wesley claimed to have experienced the divine light and taught that everyone who awakens from sin shall see God's light.[85] The prayer by John Wesley that most moves me is the following one:

> O Thou who dwellest in the light which no man can approach, in whose presence there is no night, in the light of whose countenance there is perpetual day; I, thy sinful servant . . . who live [*sic*] by thy power this day, bless and glorify thee for the defence of thy almighty providence . . . and humbly pray thee, that this, and all my days, may be wholly devoted to thy service.[86]

Another prayer by John Wesley reminds me of the many times I arose at 3 a.m. and worshiped with the monks in the Justinian Chapel in St. Catherine's Monastery. Surely all of us would have felt that this prayer by John Wesley was perfectly couched:

> O thou eternal Fountain of all wisdom, whom I cannot see or know but by the means of thy own light, vouchsafe to manifest thyself to my soul, and teach me to know aright thee the only true God, and Jesus Christ whom thou hast sent.[87]

This prayer could have been written—and would surely be appreciated—by the monks I know so well in St. Catherine's Monastery.

In "Christ, Whose Glory Fills the Skies," penned in 1740, Charles Wesley salutes Christ as "the true, the only light" and calls on Christ: "[the] Day-spring from on high, be near; / Day-star, in my heart appear." In "Praise the Lord Who Reigns Above," composed in 1743 and based on Ps. 150, Charles Wesley ends the second verse with these words: "all the powers of music bring, / the music of the heart." These words show that Charles Wesley was often close to Hesychasm, although he seems never to mention the term. Having completed my present research, I was pleased to read Ioann Ekonomtsev's insight that Charles Wesley's hymns "are surprisingly close in the content and spirit of the poetry of Symeon the New Theologian, who is the forerunner of the hesychast tradition in the East."[88] Like the Hesychasts, Charles Wesley, especially in his "Jesus, Lover of My Soul," urged those who sang the hymn to seek "human perfection in the image of God."[89]

We have seen that both the Methodists and the Greek Orthodox place prayer and worship above systematic theology. Both express thought in praise. Both shun academic theology for mystical liturgy. As Vladimir Lossky states,

> The eastern tradition has never made a sharp distinction between mysticism and theology; between personal experience of the divine mysteries and the dogma affirmed by the Church. . . . Far from being mutually opposed, theology and mysticism support and complete each other. . . . There is, therefore, no Christian mysticism without theology; but, above all, there is no theology without mysticism.[90]

For Lossky, and for Greek Orthodox Christians, the great theologians are not Barth or Tillich; they are the author of the Fourth Gospel, St. Gregory of Nazianzus (329–389), and St. Symeon the New Theologian (949–1022).[91] I am convinced that the Wesleys would be in agreement with Lossky's claim that there is "no Christian mysticism without theology; but above all, there is no theology without mysticism."

Reflections on the somatic experience of the *noumena* would not be complete without some mention of the sacraments, especially the Eucharist.[92] During the celebration of the Lord's Supper, we Methodists and Orthodox join with all Christians. Before the universal table, all of us—past, present, and even future worshipers—unite as we all kneel before the grace of God. Eating the bread and drinking from the cup is more than a re-enactment of what Jesus did long ago during Passover in Jerusalem. It is imbibing God's love and becoming one with the Eternal. In celebrating the Eucharist, we affirm the *imago dei* and leave behind forever the *mea culpa.* Our full being inherits the promise of eternal life. The Eucharist defines the mystery of salvation by affirming it. Ignatius of Antioch said it well, for all of us, when he stressed that there is only ἕνα ἄρτον and labeled the Eucharist φάρμακον ἀθανασίας, "the medicine of immortality."[93]

Perhaps too boldly, I offer these reflections for discussion. May my lack of expertise in Wesley studies and in Greek Orthodoxy not distort the presentation of some thoughts that may be worthy of reflection and improvement. My hope is that one who has focused on the origins of "Christianity" within Judaism may help others hear the wisdom of Wesley, who sought to judge all theology by the mutually supportive norms of Bible and apostolicity.

Both Methodists and the Greek Orthodox find God's Word in the past, in scripture. They find it appearing afresh each day. They experience and know that God comes to us even from the future. Indeed, for both ways God's Word unifies our concept of time.

Conclusion

The bureaucracy and episcopal system of the The United Methodist Church and the Greek Orthodox Church often dim the focus that make these two similar ways of being Christian so important and attractive. The ecclesiastics and bureaucrats fail too often to see the need to help the individual grow spiritually and to ascend, as John Climacus stated, so as to be near God. Or, as John and Charles Wesley affirmed, to move on to perfection, perhaps within this life (John) or only at the end of it (Charles), is the goal of the Christian *viator*. Indeed, so many people are leaving the institution called the "church" for spiritual reasons. They have not found in the institution what the church alone can offer: spiritual nourishment and grace—supplied by the presence of God—to move on to perfection. How does this insight need to be clarified today? The answer is: Quite simply, not as a belief but as the most assured fact of our existence. And the assurance is grounded in our experience of the *noumena*, the awesome oneness with Light.

Most importantly, both paths to God are distinguished within Christendom by the emphasis on praise, not prose. For both paths, the purest forms of systematic theology are those that do not shape experience by isolating and selecting special aspects of it to form a system. Concentrating on church dogmatics (as with Barth) or a systematic theology (as with Tillich) puts too much emphasis on the intellect and demands excluding elements that have been experienced. The purest form of dogmatics is the one which is not categorical. In Methodism and in Greek Orthodoxy, systematic theology and dogmatics are played out within the realm of liturgy. In praising our Creator, we synthesize all experiences and thoughts; we transcend categories in the affirmation of praise and celebration.

We representatives of Methodism and Greek Orthodoxy have come together on Crete, which is a singularly important location. Here European culture began to flourish, and from here, influences sped eastward to shape the last phases of the Canaanite culture that the Israelites confronted when they entered the "Promised Land." We shake hands in a somatic and intellectual commitment to ecumenism, which, as the great Methodist theologian Robert E. Cushman stated, is "the end-product of the love of God whereby he sent his Son into the world for the redemption of humankind." Cushman continued by stressing that "ecumenicity is wholeness and unity of the historic and undivided Catholic Church."[94]

I write these words mindful of the tragedy of "the Great Schism" that from the ninth to the thirteenth centuries has bifurcated Christendom into East and West. This sad division was placarded by the Fourth Crusade and the burning of Constantinople by the Crusaders in 1204. Ever since the Reformation of the sixteenth century, Christianity has divided and subdivided. Our mandate is to seek reconciliation and to build bridges towards a global Christianity. The success of such endeavors is insured, since, as Ioann Ekonomtsev states, it is easy to stress "the great importance of the Wesley phenomenon as a spiritual bridge between the two related Christian cultures of the East and West."[95] This way is paved, on the one hand, by John Wesley's own knowledge of and quotation of the Greek Fathers.[96] As S T Kimbrough, Jr. points out from the first consultation on "Orthodoxy and Wesleyan Spirituality" in January 1999, specialists and representatives of Methodism and Greek Orthodoxy concur that there "is a strong presence of the theology and spirituality of the early church fathers in the writings and practice of the Wesleys."[97] The way is paved, on the other hand, by the stress within both Methodism and Greek Orthodoxy on praise and prayer. When we pray and worship together, the differences often percolating in theological debates ebb away as inconsequential.

This focus in Methodism and in Greek Orthodoxy is not only a bridge to a stronger relation of appreciation between the two paths; it is itself proof of a shared theology and Christology. In the phenomenology of gathering as one community called into existence by God through Christ, we move towards the only Perfect One and begin to realize our own perfection, which is possible only through God's grace.

Let our joint sessions serve as a major step toward and an indication of the success of the prevalent movement for unity, the uniting of East and West, and the development of a global Christianity. Let our focus be not only on what unites Methodists and Greeks; let it be on our common origins—especially Jesus Christ, who lived in the East—and on the early centuries when we were all one.

One of the formative insights I inherit from John Wesley is the affirmation that "The world is as my parish."[98] Thus, it is appropriate to conclude by quoting the "Prayer of Thanksgiving" as printed in *The United Methodist Book of Worship*:

> By your Holy Spirit make us one with Christ, one with each other,
> and one in ministry to all the world;
> through Jesus Christ our Lord. Amen.

Surely our final words, as we dream about a world in which all humans are sustained and uplifted by peace, are those of our Lord:

> Πατερ ἡμῶν . . .
> ἐλθέτω ἡ βασιλεία σου·
> γενηθήτω τὸ θέλημά σου,
> ὡς ἐν οὐρανῷ καὶ ἐπὶ τῆς γῆς·[99]

Addendum

When I began this essay, I imagined that my argument and position would be branded as perhaps original but certainly controversial. I was pleasantly surprised to hear from many of the other participants in the conference that my ideas were shared by many others. I am delighted to learn that it is by no means scandalous to claim that Methodists and the Orthodox employ liturgy to express theology. Indeed, some

Orthodox scholars maintain in the present volume that Orthodox theology is best expressed in and through liturgy. John and Charles Wesley would have been pleased, I am certain, by the joint stress on expressing theology through music and poetry; that is, through a common liturgy. S T Kimbrough, Jr. has convinced me (and he knows more about Charles Wesley than I ever will) that Charles Wesley obtained many of his theological reflections, shared via hymns, from the Book of Common Prayer of the Church of England. If there is anything original about my paper, perhaps it is my stress on the "somatic experience of God" in the Wesleys and the Orthodox. I am also convinced more can and should be made of the insight that the uniqueness of John Wesley's theology may well lie in his "collegial formula for theological enrichment."

When I shared some of these thoughts, *viva voce*, with D. Moody Smith, a United Methodist minister who has been a professor at Duke Divinity School, he told me they reminded him of Geoffrey Wainwright's publications. He urged me to consult Wainwright's work. I had heard about Wainwright but had never had the opportunity to read his books, *Christian Initiation* (1969), *Eucharist and Eschatology* (1971), and *Doxology: The Praise of God in Worship, Doctrine, and Life* (1980).[100] I obtained a copy of *Doxology* and found much in it that resonated with my own reflections on theology and praise. It seems odd now to observe that I have not yet used the word "doxology," yet this term is synonymous with many words found on the preceding pages.

Perhaps, I should explain the research that has helped shape the previous reflections. There were experiences that grounded theological reflections in phenomena, especially the days I stood in the ruins of the last Nestorian villages, which are east of the Great Zap River, and a moment of truth when I stood in a horrifying spot in Auschwitz.[101] My thoughts evolved from years of studying the great systematic theologians (perhaps perfunctorily). I found Thomas rich and enduring, but found his work too focused on abstracted thoughts and not sufficiently grounded in the unsystematic chaos that shapes all our lives. I learned much from Calvin, but felt a chill in his halls of mathematically rigorous systematics. I once was moved by Tillich, but was disappointed by his fear of the historian and failure to engage the fruits of the study of the historical Jesus (surely a product of his time). G. von Rad with his *Heilsgeschichte* and W. Eichrodt with his stress on covenant have made permanent contributions to the study of Old Testament theology, but von Rad missed unifying forces in the records, and Eichrodt failed to represent the variety of thoughts preserved in the Hebrew Bible.[102] Each of these luminaries also failed to perceive the celebration of nature and creation found in the Psalms. This appreciation, however, appears in the Wesleys, the Orthodox, and Wainwright. R. Bultmann's theological reflections are profound, but the historical Jesus cannot be merely the presupposition of New Testament theology, and the mere "that" (*dass*) that Jesus existed is insufficient reason for Jews—and later "Christians"—to have followed him. My appreciation of the theology of praise evolved—from 1962 to the present—through decades dedicated to the study of the *Odes of Solomon*, the *Psalms of Solomon*, the *Thanksgiving Hymns*, the *Prayer of Manasseh*, the *Angelic Liturgy*, the *More Psalms of David*, and the *Hellenistic Synagogal Hymns*. The study of Jewish mysticism—especially the search for its origins—made me sensitive to mysticism in the Wesleys and prompts me to ponder how much Jewish mysticism, especially the *Hekhalot* texts (medieval Jewish mystical texts), may have influenced them. Surely, reminiscent of the "descent into the chariot" and the ascension to the heavenly throne room of the Jewish mystics are the words of Charles Wesley, with which Wainwright ends *Doxology*:[103]

> Finish then Thy new creation,
> Pure and spotless let us be;
> Let us see Thy great salvation,
> Perfectly restored in Thee;
> Changed from glory into glory,
> Till in heaven we take our place,
> Till we cast our crowns before Thee,
> Lost in wonder, love, and praise.

While I doubt Wainwright's *Doxology* is "A Systematic Theology,"[104] I am convinced that his approach helps replace systematic theology. The phenomenologists have urged us to be aware of systems; these are by definition so removed from phenomena that they represent only themselves and not the variegations of life. Wainwright rightly stresses the importance of "open systems"[105] and points out the universal and inclusive in music and praise.[106] The doxological aspect of religion (and not only Christianity) has united many dispersed peoples, from those in a Madison Avenue church to those who composed the Afro-American spirituals, and from those who follow the lyrics in India to those who repeat the Eastern odes. With the reflections by F. A. Zaccaria, we may perceive that the agreements between the liturgy in the East and West adumbrate a future universal Church.[107]

If Wainwright is correct to describe Protestants as those who have customarily used doctrine to control worship, and Roman Catholics as those who have tended to employ worship to support doctrine, then I would urge that we restore doxology to its original place in the Psalms[108] and in the pre-Pauline hymns in Colossians and especially Philippians.[109] Praise must not be controlled by dogma, theology, or a *magisterium*. When worship is pure and authentic, there is no need for doctrine or systematic theology; in fact, each of them has tended to erode purity and authenticity. What is needed is neither *lex orandi* ("the law of praying") or *lex credendi* ("the law of believing"); what is required is *lex orandi et lex credendi*—provided the emphasis is placed not on "law" but on the vitality of *laudamus*. Doxology thus may remain ever fresh and free. This is the path—not *in patria* but *in via*—taken by both Methodists and the Orthodox, as Wainwright points out.[110] Wesley stated this point well in his preface to *A Collection of Hymns for the Use of the People Called Methodists*: "[The Hymn Book] is large enough to contain all the important truths of our most holy religion."[111]

Our liturgy must be grounded in the earliest traditions, especially those in the Bible, refined by the clear presence of the Holy Spirit over twenty (probably thirty) centuries, and eventually purified in and for a pure heart. As the individual, privately or collectively, ascends in thought and being to the ever-present Creator, the *cor ad cor loquitur* evolves to periodic silences. The ineffable One and the *mysterium tremendi* often reside in, and are articulated through, silence.[112] From such elevated experiences comes the freedom for theological differences, whereby opposing opinions are allowed, even encouraged, so that with Paul we can proceed doxologically Τῇ ἐλευθερίᾳ οὖν, ᾗ Χριστὸς ἡμᾶς ἠλευθέρωσε, "to the freedom, therefore, to which Christ has freed us" (Gal. 5:1).

Endnotes

[1]Unless otherwise noted, quotations from John Wesley's works are taken from *The Works of John Wesley*, 14 vols., ed. Thomas Jackson (Grand Rapids: Baker, 1996, 3rd ed [reprint of the 1872 edition]).

[2]As I have written the following work, I have thought of the many enriching conversations I have enjoyed with his eminence Archbishop Damianos, Professor John Karavidopoulos, and Professor Savas Agourides.

[3]As is customary, I will use "Greek Orthodoxy," "Greek Christianity," and "the Greek church" as synonyms. In the following work, I have focused on John and Charles Wesley. I do so because I am convinced that the revival of theological thought within Methodism must be guided, in freedom, by John Wesley's own practical theological reflections, and that the 1988 "Doctrinal Standards and Our Theological Task" is founded on the freedom of theological inquiry that has its stimulus in John Wesley.

[4]These personal comments seem necessary since most of the members of this consultation do not know each other. It is thus germane to clarify one's experiences and perspectives.

[5]As Kallistos Ware points out in "Eastern Christianity," *The Encyclopedia of Religion*, 4.558–76 (notably 4.565), there were Byzantine Thomists, notably Demetrios Kydones (c. 1324–c. 1398) and Gennadios Scholarios (c. 1405–c. 1478). Obviously, I am not suggesting that Thomism cannot be aligned with Greek Orthodoxy; rather, I am convinced that there is much in the *Summa Theologica* that is close to Greek Orthodoxy, notably that such doctrines as the Trinity, original sin, the incarnation, salvation, and the resurrection of the body are revealed as true to us not by reason but by faith. The "Doctor of the Church" (the title given to St. Thomas by Pope Pius V in 1567) emphasized the incarnation and the sacraments; these emphases suggest a possible bridge between Thomism and Greek Orthodoxy.

[6]The quotations are derived from Ronald P. Patterson, et al., eds., *The Book of Discipline of the United Methodist Church 1984* (Nashville: United Methodist Publishing House, 1984), 43–44.

[7]The words are from James H. Rigg, *The Churchmanship of John Wesley* (London: Wesleyan Methodist Book Room, 1886), 65–66.

[8]See esp. Question 5; it is re-presented on page 219 of Colin W. Williams, *John Wesley's Theology Today* (Nashville: Abingdon, 1960). I use this book, because it was my *vade mecum* during my divinity years at Duke University. I am excited about the recent Methodist desire to trace present-day worship back to the synagogue and the "worship as Jesus and his earliest disciples knew it . . ." (*The United Methodist Book of Worship*, 13).

[9]See *The Book of Discipline*, Article XXI.

[10]See Stanley Samuel Harakas in "Greek Orthodox Church," *The Encyclopedia of Religion*, 6.95–99 (notably 6.97). Contrast Ware, who in *The Encyclopedia of Religion*, 4.559, reports that there are 8 million Orthodox in Greece. I know the approximate size of Methodism in America from over sixty years of living the life of a Methodist and intermittently reading the surveys.

[11]Kallistos Ware, *The Encyclopedia of Religion*, 4.561.

[12]See Charlesworth, ed., *Jesus and Archaeology: The Millennium Celebration in Jerusalem* (Grand Rapids: Eerdmans, 2003). Also see S. Freyne, "Jesus and the Urban Culture of Galilee," in *Galilee and Gospel: Collected Essays* (Tübingen: Mohr Siebeck, 2000), 183–207.

[13]*The Works of John Wesley*, 5.346.

[14]Ibid., 1.274, 451; 3.23, 28, 385.

[15]Ibid., 13.119.

[16]Ibid., 2.3; 3.40; 4.90, 116, 143.

[17]*Philokalia*, 4.58. All excerpts from the *Philokalia* are from G. E. H. Palmer, Philip Sherrard, and Kallistos Ware, trans., *The Philokalia: The Complete Text*, 4 vols. (Boston: Faber and Faber, 1979–1995).

[18]Ibid., 4.127.

[19]Ibid., 4.215.

[20]Ibid., 4.310.

[21]See John Wesley, *Explanatory Notes Upon the New Testament* (New York, n.d. [London, 1775]). Also see J. H. Charlesworth, "The Wesleys and the Canon: An Unperceived Openness," *Proceedings of the Charles Wesley Society* 3 (1996): 63–88; esp., 72–81.

[22]John Wesley, "The Unity of the Divine Being," *The Works of John Wesley*, 7.264–273.

[23]I owe these thoughts to Kallistos Ware in *The Encyclopedia of Religion*, 4.570.

[24]I am indebted to Kallistos Ware in *The Encyclopedia of Religion*, 4.570 for these insights and the quotation.

[25]All quotations of Charles Wesley's hymns are from Carlton R. Young, ed., *The United Methodist Hymnal: Book of United Methodist Worship* (Nashville: United Methodist Publishing House, 1989).

[26]Thomas A. Langford, gen. ed., *The United Methodist Book of Worship* (Nashville: United Methodist Publishing House, 1992), 13.

[27]J. H. Charlesworth, ed., *The Old Testament Pseudepigrapha*, 2 vols. (Garden City, NY: Doubleday, 1983–1985).

[28]J. H. Charlesworth, "The Wesleys and the Canon: An Unperceived Openness," 63–88.

[29]Scott J. Jones, *John Wesley's Conception and Use of Scripture* (Nashville: Kingswood, 1995), 59.

[30]Ibid.

[31]John Wesley warns that this theme does not allow for "any kind of *practical* latitudinarianism." Rather, a catholic spirit must be both scriptural and rational. See John Wesley's sermon on "Catholic Spirit," in *The Works of John Wesley* (3rd ed.), 5.492–504.

[32]John Wesley, *The Works of John Wesley*, 1.499.

[33]Ibid., 1.497–499.

[34]Ibid., 500–501.

[35]Ibid., 495.

[36]Ibid., 503.

[37]Thomas A. Langford, ed., *Doctrine and Theology in the United Methodist Church* (Nashville: Kingswood, 1991), 14.

[38]John R. Tyson, "Christian Perfection and Its Pretenders," in *Charles Wesley: A Reader*, John R. Tyson, ed. (Oxford: Oxford University Press, 1989), 365.

[39]Grace was rightly chosen as the theme for Langford's Festschrift: Robert K. Johnston, et al., *Grace upon Grace: Essays in Honor of Thomas A. Langford* (Nashville: Abingdon, 1999).

[40]Charlesworth, ed. and trans., *The History of the Rechabites: The Greek Recension* (Texts and Translations 17; Pseudepigrapha Series 10; Chico, CA: Scholars Press, 1912), 51.

[41]Ibid., 496–497.

[42]This reading is appreciably different from the Greek text used by most New Testament scholars (Aland ed., XXVII). I use the text of a Greek New Testament given to me on Mt. Athos: *Η ΚΑΙΝΗ ΔΙΑΘΗΚΗ* (Mt. Athos, 1992), 456.

[43]See, for example, the statement in *The Book of Discipline*: John Wesley's "collegial formula for doctrinal guidance was unique in Christendom" (43).

[44]Ibid., 40.

[45]Ibid., 82.

[46]He was chief librarian during my early years in the monastery. He later died of cancer, yet praising God for life and for the physicians. The love we shared transcended theological subtleties.

[47]*Philokalia*, 4.270.

[48]Charlesworth, *Rule of the Community* (The Princeton Theological Seminary Dead Sea Scrolls Project, vol. 1, Tübingen: Mohr [Siebeck] and Westminster John Knox, 1994), 45–49.

[49]*Philokalia*, 1.60.

[50]Charlesworth, *The Odes of Solomon: The Syriac Texts* (Texts and Translations 13; Pseudepigrapha Series 7; Chico, CA: Scholars Press, 1977), 67.

[51]John Wesley, "Thoughts on the Power of Music," *The Works of John Wesley*, 13.470–473. Wesley also admired the Scotch and Irish airs; he was convinced that they are "composed, not according to art, but nature; they are simple in the highest degree. There is no harmony, according to the present sense of the word, therein; but there is much melody."

[52]Hans Küng, *Mozart: Traces of Transcendence*, trans. John Bowden (London: SCM, 1992), 33.

[53]*The Book of Discipline*, 44.

[54]Ibid., 81.

[55]See especially J. R. Tyson, "Christian Perfection and Its Pretenders," in *Charles Wesley: A Reader*, 360–97.

[56]John Wesley, *The Works of John Wesley*, 11.446.

[57]Tyson, ed., *Charles Wesley: A Reader*, 370.

[58]Priestmonk Christodoulos, *Elder Paisios of the Holy Mountain* (Holy Mountain, 1998), 86.

[59]Charlesworth, *The Rule of the Community*, 49.

[60]Charles Wesley, "The Promise of Sanctification," in *The Works of John Wesley*, 2.20–22.

[61]John Wesley, "On Christian Perfection," *The Works of John Wesley*, 11.448.

[62]Ibid., 6.1–19; the quotation is on page 1.

[63]Ibid., 6.411–24.

[64]John Wesley, "Brief Thoughts on Christian Perfection," *The Works of John Wesley*, 11.446.

[65]Ibid., 5.

[66]John Wesley, *The Works of John Wesley*, 6.414.

[67]Ibid., 6.

[68]A fragment of the *Ladder of Paradise* was discovered in the mid-seventies in St. Catherine's Monastery; conceivably it is from the autograph, since it seems to date from the seventh century. The portion found is from Logos A, 3–4, according to P. Trevisan, ed., *Scala Paradisi* (Corona Patrum Salesiana Serie Greca 8; Turin: Societé Editrice Internazionale, 1941). A photograph of this fragment was published in Charlesworth, *The New Discoveries in St. Catherine's Monastery: A Preliminary Report on the Manuscripts* (American Schools of Oriental Research Monograph Series no. 3; Winona Lake: Eisenbrauns and the American Schools of Oriental Research, 1981) Plate II, or 18–19.

[69]I have taken the excerpts from John Climacus, *The Ladder of Divine Ascent*, trans. Colm Luibheid and Norman Russell, with an introduction by Kallistos Ware (New York: Paulist, 1982).

[70]See esp. Kallistos Ware in John Climacus, *The Ladder of Divine Ascent*, 7. John Wesley constantly bases his insights on "experience"; see, e.g., *The Works of John Wesley*, 1.279.

[71]*Philokalia*, 4.125.

[72]Sergius Bulgakov, *The Orthodox Church*, trans. Thomas Hopko (Crestwood, NY: St. Vladimir's Seminary Press, 1988 [revised translation]), 147.

[73]For these insights, I am grateful to Kallistos Ware in *The Encyclopedia of Religion*, 4.567.

[74]*Philokalia*, 4.331–342.

[75]See esp. "The Declaration of the Holy Mountain in Defence of Those Who Devoutly Practise a Life of Stillness" (*Philokalia*, 4.418–425).

[76]*Philokalia*, 4.380.

[77]Constantine N. Tsirpanlis, *Introduction to Eastern Patristic Thought and Orthodox Theology* (Collegeville, MN: Liturgical Press, 1991), 7.

[78]Ibid., 567.

[79]*Philokalia*, 1.11.

[80]John Breck calls for a biblical exegesis and hermeneutic that transcends the normal historical-critical method and is enriched by patristic hermeneutics. See his *Scripture in Tradition: The Bible and Its Interpretation in the Orthodox Church* (Crestwood, NY: St. Vladimir's Seminary Press, 2001).

[81]*The Works of John Wesley*, 1.103; the entry for Wednesday, 24 May 1738.

[82]Ibid., 11.227.

[83]For a discussion of the divine energy, especially in Gregory of Nazianzus, Saint Basil, Cyril of Alexandria, John of Damascus, Athanasius, and Gregory Palamas, see Panagiotis N. Trembelas, *Dogmatique de L'Église Orthodoxe Catholique*, 3 vols., trans. Pierre Dumont (Paris: Éditions de Chevetogne, 1966–1968), 1.261 and 1.355–61.

[84]John Wesley, *The Works of John Wesley*, 1.497.

[85]Ibid., 5.32.

[86]Ibid., 11.218.

[87]Ibid., 267.

[88]Ioann Ekonomtsev, "Charles Wesley and the Orthodox Hesychast Tradition," in S T Kimbrough, Jr., ed., *Orthodox and Wesleyan Spirituality* (Crestwood, NY: St. Vladimir's Seminary Press, 2002), 233–240; the quotation is on 238.

[89]Ibid., 239.

[90]Vladimir Lossky, *The Mystical Theology of the Eastern Church* (Crestwood, NY: St. Vladimir's Seminary Press, 1976), 8–9.

[91]Ibid., 9.

[92]Much more may be said, but time and space allow only these few comments on the sacraments. I am grateful to Professor Clifton Black for urging me to include some thoughts on the sacraments.

[93]Ignatius, *To the Ephesians* 20:2; for the Greek text, see K. Lake, *The Apostolic Fathers* (LCL 24; Cambridge, MA: Harvard University Press; London: Heinemann, 1965), 194.

[94]R. E. Cushman, *Faith Seeking Understanding* (Durham, NC: Duke University Press, 1981), 284.

[95]Ioann Ekonomtsev in *Orthodoxy and Wesleyan Spirituality*, 240.

[96]R. P. Heitzenrater surveyed John Wesley's use of the early church Fathers; see his "John Wesley's Reading of and References to the Early Church Fathers," in *Orthodoxy and Wesleyan Spirituality*, 25–32. Heitzenrater suggests that John Wesley often obtained knowledge of the church Fathers indirectly, the "ideas of the Fathers were in the air" (30).

[97]S T Kimbrough, Jr. in *Orthodoxy and Wesleyan Spirituality*, 12.

[98]Cited, for example, in Ronald P. Patterson, et al., eds., *The Book of Discipline of the United Methodist Church*, 8.

[99]*H KAINH ΔIAΘHKH* (Mt. Athos, 1992), 13.

[100]G. Wainwright, *Doxology: The Praise of God in Worship, Doctrine, and Life—A Systematic Theology* (New York: Oxford University Press, 1980, 1984).

[101]Such reflections are still too private; they do not even appear in my "Fear: A Perennially Present Anguish," in *Overcoming Fear Between Jews and Christians*, ed. Charlesworth (New York: American Interfaith Institute, Crossroad, 1992).

[102]For further reflections, see Charlesworth and W. P. Weaver, eds., T*he Old and the New Testaments: Their Relationship and the "Intertestamental" Literature* (Faith and Scholarship Colloquies; Valley Forge, PA: Trinity Press International, 1993).

[103]Wainwright, *Doxology*, 462; also see 204.

[104]I doubt Wainwright's *Doxology* may be categorized as a "complete systematic theology written from a liturgical perspective" (464, note 12). It is clearly, however, a theology written from a doxological perspective.

[105]Ibid., 435.

[106]Ibid., 215.

[107]See Wainwright, *Doxology*, 220.

[108]We must protect the Psalms from being interpreted only ecclesiologically and christologically. Wainwright recognizes these failures to appreciate the original piety of the Psalms. See Wainwright, *Doxology*, 210–12.

[109]Wainwright's words are on target: "The paradox of the *sub contrario* and the strange continuity of the *communicatio idiomatum* depend on a view of Christ which is already adumbrated in the hymn of Philippians 2:5–11" (*Doxology*, 205).

[110]Ibid, 200–14.

[111]Wesley, as cited by Wainwright in *Doxology*, 201.

[112]See Wainwright, *Doxology*, 216: "How adequate are words to express the inner experience with God?"

7

The Authority of Scriptural Interpretation: An Orthodox Perspective on the Positions of John Wesley and Modern Methodism

Tamara Grdzelidze

The main interest of this paper lies between John Wesley, modern Methodism, and the Orthodox church, and the ways in which they respectively understand the authority of scriptural interpretation. The argument is that the three share a common understanding of the authority of scriptural interpretation but that the ecclesiological frameworks of this pneumatological understanding differ. The Orthodox have a very strong ecclesiological discernment of the issue, modern Methodism has a rather loose ecclesiology, while John Wesley shows less concern for the issue of ecclesiology in relation to the authority of scriptural interpretation.

First of all, the authority of scriptural interpretation as a foundation for teaching in the church is taken as an *a priori* fact for this paper. It is also assumed that teaching and decision-making are the means of the exercising of authority in the church. Moreover, John Wesley, modern Methodism, and the Orthodox church all share a christocentric view of church authority and a belief in its historical development: the development from Christ and the Holy Spirit to the apostles, the early ecclesial communities, and Holy Scripture (Acts 1:24. 15:22–28).

Authority as scriptural interpretation under the Holy Spirit, transmitted by the apostles and the first communities, became the norm for the entire church. Modern bilateral dialogues display a systematic mapping of this authority in the church. From the bilaterals, we understand that church authority and biblical interpretation always emerge in the same context.

Biblical Interpretation as "the Way to Heaven"

According to Methodist scholarship, scripture for John Wesley is both the source and the norm for truth, and reading the scriptures is also one of the means of grace. According to Wesley, the authority of scripture is manifold: it gives an explanation to events; it inspires the faithful with language, images, narrative structures. In the system of authorities, scripture has a leading role: "Scripture alone is our authority, yet scripture is never alone."[1]

When Wesley writes, "I sit down alone: only God is here; in His presence I open and read this book to find the way to heaven," he bears witness to the strong presence of the Holy Spirit in reading through the biblical verses. If reason guides the faithful as far as it can go, the Holy Spirit, superseding reason, acts towards the end; it is the Holy Spirit that brings about the authority of scripture, whose purpose is salvation of the individual: the restoration of the human being from sin through justification back to holiness. While holding, in accordance with the Anglican Articles of Religion, that "Holy Scripture containeth all necessary things to salvation," Wesley, in his *Address to the Clergy* of 1756, considers the early Christian writers to be "the most authentic commentators on Scripture, as being both nearest the fountain and eminently endued with that Spirit by whom all Scripture was given" (1:2).

Two epicletic hymns of the Wesley brothers also bear witness to the Wesleyan pneumatology: "Spirit of faith, come down / Reveal the things of God" and "Come, thou everlasting Spirit / Bring to every thankful mind." The Spirit is a true recorder of Christ's passion; the same Spirit speaks in our hearts and reveals Christ's salvation by preaching of his gospel to the faithful.[2] True, the second of these texts figures in the *Hymns on the Lord's Supper*, and John Wesley gave a positive account of "frequent communion," yet in the Wesleyan correlation between the Holy Spirit, scripture, and authority, no space is left for church. In the Orthodox case, however, it is in the church that, by the Word of God and through the Spirit, Christian holiness is achieved.

In the Orthodox understanding, the Word of God is properly proclaimed—taught and heard—in a liturgical context, and it is *there* that it reveals its eschatological quality. When the Orthodox claim their major hermenutical key to be writings of the church fathers, this includes the ecclesial context, since most of these writings were first preached or meant to be read in the church. According to the Orthodox belief, biblical witness in the church has canonical authority only insofar as it receives the gospel message, inteprets it correctly, and transmits it in the church so that others might believe. (1 Cor. 15:1–11). Thus biblical interpretation is also about reception in the church; it reaches those with whom the Spirit dwells; and it requires a synergy between humankind and God. The Orthodox reveal a very strong ecclesiological basis for the work of the Holy Spirit regarding the authority of scriptural interpretation.[3]

It is clear that *authoritative teaching and decision-making* have been viewed in the framework of a strong pneumatology by John Wesley, modern Methodism, and the Orthodox church. According to several bilateral dialogues in which either the Orthodox or the Methodists have been involved, the authoritative expressions of the manifold action of the Holy Spirit emerge in various measures as scripture, decisions of ecumenical councils and of local synods, the teaching of the holy fathers, and liturgical texts and rites. Some of these actions are presented in a less explicit way by John Wesley and modern Methodism.

In 1992–93, in preparatory steps for a dialogue between the World Methodist Council and the Orthodox churches which took place at the Ecumenical Patriarchate of Constantinople, Methodist and Orthodox theologians posed the question: "How do Orthodox and Methodists understand the work of the Holy Spirit as the shaper of the Christian community across time as well as the source of faith for each believer in every present moment?"[4] They recalled a lecture on the Holy Spirit given by Father

John Meyendorff twenty years earlier at the Oxford Institute of Methodist Theological Studies. Father Meyendorff had given a good exposition of the Orthodox understanding of the work by the Holy Spirit that maintains the community through history. The Spirit "created the apostolic ministry at Pentecost," said Fr. John. That ministry serves the teaching of the church as it is inspired and guided by the Holy Spirit. In the same context, Fr. John gave full credit to the work of the Holy Spirit by saying that different churches recognize the same Spirit in each other, the same Spirit granted at Pentecost. Recognition of the Holy Spirit is an act of interpretation, a cognitive act. Therefore it is a very important statement from the point of view of Orthodox ecclesiology to say that the church recognizes the authority of another Christian community by virtue of the Holy Spirit's transmitting and guiding its teaching.

According to the "theological guidelines: sources and criteria" set out by the 1992 General Conference of the United Methodist Church, "the biblical authors, illumined by the Holy Spirit, bear witness that in Christ the world is reconciled to God. The Bible bears authentic testimony to God's self-disclosure in the life, death and resurrection of Jesus Christ as well as in God's work of creation, in the pilgrimage of Israel, and in the Holy Spirit's ongoing activity in human history."[5] This could be a part of an Orthodox statement, but only a part. So what is it that makes such a big difference between the Methodist and the Orthodox teachings on the Holy Spirit? Perhaps it is the "mystery" that is a concept commonly referred to in Orthodox theology?[6] Mystery is one of the foundations of the Orthodox sacramental theology and casts light on Orthodox ecclesiology.

Although for both churches the primacy of scripture is a critical norm for life in the church, the Methodists have a problem in grasping how the Orthodox account for failings in the life of the church. I do not know whether a satisfactory answer has been found. However, by referring to our different ecclesiologies, one may seek an appropriate answer. The Orthodox church has a sacramental nature, and accusations or criticisms brought against it on the plane of history are not applicable to it.

The emphasis on the sacramental nature of the church underlines the divine aspect in the church's life. Christ through the Holy Spirit is *the* mystery of God's presence in the world. The sacramental nature of the church gives rise to inaugurated eschatology when the faithful are fully incorporated into Christ. In Protestantism in general, on the other hand, the details of sacramental theology are less developed.

For the Orthodox the active presence of God in the church and the worldly accomplishment of his presence are crucial to the nature of the church. Thus the church is seen as a divine-human reality very much in the spirit of the Chalcedonian Christology. It is in the church, the Orthodox believe, that the faithful experience the restored communion of God with the world. "It is very important that an ecclesiology should keep this curious and unique dialectic between unshaken communion in essence and brokenness in existence in the whole creation. This is because the *ekklesia* as sacramental communion is absolutely holy, and a sure guarantee for sharing in the full communion with God by his grace, but all men yet remain sinful."[7]

Perhaps it will be helpful to remind ourselves that John Wesley's admiration for the early church of the first three centuries was counterbalanced by his viewing the Constantinian church as a fall from grace. Such a "breach" has never been a point of reference in the Orthodox tradition.

Councils as a Source of Authoritative Teaching

Along with the recognition of Christianity as the official state religion and the increase of worshipping communities, theological problems multiplied. Those problems, originating from errors in teaching, considerably affected the authority of the church. A solution to the restoration of authortiy was found in the gathering of ecumenical councils. Without the multiplicity of communities and theological errors—in other words, without the spread of Christian teaching throughout the Roman Empire and beyond—there would have been no need to "restore" the church authority. Whatever the implications of the ecumenical councils, their goal was to correct the distorted teaching which threatened the church's authority, for the church as an institution maintains its authoritative teaching precisely through its being exercised universally.

From the dialogue between the World Methodist Council and the Roman Catholic Church, we see that both parties accept the authority of the first ecumenical councils but also make a clear statement about accepting the possibility of further developments in matters of authority through new councils whenever there is a need. For the Methodists, this occurs through the Conference, which is understood as an exercise of corporate *episcope* for the service of the church; it is close in concept to a council and college of bishops, though Methodist Conferences involve laity more formally in a decision-making process. In any case, and both Methodists and Roman Catholics see here a continuing process. Thus the Nairobi Report of 1986 states, "At different moments of history it is sometimes necessary to clarify the contents of Christian faith, and even to define the limits of orthodoxy. For this reason the Christian church convenes in councils, whose purpose it is to bring into sharper focus various aspects of Christian belief. Properly understood, the decisions of the ecumencial councils, which met in the first centuries, command assent throughout the whole church, and there is no reason to think that at the end of the patristic era God stopped enabling his church to speak in such a way. Other occasions have called, and may still call, for such authoritative guidance."[8] To me it seems that this position of modern Methodism is not what John Wesley would endorse.

In Anglican-Orthodox dialogue, it was pointed out that "the Scriptures contain the witness of the prophets and apostles to the revelation of himself which God the Father made to man through his Son in his Holy Spirit. The councils maintain this witness and provide an authoritative interpretation of it."[9]

For the Orthodox, any idea of change with reference to doctrine is a real stumbling block. However, as becomes evident from bilateral dialogues in which they take part, the Orthodox claim openness to some renewal within the limits set by the ecumenical councils. The ecumenical councils accepted a certain understanding of the scriptures, and on the basis of this understanding, they formulated the authoritative interpretations as doctrine. Could we say that councils accepted a faith-based (and faith-tested) interpretation of scripture as a methodological tool? But this is another matter.

For the Orthodox church, authoritative teaching acquires its fullness in the practice of synodality. So also in Methodism. In spite of the fact that both churches acknowledge the leading role of an ecclesial assembly in authoritative teaching and decision-making, still they differ greatly in the structural arrangement of such a gathering:

- The role of laity in the Methodist Conference considerably exceeds the part played by laity in authoritative teaching and decision-making in the Orthodox church.
- Continuation of apostolic authority by the personal link of episcopal succession is an important aspect of Orthodox ecclesiastical authority, but this is not so in Methodist churches.

Here, indeed, we see that Constantinian church policy contributed a lot to authoritative teaching as it is understood in the Orthodox church. Paradoxically, the Methodists in their bilateral talks and agreements emphasize the crucial role of their Conferences for church identity, and the Conference for its part has been a means of maintaining authoritative teaching within the church. Methodist Conferences also acknowledge the importance of the creeds and doctrinal decrees of the early ecumenical councils. The 2001 Brighton Report from the Methodist-Roman Catholic dialogue stated, "In Methodism the Holy Scriptures are believed to contain all things necessary to salvation. At the same time, Methodists' reading of the scriptures is guided by the early creeds and councils and certain standard texts, such as the sermons of John Wesley, his [*Explanatory*] *Notes* [*Up*] *on the New Testament*, and the Articles of Religion."[10] So if ecumenical councils were regarded by John Wesley as dating from after the Constantinian "fall," Methodism today attributes to them a special place next to scripture and the heritage of John Wesley and thus makes them a part of the whole authoritative teaching of the Methodist churches.

Tradition as a Source of Authoritative Teaching

Often the regional Orthodox churches refer to tradition when trying to express the authority of universal teaching, but, as becomes clear from bilaterals, modern Methodism also acknowledges the necessity to refer to a tradition when exercising universal teaching in the church. It should be mentioned, however, that tradition is not very highly regarded in the above mentioned "theological guidelines: sources and criteria" stated by the 1992 General Conference of the United Methodist Church. On the other hand, in a dialogue with other churches, Methodists underline the importance of linking scripture and tradition in matters of authority. According to the 1971 Denver Report of the Roman Catholic-Methodists Dialogue,[11] Christ speaks of authority in terms of service and discipleship; Christ's authority is a manifestation in faith not of servants but of sons. Only an authority given in love and received in love expresses the deepest meaning of the word for Christians. In the Honolulu Report of 1981, the following was stated: "Scripture in witness to the living tradition from which it arose has a normative role for the total tradition of the church as it lives and is guarded still by the Spirit of truth."[12] The dual fact—that a tradition forms a particular interpretation of scripture and that, at the same time, this interpretation becomes normative for this tradition—brings about the dialectics of the normative nature of scripture within a tradition. A similar formulation comes from the Nairobi Report of 1986: "The scriptures bear permanent witness to the divine revelation in Christ and are normative for all subsequent traditions."[13]

Most churches agree that tradition is a significant aspect of Christian identity. However, the various foci used by the churches make tradition an uneasy issue. The Orthodox explicitly emphasize the importance of tradition, which is often described as the patristic interpretation of scripture. Therefore it is remarkable for the Orthodox in a dialogue with other churches to reach the following agreement: "The mind (*phronema*) of the fathers is of lasting importance for our understanding of the Christian faith."[14] The Orthodox and Anglican partners express their dynamic vision of the tradition by saying "there exists freedom and variety within the one tradition of the church";[15] and this is a post-Montreal attitude that has been widely reflected in international dialogues.

Does the above mentioned allow us to raise a question about a shift in modern Methodism towards a search for stronger ecclesiological implications? If that is so, how is this "change" to be interpreted? Is it the influence emerging from the ecumenical commitment of the Methodist churches? Is it the influence of ecclesiology of the "older" churches?

Endnotes

[1]Scott J. Jones, *John Wesley's Conception and Use of Scripture* (Nashville: Kingswood, 1995), 219.

[2]See Geoffrey Wainwright, "Tradition and the Spirit of Faith," in his *Methodists in Dialogue* (Nashville: Kingswood, 1995), 161–178, here especially 173–175.

[3]One of the reasons why some Orthodox theologians refuse to consider commentaries on the Eucharistic rite by the same church fathers as having the same authority is that they are not meant to be preached in the church.

[4]See Wainwright, *Methodists in Dialogue,* 161–162.

[5]Quoted in Wainwright, *Methodists in Dialogue,* 177.

[6]It seems that "mystery" is something which is not quite there in Methodism, but it is something which attracts modern Methodism. See Wainwright, *Methodists in Dialogue,* 179–85 on "the Orthodox Role in the Ecumenical Movement." In Charles Wesley's hymns, however, there is a strong emphasis on "mystery."

[7]Nikos A. Nissiotis, "The Church as a Sacramental Vision and the Challenge of Christian Witness," in *Church-Kingdom-World: The Church as Mystery and Prophetic Sign,* ed. Gennadios Limouris, Faith and Order Paper No. 130, 109.

[8]Methodist–Roman Catholic Dialogue, Nairobi, 1986, paragraph 65, in *Growth in Agreement II,* 594–95.

[9]Anglican-Orthodox Dialogue, Moscow, 1976, paragraph 13, in *Growth in Agreement I,* 43.

[10]"Speaking the Truth in Love: Report of the Joint Commission for Dialogue between the Roman Catholic Church and the World Methodist Council," 1997–2001, 22.

[11]Roman Catholic–Methodist Dialogue, Denver, 1971, 106, in *Growth in Agreement I,* 332–333.

[12]Roman Catholic–Methodist Dialogue, Honolulu, 1981, 34, in *Growth in Agreement I,* 377.

[13]Roman Catholic–Methodist Dialogue, Nairobi, 1986, in *Growth in Agreement II,* 594.

[14]Anglican-Orthodox Dialogue, Dublin, 1984, paragraph 91, in *Growth in Agreement II,* 100.

[15]Ibid., paragraph 92.

8

God's Word Proclaimed: The Homiletics of Grace and Demand in John Chrysostom and John Wesley

Frances Young

The approach and perspectives of this paper are inevitably colored by the facts that I am a Methodist and a scholar of Greek Patristics: I look for convergences. In this study, I shall compare the preaching of John Chrysostom and John Wesley. My conclusion will be that these two famous preachers, each in his different historical, social, and indeed liturgical contexts, drew from scripture the same fundamental message: the inseparability of grace and demand. This was both gospel and challenge. It both shaped the Christian life and undergirded the worship of the heart.

To show this, I propose to put the preaching of each John in context; compare their preaching style and message, noting how both hold together faith and works; consider the liturgical context of their preaching; and explore the significance of their common homiletic thrust on grace and demand for worship in each of our traditions.

My project is, of course, fraught with difficulties. The first concerns the link between preaching and worship. A good deal of John Wesley's preaching took place in the highways and byways, not in a liturgical context at all. But my argument would be that it is no accident that the Wesleys generated an explosive outpouring of hymns and created a Eucharistic movement in an Anglican church that had ceased seriously to be sacramental. The development of characteristically Methodist worship put the proclamation of the Word firmly at the heart of it. For our tradition, worship and preaching belong together theologically, and there is a profound coherence between John Wesley's preaching and the Wesley hymn-writing, not least in the use of scripture.

The difficulty with setting John Chrysostom's preaching into liturgical context is somewhat different: it lies in the question of how much liturgical and homiletic material genuinely goes back to his time and his voice. My plea would be that that does not matter: for our purposes it is the Chrysostom received within the Orthodox tradition, including the liturgy attributed to him, which is of significance.

A second area of difficulty presents itself: from each John, we have written homilies or sermons, but it would seem that each normally preached with much spontaneity and a good deal of spur of the moment response to the congregation. It is difficult to reconstruct their non-verbal communication, the inflections and attitudes, which projected personality or powerful conviction. It is difficult even to know what they really preached, as distinct from what the published texts reveal.

Most of John Wesley's preaching was extempore, and apart from a few special sermons preached, for example, to the University of Oxford on specific occasions, the published sermons were not actual sermons as delivered; rather, they were published as "models"—the sort of doctrines to be preached and the way to preach them. To read the published sermons of John Wesley is to enter the world of the eighteenth-century rationalist, ordering his points in beautiful sequence; one wonders how on earth this could bring people to their knees and provoke mass conversions among the poor and illiterate.

A similar difficulty exists with the homilies of John Chrysostom, though certainly it seems as if some of his were taken down by stenographers as he spoke, and we even have amusing asides recorded which give a vivid impression of the kind of conditions under which he preached. Clearly, huge crowds packed into the basilicas of Antioch and Constantinople, and Chrysostom even warns people to watch out for pickpockets in the crush! But not all the homilies have come to us in this way; some seem to have been deliberately put together for publication. The limits of our knowledge of the circumstances of Chrysostom's preaching has been emphasized by Wendy Mayer in recent writings.[1]

Yet, making allowance for these difficulties, it is possible to deduce something of the style and content of the preaching of both these great Christian orators, one of whom entranced fourth-century Antioch only to offend those in high places in Constantinople, the other of whom swept eighteenth-century England off of its feet but was excluded from the Established Church. Let's proceed to put each in context.

Chrysostom was a priest at Antioch from 386–398, and from then until 404, Patriarch of Constantinople. His sermons give a vivid picture of the corrupt life of both cities and the problems of the church in that particular society. There was a reaction towards worldliness after the rigors of severe persecutions, and as Christianity became the established religion of the Empire, a vast influx of new Christians who "had the name of Christ in their mouths rather than their hearts."[2] Society was no longer simply pagan, but neither was it Christian. Crowds flocked to the churches to applaud Chrysostom's rhetoric and behaved as if they were at the theatre, and they no longer flocked if there was the counter-attraction of a real theatre production or circus races. Social conditions were hard; at one end of the scale was extreme poverty, and slavery was among social norms; at the other end of the scale was the acme of riches coupled with greed, cruelty, and exploitation of the poor. The situation was even more severe in Constantinople, where the imperial court set the tone. With these conditions in mind, the prevailing moralistic tone of Chrysostom's preaching is hardly surprising, even though at first sight it appears that works, not faith, is his emphasis, and the Greek word *agape*, like the English word *charity*, has been reduced to almsgiving.

Chrysostom's primary purpose, then, was to educate an essentially pagan society in the Christian way, and this meant a great deal of straightforward instruction. Most of his sermons are series of exegetical homilies, preached commentaries, which took his congregations through books of the Bible, sometimes covering quite extensive passages in one go. His listeners had to be introduced to the content and meaning of scripture, often beginning with no knowledge at all. For the most part, the homilies seem diffuse and unplanned. Chrysostom apparently picked up the text of the book he was preaching on, read out a few words, spoke a general introduction, and then followed through the text, carefully explaining words and phrases, expounding it verse by verse, rather as the schoolmaster of his day would go through one of the classics, Homer or Thucydides. After a time, particularly if a theme or phrase struck him as pertinent to the current situation, he would digress into a long exhortation, which often bore scant relation to the content of the exegetical section of his homily. This digression would normally be on one of his favorite moralistic themes: the evils of riches, almsgiving, voluntary poverty, the immoralities of the theatre, and so on. Occasionally it dealt with an issue that was alive at the time—for example, whether repentance was possible after baptism.

This method of preaching meant that Chrysostom often dealt with a vast range of topics, sometimes entirely unrelated, within the compass of a single homily. This was clearly regarded as unusual even in his own time; rhetorical convention expected a particular speech to cover a particular topic, with all the tricks of the trade employed to embellish it to maximum effect. So Chrysostom's

> hearers once asked him why he often spoke of entirely different things in one and the same sermon. He justified himself by saying that as a physician did not treat all diseases with the same medicine, but administered to each one what was most useful, so the preacher did not venture to offer the same medicine to all his listeners, but must prepare several so that each one might go home with a suitable means of salvation. "Therefore," he said, "I speak now of avarice and reproach the sensual life; then I touch on continence, and after that praise almsgiving and encourage everyone to it and all other good works."[3]

This diffuse and unplanned method of sermon construction is hardly to our taste and, as one scholar once put it, "would be crossed out by anyone taking a sermon class."[4] Yet in educational terms, it had its advantages in Chrysostom's day, and it apparently did not turn off his hearers. It communicated the content of scripture to largely ignorant congregations, and it fostered a range of basic moral attitudes as well as providing practical advice on the decent ethical standards to be expected in a supposedly Christian society. One of the things Chrysostom tried to do was to bridge what was then a widening rift between the perfectionist ideals of the monks and the daily lives of ordinary Christian people. And, however disjointed, whatever Chrysostom said was relevant to his time and rooted in scripture.

John Wesley became notorious for open-air evangelism. Yet he did not take to field preaching easily. He did so only after scores of pulpits in England had been closed to him and he was summoned to it by George Whitefield. Wesley was preaching in an England whose social conditions were not entirely unlike those of Chrysostom's Antioch: the gap was wide between rich and poor, the respectable gentleman and the inmate of the workhouse or prison. It was the England of Hogarth in which Wesley preached the gospel of Christ. He faced savage, brutal, poverty-stricken masses, and on the edge of the crowd, the curious rich conspicuously hidden in their carriages. Is it any wonder that it was a deep ethical concern that motivated both of these preachers;

and that it was the Christian way of *agape* that was the basis of a real attempt to preach practical Christian morality in their respective contemporary situations?

The structure of Wesley's sermons provides a striking contrast to those of Chrysostom. His preaching is thematic and follows a prepared plan whose subdivisions are often announced in advance. Even within the subdivisions, it's easy to discern the outline. The obvious care over the structure, sometimes with paragaphs of different sections beautifully balanced, sometimes with paragraphs arranged in a magnificent logical progression, is a real joy to anyone with a tidy mind and provides a clear and obvious contrast to the apparently muddled sermons of Chrysostom. Yet this too has its dangers: texts may be broken down into over-schematized components, or a treatise may be constructed which is far removed from the text to which it is nominally attached. Perhaps the most notorious example of the latter problem is the sermon on "The Almost Christian." The text is "Almost thou persuadest me to be a Christian" (Acts 26:28), and the sermon consists of a powerful contrast between the "Almost Christian" and the "Altogether Christian." No one can deny the effectiveness of the sermon, but "Wesley's warmest admirer must admit that this is an example of how not to treat a text."[5]

Structure and style, then, are so different that the two preachers hardly appear at first sight to have much in common. Besides this, Wesley's published sermons are for the most part isolated expositions of congenial texts. Wesley did not face the same congregation day after day as Chrysostom did, and in any case, his intention in publishing his sermons was to indicate his stance and approach on various doctrinal and practical issues, which were to the fore in the evangelical revival. There is one set of exegetical sermons from Wesley's pen, namely the series on the Sermon on the Mount, so it should be fruitful to make some comparisons between these and Chrysostom's sermons on the same chapters of Matthew's Gospel.

Both are now preaching in the exegetical tradition and dealing with texts as they stand, interpreting them for their hearers. The fact that the text is ethical in content means that Chrysostom's exhortations are much more integrated with his exegesis than usual, and his sermons therefore give a greater impression of unity, clarity, and dependence on the text before him. Wesley too appears in a different light in many of these sermons. He is now concerned with following through the text, sometimes, like Chrysostom, covering a very lengthy passage in one sermon. But even here, his preaching never becomes chaotic or diffuse. His careful plan is ever before us. It may be a simple plan whereby he carefully follows the verses in order, showing their relationship and dealing with each in turn, but always there is a feeling of systematization of a kind that Chrysostom never attempted.

The superficial impression on first reading the sermons of these two preachers is therefore one of contrast. This is further enhanced by the differences in their approach to sermon illustration. Chrysostom uses the stock tropes of Greek rhetoric: storms at sea, competitors in chariot races, and many others. One of Wesley's most characteristic methods of illustration is to compose character sketches—the pictures of "the Almost Christian" and "the Altogether Christian" are typical. These sketches, however, mostly consist of collages of scriptural allusion and are couched in scriptural language, and since Chrysostom's most frequent illustrative method is to cross-reference scriptural texts, stories, and characters, there is a common source and a common approach to dramatic and telling use of the basic material they share.

This is typical of the situation: a first impression of utter dissimilarity, but a deeper consonance revealed by more careful study of the content. Both preachers were obviously soaked in scripture. The Greek of Chrysostom is steeped in phrases from the Greek Old and New Testaments, and his work is full of quotation from scripture. John Wesley's language has similar characteristics: scriptural phrases from the Authorized Version are built into his English sentences, and scriptural sentences are assembled into paragraphs. Exegetical procedures are also similar: when a text is expounded by either, it is broken down into distinct ideas and then put together again to form a full picture of what the text is getting at.

A clear example of this is the exposition of the Beatitudes. Each asks, "Who are the poor in spirit?" Each answers in terms of humility and dependence on God, as distinct from pride, the attempt to be equal with God, the sin of Adam. Each asks the same question of each Beatitude, and each Beatitude is then interpreted in terms of Christian virtues and stages in the Christian life. The words are related to the effects of God's gracious gift of salvation. Thus the individual elements are expounded and then put together to form a complete picture of life in Christ, culminating in the inevitability of persecution. The details of the exposition produced by each preacher may be different, but their method of tackling it is very much the same.

So Chrysostom sums up thus:

> Therefore you see in each instance, by the earlier precept making way for the following one, he has woven a sort of golden chain for us. So first he that is humble will surely mourn for his sins; he that so mourns will be meek and righteous and merciful; he that is merciful, righteous and contrite, will, of course, be also pure of heart; and such a one will be a peacemaker too; and he that has attained to all these will be moreover arrayed against dangers, and will not be troubled when evil is spoken of him and he is enduring trials innumerable.[6]

For Wesley too the sum of the Beatitudes characterizes what Christians are to be and what they are to do—how inward holiness is to exert itself in outward conversation.

Both preachers assume the unity of scripture and make indiscriminate use of passages from one context or author to illuminate passages found elsewhere. Wesley explains that the merciful who are to obtain mercy are those who love their neighbors as themselves. This opens the way to full-scale exegesis of Paul's hymn to love in 1 Corinthians 13. That chapter is also a favorite of Chrysostom's, to which he easily digresses when expounding other texts. Once modern exegetes would have condemned this procedure, chiding Wesley for importing the whole of Paul's doctrine of justification by faith into the Beatitudes. Yet it was a universal exegetical technique before modern criticism, and it enables each of our preachers to proclaim the central core of the gospel message for the congregations of his own time.

I have suggested that the central core common to both and underlying the many differences we have observed is to be summed up in the twin emphases grace and demand. The theme of grace was central for John Wesley, who had learned the doctrine of justification by faith alone from the Reformers. Humanity cannot earn salvation; it can only accept it from God. "Justifying faith . . . is a sure trust and confidence that Christ died for my sins, that he loved me and gave himself for me." "Acceptance must depend, not on us, but on him that calleth us."[7]

John Chrysostom, in a different context and centuries before the Reformation, could hardly be expected to focus on this theme so explicitly. Recent studies of Paul's theology have differentiated the thrust of Paul's likely meaning in his own context from the Reformation reading of Paul to which Wesley was committed. Yet Chrysostom too is sure that salvation depends upon God's gracious acceptance, not on any deserts of our own. It is as well to remember that Chrysostom's near contemporary, the historian Socrates, found his preaching inexplicable, precisely because it offered the possibility of repentance over and over again. This seemed to Socrates incompatible with Chrysostom's own zeal for ascetic virtues and holiness of life, as well as contrary to the decree of a recent synod of bishops that repentance was possible after baptism only once. Chrysostom, says Socrates,

> did not scruple to say "Approach, although you may have repented a thousand times." For this doctrine, many even of his friends censured him.[8]

Socrates clearly thought that Chrysostom's judgmental attitude to the court and to his fellow clergy lay at the root of his downfall; yet he recognizes that his sermons imply that God in his mercy always holds the invitation to repentance open.

In fact, the most persistent theme in Chrysostom's preaching was God's *philanthropia*, his love towards humanity. One reason for his popularity was that he could lash the rich and hypocritical with cruel wit while offering the poor and the sinner the mercy of a kind and loving Father. God's *philanthropia* meant that human beings were called upon to show love and consideration for all. God's mercy (*eleemosyne*) should induce Christians to *eleemosyne*; the sense has now shifted to alsmgiving, but this was the practical outworking of Christian *agape* in the environment in which Chrysostom was preaching. It was God's *eleemosyne* which reconciled us; Chrysostom in one passage pictures her as a dove interceding on our behalf at the judgment, taking us under her wings.

> Beloved, let us strive after her through whom we are saved. Let us love her, let us value her more than money.[9]

God prizes her more than sacrifice, he goes on. Nothing is more characteristic of a Christian than *eleemosyne* (almsgiving). But it does not stem from us first, for God has already shown his mercy (*eleemosyne*) towards us.

In this passage, we can see how very aware Chrysostom was that neither God's grace nor human effort was sufficient for salvation without the other. He often couples both emphases:

> In willing lies everything, with grace from above.[10]

Chrysostom's moral exhortations may give the impression that he preached a doctrine of salvation by works, but he was a great admirer of Paul, and his *Homilies on Romans* are particularly revealing. On Romans 1:17, he points out that it is "not your own righteousness, but that of God . . . For you do not achieve it by toilings and labours, but you receive it as a gift from above, contributing only one thing from your own store, namely 'believing.'" On Romans 3:24–5, Chrysostom asks, "What is the 'declaring of righteousness'?" And he replies,

> Like the declaring of riches means not merely that he is rich himself, but also makes others rich; or of his life, not only that he himself is living but also that he makes the dead to live; and of his power, not only that he is powerful but also that he makes the feeble powerful; so also is the declaring of his righteousness, not only that he himself is righteous, but that he also makes them that are filled with the putrefying sores of sin suddenly righteous . . . Doubt not, then; for it is not of works but of faith.[11]

Chrysostom says of his own work that "that is our only care day and night, that all of you may become holy and perfect." This explains the combination of grace and demand in his preaching. All is of God, and we should pray for divine help; yet it is unrealistic to think that people do not need advice and even inducements for the practical outworking of faith in life. So Chrysostom is not averse to suggesting that we may make God our debtor by good deeds; indeed, he suggests that almsgiving is a way of purchasing heavenly securities! Such a doctrine of merit would become unacceptable in the post–Reformation West, yet the demand of the gospel could never be ignored. That was what Wesley grasped and constantly reiterated, even as he preached a gospel based on justification by faith. Wesley's doctrine of Christian perfection or scriptural holiness is the eighteenth-century parallel to the holiness and perfection that Chrysostom labored to realize in his congregations.

On May 24th, 1738, Wesley's heart was "strangely warmed"as he listened to someone reading from Luther's *Commentary on the Epistle to the Romans.* This seems to have been the culmination of a long process whereby Wesley came to accept the doctrine of justification by faith not works. His sermon on Ephesians 2:18, "By grace are ye saved through faith," was preached at St. Mary's Oxford a few weeks later, and it is by no means his only exposition of this doctrine. Wesley, of all people, could not be accused of preaching justification by works.

Yet a great many of his sermons are moralistic, and Christian conduct is his main concern. The reason for this is clearly seen in his two sermons on "Law established through faith," based on Romans 3:31. Here he enquires first: Which are the most usual ways of making void the law through faith? He then deals, amongst others, with those who say that faith supercedes the necessity of holiness. He argues that under the covenant of grace

> the manner of man's acceptance is this: the free grace of God through the merits of Christ gives pardon to them that believe; that believe with such a faith as, working through love, produces obedience and holiness.[12]

> Now all good works, though as necessary as ever, are not antecedent to our acceptance, but consequent upon it.[13]

> We are doubtless justified by faith. This is the corner-stone of the whole Christian building. We are justified without the works of the law as any previous condition of justification; but they are an immediate fruit of that faith whereby we are justified. So

> that if good works do not follow on faith, even all inward and outward holiness, it is plain that our faith is nothing worth; we are still in our sins.[14]

> We establish the law when we so preach faith in Christ as not to supercede, but to produce holiness . . . Faith itself, even Christian faith, the faith of God's elect, the faith of the operation of God, still is only the handmaid of love. As glorious and honourable as it is, it is not the end of the commandment. God has given this honour to love alone: love is the end, the whole end of every dispensation of God, from the beginning of the world to the consummation of all things. And it will endure when heaven and earth flee away; for love alone "never faileth." Faith will totally fail; it will be swallowed up in sight, in the everlasting vision of God.[15]

Because his sermons are full of this kind of defense, Wesley's presuppositions about the relation of faith and works are much clearer to us than is the case with Chrysostom. Yet Chrysostom outlined a not dissimilar position, also referring to Romans 3:31. Christ fulfilled the law in two senses: he fulfilled it himself and

> he did the same through us also: for this is the marvel, that he not only fulfilled it himself, but he also granted this to us likewise . . . For since the law was labouring at this, to make men righteous, but had not the power, he came and brought in the way of righteousness through faith, and so established what the law desired; and what the law could not by letters accomplish, this he accomplished by faith.[16]

This fulfilling of the law has to be worked out in practical ways. Christ provided the example; Christians have to follow it. Faith is of no avail without works. Both Chrysostom and Wesley realized that neither active antinomianism nor passive waiting for a miracle could produce holiness. The gospel of grace had to be matched by challenging people with its demand.

The preaching of Chrysostom and Wesley is full of the same ethical concern, the same call to respond through a life of good works, a life of love, to the love and mercy of the God of grace who saves humanity. Neither of them shrinks from the responsibility of giving guidance on how this is to work out in practical terms. Although the practical advice has something of a different flavor in the different cultural contexts, Wesley's call to self-giving and good works is recognizably the same as the preaching and concern of Chrysostom. Both were anxious about the responsible use of wealth and care for the poor. Both were equally prepared to stick their necks out by condemning those in high places who compromised their Christian profession by their style of life.

For Chrysostom, problems arose because he insisted on preaching the ascetic and puritanical ideals of the monk as the standard to which all Christians should aspire. Simplicity, purity, holiness, an independence of worldly goods and concerns, concern rather for the poor and the kingdom of heaven—such were the perfections Chrysostom preached, while offering through Christ the promise of God's grace, love, and forgiveness if only repentance were forthcoming. For Wesley, true Christianity was a complete change of heart wrought in a person by acceptance of Christ alone in faith, which then worked out in practical terms in the expression of "love, joy, peace, long-suffering, gentleness, goodness" (Gal. 5:22, a favorite text of his); it meant the

Christian's involvement with his neighbor and responsibility for him. It was this deep ethical concern that made him write:

> I find more profit in sermons on either good temper or good works than in what are vulgarly called Gospel sermons. . . . Let but a pert self-sufficient animal, that has neither sense nor grace, bawl out something about Christ and his blood, or justification by faith, and his hearers cry out, "What a fine Gospel sermon!"[17]

> If we duly join faith and works in our preaching, we shall not fail of a blessing. But of all preaching, what is called gospel-preaching is the most useless, if not the most mischievous; a dull, yea or a lively, harangue on the sufferings of Christ or salvation by faith without inculcating holiness. I see more and more that this naturally tends to drive holiness from the world.[18]

Noticeably, both Chrysostom and Wesley demand holiness. Unless the message of grace produces fruits of repentance and reform, it is shallow and indefensible, yet moralizing without the compassion of the gospel has also proved incapable of effecting these fruits. For both read Paul as saying that the law simply sets a standard which people cannot live up to. Response to what God has done for us is the only effective "fulfilling of the law." Chrysostom and Wesley, each in his own way, recognized that God and humankind need to work together in producing a new world. God's gift and the human response both belong to the saving process.

Given the similarities, it is an interesting question how far Wesley was dependant upon Chrysostom. We know that he read him along with other patristic literature, Chrysostom's name almost invariably appearing among the Fathers listed as significant in various places in his voluminous writings. We also know that he took seriously the way scripture was interpreted by the Fathers: according to the Journal, on his trip across the Atlantic, Wesley daily checked his reading of scripture against the early authors. Furthermore, Wesley was especially interested in the so-called Anglican Homilies, sermons authorized at the time of the Reformation for use in English churches. Wesley used a number of patristic "proof-texts," which he published in an abbreviated version as a pamphlet in 1738. Several quotations from Chrysostom are reproduced, including the following sentence, which Wesley found in the *Homilies on Matthew*:

> Faith is full of good works, and as soon as a man believes, he shall be adorned with them.

That, however, alerts us to the most likely medium of Wesley's acquaintance with Chrysostom: his works came to Wesley through the filters of the Anglican tradition, and in particular the syllabus he read at Oxford. If Chrysostom had any direct influence, it was because he confirmed Wesley's own reading of scripture. It was their common facility in bringing different scriptures to bear upon one another that produced their common "synergistic" approach. The other thing they shared was an endeavor, conscious or unconscious, to bring into ordinary life the "perfectionism" of monastic ideals. Faith and works are inseparable in the human response to God's gracious salvation.

The theme of this consultation is worship and devotional life, and in what remains of my time, I should make some attempt to relate this paper to our larger endeavor. This exploration of similarities and differences in the preaching of a key historical figure in each tradition is intended to show how a common reading of the core message of the Bible undergirds the spiritual life of each tradition. But even more to the point is to draw out of this common emphasis on grace and demand the consequences for the worshipping heart. Culturally, the Orthodox liturgy and Methodist informality seem poles apart. But by approaching each with the same question, I suggest, we find a deeper consonance, at least where each is at its best. That question is this: how is grace and demand articulated in worship?

We have observed Chrysostom's way of focussing on God's *eleemosyne* as the ground of human *eleemosyne*. To one but little versed in Orthodox liturgy, one of the most striking things about it is the constant expression of humility before God and the cry for mercy. Approach to God is only possible because of the gracious economy of the Trinity, and the human response must be one of contrition and awe. Whatever else happens in the liturgy—and the lections from scripture will color each particular occasion—that fundamental attitude recognizes that receiving God's mercy and grace makes demands. There is nothing casual about the Christian life. God is both trustworthy and terrifying. Judgment and love are two sides of the same coin. The invocation of the saints reinforces the demand for holiness, to become like them, while at the same time offering the comfort of their intercession.

There is a sense in which Chrysostom's preaching reflected, or perhaps shaped, the grace and demand articulated in the liturgy. His *Homilies on the Psalms* are a wonderful expression of what it means to praise God, to know God's love, and yet at the same time demand an approach of self-abasement that changes one's life. To explore some of his more thematic preaching would reinforce that conclusion: for example, the series on God's incomprehensibility, though dealing with a doctrinal issue of the day, does so by evoking a profound sense of God's otherness and of the respect that that must induce. Chrysostom's preaching coheres with the liturgical setting, and both create a sense of the demands made by the grace of God.

Would that Methodist worship had the same effect! We experience rather too much of Wesley's pert preachers and the soft gospel of comfort and joy. If we return to the roots of our tradition, however, we find Wesley equally insistent upon the awesomeness of approaching God:

> "A Christian" cannot think of the Author of his being without abasing himself before him, without a deep sense of the distance between a worm of earth and him that "sitteth on the circle of the heavens." In his presence he sinks into the dust, knowing himself to be less than nothing in his eye and being conscious, in a manner words cannot express, of his own littleness, ignorance, foolishness.[19]

The attitude is "awful reverence" and "tenderest gratitude." All the Christian needs to know is that God is love, and that he or she is to be conformed to that likeness—grace and demand:

> This is Christian faith in the general notion of it. In its more particular notion, it is a divine evidence or conviction wrought in my heart that God is reconciled to me through his Son, inseparably joined with a confidence in him as a gracious, reconciled Father.[20]

Historically, the Wesley hymns are characteristic of Methodist worship and devotion. In some quarters, this needs reclaiming in our tradition. They are an expression of this grace and demand. I end with some examples:

Saviour, and can it be
That thou shouldst dwell with me?
From thy high and lofty throne,
Throne of everlasting bliss,
Will thy majesty stoop down
To so mean a house as this?

Yet come, thou heavenly Guest,
And purify my breast;
Come, thou great and glorious King,
While before thy cross I bow,
With thyself salvation bring,
Cleanse the house by entering now.[21]

Behold the servant of the Lord!
I wait thy guiding eye to feel,
To hear and keep thy every word,
To prove and do thy perfect will:
Joyful from all my works to cease,
Glad to fulfill all righteousness.

Me if thy grace vouchsafe to use,
Meanest of all thy creatures, me,
The deed, the time, the manner choose,
Let all my fruit be found of thee:
Let all my works in thee be wrought,
By thee to full perfection brought.[22]

Endnotes

[1]E.g., Wendy Mayer, "John Chrysostom: Extraordinary Preacher, Ordinary Audience," in *Preacher and Audience: Studies in Early Christian and Byzantine Homiletics*, ed. Mary B.Cunningham and Pauline Allen (Leiden: Brill, 1998), 105–137.

[2]Donald Attwater, *St. John Chrysostom* (London: P. Harvill, 1959), 12.

[3]Dom Chrysostomos Baur, *John Chrysostom and His Time*, Eng. trans. by M. Gonzaga (London: Sands, 1959, 1960), 213.

[4]S. L. Greenslade, an unpublished paper on communication in the early church.

[5]John Lawson, *Notes on Wesley's 44 Sermons* (London: Epworth, 1946), 11.

[6]*Homilies on Matthew xv.6*, P. Migne, *Patrologia Graeca* (henceforth PG), vol. 57, col. 230. English translation in *Nicene and Post-Nicene Fathers* (henceforth NPNF), 1st series, vol. xi, 378, adapted.

[7]Sermon V, "On Justification by Faith": iv.2, 7, John Wesley, *Sermons on Several Occasions*, 1st series (London: Epworth, 1944), 57, 59–60.

[8]Socrates, *Historia Ecclesiastica*, vi.21; text in Migne, PG 67.725.

[9]*Homilies on Hebrews* xxxii.3; text in Migne, PG 63.224, Eng. trans. by Frances Young.

[10]Ibid., xiii.5.

[11]*Homilies on Romans* vii.2, Migne, PG 60.414, NPNF, first series, xi.378 adapted.

[12]*Sermon* xxx.ii, 401.

[13]Ibid.

[14]*Sermon* xxx.ii.6, 402.

[15]*Sermon* xxx.ii.1, 410–11.

[16]On Matt. 5:17.

[17]Letter to Miss Bishop, October 8, 1778; John Telford, ed., *The Letters of John Wesley* (London: Epworth, 1931).

[18]Letter to Charles Wesley, November 4, 1772, ibid.

[19]*A Plain Account of Genuine Christianity* I.2ff. and II.7, as quoted by Albert Outler, *John Wesley* (London: Epworth, 1931), 183ff., 189.

[20]Ibid.

[21]John and Charles Wesley, *Hymns on the Lord's Supper* (Bristol: Farley, 1745), hymn 43, p. 32, stanzas 1 and 3.

[22]This poem was first published in 1745 and was appended to John Wesley's pamphlet *A Further Appeal to Men of Reason and Religion,* which was Wesley's response to those who had opposed his teaching and preaching in the fields. It was later published in *Hymns and Sacred Poems,* 2 vols. (Bristol: Farley, 1749), 1:206–7, stanzas 1 and 2 of 4 stanzas.

9

Lancelot Andrewes: A Bridge between Orthodoxy and the Wesley Brothers in the Realm of Prayer

Nicholas Lossky

Anyone who studies the Anglican tradition, from which Methodism was born, is bound to encounter the names of the two men who gave the English Church its very particular spirit. As T. S. Eliot wrote in 1928, "if the Church of Elizabeth is worthy of the age of Shakespeare and Johnson, that is because of Hooker and Andrewes."[1] Most people interested in sixteenth-century English literature have read at least a page or two of Richard Hooker's *Treatise of Ecclesiastical Polity* because his style is still appreciated and extracts are quoted in prose anthologies. Just as Bossuet's sermons are read by lovers of the French language, Hooker may be appreciated even by those who do not believe in God. The case of Lancelot Andrewes is very different. As Eliot says, "The sermons of Andrewes are not easy reading. They are only for the reader who can elevate himself to the subject." Yet he also says of these sermons that "they rank with the finest English prose of their time, of any time."[2] And let me add that Andrewes, in Eliot's view, "is the first great preacher of the English Catholic Church."[3]

It is significant that the sermons of Lancelot Andrewes, read in his own day, gathered after his death by Archbishop William Laud and Bishop John Buckeridge (1629), were not published again after the late seventeenth century, when the taste for preaching completely changed. The "metaphysical" (in fact patristic) style of Andrewes was replaced by a polished manner of preaching corresponding to a different approach to theology. This more or less coincided with the departure of the Non-Jurors into schism. Andrewes's sermons were rediscovered by the Tractarians and reprinted in the *Library of Anglo-Catholic Theology* in the middle of the nineteenth century (11 volumes, 1841–1854).

It is, however, interesting to note that if the style of Andrewes's preaching was no longer appreciated and considered too difficult to read (as it still is by the majority today), his theology did not disappear. The reason is simple to understand. If the sermons were no longer printed in the eighteenth and early nineteenth centuries, Andrewes's reputation as a great churchman never died, and his *Private Devotions* (*Preces Privatae*) were frequently published and republished, starting from 1630 (Henry Isaacson, Andrewes's amanuensis). This book of prayers was used by all kinds of Christians, not only those generally described as Anglo-Catholics. There even exists a French adaptation done by Roman Catholics, printed in 1946 (long before the second Vatican Council) and reprinted in 1981 (unfortunately with exactly the same introduction, still expressing the pre–Vatican II vision of the English Reformation).

I personally suspect that many of those whose leanings were rather "Protestant" did not really know what they were in fact using for praying. Indeed, it was only in 1903 that the great English liturgist F. E. Brightman produced his invaluable annotated translation, which provides all the sources.[4] Brightman, as we all know, remains even today one of the greatest experts of all liturgies, Eastern as well as Western. He was therefore particularly well qualified to detect both the actual verbatim quotations from the different liturgical traditions, Jewish and Christian, and Andrewes's developments in the style of the sources he used. One should never forget that this book was his private prayer book and was not meant for publication. According to some of his contemporaries, he died with this book in his hands.

One of the most interesting features of F. E. Brightman's English version of Lancelot Andrewes's *Preces Private* is the fact that in the notes, he points to most of the parallel correspondences between the prayers and the sermons. As he himself says in the Introduction, "The devotions are in fact an abstract of the sermons, the sermons a development and expansion of the devotions. The things which he delivers to the Church are the things in which he habitually 'exercises himself day and night'; they have been proved and tested in his own heart; and the essence of his public teaching is distilled into suggestion for his own devotion."[5]

Now, the sermons of Lancelot Andrewes are thoroughly theological. He dealt with every point of doctrine that he considered to be of importance for the enlightenment of his audience, which was as mixed as audiences of the plays of Shakespeare—the courtiers were accompanied by their households and not reduced to the most enlightened minds of the nobility as was the court of Versailles in the eighteenth century. The point that F. E. Brightman is making deserves to be expanded a little. But before proceeding with the expansion, I need to offer an apology.

Ten years ago, Canon A. M. Allchin delivered a paper, "The Epworth-Canterbury-Constantinople Axis," which dealt with a subject very close to mine here today: the relation between the Wesley brothers and Eastern Orthodoxy. In this excellent paper, referring as was most natural to Lancelot Andrewes, my friend A. M. Allchin quoted my own work on the learned and saintly bishop of Winchester; he had also done the same in his remarkable book on *Participation in God: A Forgotten Strand in Anglican Tradition* (London, 1988), one chapter of which deals with Charles Wesley. I must therefore apologize for a certain amount of repetition of what Canon Allchin and I have already said in the past.

The repetition concerns the fact that for Andrewes, as for the Wesley brothers, as well as for many great Christians before and after them, theology is anything but abstract intellectual constructions or speculation about God, a province of knowledge reserved for professors of "systematic" theology (a rather unpalatable phrase in my opinion), separate from the rest of the human relation with God. Anyone who has read Vladimir Lossky's *Mystical Theology of the Eastern Church* will remember that in the first chapter, my father, who was also my professor of dogmatics, clearly expresses the traditional orthodox view—"orthodox" is here used not in the "confessional" sense of the word—that any theology worthy of the name can only be mystical, provided of course that the latter notion of mysticism is properly understood. Mysticism is not something reserved for a few exceptional human beings (such as the fourteenth-century Rhenish or English mystics) but the calling offered to all baptized believers, what many today would call spirituality. Incidentally, in this same first chapter, the notion of an *Eastern* theology is also rejected.

For Vladimir Lossky, as for the Wesley brothers (whom he did not know!), as for Lancelot Andrewes (whom he did not know either!), or for Geoffrey Wainwright, a great Methodist of our own time, theology without the "spiritual," doxological (or I would say liturgical) dimension is nothing but dry abstraction. Conversely, "mysticism" or spirituality without theology, in the sense of contemplation of the triune God, is nothing but "enthusiasm" in the seventeenth and eighteenth centuries' derogatory sense of the word. What all these people have in common is the one and the same source or spring: the patristic experience of God, deeply rooted in the scriptures and the liturgy of the Church.

Lancelot Andrewes was deeply immersed in patristic theology, which he preached to his contemporaries and through them to all the following generations. It is mainly through the Non-Jurors (who continued in Andrewes's theological spirit) that the Wesley brothers were acquainted with this relation with the early Church. Patristic theology is to be distinguished from what might be termed an archeological, philological knowledge of the Fathers. Anyone can read the Fathers and remain totally on the surface (and even be an agnostic; I have known such scholars in my French university). The discovery of patristic theology is something quite different from knowledge of the Fathers. It consists in living the experience of God like the Fathers. And the Fathers' experience of God is an ecclesial experience of God. Everyone will remember the famous judgment of William Chillingworth published in 1638 (twelve years after Andrewes's death): "I see plainly and with mine own eyes that there are Popes against Popes, Councils against Councils, some Fathers against others, the same Fathers against themselves, a Consent of Fathers of one age against a Consent of Fathers of another age, the Church of one age against the Church of another age."[6]

Andrewes, and for that matter all intellectually honest Orthodox, could subscribe, at least partly, to this view of Church history. However, both Andrewes and the intellectually honest Orthodox would temper this judgment with a view of tradition as the living breath of the Holy Spirit, the critical spirit of the Church.[7]

What Lancelot Andrewes tried to convey to his audience in his "solemn sermons" (as Bishop John Buckeridge called them in his funeral sermon) is full of Orthodoxy in more ways than one. At this stage, let us mention only a few matters. First of all, he preached an extremely "realistic" approach to the Incarnation: the wondrous mystery of God's taking on humanity has consequences, which concern the human body as well as the human soul. The body must take an active part in prayer. In this respect, Andrewes insists on the importance of "worshipping, falling down, kneeling before the Lord" (Ps. 95:6). This physical dimension of the Incarnation not only means that God has made himself visible, especially on Mount Tabor; it also implies that all matter is called to sanctification, transfiguration. The whole of creation is thus concerned.

Secondly, Andrewes's Christology might be termed pneumatological. He insists very much on the inseparable yet distinct action of the Son and the Spirit, "the two hands of the Father" (Irenæus) who collaborate in the divine dispensation. Jesus Christ became man in order to manifest the Holy Trinity. Thus, the baptism of Christ plays a very important part in Andrewes's preaching. His Christology is therefore trinitarian. To this we shall return later in connection with the Wesley brothers.

Just one more element of Orthodoxy, among many that could be pointed to, may be suggested here in connection with the preaching. It is my impression that we can read between the lines a fumbling for something close to a distinction between the essence of God and the divine energies. This seems to me to appear in the context of the gift of the Holy Spirit in the pentecostal sermons. I am not suggesting that Andrewes knew St. Gregory Palamas. But there is no doubt that he knew St. Gregory of Nyssa, who, as Cardinal Jean Daniélou admitted in 1944, already expressed such a distinction.

Let us now return to what F. E. Brightman so aptly said about the relation between the sermons and the devotions of Lancelot Andrewes: "The devotions are in fact an abstract of the sermons, the sermons a development and expansion of the devotions." Andrewes therefore preached from experience, just like John Wesley. He is known to have spent over five hours a day at prayer. In fact, along with his episcopacy, he lived a very monastic life for an Orthodox observer.

Concerning his conception of preaching and its relation with prayer, he sternly tells his audience:

> For what? Is the pouring of the Spirit to end in preaching? And preaching to end in itself, as it doth with us? A circle of preaching, and in effect nothing else, but pour in prophesying enough, and then all is safe? No; there is another yet as needful, nay, more needful to be called on, as the current of our age runs, and that is, "calling on the Name of the Lord."
>
> This, it grieveth me to see how light it is set; nay, to see how busy the devil hath been, to pour contempt on it, to bring it in disgrace with disgraceful terms; to make nothing of Divine service, as if it might be well spared, and *invocaverit* / Acts 2, 21 / here be stricken out.[8]

In his book of private devotion, which, as has already been said, was constantly reprinted and therefore very much used by all sorts of people, there are very many elements familiar to the Orthodox. As was suggested earlier, these elements were not necessarily recognized for what they are by people inclined towards Protestantism. An interesting case is that of A. Whyte, who wrote a book titled *Lancelot Andrewes and his Private Devotions* (Edinburgh, 1896). His view is that the very penitential aspect of the *Preces Privatæ* is due to Andrewes's bad conscience on account of his role in the Essex divorce case. This is a perfect example of someone who has never even heard of the tradition that characterizes the Desert Fathers, let alone reading any literature so familiar to the Orthodox. Instead of a sense of sin, A. Whyte had a purely moralistic attitude. Such was not the case of the Wesley brothers, who did have a sense of sin.

The *Preces Privatæ* of Lancelot Andrewes clearly reveals what kind of spiritual life he led and what kind of theology he preached. The book is full of quotations and adaptations from Holy Scripture, of course, but Holy Scripture as it is used by the liturgical traditions of both East and West (as well as the synagogue). It is also full of liturgical quotations from sources which any Orthodox even vaguely conversant with his or her liturgical life will immediately recognize. The main sources are the Syro-Byzantine *Horologion*, the liturgies of St. Basil the Great, of St. John Chrysostom, and of St. James.

Here is a very obvious example taken from Evening Prayers:

> O gladsome light of the holy glory of the immortal Father,
> heavenly, holy, blest, O Jesu Christ,
> being come to the going down of the sun,
> seeing the evening light,
> we hymn the Father and the Son
> and the Holy Spirit of God.
> Worthy art Thou at all times to be hymned with holy voices,
> Son of God, which givest life:
> therefore the world doth glorify Thee.[9]

And here is an example from Morning Prayers:

Glory be to Thee, O Lord, glory be to Thee.

1. To enter on this and every day, a perfect holy peaceful healthful sinless day: let us ask of the Lord. Grant it, O Lord.

2. An angel of peace, a faithful guide, a guardian of our souls and bodies, tarrying round about me [cf. Ps. 34:7] and suggesting to me always what things are wholesome: let us ask of the Lord.

3. The forgiveness and the remission of all our sins and of all our offences, let us ask of the Lord.

4. What things are good and expedient for our souls, and peace for the world, let us ask of the Lord.

5. To accomplish the residue of our lifetime in repentance and godly fear, in health and peace, let us ask of the Lord.

6. Whatsoever things are true, whatsoever things are honest, whatsoever things are just, whatsoever things are pure, whatsoever things are lovely, whatsoever things are of good report, if there be any virtue and if there be any praise, that we may think on these things and practise these things [cf. Phil. 4, 8], let us ask of the Lord.

7. That the end of our life be Christian, sinless, shameless, and (if it like Thee) painless, and a good defense at the appalling and fearful judgement-seat of Jesus Christ our Lord, let us ask of the Lord.[10]

These are but one or two examples to show how close to Orthodox life Andrewes's spiritual experience was. This spiritual (and theological) experience, as we see, comes through the liturgy. There are many other passages that might have been quoted from the sacramental, eucharistic prayers of St. Basil, St. John Chrysostom, and St. James. Let us simply note in passing that Andrewes, like so many monastic figures in the history of the Church, prayed privately in ecclesial, liturgical terms. In his cell, he was conscious of belonging to the Church. He is never an individual with a vertical type of piety.

The same could be said about the extraordinary hymnography of Charles Wesley. Here, in poetical form, we find an expression of the Church's experience of God. Much of the theology is of the school of Andrewes. It is a trinitarian theology, with a Christology inseparable from pneumatalogy. As for the divine dispensation, Charles Wesley insists many times on the fact that Christ "died for all" and that grace is offered to all.[11] The poetical form, often magnificent, is also something that links Charles Wesley with Orthodox practice: the non-Greek Orthodox should never forget that in the original, most of our Syro-Byzantine hymnography is in rythmic poetry (most of the time untranslatable).

Probably the most interesting and most important aspect of theology which links the Wesley brothers with Orthodoxy through the patristic theology of Lancelot Andrewes's school concerns the nature of salvation offered to all. This is what the Orthodox generally call "deification," an objectionable word for many Western ears: it smacks of pantheism or some sort of quietism (the "already" excludes the "not yet"). In reality, this deification is exactly the same as "participation" (Richard Hooker's favorite theme), and it implies what the Orthodox, in their jargon, call "synergy," which is clearly present in Andrewes's theology. This means that there is nothing automatic about salvation, which is "offered," not imposed on believers whom God has created free.

This notion of deification is based on a verse in the New Testament, found only once but nevertheless present, about the "exceeding great and precious promises: that by these ye might be partakers of the divine nature" (2 Peter 1:4). This quotation is the favorite one of Lancelot Andrewes, and there are adaptations of it in several of Charles Wesley's hymns. St. Peter's bold statement, as we all know, has been adapted in a no less bold form by the patristic tradition. It is the famous sentence ("God became man that man may become God") constantly used in variously adapted forms by Lancelot Andrewes, who calls this "the royal exchange."

As T. S. Eliot put it, Lancelot Andrewes is very difficult to quote on account of the extremely close-knit quality of his sermons: they are "too well built to be readily quotable."[12] Here, however is one paragraph, which epitomises the doctrine of θέωσις and at the same time strongly emphasizes the role of the Holy Spirit in the divine dispensation, another characteristic feature of Andrewes's preaching. The passage, by now, is well known because those of us who work on Andrewes keep quoting it:

> The Holy Ghost is the Alpha and Omega of all our solemnities. In His coming down, all the feasts begin; at His annunciation, when He descended on the Blessed Virgin, whereby the Son of God did take our nature, the nature of man. And in the Holy Ghost's coming they end, even in His descending this day upon the sons of men, whereby they actually become "partakers" θείας κοινωνοὶ φύσεως, "of His nature, the nature of God" (2 Pet. 1:4). Of which His last and great coming, in this text

(John 14:15–16) is the promise, and at this time the performance; that as promise and performance, so the text and time agree.[13]

More allusive, but no less rich, are the references to the same participation in God to be found in Charles Wesley's hymns. Here are one or two examples:

Let earth and heaven combine,
    Angels and men agree,
To praise in song divine
    The incarnate deity,
Our God contracted to a span[14]
Incomprehensibly made man.

He deigns in flesh to appear,
    Widest extremes to join;
To bring our vileness near,
    And make us all divine:
And we the life of God shall know,
For God is manifest below.

Made perfect first in love,
    And sanctified by grace,
We shall from earth remove,
    And see his glorious face:
Then shall his love be fully showed,
And man shall then be lost in God.[15]

Commenting on this hymn, Canon A. M. Allchin emphasizes the fact that "the doctrine being stated is not something abstract; it is constantly turning into worship"; the relation between theology and liturgy is thus clearly stated.[16]

We also find an emphasis on the role of the Holy Spirit as the agent of participation in God. Here is one verse of a well-known hymn:

Come Holy Ghost, all-quickening fire,
    Come, and in me delight to rest;
Drawn by the lure of strong desire,
    O come and consecrate my breast;
The temple of my should prepare,
And fix the sacred presence there.[17]

And here are one or two lines directly concerned with the theme of deification:

Thy kingdom come to every heart,
And all thou hast, and all thou art.[18]

For us he uses all his powers,
And all he has, or is, is ours.[19]

Since the Son hath made me free,
Let me taste my liberty;

Heavenly Adam, Life divine,
Change my nature into thine.[20]

Here we have a statement of freedom and what seems to me a clear reference to 2 Peter 1:4.

We know that the pope, His Holiness John Paul II, has written a Pastoral Letter titled *Orientale Lumen* in which he expounds and praises the Eastern doctrine of the deification of man. The Jesuits asked me to write a review of this text. I expressed all my admiration for the doctrine and the pope's text. Only I raised the question: "why should this doctrine be regarded as Eastern, whereas it is universally scriptural, patristic, and Christian?" And I quoted such men as Lancelot Andrewes and the Wesley brothers, and recalled that, after all, the first to use the famous adage "God became man that man may become God" was St. Irenæus, who certainly was a Greek but was also bishop of Lyon, which is not exactly the East. It is also used by St. Augustine, who was anything but an Easterner, and St. Augustine was quoted by no less a Westerner than St. Thomas Aquinas. It is therefore about time that we all receive this doctrine as universally Christian. We may then recognize that Lancelot Andrewes is truly a bridge, and that in more senses than one.

Endnotes

[1]*For Lancelot Andrewes* (London: Faber and Gwyer, 1928), 17.

[2]Ibid., 14.

[3]Ibid., 18.

[4]*The Preces Privatae of Lancelot Andrewes, Bishop of Winchester*, translated with an introduction and notes by F. E. Brightman (London: Methuen, 1903).

[5]Ibid., li.

[6]William Chillingworth, *The Religion of the Protestants: A Safe Way to Salvation* (1638), quoted in *Anglicanism: The Thought and Practice of the Church of England Illustrated from the Religious Literature of the Seventeenth Century*, compiled and edited by the late Paul Elmer More and Frank Leslie Cross (London: SPCK, 1935; reprinted 1962).

[7]V. Lossky, "Tradition and Traditions," in *The Meaning of Icons*, revised English edition (Crestwood, NY: St. Vladimir's Seminary Press, 1982).

[8]Lancelot Andrewes, *Works*, in *Library of Anglo-Catholic Theology* (LACT), 11 vols. (Oxford: Parker, 1841–1854), vol. 4, Whitsun 11:319.

[9]Brightman, 104.

[10]Ibid., 24–25.

[11]*A Rapture of Praise: Hymns of John and Charles Wesley*, selected, arranged, and introduced by H. A. Hodges and A. M. Allchin (London: Hodder and Stoughton, 1966), 79, 84, 83, among others.

[12]Eliot, 14.

[13]Andrewes, vol. 3, Whitsun 3:145–146.

[14]This image is clearly inspired from one of Lancelot Andrewes's Nativity sermons.

[15]*A Rapture of Praise*, 58–59.

[16]A. M. Allchin, *Participation in God: A Forgotten Strand in Anglican Tradition* (London: Darton, Longman and Todd, 1988), 27.

[17]*A Rapture of Praise*, 74–75.

[18]Ibid., 152.

[19]Ibid., 153.

[20]Ibid., 121.

PART 3

Wesleyan Scriptural Understanding and Practice

10

Scripture and Tradition in the Wesleyan Tradition

Ted A. Campbell

Précise: A notion of "tradition" as embracing the continuity of divine work in history became a prominent conception for American Methodists in the later twentieth century when, under the influence of the ecumenical movement, American Methodists began to develop a sense of their own connection to the Christian "tradition." This rediscovered notion of tradition had roots in John Wesley's view of ancient Christianity. It was made formal in the 1972 statement "Our Theological Task," which has been very widely received, and it has been complemented by Methodist use of the Nicene-Constantinopolitan Creed, liturgical revision reflecting the practices of the ancient Christian community, restoration of the permanent diaconate, and a growing sense of Methodism as a distinct Christian "tradition."

Context: *Tristesse Œcuménique*

I approach this subject primarily as a student of Methodist life and thought, but also as a participant (since 1992) in the Faith and Order Commission of the National Council of the Churches of Christ in the United States, where Methodists and Orthodox and others have engaged in significant dialogue. I also remember fondly my days in Oxford when then Archimandrite (now Bishop) Kallistos Ware was my tutor in patristic studies, and he introduced me to some aspects of Orthodox life from his own experience. In writing an earlier book titled *Christian Confessions* (1996), I attempted to give a concise account of historic Orthodox teachings in an ecumenical framework, and in this, I also consulted with Orthodox scholars.

One of the convictions that grows from my own ecumenical experience is that it is extremely important in ecumenical discussions to be aware of and even to experience the depth of our separation from each other. One of my mentors, Albert Outler, used the expression *la tristesse œcuménique* to describe "the ecumenical sadness that Christians feel who see their eager will to unity frustrated."[1] Methodists have contributed to the reality of Christian separation, and in fact, our own tradition has reflected at many points the kind of ecumenical misrepresentations that have characterized generations of Christians prior to the advent of the ecumenical movement in the twentieth century. I am afraid that John Wesley himself was no exception in this regard. The following words are painful to repeat, but they do reflect, I am afraid, what many Western Christians believed about Eastern Christians in the eighteenth century. In his sermon "The General Spread of the Gospel" (1783), John Wesley wrote,

> 5. And little, if at all, better than the Turks [i.e., Muslims in the Ottoman Empire] are the Christians in the Turkish dominions, even the best of them, those that live in the [Peloponnesus], or are scattered up and down in Asia. The more numerous bodies of Georgian [and Transcaucasian] Christians are a proverb of reproach to the Turks themselves, not only for their deplorable ignorance, but for their total, stupid, barbarous irreligion.
>
> 6. From the most authentic accounts we can obtain of the southern Christians, those in Abyssinia, and of the northern Churches, under the jurisdiction of the Patriarch of Moscow, we have reason to fear that they are much in the same condition, both with regard to knowledge and religion, as those in Turkey. Or if those in Abyssinia [here Wesley appears to have reference to all of the Oriental Orthodox churches of Africa] are more civilized and have a larger share of knowledge, yet they do not appear to have any more religion than either the Mahometans or pagans.[2]

A couple of things must be said about this. First, many Orthodox would acknowledge the problems with Orthodoxy in the period of Ottoman domination, the period that also involved the "Western captivity" of the Eastern churches. Secondly, it is fair to recognize John Wesley's homiletical ploy in this account. Wesley's ploy is that of the prophet Amos; namely, to condemn the sins of all the nations around one's own, and then to focus on the sins of one's own nation. So a few paragraphs later, Wesley considers the supposed Christians of England and France—both Protestant and Catholic—and he concludes, ". . . do they 'walk as Christ also walked'? Nay, they are as far from it as hell is from heaven."[3]

My point here is simply that we cannot take much for granted in Orthodox-Methodist dialogue. Although some dialogues have been carried on between Orthodox and Western Christian leaders since the 1920s, we have to remain extraordinarily cautious, especially since we know that there have been historic misrepresentations of each other's traditions. The ultimate reason for our *tristesse œcuménique* is that while professing a common faith in Christ, we do not in fact share communion (*koinonia*), certainly not in the formal sense of mutual and visible eucharistic hospitality, and seldom even in the more informal sense of *koinonia* as "fellowship" (*sobornost*?) with each other. We are visibly divided, and our conversations have to take this condition of visible division as their underlying context. The fact that there are now at least a hundred Methodist congregations within the historic bounds of the patriarchate of Moscow, moreover, brings a certain urgency to our discussions.

The Problem: Scripture and Tradition in Wesleyan Life

I turn now to the specific issue of scripture and tradition in Wesleyan life. The broad context for this is that Methodists are the heirs of a distinctively Western mode of viewing history that has prevailed since the time of the Renaissance, according to which ancient history (Greek and Roman antiquity) was valued highly, the "Middle Ages" were devalued, and European modernity was valued positively. Indeed, the very terms Renaissance and Reformation imply this particular understanding of history. Applied to the narrative of Christian community, this understanding of history valued the early Christian church positively, it deprecated the church in the "dark ages," and again valued positively the church as it was renewed or "reformed" in European modernity.

Critical in this interpretation of history was a deprecation of the notion of "tradition." This can be seen very clearly in the first Homily of the Church of England, which urges Christians to

> . . . search for the well of life in the books of the New and Old Testament, and not run to the stinking puddles of men's traditions, devised by men's imagination, for our justification and salvation.[4]

The term tradition obviously carried pejorative connotations at the time of the Reformation, even among Anglicans, who have often distinguished themselves as being more open to tradition than other churches of the Reformation era. On this view, tradition was set against scripture, with the presupposition that the scriptures, rightly understood by careful study of their original languages, could norm the life of the church. The scriptures themselves were understood to be the best interpreters of scripture, not the subsequent traditions of the churches.[5]

A. *Scripture and Tradition in Methodist Doctrinal Standards*

Formal Methodist doctrine reflects this understanding of the authority of scripture. The Articles of Religion and Confession of Faith of the United Methodist Church follow classic Protestant affirmations about scripture in affirming that the scriptures alone teach what is necessary for salvation. In the words of the fifth Article of Religion,

> The Holy Scripture containeth all things necessary to salvation; so that whatsoever is not read therein, nor may be proved thereby, is not to be required of any man that it should be believed as an article of faith, or be thought requisite or necessary to salvation.[6]

In Protestant parlance, this teaching is referred to as the doctrine of the "sufficiency" of the scriptures. The doctrine usually holds that the scriptures contain everything we need to know for the reform of the church, as well as for human salvation. An implication of this doctrine is that subsequent Christian traditions, including the teachings of the Ecumenical Councils, are not considered "sufficient" for our knowledge of salvation and for the reform of the church. This implication is drawn explicitly in the original Anglican Articles of Religion, which state that "General Councils may err and have erred" in their teachings about salvation, as well as other matters. However, it may be important to note that the Methodist recension of the Articles omits this particular Article, as Episcopal (USA) recensions would do later (in 1801).

In addition to the characteristic Reformation teaching about the sufficiency of the scriptures, Methodist teachings also affirmed the unity of the scriptures and the clarity of the scriptures—the notion that although there may be obscure passages of scripture, the general meaning of the Bible is clear enough, especially when studied with reference to the original languages in which it was written, that an unprejudiced reader can know what is necessary for salvation and for the reform of the church. Although one can argue that the related ideas of the infallibility or inerrancy of the scriptures (affirmed by Catholics as well as Protestants in the Reformation age) are presupposed by Methodist teachings, they are not explicitly affirmed by American Methodist doctrinal standards, as they are by the doctrinal standards of other Protestant traditions.[7] These doctrinal standards, in general, do not allow a significant place for tradition as an authority for Christian faith and life.

B. *Scripture and Tradition in John Wesley's Thought*

In terms of our formal doctrinal standards, then, Methodists affirm teaching about the authority of the scriptures reflecting for the most part the inheritance of the Reformation with its pejorative understanding of tradition. We may, however, consider some ways in which John Wesley's own thought may add some important nuances to this. Not every one of John Wesley's opinions has the status of doctrine for Methodists (we can thank divine providence for this), but John Wesley's thought does have a kind of informal canonical status for Methodists, and certain of his *Sermons on Several Occasions* and *Explanatory Notes upon the New Testament* hold a degree of formal doctrinal authority in British as well as American Methodist churches.

John Wesley was the heir of a particular tradition of Anglican patristic study that had developed in the late 1500s and the 1600s in response to Puritans.[8] This Anglican tradition—we refer to it as "Caroline" Anglicanism—saw the Church of England as the true heir of the "primitive" church—that is, the church of the earliest centuries, through at least the fourth century. Caroline Anglicans argued that the episcopal polity of the Church of England replicated the polity of the early church, that the liturgy of the Church of England faithfully reflected the liturgy of the primitive church, and that the doctrines of the Church of England reflected the doctrinal inheritance of the early fathers and the earliest Ecumenical Councils, with the further refinement of doctrines about human nature and salvation as clarified in the Reformation. The so-called Apostolic Fathers played a particularly crucial role for Anglicans and their Gallican counterparts in France: the corpus of the Apostolic Fathers had only recently been identified as such by Gallican and Anglican scholars, who saw in these second-century authors an ecclesiastical polity that was episcopal and yet not papal, and a form of Christian doctrine that did not legitimate the Augustinian leanings of their Puritan or Huguenot interlocutors.

John Wesley had studied early Christian literature, and he had read a great deal of the Anglican literature that valued their connection with the early church. Like many Anglicans before him, John Wesley believed that the first three Christian centuries were an exemplary period of particular holiness.

In his own edition of the Apostolic Fathers, Wesley repeated the opinion of Archbishop William Wake, that the Apostolic Fathers were the best interpreters of the New Testament, since they lived close to the time of the New Testament authors and were in a stronger position to understand their meaning.[9] One can see this principle in practice in Wesley's argument that because fasting was practiced on Wednesdays and Fridays in the early church (here following Tertullian, *De Ieiunio*), Christians should observe the Wednesday and Friday half-day fasts as a faithful interpretation of Jesus's teaching about fasting.[10] Scott Jones's work *John Wesley's Conception and Use of Scripture* points out Wesley's interpretation of scripture in this way, as has my own study *John Wesley and Christian Antiquity*;[11] the relevance for our discussion is that in this particular way of interpreting scripture, John Wesley seems to depart from the Reformation understanding of scripture as its own best interpreter, and Wesley seems to allow that something we would identify as Christian tradition can in fact serve as a normative means of interpreting the meaning of the Bible.

Nevertheless, Wesley's views of Christian antiquity interpreting the Christian scriptures did not become part of the doctrinal inheritance of Methodist life, at least in the United States. Moreover, as I think Professor Heitzenrater's essay will also point out, Wesley does not seem to have held a notion of tradition as embracing the continuity of God's work in history.[12] In this sense, we must acknowledge that Wesley's vision of Christian history, far from the Orthodox understanding, saw the Christian story as significantly interrupted by the Middle Ages, however he may have modified the precise boundaries of the Middle Ages in deference to his positive understanding of Christian antiquity.

C. *Scripture and Tradition in Subsequent Methodist Life*

To my knowledge, subsequent Methodist life from the time of John Wesley through the beginning of the twentieth century continued to devalue tradition. Methodist works of systematic theology, many of them approved for study by the General Conferences, discussed the authority of scripture without reference to subsequent Christian tradition.[13] The rise of theological liberalism, prominent in Methodist life from the late nineteenth century, contributed to an even greater suspicion of Christian history in the Middle Ages and beyond. I think it is fair to say that, with the exception of the regular recitation of the Apostles' Creed, Methodist life in the nineteenth century proceeded generally without reference to Christian history or tradition past the New Testament age, except when Methodists needed to differentiate themselves from Catholics. A possible exception to this might be seen in the architecture of urban Methodist churches in the late nineteenth century and early twentieth century, where the Gothic style so prominent in Victorian culture prevailed.[14] My rather uneducated guess on this, though, would be that this reflected a popular trend in church architecture rather than a positive valuing of the Middle Ages, as it had been for Victorian Anglicans.

Methodist Appropriation of Tradition in the Twentieth Century

It has only been in the last half of the twentieth century that Methodists have come to value tradition in a more positive way. This is undoubtedly due to Methodist exposure to other Christian traditions as a result of the ecumenical movement.

Presupposing the spiritual unity of Christians, the twentieth-century ecumenical movement sought to address the "visible disunity" of the churches, at first in response to concerns about the missionary outreach of the churches. At first, an overwhelmingly Protestant movement, the ecumenical movement was enriched by the participation of Orthodox since the 1920s and the participation of Roman Catholics from the 1960s.

Issues of scripture and tradition were addressed very directly by the plenary gathering of the Faith and Order Commission of the World Council of Churches, which met in Montreal in 1963, at the same time as the Second Vatican Council, which had been under way since 1962. In its attempt to deal with the thorny issues surrounding the authorities of scripture and tradition in Protestant and Orthodox churches, the Montreal plenary distinguished between Tradition (with an uppercase "T") as "the Gospel itself," and traditions (with the lowercase "t") as denoting denominational (or confessional) and cultural expressions of the Christian faith.[15] The identification of Tradition in the prior sense fit nicely with contemporary New Testament research that had focused on oral traditions underlying and preceding the Christian scriptures. The Montreal statement, in general, allowed Protestants a new and positive understanding of tradition.

Methodist theologian Albert C. Outler was a leading participant in the Montreal conference. He had just been elected president of the American Society of Church History at the time of the Montreal Faith and Order conference in 1963, and was at that time participating as a Protestant observer in the Second Vatican Council. As a student of Robert L. Calhoun at Yale, Outler had imbibed a rich and newly discovered Protestant appropriation of the history of Christian doctrine. Moreover, and quite relevant for our present inquiry, Outler had worked in the 1950s with Father Georges Florovsky, then Dean of St. Vladimir's Seminary in New York, to set the agenda for the discussion of "Scripture, Tradition and Traditions" that occurred in Montreal. The Montreal language about "Scripture, Tradition and Traditions" was incorporated into the Second Vatican Council's statement on Holy Scripture, *Dei Verbum*. In a presidential address to the American Catholic Historical Association in 1972, Outler noted how the idea of tradition had come to prominence among ecumenically oriented Protestants in the previous decade.[16]

In the midst of all of these discussions about scripture and tradition with Orthodox, Catholic, and Protestant leaders in the 1960s, Outler was asked to give the sermon at the Uniting Conference of the United Methodist Church in 1968, and at that Conference was asked to chair a Theological Study Commission to reconcile the inherited doctrinal statements of the Methodist Church (USA) and the Evangelical United Brethren Church. Under Outler's leadership, the Commission decided to keep the two earlier denominational statements but to add to them a contemporary reinterpretation of doctrine for United Methodists. The 1972 General Conference approved this interpretative statement, though not with the same level of doctrinal authority as the historic statements. (I would note that this was the same year as Outler's presidential address to the American Catholic Historical Association.) The 1972 doctrinal interpretation, titled "Our Theological Task," included the first formulation of what was subsequently called the Wesleyan Quadrilateral. This doctrinal statement gave United

Methodists their first formal affirmation of tradition as a source and norm of doctrinal authority, and throughout the document, one can see the marks of Outler's involvement with Faith and Order discussions of scripture and tradition.

It is particularly important to note the remarkable acceptance of this 1972 document within the church. Within a few years, the criteria of scripture, tradition, experience, and reason were referred to as the Wesleyan Quadrilateral, with the accompanying "myth" that they were formulated as such by John Wesley himself.[17] The statement was revised by General Conference action in 1988, making clearer the priority of scripture within the quadrilateral, with a revision (see the following) of its statement on the authority of tradition. It is worth noting the prominent place that the statement of the Wesleyan Quadrilateral has occupied in United Methodist life. Doctrinal statements often pass with little recognition. The fact that this statement has been so frequently alluded to and discussed in United Methodist circles means that it has enjoyed a strong degree of what in ecumenical circles we call "reception"; that is, the actual use of it as a doctrinal formulation in the church, with the degree of consensus that is reflected in that use. Even the myth of Wesleyan authorship seems to demonstrate the importance that United Methodists have attached to the quadrilateral.

The 1972 statement about tradition in "Our Theological Task" is brief and makes explicit reference to "contemporary Faith and Order discussions of 'Tradition and Traditions.'" It identifies three senses of tradition: tradition as process, tradition as reflecting the diversity (and division) of the churches, and then a "transcendent" sense:

> In a third sense, however, "the Christian tradition" may be spoken of transcendentally: as the history of that environment of grace in and by which all Christians live, which is the continuance through time and space of God's self-giving love in Jesus Christ. It is in this transcendent sense of *tradition* that Christians, who have been isolated from one another by various barriers of schism, race and rivalries, may recognize one another as Christians together.[18]

This "transcendent" sense of tradition appears to answer to what the Montreal Faith and Order Conference called Tradition, with a capital "T", although the Montreal statement was bolder, referring to tradition in this sense as "the Gospel itself." The 1988 revision of the United Methodist statement about Tradition in "Our Theological Task" is expanded but deletes the earlier references to the Faith and Order discussions of "Tradition and Traditions" and focuses on tradition as "[t]he story of the church." It does refer to tradition as "the history of that environment of grace in and by which all Christians live, God's self-giving love in Jesus Christ" but omits the phrase "the continuance through time and space *of* [this author's italics] God's self-giving love in Jesus Christ."[19] I do not know how deliberate this alteration was, but it seems to weaken the sense of tradition as the continuity of divine grace through history.

The preface to the United Methodist doctrinal standards in the 1988 *Book of Discipline* refers to "the apostolic witness to Jesus Christ as Savior and Lord, which is the source and measure of all valid Christian teaching."[20] Following this, the statement asserts that

> The determination of the canon of Christian Scripture and the adoption of ecumenical creeds such as the formulations of Nicaea and Chalcedon were of central importance to this consensual process. Such creeds helped preserve the integrity of the church's witness, set boundaries for acceptable Christian doctrine, and proclaimed the basic elements of the enduring Christian message. These statements of faith, along with the Apostles' Creed, contain the most prominent features of our ecumenical heritage.[21]

I hope that this is true—although if it is, of course, it would seem to commit United Methodists to understanding the Blessed Virgin as *Theotokos* (as per the Chalcedonian Definition), and that will come as news to many of our United Methodist comrades! My concern, though, is that having made what I consider to be a fine affirmation of Christian Traditionin the "transcendent" sense, this understanding of tradition is not as clearly enunciated in the section on tradition in "our Theological Task," where tradition seems largely identified with that which we value in the history of the Christian community.

Other aspects of our church life show how United Methodists in the same period became conscious of our connection to the broader history of the Christian community. The *Hymnal* of 1964 was the first American Methodist hymnal to include the Nicene-Constantinopolitan Creed. The process of liturgical renewal among Methodists led to a series of reforms in the 1940s and 1960s that brought Methodists more into line with Anglican and Protestant liturgical traditions. Further development of liturgical renewal in the 1970s and beyond led Methodists, along with Roman Catholics and others, to adopt liturgical rites grounded in the ancient liturgies of the Christian tradition, including the restoration of the *epiclesis* in the *anaphora*, as Karen Westerfield-Tucker discusses in chapter 18 of this volume. In the last decade (the 1990s), United Methodists moved to restore the permanent diaconate and approved ecumenical statements affirming the threefold ordained ministry of deacons, priests, and bishops.[22] A host of historical works in the 1980s and beyond, including my own doctoral dissertation, later published as *John Wesley and Christian Antiquity* (1991), examined Methodism's connection to the ancient and medieval church, Eastern and Western.[23]

Perhaps one of the most important signs of Methodism's rediscovery of the meaning of Christian tradition was the growing sense that Methodism itself was a discrete Christian tradition, here answering to the sense of traditions defined at Montreal. Evidence of this would be the host of books and articles bearing the phrase "... in the Wesleyan Tradition" that appeared in the 1980s and 1990s. British Methodist ecumenist Geoffrey Wainwright argued in 1982 that Methodists through the world should develop an understanding of the Methodist movement as a religious movement existing through a number of particular ecclesial communities. His ecumenical vision was grounded in the observation that John Wesley did not intend the formation of an independent "church," and Methodism's "ecumenical vocation" could be grounded in its original sense of calling as a religious movement or "society," rather than claiming in any sense the fullness of "church."[24]

Conclusion

This chapter suggests that a notion of tradition as embracing the continuity of divine work in history became a prominent conception for American Methodists in the later twentieth century when, under the influence of the ecumenical movement, American Methodists began to develop a sense of their own connection to the Christian tradition. This rediscovered notion of tradition had roots in John Wesley's view of ancient Christianity. It was made formal in the 1972 statement "Our Theological Task," which has been very widely received, and it has been complemented by Methodist use of the Nicene-Constantinopolitan Creed, liturgical revision reflecting the practices of the ancient Christian community, restoration of the permanent diaconate, and a growing sense of Methodism as a distinct Christian tradition.

If we ask how Methodists and Orthodox might better work through such dialogue for mutual understanding, I would point to the proposals and questions laid out by Methodist Outler and Orthodox Florovsky in the 1950s, and I would call special attention to the fourth (last) question they consider:

> The church had a common history for many centuries and this common history was the common background of all existing denominations, The real question, however, is how and why did the ways of development fragment? When and why did diversity become divisive?
>
> a. Is there a describably common tradition in all existing communities which call and profess themselves Christian?
>
> b. When and how do "additions to" or "deviations from" the primitive or initial tradition alter the character and import of faith and order?
>
> c. Can we account for the evolution and variety of teaching, polity, and liturgy in a non-polemical and truly ecumenical manner?
>
> d. How far can we recognize the essential complex of *kerygma* and *paradosis* in other Christian communities than our own?[25]

Paradosis, awkwardly rendered into English as "traditioning," is a particularly difficult matter for Protestants and for Americans. It is difficult for Protestants because the Reformation represents an intentional discontinuity within the history of the Christian community. It is difficult for Americans because to be an American is, almost by definition, to be cut off from one's deeper historical and cultural roots. And yet, there is a deep yearning, prominent in "postmodern" culture, to understand oneself and one's own community as being tied to deeper roots.

I wonder if Outler and Florovsky had 1 Corinthians 15:3–4 in mind. It is a passage in which St. Paul gives the *kerygma* as he had received it, utilizing *paradothenai*, the verb associated with "traditioning." "For I handed on to you as of first importance what I in turn had received," Paul wrote, and the message he had received and handed on was as follows:

> that Christ died for our sins
> in accordance with the scriptures,
> and that he was buried

and that he was raised on the third day
in accordance with the scriptures. (1 Cor. 15:3b–4)

These words lie at the basis of the historic Christian creeds. They express the *kerygma* known to generations of Methodists in the words of the so-called Apostles Creed, known to centuries of Orthodox Christians in the words of the Nicene-Constantinopolitan Creed. But how, I wonder, shall we, today, answer Outler's and Florovsky's question about "How far [we] can recognize the essential complex of *kerygma* and *paradosis* in each other's communities?"

The term tradition still bears negative connotations in Protestant communities; it is often used in a manner that implies "insignificant." But if I understand anything about how Orthodox Christians value tradition, it is that for the Orthodox, tradition has above all to do with the gospel—it has to do with Christ. We need to talk about this, about the gospel. If there is any consolation for our own experience of *tristesse œcuménique*, it is surely in the gospel of Jesus Christ. "To [God] be glory in the church and in Christ Jesus to all generations, forever and ever. Amen" (Eph. 3:21).

Endnotes

[1]Albert C. Outler, "Our Common History as Christians," in Paul Minear, ed., *The Nature of the Unity We Seek* (St. Louis, MO: Bethany Press, 1958), 81, here referring to comments by Pierre Maury.

[2]John Wesley, "The General Spread of the Gospel" (1783), 5–6, in Albert C. Outler, ed., *Sermons* (Bicentennial Edition of the Works of John Wesley), 4 vols. (Nashville: Abingdon, 1984–1987), 2:487.

[3]Ibid., 7, in Outler, ed., *Sermons*, 2:488.

[4]Homily 1, in John Leith, ed., *Creeds of the Churches*, third edition, revised (Atlanta: John Knox, 1983), 232.

[5]On Protestant understandings of scripture in general, cf. Ted A. Campbell, *Christian Confessions* (Louisville, KY: Westminster John Knox, 1996), 133–144. Some important *loci* for Protestant understandings of scripture are as follows: the Augsburg Confession, preface (in Leith, 65), cf. conclusion of the section of initial articles, the preface to the section on disputed matters, and the conclusion to the Confession (in Leith, 78–79, 106); the Formula of Concord, Epitome, introduction 1, in Theodore G. Tappert, tr. and ed., *The Book of Concord: The Confessions of the Evangelical Lutheran Church* (Philadelphia: Fortress, 1959), 464; Philip Schaff, ed., *The Creeds of Christendom: With a History and Critical Notes*, 3 vols. (New York: Harper and Row, 1931; reprint edition, Grand Rapids, MI: Baker, 1993), 3:93–94; the Second Helvetic Confession 1, in Leith, 132–34, Schaff 3:237–38, 831–33; the Westminster Confession 1, in Leith, 193–96, Schaff 3:600–6; the Anglican Articles of Religion 6–7, in Leith, 267–69, Schaff 3:489–492; the Anglican Homilies "A Fruitful Exhortation to the Reading and Knowledge of Holy Scripture" and "The Second Part of the Sermon on the Knowledge of Holy Scripture," in Leith, 231–39.

[6]United Methodist Church Articles of Religion no. 5, here quoted from Ted A. Campbell, *Methodist Doctrine* (Nashville: Abingdon, 1999), 102.

[7]Cf. Richard A. Muller, *Post-Reformation Reformed Dogmatics*, vol. 2, *Holy Scripture: The Cognitive Foundation of Theology* (Grand Rapids, MI: Baker, 1993), 51–86 on the issues of inerrancy and infallibility at the time of the Reformation.

[8]Ted A. Campbell, *John Wesley and Christian Antiquity: A Study of Religious Vision and Cultural Change* (Nashville: Kingswood/Abingdon, 1991), 11–20.

[9]Preface to the Apostolic Fathers in John Wesley, ed., *A Christian Library: Consisting of Extracts from and Abridgements of the Choicest Pieces of Practical Divinity Which Have Been Published in the English Language*, 50 vols. (Bristol: Felix Farley, 1749–1755), 1:i.

[10]Cf. John Wesley, *Sermons* 27:I:6, in Outler, ed., 1:596–597. One has to admit at this point that this view of fasting was grounded not in Wesley's study of the Apostolic Fathers, but in his reading of such later

literature as Tertullian. Although the *Didache* has reference to the Wednesday and Friday fasts, it was not known until the very late nineteenth century. Wesley's convictions about the normative nature of the fasts of the early church can be seen in some of the material that Wesley himself edited: [Claude Fleury] *Manners of the Ancient Christians*, ed. Wesley, 5:1 (1798 edition, p. 14); Anthony Horneck, "Letter to a Person of Quality," ed. Wesley (*Christian Library*, first edition, 29:134); William Cave, *Primitive Christianity*, ed. Wesley, I:VII:4 (*Christian Library*, first edition, 31:187); [Mosheim], *Concise Ecclesiastical History*, ed. Wesley, I:II:IV:10 (1781 edition, 1:72). Mosheim regarded the Wednesday and Friday fasts as being of first-century, if not apostolic, origin.

[11]Scott J. Jones, *John Wesley's Conception and Use of Scripture* (Nashville: Kingswood/Abingdon, 1996), 169–75; Campbell, *John Wesley and Christian Antiquity*, 108–113.

[12]Cf. my article "The Interpretative Role of Tradition," in Stephen Gunter, Ted A. Campbell, Scott J. Jones, Rebekah Miles, and Randy Maddox, *Wesley and the Quadrilateral: Renewing the Conversation* (Nashville: Abingdon, 1997); Ted A. Campbell, "The 'Wesleyan Quadrilateral': The Story of a Modern Methodist Myth," in *Methodist History* 29:2 (January 1991): 87–95; also published in Thomas A. Langford, ed., *Doctrine and Theology in the United Methodist Church* (Nashville: Kingdwood/Abingdon, 1991), 154–161; "Christian Tradition, John Wesley, and Evangelicalism," *Anglican Theological Review* 74:1 (Winter 1992): 54–67.

[13]Richard Watson's *Theological Institutes*, which served as a first theological textbook for generations of American as well as British Methodist preachers gives evidences of the truth and authority of the scriptures, then defends Methodist teachings grounded in scripture with no reference to the authority of subsequent Christian tradition. Richard Watson, *Theological Institutes: Or, a View of the Evidences, Doctrines, Morals and Institutions of Christianity*, 2 vols. (New York: Carlton and Phillips, 1854), 1:70–262, on the evidences of the truth and authority of scripture.

[14]Or, as an interesting extension, the Italian Renaissance church architecture at Lovely Lane Methodist Church in Baltimore, as designed by architect Stanford White and built for the 1884 Methodist centennial.

[15]World Council of Churches, Faith and Order Commission, "Scripture, Tradition, and Traditions," paragraphs 46–47, in Hans-Georg Link, ed., *Apostolic Faith Today: A Handbook for Study* (Faith and Order Paper No. 124; Geneva: World Council of Churches, 1985), 82.

[16]Albert C. Outler, "History as an Ecumenical Resource: The Protestant Discovery of 'Tradition,' 1952–1963," presidential address, American Catholic Historical Association, 28 December 1972, in *Catholic Historical Review* 59:1 (1973): 1–15.

[17]The subject of my article "The 'Wesleyan Quadrilateral': The Story of a Modern Methodist Myth" (cited above).

[18]*The Book of Discipline of the United Methodist Church* (Nashville: United Methodist Publishing House, 1972), 70, 76–77.

[19]*The Book of Discipline of the United Methodist Church* (Nashville: United Methodist Publishing House, 2002), 104, 80.

[20]*Book of Discipline* (1988), 101, 41–42.

[21]Ibid., 101, 42.

[22]"The COCU Consensus," in Joseph A. Burgess and Jeffrey Gros, F.S.C., eds., *Growing Consensus: Church Dialogues in the United States, 1962–1991* (Ecumenical Documents V; New York: Paulist, 1995), 42. *Baptism, Eucharist and Ministry* (Geneva: World Council of Churches; 1982 printing), 4.

[23]On this matter, cf. my article "Back to the Future: The Wesleyan Quest for Ancient Roots: The 1980s," *Wesleyan Theological Journal* 32:1 (Spring 1997): 5–16.

[24]Geoffrey Wainwright, "Ecclesial Location and Ecumenical Vocation," in M. Douglas Meeks, ed., *The Future of the Methodist Theological Traditions* (Nashville: Abingdon, 1985), 93ff.

[25]Outler's note: Cf. *Faith and Order Commission Paper 17*, 31–33; the document is cited in the Outler article "History as an Ecumenical Resource" (see above), 7.

11

Charles Wesley's Lyrical Commentary on the Holy Scriptures

S T Kimbrough, Jr.

Introduction

In 1762, Charles Wesley published *Short Hymns on Select Passages of the Holy Scriptures.*[1] Volume 1 included 1,160 poems on the Old Testament and volume 2 contained 318 poems on the Old Testament and 871 poems on the New Testament for a total of 2,349. *Short Hymns* appeared only in one additional, but abbreviated, posthumous (Wesley died in 1788) edition: volume 1 in 1794 and volume 2 in 1796. The edition included 203 fewer poems, for a total of 2,145. Charles continued to rework some of the poetry in the 1762 edition, as a comparison with unpublished manuscripts from the period following the publication of *Short Hymns* indicates. For example, in volume 2 the poem on John 19:26–27 ("Behold thy son: behold thy mother") appears in a later manuscript (MS John) in identical form, with the exception that the word "mankind" in line seven has been changed to "thy saints."

We would thine aged followers give
    The honour to a parent due,
We would the young with love receive,
    Purer than nature ever knew.
Saviour, bestow th'intend'ring grace,
    Us in a new relation join,
So shall we all *mankind*[2] embrace,
    And love them with a love like thine.
        (SH 2:232, Hymn 383; see MS John, 412)

Wesley began MS John on December 3, 1763, and completed it on April 30, 1764.

Short Hymns is one of the largest lyrical commentaries on the Holy Scriptures in the English language. In most instances, his brother John edited his poetry before publication; however, Charles published the 1762 work, as he had *Hymns and Sacred Poems* (1749), independently of John. Thus, Charles expressed himself without the theological, linguistic, or literary editing of his brother and in *Short Hymns* shaped his thoughts on gradual sanctification, perfection, and mysticism which John might have altered had he edited the work. The 1762 volumes contain valuable biblical, theological, social, ecclesiastical, and poetical insight for the study of Holy Scripture, English and church history, literature, and theology.

Short Hymns is a collage of biblical allusions. Wesley begins with Genesis and concludes with the book of Revelation, writing over 2,000 poems which encompass every book of the Bible. He proceeds chronologically through the scriptures, except in poems on the Gospel of Luke in which he fills out the seven last words of Jesus from the cross with passages from the Gospels of Matthew and John.[3] Unlike many of his lengthy poetical expositions of biblical passages[4] in other publications, the poems in *Short Hymns* are usually brief, consisting of one or two stanzas. Poems of five or six stanzas do occur, but they are not the norm. Therefore, the focus is generally on a central idea, word, or phrase of a passage. Wesley preceded each poem with a scriptural quotation and reference. To save space, he often abbreviated a lengthy verse and added "etc." at the point of interruption. At times, he wrote more than one poem on the same biblical passage. In such instances, he quoted the biblical verses only before the first poem in the series.

The title contains the word "hymns" and suggests that all of the 2,349[5] poetical entries in the two volumes are hymns. That is far from the case. More properly they should be called "sacred poems," as Wesley had done in earlier works. Although some of the poems did make their way into hymn books, one may not consider the 1762 work as a two-volume hymn book. Some of those which have appeared in hymn books over the years include:

"Captain of Israel's host and guide," 1:42, Hymn 133
"O thou who camest from above," 1:57, Hymn 183
"A charge to keep I have," 1:58, Hymn 188
"Lord, in the strength of grace," 1:194, Hymn 621
"Thou shepherd of Israel, and mine," 1:294, Hymn 931
"'Tis finished! the Messiah dies," 2:234, Hymn 387
"Come, let us use the grace divine," 2:36, Hymn 1242
"Come then, and dwell in me," 2:298, Hymn 569
"The causeless, unexhausted love," 1:53, Hymn 169

It should be noted that "O thou who camest from above" is of particular historical and theological importance, since John Wesley is reported to have referred to its second stanza as expressive of his own testimony of faith.

Jesus, confirm my heart's desire
　　To work, and speak, and think for thee,
Still let me guard the holy fire,
　　And still stir up thy gift in me,
Ready for all thy perfect will
　　My acts of faith and love repeat,
'Till death thy endless mercies seal,
　　And make my sacrifice compleat.

(SH 1:57, Hymn 183)

"Come, let us use the grace divine" is also of extreme importance, for it became known as the "Covenant Hymn" included in John Wesley's Covenant Service, which was celebrated at the turn of each new year.

In *Short Hymns*, Charles Wesley demonstrated how the art of poetry often gets to the heart of a biblical passage without the advantages or disadvantages of biblical criticism. He achieved this frequently by the turn of a phrase or by his ingenious use of alliteration, assonance, repetition, structure, and rhyme. Unquestionably, his knowledge of Hebrew, Greek, and Latin provided him with a reservoir of linguistic resources which not only helped him grasp the meaning of Holy Scripture but enriched his poetical vocabulary. This strong linguistic background and a vast knowledge of the Authorized Version of the Bible are reflected in his diction, language style, and thought. His frequent preference for the Coverdale version of the Psalms (1535) was no doubt due in part to its retention in the Book of Common Prayer[6] and Wesley's regular use of it in the worship of the Church of England.

Short Hymns clearly illustrates, however, that Wesley was not slavishly bound to the Authorized Version of the Bible (1611), which was already 150 years old at the time. His knowledge of biblical languages helped him to see its disadvantages and imperfections. Therefore, he often made notations enclosed in brackets within biblical verses which he cited in *Short Hymns* (e.g., [Heb.] or [Gr.]) to indicate a more accurate or alternate translation of his own. In volume 2 in the New Testament section, he also made occasional reference to his brother John's *Explanatory Notes upon the New Testament*, on which he had collaborated seven years earlier (1755). It is significant that in hundreds of instances, John Wesley anticipated, in the volume just mentioned, translation changes that were made in the revision of the Authorized Version in 1881. Both brothers produced major works on the Bible: John, *Explanatory Notes upon the New Testament*; Charles, *Short Hymns on Select Passages of the Holy Scriptures.*

The following is a tabulation of Charles's literary output in *Short Hymns.*

	Lines of Poetry	Stanzas
Vol. 1 (Old Testament)	10,903	1,241
Vol. 2 (Old Testament)	3,320	446
Vol. 2 (New Testament)	8,912	1,306
Totals	23,135	2,993

According to Frank Baker's calculations, Wesley wrote approximately 180,000 lines of poetry and 27,000 stanzas.[7] Therefore, *Short Hymns* contains some 12.8 percent of the total number of lines and 11 percent of the total number of stanzas he produced.

In the succeeding discussions, all poetical references are to stanzas from *Short Hymns*, unless otherwise indicated, and each quotation of or from a poem is followed by a designation of the volume, page, and hymn numbers respectively. The word "hymn" is used as a designation for each poem, since it is Wesley's own terminology in the two volumes. Scripture passages are quoted from the Authorized Version (AV) or the King James Version of the Bible as Wesley published them, unless otherwise indicated.

The Holy Scriptures

In the "Preface" to *Short Hymns on Select Passages of the Holy Scriptures*, Wesley expresses his debt to three scholars upon whose works he relied for the interpretation of scripture: "Many of the thoughts are borrowed from Mr. Henry's Comment, Dr. Gell on the Pentateuch, and Bengelius on the New Testament."[8] The first reference is to the biblical commentary of Matthew Henry, which enjoyed extensive popularity and influence in the eighteenth-century English church. As Thomas Jackson has pointed out, "Some of his [Wesley's] eminently beautiful hymns, strange as it may appear, are poetic versions of Henry's expository notes."[9] Dr. Gell was a distinguished biblical scholar and clergyman who lived in London. Wesley is no doubt referring to his "Amended Translation" of the Pentateuch. Some poems in *Short Hymns* indicate that Gell's idea of the possibility of God's people being saved from all sin in this present life influenced Wesley.[10] One suspects also that Gell's mystical tendencies influenced him as well. Charles Wesley had become intimately acquainted with the work of Bengelius, a Lutheran minister and an erudite scholar, while collaborating with his brother John on *Explanatory Notes upon the New Testament*, since John had drawn heavily on Bengelius's work.

Authority of Scripture

Charles Wesley's concept of the authority of scripture is made crystal clear in lines based on Isaiah 8:20.

Doctrines, experiences to try,
We to the sacred standard fly,
Assur'd the Spirit of our Lord
Can never contradict his word:
Whate'er his Spirit speaks in me,
Must with the written word agree;
If not: I cast it all aside,
As Satan's voice, or nature's pride.
(SH 1:310, Hymn 973)

In writing on Ezekiel 37:3–4, he perceived the possibility of new life for dry bones through the divine energy of the word.

All-good, almighty Lord,
Thou know'st thine own design,
The virtue of thine own great word,
The energy divine.
(SH 2:51, Hymn 1273)

He understands the word to be sufficient for human completeness (Deuteronomy 4:2).

All thy word without addition
Renders us for glory meet,

Fits us for the blissful vision,
 Makes the man of God compleat.
 (SH 1:89, Hymn 278)

Though strangely based on Ezekiel 37:25, Wesley writes:

Trusting in the literal word,
 We look for Christ on earth again:
Come, our everlasting Lord,
 With all thy saints to reign.
 (SH 2:56, Hymn 1284)

Is he then to be understood as a biblical literalist? A qualified answer must be given, for it can be yes only in the sense that the believer may have utmost confidence that the promises of God in scripture are not empty ones. God fulfills them. As for slavish, biblical literalism, which would impute words with power God alone possesses, in reflecting on John 6:63, Wesley expresses reservations.

The word in the bare literal sense,
 Tho' heard ten thousand times, and read,
Can never of itself dispense
 The saving power which wakes the dead;
The meaning spiritual and true
 The learn'd expositor may give,
But cannot give the virtue too,
 Or bid his own dead spirit live.
 (SH 2:249, Hymn 429)

Without question, for Wesley it is Christ who unseals God's word with saving wisdom. 2 Timothy 3:15 evokes this response.

1. If faith in our dear dying Lord
 The sacred instrument applies,
The virtue of his hallowing word
 Shall make us to salvation wise,
Wise our high calling's prize t'attain,
 And everlasting glory gain.

2. Jesus, the Spirit of faith bestow,
 Who only can thy book unseal,
And give me all thy will to know,
 And give me all thy mind to feel,
Fill'd with the wisdom from above,
 The purity of heavenly love.
 (SH 2:337, Hymn 663)

The poem based on Revelation 1:3, "Blessed is he that readeth, and they that hear the words of this prophecy, and keep those things which are written therein," is Wesley's lifelong plea and reveals the impetus for his poetical exposition of scripture.

He constantly desires eyes and ears which grasp and appropriate the meaning of the word.

1. Come, divine Interpreter,
    Bring me eyes thy book to read,
Ears the mystic words to hear,
    Words which did from thee proceed,
Words that endless bliss impart
Kept in an obedient heart.

2. All who read, or hear, are blest,
    If thy plain commands we do,
Of thy Kingdom here possesst,
    Thee we shall in glory view,
(When thou com'st on earth t'abide)
Reign triumphant at thy side.
(SH 2:412, Hymn 821)

Scriptural Language and Translation

Wesley breathes the language of scripture: its metaphors, similes, imagery, and phrases, particularly those of the Authorized Version (AV). However, he diverges from it on numerous occasions in an attempt to be more accurate in translation, meaning, and interpretation. Wesley's phrase "Father of eternity" ("Everlasting Father" in the AV) for Hebrew אֲבִי עַד (*'avi 'ad*) (Isa. 9:5) in his poem on Isaiah 9:6–7 is a rigid, literal rendering.

The Almighty God is He,
    Author of heavenly bliss,
The Father of eternity,
    The glorious Prince of peace.
(SH 1:312, Hymn 980)

He is faithful to the proper meaning of the Hebrew adjective קְלֹקֵל (*ḳelloḳel*), describing the bread or food in the wilderness in his poem on Numbers 2:15, when he opts for the translation "vile" rather than "light" (AV). Thus he writes:

Who murmur in the wilderness
    By daily wonders fed,
May loath the comforts of thy grace
    As despicable bread.
(SH 1:77, Hymn 245)

There is certainly a difference between translating Deuteronomy 10:12, "What doth the Lord *require* of thee" (AV) and "What doth the Lord *request* of thee." Within the verse after "require," Wesley adds: "[Heb. request, intreat, petition]." The verb is the common Hebrew verb meaning "to ask," שָׁאַל (*sha'al*). Wesley exercises the freedom of translating it as "request" and writes:

May we not grant our God's request,
And serve thee with an heart sincere,
With thy prevenient spirit blest,
Inspir'd with thy ingenuous fear,
And strengthen'd by sufficient grace
To walk in all thy righteous ways!
(SH 1:98, Hymn 309)

When Wesley quotes Deuteronomy 10:12–13 immediately following as the preface to another poem, he substitutes the word "request" for "require" once again, but with no comment.

In Deuteronomy 33:28, Wesley translates עֵי (*'e*) (the construct form of עַי [*'ai*]) as "eye," not "fountain" as in the AV: "The fountain of Jacob shall be upon a land of corn and wine: also his heaven shall drop down dew." Once again Wesley's verse reflects his rendering.

Meanest of Jacob's race,
By Jordan's stream I stand,
And lo! Mine eye of faith surveys
The wide extended land!
(SH 2:112, Hymn 349)

Wesley stands reasonably alone in this translation, for most English versions have "fountain." There are two identical words in Hebrew which mean "eye" and "fountain." Wesley exercises the freedom of translation by choosing "eye," which indeed changes the nuance of meaning in the text.

The last phrase of Daniel 9:24 reads: "To anoint the most holy" (AV). For the Hebrew קֹדֶשׁ קָדָשִׁים (*ḳodesh ḳodashim*), Wesley prefers literally "holiness of holinesses," which then becomes the first line of the following poem.

Holiness of Holinesses
On a sinful world bestow'd,
Jesus, all the nations blesses,
Consecrates our souls to God.
(SH 1:64, Hymn 1307)

Wesley was aware of the problem in the Authorized Version of taking little note of the Greek definite article. For example, its translation of τὸν καλὸν ἀγῶνα in 2 Timothy is "a good fight," but Wesley properly translates "*the* good fight."

"I *the*[11] good fight have fought,"
O when shall I declare!
The victory by my Saviour got
I long with Paul to share.
(SH 2:338, Hymn 665)

Henry Bett points out another instance in which Wesley differs from the AV in reference to the definite article in a poem (not found in *Short Hymns*) based on

2 Timothy 4:8, "Henceforth there is laid up for me a crown of righteousness, etc." Bett states, "But the Greek is ὁ τῆς δικαιοσύνης στέφανος, 'the crown of righteousness.' So Wesley renders in the *Notes* [*Explanatory Notes upon the New Testament*]. And so constantly in the hymns."[12] Then he quotes the lines:

The[13] glorious crown of righteousness
To me reached out I view,
Conqueror through Him, I soon shall seize
And wear it as my due.

In a poem in *Short Hymns* based on the same passage, however, Wesley adheres to the AV, contrary to Bett's claim that he "constantly" translates "*the* crown."

A[14] crown of righteousness
There is laid up for me,
Who keep the faith, and win the race
And get the victory.

In the concluding lines of stanza three of this poem, he does speak of "the crown," but it is a reference to "a crown of righteousness" in stanza one.

Thou promisest to give
The[15] crown at that glad day
To all who lovingly believe
And for thy coming stay.
(SH 2:339, Hymn 668)

Another example by Bett of how Wesley seeks to bring out the proper significance of Greek words is not supported by poems in *Short Hymns*. The reference is to the use of the word στέφανον in Revelation 2:10, "Be thou faithful unto death, and I will give thee a crown of life" (AV), τὸν στέφανον τῆς ζωῆς. Bett shows that the word more properly should be translated "wreath" or "garland" and that Wesley follows this rendering in nearly every case. He then gives two examples, which are not in *Short Hymns*. However, in a poem based on the above passage in *Short Hymns*, Wesley follows the AV and uses "crown":

And when I lay this body down,
Reward with *an*[16] immortal crown.
(SH 2:416, Hymn 831)

Bett also refers to 2 Timothy 4:8, where Wesley uses "wreath"; however, the hymn in *Short Hymns* just quoted is based on this passage and uses "crown."

In spite of occasional inconsistencies in his rendering the text as found in the AV and in Hebrew or Greek, one can say that in most instances, where there are viable options, Wesley followed the most authentic translation available to him through his linguistic knowledge and the language sources accessible at the time. It is very clear that he exercised a freedom to approach the text with an attempt to produce an authentic rendering. It is also clear that he is not always consistent and that he sometimes quite arbitrarily follows the AV or his own translations without explanation.

At times, he is successful in correcting inadequate translations of the AV. For example, 1 Peter 5:7 reads, "Casting all your care [μέριμαν] upon Him, for He careth [μέλει] for you" (AV). Here two different Greek words are translated by the same word "care" in English. Wesley understands that the first word is more appropriately translated "trouble" and writes:

O Lover of sinners, on thee,
    My burden of *trouble* I cast,
Whose *care*[17] and compassion for me
    Forever and ever shall last.
(SH 2:396, Hymn 778)

The word μαθητεύσατε is translated "teach" in the AV of Matthew 28:19, "Go ye therefore, and *teach* all nations." "Teaching" is a proper rendering of διδάσκοντε in the next verse: "teaching them to observe all things whatsoever I have commanded you." However, μαθητεύσατε means "make disciples of," and this is Wesley's preferred reading in a poem on this passage.

Let them thy promis'd presence find,
Sent to baptize into thy Name,
Sent to a lost world for thine to claim,
Sent to disciple all mankind.
(SH 2:197, Hymn 275)

Mark 11:22 reads, "Have faith in God" (AV), but Wesley adds "[Gr. the faith of God]" and writes:

I want the true divinity,
The faith of God, the power in me.
Jesus, the power of God thou art,
Inspeak thyself into my heart,
Command my heart the faith to have
Which saves, and shall for ever save.
(SH 2:208, Hymn 312)

This is a grammatically difficult phrase, ἔχετε πίστιν θεοῦ, and found nowhere else. One finds related phrases such as πίστεως ἐπὶ θεόν in Hebrews 6:1 and εἰς τὸν θεόν in John 14:1. Wesley has gone his own way and chooses a literal rendering of the genitive θεοῦ, "of God."

While Wesley offered no extensive prose commentary to the biblical passages upon which he based his poetry, occasionally there are brief footnotes, mainly in the New Testament section of volume 1 of *Short Hymns.* For example, 2 Corinthians 13:11 has the following footnote: "Be perfect, i.e. aspire to the highest degree of holiness.—Mr. W.'s *Notes.*"[18]

Infrequently, a word or phrase in a poem will be explained in a footnote. For example, in a poem on Galatians 5:24, line 3 of stanza 3 has a footnote.

But taught of God, we surely know,
    The man of desparate wickedness
Shall weaker still and weaker grow,
    And ling'ring die by slow degrees.
(SH 2:310, Hymn 602)

The footnote reads, "True believers have nailed the flesh with all its evil passions, appetites and inclinations, as it were, to a cross, whence it has no power to break loose, but it's continually *weaker* and *weaker.* —Mr. W's *Notes.*"

While Wesley's *Short Hymns* usually offer much insight into the meaning of scripture, it must be admitted that occasionally a poem has little or nothing to do with the biblical passage upon which it supposedly is based. In 2 Kings 2:12, the words "My father, my father!" refer to Elisha, however, based on this text, Wesley wrote a hymn on Jesus's ascension and return.

Jesus, dear departing Lord,
Hang we on thy latest word,
Us who can thy word receive,
Fatherless thou wilt not leave:
Tho' we may a moment mourn,
Yet we look for the return,
Now enjoy the earnest given,
Then ascend with thee to heaven.
(SH 1:178, Hymn 568)

Likewise, one must stretch the imagination to see the relationship of the hymn supposedly based on 1 Chronicles 15:26 ("God helped the Levites that bare the ark") to the passage.

In every sacred exercise
We need the succour of the skies,
But chiefly when we preach thy word,
Or bear the vessels of the Lord:
Our power and whole sufficiency,
Jesus, is still deriv'd from thee;
And if we minister thy grace,
Thine, only thine, be all the praise.
(SH 1:192, Hymn 616)

After the first two lines, Wesley moves to a statement on homiletics, a possible Eucharistic reference, and a christological comment on Jesus as the source of all sufficiency.

Nevertheless, on the whole, the poems in *Short Hymns* are a reservoir of biblical insight. An excellent example is the poem on Judges 10:15, "We have sinned, do thou unto us whatsoever seemeth good unto thee, deliver us only, we pray thee, this day."

Lord, I have sinn'd, but now relent,
    And groan beneath my guilt,

Humbly accept my punishment;
    Do with me what thou wilt:
For this, and only this I pray,
    From all my sins release,
And save throughout my evil day,
    And bid me die in peace.
                    (SH 1:130, Hymn 404)

This is an excellent interpretation which personalizes precisely what Israel does; namely, pray for deliverance.

Theological Ideas

Short Hymns is a veritable compendium of biblical and theological ideas seen through the eyes of the poet-priest Charles Wesley. Historically, there has been a tendency to cast him and his brother into one theological mold, whereby to speak of the thought of one meant to speak of the thought of the other. To be sure, John often edited Charles's poetical work for publication, and one can find numerous instances in which John changed what he found to be theologically objectionable, at least in his view, to a more acceptable form. Hence, it is understandable that in the theology expressed in much of Charles's poetry edited by John there is much ground shared by both, particularly as regards those hymns which survive in hymnals. It must be added, however, that even without John's editorial changes, there is a common theological foundation, one rooted in the authority of scripture, the early church, the eighteenth-century Church of England, the sacraments and prayers of the church, and the Holy Trinity. In the case of *Short Hymns*, there are two volumes of 2,349 poems written and edited *only* by Charles Wesley.

Since he covers vast amounts of material from almost every book of the Bible, it is only natural that a broad spectrum of theological concerns is found here. Therefore, these volumes are particularly valuable, along with *Hymns and Sacred Poems* of 1749 (also written and edited *only* by Charles), for the uniqueness of his thought, as well as the aspects of theology shared commonly with John.

The following discussion is a brief summary of major theological ideas expressed in *Short Hymns*, but it is not intended as a critical study of them in the light of the full breadth of all of Charles's poetry and prose. They will be delineated here as expressed through Charles's own interpretative skills in the two volumes of *Short Hymns.*

The Holy Trinity

A. *God the Creator*

The God of whom Wesley writes is the God of Holy Scripture and history: the God of the Old and New Testaments. Deuteronomy 33:26 ("There is none like unto the God of Jeshurun, who rideth upon the heaven in thy help, and in his excellency on the sky") is the basis for an interesting description of God. Note that it is written in the third person.

1. God of the upright ones,[19]
Who can with Him compare!
He makes the house of Israel's sons
His everlasting care:
Jehovah's rapid course
What can resist, or shun,
When heaven is his manag'd horse,
And brings the Thunderer down!

2. Glorious in majesty,
He takes the whirlwind's wings,
Sublime he rides upon the sky,
And help to Israel brings,
His people's sure defence
He takes them to his breast;
And safe in his Omnipotence
They shall forever rest.
(SH 1:110, Hymn 345)

In the succeeding hymn on the next verse, Deuteronomy 33:27 ("The eternal God is thy refuge, and underneath are the everlasting arms"), Wesley immediately shifts to the first person and the New Testament.

1. Secure in Christ I dwell,
Jeshurun's God is mine,
I feel it now, by faith I feel
Th'eternal strength divine;
My refuge in distress,
In every trying hour,
Jesus, thy saving name I bless,
And shout within my tower.
(SH 1:110, Hymn 346)

Charles Wesley harbors no Marcionite theology. God is the God of the Hebrew and Greek scriptures, and God is a God of grace *and* law in both testaments. One meets no antinomianism here.

1. Moses, when dead, himself survives,
He always in his precepts lives;
Tho' sinners dream his office o'er,
He loses nothing of his power,
His sight is as the eagle's strong,
And Sinai thunders in his tongue.

2. Think not the law thro' faith made void,
Its vigour cannot be destroy'd:
It marks our hearts with quickest eye,
And doth our smallest faults espy,
It seizes with almighty hands,
And holds us in eternal bands.

3. It holds us, when by grace set free
From curse, and fear, and penalty;
The easy yoke of Christ we prove,
Bound to obey the God we love;
And when these heavens are past away,
We still shall glory to obey.
(SH 1:114, Hymn 353)[20]

The word of God in the Old Testament is extended and fulfilled in the Word made flesh in the New Testament, but it is one and the same word. The Old Testament דָּבָר (*davar*) (word) and the New Testament λόγος (word) are one. Hence, Wesley views the word in Deuteronomy 30:14 ("The word is very nigh unto thee, in thy mouth and in thy heart") as the word in Christ.

My God, from whom the precept came,
Doth power divine therewith impart,
When Jesus I desire, and name,
The Word is in my mouth and heart;

I feel it intimately near,
Soon as my heart believes him true,
And conscious of his presence here,
Thro' Jesus I can all things do.
(SH 1:104, Hymn 326)

The law of the Old Testament finds full affirmation and completion in the revealed Love of the New Testament. It is not weakened, rather strengthened.

Father, thy merciful design
We see, and joyfully approve,
Thou kindly dost thy laws injoin,
To make us happy in thy love:
With joy we own the gracious end
For which thy laws were all bestow'd,
Thou dost by each command intend
Our present and eternal good.
(SH 1:91, Hymn 285, based on Deuteronomy 5:29)

Wesley's theology of God, however, is above all a theology of mystery. God is knowable and unknowable, revealed and unrevealed. He stands firm in faith and the assurance of redemption in the revealed word of God, who is Love and whose revelation in the Word made flesh is a personalization of Love individually and corporately.

At the moment in which Wesley thinks he comprehends, however, he stands in total awe of that which he does not know—the Mystery of mysteries yet to be revealed, yet to be known, and which he may never know.

An eloquent expression of Wesley's theology of the mystery of God is found in a poem based on Deuteronomy 7:7–8, "The Lord did not set his love upon you because ye were more in number than any people, but because the Lord loved you."

What angel can explain,
The love of God to man,
The secret cause assign
Of charity divine?
Nothing in us could move,
Deserve, or claim his love:
'Tis all a mystery,
And must forever be!

(SH 1:93, Hymn 293)

Finally, there is perhaps no finer statement of Charles Wesley's theology of the knowledge of God than his reflection on Job 11:7, "Canst thou searching find out God? Canst thou find out the Almighty unto perfection?"

1. Shall foolish, weak, short-sighted man
 Beyond archangels go,
The great almighty God explain,
 Or to perfection know?
His attributes divinely soar
 Above the creatures' sight,
And prostrate Seraphim adore
 The glorious Infinite.

2. Jehovah's everlasting days,
 They cannot number'd be,
Incomprehensible the space
 Of thine immensity;
Thy wisdom's depths by reason's line
 In vain we strive to sound,
Or stretch our labouring thought t'assign
 Omnipotence abound.

3. The brightness of thy glories leaves
 Description far below;
Nor man, nor angels' heart conceives
 How deep thy mercies flow:
Thy love is *most* unsearchable,
 And dazzles all above;
They gaze, but cannot count or tell
 The treasures of thy love.

(SH 1:231, Hymn 729)

Wesley understood the God of Holy Scripture to be triune: Father, Son, and Holy Spirit. An interesting poem on the Incarnation is a response to Solomon's prayerful question before the altar in 1 Kings 8:27: "But will God indeed dwell on the earth?" In the first stanza, Wesley uses only the name Jehovah for God. While there is only a calculated guess as to how the Hebrew name for God, *YHWH* (which was never pronounced), should be vocalized, Jehovah was commonly accepted in Wesley's time. He intended to show here that the God of the Old Testament is the God of the Incarnation. Jehovah and the triune God are one and the same. Jehovah, who dwelled on earth among the Hebrews, still resides on earth but is revealed as Father, Son, and Holy Spirit.

1. He did: the King invisible,
Jehovah, once on earth did dwell,
And laid his majesty aside:
Whom all his heavens cannot contain,
For us he liv'd, a mournful man,
For us a painful death he died!

2. Still the great God resides below,
(And all his faithful people know
He will not from his Church depart)
The Father, Son, and Spirit dwells,
His kingdom in the poor reveals,
And fills with heaven the humble heart.
(SH 1:167, Hymn 533)

The fact that Wesley, however, sees the plural verb, "Let us make," and perhaps the plural of the name for God, אֱלֹהִים (*'elohim*), as evidence for the Trinity in Genesis 1:26 is indeed questionable ("Let us make man in our image"), but it was not uncommon in Wesley's day.

Father, Son, and Holy-Ghost,
In Council join again
To restore thine image, lost
By frail apostate man.
(SH 1:4, Hymn 5)

There is no linguistic foundation for Wesley's conclusion about the Trinity here. What he wishes to convey, however, is that the God of Scripture is an eternal whole whose revelation is ongoing.

B. *God the Son, Jesus Christ*

The revelation of the one eternal God throughout scripture discloses God as Father, Son, and Holy Spirit. Wesley's passion for this view leads him often to christologize the Old Testament. His fervor for the gospel and for the overwhelming revelation of God in the redemptive love of Christ forces an evangelization of the Old Testament that is at times most unfortunate. He sees Christ almost everywhere in the Old

Testament. It is a spiritualized view which allows the concept of Trinity to preempt all biblical revelation and place it on one level. It does not allow the cascading power of the unfolding revelation of God in scripture to have its full impact as it moves from Genesis to Revelation. Almost all messianic passages in the Old Testament are unequivocally about Jesus in his view.

The "word" in Deuteronomy 30:14 is Christ.[21] The "rock" in Deuteronomy 32:4 is Christ.[22] He finds innumerable prototypes for Christ in the Old Testament: Moses, Joshua, Elijah, Cyrus. In volume 1, and in the Old Testament section of volume 2, of *Short Hymns*, one finds poems on almost all primary aspects of Christ's life as revealed in the New Testament: childhood, ministry, death, resurrection, ascension, return. Wesley is at his best when he allows the Old Testament to interpret his relationship with Christ, rather than interpret the Old Testament with Christ. For example, he does not say that the "light" in Genesis 1:3 is Christ per se. Rather, "Let there be light" becomes the anticipation of new creation; namely, spiritual creation.

Let there be light (again command)
　　And light there in our hearts shall be,
We then thro' faith shall understand
　　Thy great mysterious Majesty,
And by the shining of thy grace
Behold in Christ thy glorious face.
(SH 1:4, Hymn 4)

Here Wesley allows the passage to illuminate his spiritual journey.

In another instance, he allows the messianic anticipation of a passage (Isaiah 11:1) to retain its power without imposing a christology upon it.

Branch of Jesse's stem, arise,
　　And in our nature grow,
Turn our earth to paradise,
　　By flourishing below:
Bless us with the Spirit of grace
　　Immeasurably shed on thee,
Pour on all the faithful race
　　The streaming Deity.
(SH 1:314, Hymn 983)

While Wesley writes a moving hymn on Job 19:25–27, having to do with Jesus as redeemer, he projects a unilinear view that the גֹּאֵל (*go'el*) (redeemer) of this passage is Jesus. One might defend his perspective by saying that he is writing in the first person, and when he reads, "I know that my Redeemer liveth," he can think only of Jesus because that is his experience of a redeemer; therefore, he is not writing about Job's experience. Undoubtedly, he spiritualizes the text. This may have some validity, but it preempts, if not nullifies, Old Testament history and human experience of thousands of years in relationship to God and creation, and allows them to have little or no validity on their own, or such an interpretation serves only a christological understanding of history.

What often saves his christological view of the Old Testament is that it is couched in his own personal experience of God. His paraphrase of Isaiah's outburst of thanksgiving, "Sing to the Lord a new song, and his praise from the end of the earth; ye that go down to the sea" (Isaiah 42:10), begins:

1. Thanksgiving and praise to Jesus belongs.
   He claims for his grace New-Testament songs:

   Our Saviour and lover in hymns we proclaim.
   And all the world over rejoice in his name.

(SH 1:342, Hymn 1045)

As a paraphrase of Isaiah's rejoicing, it is inappropriate. As a Christian hymn precipitated by responding to Isaiah's admonition to sing a new song to the Lord, it is authentic. The authenticity, however, is found in Wesley's experience, not Isaiah's. This is the key to understanding his christology as it relates to scriptural interpretation and the Old Testament in particular. His experience of Christ dominates his response to scripture, and it is problematical mainly when he projects it into the experience of human beings within scripture, Old or New Testament, as though it were theirs. The overall thrust of Wesley's christological understanding of scripture, however, is that the knowledge and experience of the redemptive revelation of God in Christ is the goal toward which the whole of the Bible points. The poem on Jeremiah 31:34 ("They shall all know me") states this view succinctly for Wesley.

Essence incomprehensible,
　　Jehovah who can know
Who was, and is, and comes to dwell
　　With all his saints below!
Then the whole world shall be restor'd
　　And bow to Jesu's name,
Fill'd with the knowledge of the Lord,
　　The Infinite I AM.

(SH 2:33, Hymn 1233)

C. *God the Holy Spirit*

There is a plethora of poems on the theme of the Holy Spirit in *Short Hymns*. On the whole, they tend to emphasize the third person of the Holy Trinity as the primary means of the human experience of God. The Spirit is the means whereby the word of God is made present and powerful on earth. It is the real presence of the divine which unites us to God in Christ.

The word is unaccomplish'd still:
　　In honour of thy Son,
Father, the mystery fulfill,
　　And send the promise down;
That Spirit of universal grace,
　　That Spirit of glory pour,

And deluge all our ransom'd race
With one eternal shower.
(SH 2:73, Hymn 1333)

The poem is based on Joel 2:28, "I will pour out my Spirit upon all flesh."

The Holy Spirit also has a didactic function in human experience. When Wesley reads that the Spirit "will teach . . . all things" (John 14:26), he writes:

O that we might the Spirit find
By Jesu's grace bestow'd,
Which leads us into all the mind,
And all the things of God!
Come, Holy Ghost, thy power display,
And teach us all in one,
Teach us in Christ the living Way
To God's eternal throne.
(SH 2:259, Hymn 463)

The Holy Spirit is the liberator from sorrow, fear, and sin. It is the source of true liberty and the Spirit of health, holiness, and perfect love.

Come, then, and dwell in me,
Spirit of power within,
And bring the glorious liberty
From sorrow, fear, and sin:
The seed of sin's disease,
Spirit of health, remove,
Spirit of finish'd holiness,
Spirit of perfect love.
(SH 2:298, Hymn 569, based on 2 Corinthians 3:17)

The Holy Spirit is the source of power and strength against sin.

Holy Ghost, with grace inspire
My heart against my sin,
When I feel the base desire,
Exert thy power within;
Keep me, 'till the conflict's o'er,
That nature's will I may not do,
'Till the kingdom thou restore,
And all my heart renew.
(SH 2:308, Hymn 599, based on Galatians 5:17)

Hence, the Holy Spirit is the enabler of Christian behavior. Wesley understands the scripture and experience of God in Christ to affirm that the demeanor of persons can be positively transformed by the indwelling Spirit of God. After citing Galatians 5:22–23, "The fruit of the Spirit is love, joy, peace, long-suffering, gentleness, goodness, faith, meekness, temperance," Wesley prays:

Jesus, plant thy Spirit in me,
Then the fruit shall shew the tree,
Every grace its author prove,
Rising from the root of love.
(SH 2:309, Hymn 601)

When Wesley utilizes the language of the Old and New Testaments in speaking of the Spirit of God and acknowledges a growth in the human understanding of it culminating in the New Testament gift of the Holy Comforter, which is affirmed in the Incarnation, he often uses the language interchangeably. His christological view of scripture sees the Spirit of God in Ezekiel as one and the same with the New Testament Comforter and the Spirit of Jesus. For example, the poem on Ezekiel 37:9–10 ("Come from the four winds, O breath, and breathe upon these slain, that they may live, etc.") ends with mention of the "indwelling Comforter."

1. Come, O thou breath divine
From every quarter blow,
And whom thou didst together join,
On them thine influence shew;
Thy wonder-working power
Be here again display'd,
And now to sudden life restore
The long-forgotten dead.

2. Inspir'd at God's command
By thee, the Spirit of grace,
Let the whole house of Israel stand
And their Redeemer praise,
Host of the living God
Throughout the earth declare
The heavenly gift on all bestow'd,
Th'indwelling Comforter.
(SH 2:52, Hymn 1276)

The Church

Wesley's theological ideas of the church expressed in *Short Hymns* are characterized, as is much of his theology, by a strong tie to the Old Testament. There is even an equation of the Hebrews with the church in a hymn on Numbers 9:16.

Where is the Hebrews' God,
Who kept them night and day,
Where is the heavenly fire and cloud,
Which shew'd thy church their way?
(SH 1:63, Hymn 203)

In reflecting on Old Testament passages, he often spoke of the church in terms of its analogies and metaphors. For example, in the light of Ezekiel 37:12, the church is seen as a valley of dry bones awaiting new life.

1. Many they are and dry,
 Spread thro' the open vale,
Millions of lifeless souls they lie
 Within the Christian pale:
I pass the churches thro',
 The scatter'd bones I see,
And Christendom appears in view
 An hideous Calvary.
(SH 2:50, Hymn 1272)

From Charles Wesley's perspective, the church must be viewed in relation to Old Testament messianic fulfillment.

The Church, O God, shall find fulfill'd
 Thy sure prophetic word,
The Branch, the Man divine, shall build
 The temple of the Lord:
The temple of the Lord are these
 Who still in Christ abide,
'Till rais'd to perfect righteousness,
 And wholly sanctified.
(SH 2:106, Hymn 1422, based on Zechariah 6:12)

The messianic builder of the church of Christ, and Wesley's interpretation of a much-disputed New Testament passage, Matthew 16:18 ("Upon this Rock I will build my church"), leaves no question that for him the "Rock" is Jesus Christ.

Not on a frail sinful creature
 Dost thou build thy church below:
Thee, the Rock, divinely greater,
 Basis of our faith we know!
Rooted in thy love and grounded
 Still thy people shall prevail
Shout to see their foes confounded,
 Triumph o'er the gates of hell.
(SH 2:172, Hymn 172)

Christ is not only the church's builder but its sustainer.

Yet did its substance still remain,
For Jesus doth his church sustain.
(SH 1:370, Hymn 970, based on Isaiah 6:13)

The church is a mystical union between the body of believers and Christ, whose unity is sealed in God's love.

Myself begotten from above,
I must my Father's children love:
Born of the Spirit and the word,
Are we not brethren in the Lord,
Flesh of his flesh, bone of his bone,
His body mystical and One!
(SH 2:392, Hymn 767, based on 1 Peter 2:17)

Charles Wesley had an unswerving loyalty to the Church of England, but no biblical understanding of the church would permit him a narrow denominational view of the church as Christ's body. He is certainly a forerunner of ecumenical theology and its perception of the global church.

Not a favourite form, or name,
But for dear precious souls I care:
Bless, Saviour, our Jerusalem
That millions may her blessings share,

Prosper our church, the living few
Imploy their brethren dead to raise,
To quicken sister churches too,
And spread throughout the earth thy praise.
(SH 1:277, Hymn 875, based on Psalm 122:8)

Wesley prays for:

2. A Church which may remain
With all thy works restor'd,
Commensurate with time, obtain
The nature of her Lord;
A Church to comprehend
The whole of human race,
And live in joys that never end
Before thy glorious face.
(SH 1:392, Hymn 1160, based on Isaiah 66:21–23)

Wesley does not idealize the church beyond the reality of its brokenness in his own age or any other. He sees God's promise in Isaiah 54:11–12 as a promise to the church.

1. O thou afflicted church, forlorn
By tempest tost, by sorrow torn,
Appearing in thy last distress
I will thy ruinous state repair,
And build thee up divinely fair,
And deck with all the gems of grace.
(SH 1:366, Hymn 1104, based on Isaiah 54:11–12)

The churches of the world share a common mission.

1. Bought with the Blood
    Of very God,
The church in every nation,
    Publishes thro' earth abroad,
The God of their salvation.

(SH 2:274, Hymn 510, based on Acts 20:28)

Wesley's theology of the church is a realistic and an eschatological one. He sees it with all of its imperfections, hindrances, hypocrisies, and ineffectiveness but always with a hope of what it can become. His description of the church in the following poem is appropriate for any age.

1. Lo, the church with gradual light
    Her opening charms displays,
After a long dreary night
    Looks forth with glimmering rays,
Scarce perceptible appears,
    Until the Day-spring from on high
All the face of nature cheers,
    And gladdens earth and sky.

2. Fair as the unclouded moon,
    With borrow'd rays she shines,
Shines, but ah! she changes soon,
    And when at full declines,
Frequent, long eclipses feels,
    'Till Jesus drives the shades away,
All her doubts and sins dispels,
    And brings the perfect day.

3. Now she without spot appears,
    For Christ appears again,
Sun of righteousness, he clears
    His church from every stain,
Rising in full majesty
    He blazes with meridian light:
All th'horizon laughs to see
    The joyous heavenly sight.

4. Bright with lustre not her own
    The woman now admire,
Cloth'd with that eternal Sun
    Which sets the worlds on fire!
Bright she shall for ever shine,
    Enjoying, like the church above,

All the light of truth divine,
And all the fire of love.
(SH 1:298, Hymn 944, based on Song of Solomon 6:10)

Finally, Charles Wesley's theology of the church in *Short Hymns* suggests a strong adherence to the principle of apostolic succession; namely, the long line of ordination of clergy which originated in the New Testament and passed down through the ages via the early church. Wesley held fast to apostolic succession, within which the Church of England stood, and he was clear that the separation from Rome did not originate as an ecclesiastical one. Charles's posture on apostolic succession led him to oppose his brother John's "ordination" of superintendents ("bishops") for America in 1784.

Hebrews 5:4 ("No man taketh this honour unto himself, but he that is called of God, as was Aaron") precipitates the following lines which express Wesley's sentiments, in part, on ordination. The second stanza makes clear his opposition to dissenting views.

1. Impower'd thro' Moses's hallowing hands,
Aaron before the altar stands,
The consecrated priest of God!
Jesus *his* officers ordains:
And thus the *Christian* priest obtains
The gift of elders' hands bestow'd.

2. Ye that uncall'd the power assume,
Expect the rebels' fearful doom;
The pit its mouth hath open'd wide
For Jesu's sacrilegious foes!
Repent before its mouth it close
On all the hard'ned sons of pride.
(SH 2:351, Hymn 685)

Universalism

Short Hymns embodies a strong emphasis on universalism. Wesley did not occupy himself here, as he did elsewhere, with rather lengthy discourses against what he viewed as the particularism of Calvinism and the doctrine of election. Rather, generally he chose to affirm the all-encompassing dimension of God's love.

Lord, may not I thy promise claim,
Made to the Isles in Japheth's name?
In mercy then to me impart
The largeness of a loving heart:
An heart to no one sect confin'd,[23]
But compassing the ransom'd kind
Capacious of the Deity,
And grasping all thy gifts and thee.
(SH 1:17, Hymn 47)

The universalism one encounters in Charles Wesley is by no means limited to the divine redemptive act in Christ; rather it is found as well in God's promise to Abraham in Genesis 12:3 ("In thee shall all families of the earth be blessed"). Wesley's capitalization of "Seed" may indicate that he perceived Christ as the fulfillment of the promise of Abraham. It may simply reflect, however, his general practice of capitalizing nouns.

1. Come thou universal blessing,
Abraham's long-expected Seed,
Perfect peace, and joy unceasing
Thro' the ransom'd nations spread.
(SH 1:18, Hymn 50)

Genesis 49:10 ("Unto him shall the gathering of the people be") precipitates a prayer for universal unity in which God is addressed as the "Centre of Unity."

Centre of Unity,
Our precious Corner-stone
Collect thy people into thee,
And perfect them in one;
Break down the wall between,
Even as thou hast foretold,
And all the wandring sheep bring in,
And make us all one fold.
(SH 1:32, Hymn 98)

Christ's atonement is universal. Salvation is for all. Wesley's theology of election is a simple one: the entire world comprises the elect, for Christ has died for all. Nowhere does he make this clearer than in a poem based on John 1:29 ("Behold the Lamb of God, which taketh away the sin of the world!"). Note, however, one does not find here some kind of bland universal salvation devoid of human response. To the contrary, response, or belief, is requisite.

Did Jesus for the world atone?
"Yes; for the world of the elect:"
Love could not die for some alone
And all the wretched rest reject:
For the whole helpless world that lay
In desperate wickedness, he died,
And all who dare believe it, may
With me be freely justified.
(SH 2:241, Hymn 405)

Wesley's view of universal salvation is closely linked to an understanding of universal sin. That human nature is not originally good, he grasps from Matthew 19:17 ("There is none good but one, that is God").

None is originally good,
Good from himself, but thee:
The good thou hast on man bestow'd,
Is not his property:

By thee renew'd; yet pure and just
Himself he cannot call,
But still confesses in the dust
That thou art all in all.
(SH 2:177, Hymn 197)

On Genesis 3:24 ("God drove out the man: And he placed Cherubim, and a flaming sword, which turned every way, to keep the way of the tree of life"), Wesley pens these lines:

Spoil'd of the bliss to Adam given,
Out of my Maker's presence driven,
My fallen state I mourn;
But fondly sigh my Eden lost;
The flaming sword, and angel-host
Prohibit my return.
(SH 1:12, Hymn 32)

Humankind is driven out of the "Maker's presence," and the God-given nature of Adam no longer characterizes his identity. And Adam as generic man represents the fallen nature of all human beings. A couplet on Isaiah 65:17–18 puts it tersely.

Come, divine effectual power,
Fallen nature to restore.
(SH 1:383, Hymn 1146)

Second Chronicles 6:36 ("There is no man which sinneth not") also implies for Wesley the fallen state of humankind.

No: Every fallen child of man
Must sin in thought, and word, and deed:
But bursting our oppressor's chain
When Jesus hath his prisoners freed,
The dire necessity is o'er,
And born of God we sin no more.
(SH 1:199, Hymn 637)

Wesley is describing not a sinless state of persons after conversion but the possibility of sinning no more, a possibility he considers to be real for the redeemed child of God. His constant prayer is:

Destroy the bent to sin in me,
Cure my original malady,
And make, and keep me whole.
(SH 2:73, Hymn 1332, based on Hosea 14:4)

The poem on Isaiah 48:8 ("Thou wast called a transgressor from the womb") would seem to be a strong affirmation by Charles Wesley of a theology of original sin.

I evil from the womb have been,
Born, altogether born in sin,
In sin conceiv'd and bred,
My actual guilt's enormous load
Calls down the fiercest wrath of God
On my devoted head.
(SH 1:349, Hymn 1062)

If indeed he is speaking of original sin in a doctrinal sense, his perception of it is not always clearly delineated. In another poem, he writes:

Father, behold, I calmly wait
Thine acceptable will to prove,
Rais'd to my first unsinning state,
In perfect righteousness and love.
(SH 1:328, Hymn 643, based on 2 Thessalonians 1:11)

What is the "first unsinning state" to which he refers? Is this the state of Adam before his disobedience?

Wesley knows that all humankind is sinful and in need of God's redemption in Christ. That is the basis of his theology of sin. On the basis of scripture, however, he understands that the way in which redemption is experienced is not unilinear, not uniform for all persons.

'Tis not a sudden stroke of grace
Destroys at once the cursed race,
When first to Christ we come;
But by *degrees insensible*
The Lord shall all our sins expel,
And utterly consume.
(SH 1:93, Hymn 294, based on Deuteronomy 7:22)

This is the kind of statement which would have given John Wesley pause had he edited *Short Hymns*. In his own annotated copy of the two volumes, he adds the following marginal note to lines 1 and 4: "Both suddenly and gradually."[24]

In the light of the preceding poems, it is not surprising that Charles understands being "born again" in relation to the absence of sin. Jesus's words to Nicodemus in John 3:3 ("Except a man be born again, he cannot see the kingdom of God") elicit this response:

The truth, and blessedness, and need
Of this great change I know:
But can I witness it indeed,
Can I the tokens shew?
Marks of this birth, they all are vain
Without the Spirit's power:

Then only am I born again,
When I can sin no more.
(SH 2:242, Hymn 407)

In another place, he declares:

Away with all your boastings vain,
Proofs more substantial we demand,
Ye cannot sin, if born again,
Ye can the fiery trial stand;
The proof in facts and tempers give,
Sorrow, disgrace, and pain endure,
Live without sin, like Jesus live,
And *tell us thus* your hearts are pure.
(SH 2:217, Hymn 331, based on Luke 6:44)

Holiness and Perfection

The discussion of a theology of sin and rebirth leads quite naturally to the poems in *Short Hymns* which treat the theology of holiness. To be sure, Charles was at odds with his brother John on a number of facets of the concept of holiness, and he used *Short Hymns* to spell out his own perspective. Charles had moved to a position of gradual growth in holiness, while John wanted to leave open the possibility of a realizable holiness in this life, even holiness received instantly.[25] While holiness is a primary goal of the Christian life, Charles Wesley was opposed to any idea of instantaneous holiness in *Short Hymns*. Some of his earlier poems in *Hymns and Psalms* (1739) do hint of its possibility, but once he abandoned the idea, he did not return to it.

Ah, simple souls, who fondly dream
Of instantaneous holiness!
Tho' pride and self extinguish'd seem,
While all within is joy and peace.
(SH 2:12, Hymn 1183, based on Jeremiah 6:14)

There were those who claimed that holiness is acquired at the moment of belief. Not so, says Charles.

Nature would the crown receive
The first moment we believe,
But we vainly think to seize
Instantaneous holiness:
Faith alone cannot suffice,
Patience too much earn the prize,
Both insure the promise given,
Lead thro' perfect love to heaven.
(SH 2:355, Hymn 693, based on Hebrews 6:12)

2. "But may we not at once spring up,
"In sudden holiness mature?"
Nay; but we must the flattering hope
Renounce, and to the end endure:
The ripest fruit cannot appear,
Until the latter rain come down,
And faith's almighty Finisher
Our patience with perfection crown.
(SH 2:388, Hymn 758,based on James 5:7)

Holiness is the paradigm of the Christian's pilgrimage. Holiness is a process through which the Christian moves. It is the Christian way of life.

Thou dost not say, the seed springs up
Into an instantaneous crop;
But waiting long for its return,
We see the blade; the ear; the corn:
The weak; and *then* the stronger grace,
And *after that* full holiness.
(SH 2:201, Hymn 286)[26]

Charles Wesley's concept of perfection, being made perfect in love, is closely related, if not synonymous, with holiness.

Thou our hearts shalt circumcise,
And give us meekly to confess
Perfect love which God supplies,
Is perfect holiness.
(SH 2:287, Hymn 540, based on Romans 3:10)

Perfection and perfect love are dominant themes in *Short Hymns.* Once again, however, Charles is careful to oppose any idea of instantaneous perfection, or, that is, the possible attainment of perfect love before death.[27] He makes a strong statement on the matter in a poem based on Philippians 3:13, in which Paul says, "I count not myself to have apprehended." It suffices for Wesley as an averment against instantaneous perfection that this great apostle of the early church would make such a humble claim.

1. No; not after twenty years
Of labouring in the word!
After all his fights, and fears,
And sufferings for his Lord,
Paul hath not attain'd the prize,
Tho' caught up in the heavenly hill;
Daily still the Apostle dies
And lives imperfect still!

2. "But we now, the prize t'attain,
"An easier method see,
"Save ourselves the toil and pain,
"And ling'ring agony,
"Reach at once the ladder's top,
"While standing on its lowest round,
"Instantaneously spring up,
"With pure perfection crown'd."

3. *Such* the credulous dotard's dream,
And *such* his shorter road,
Thus he makes the world blaspheme,
And shames the church of God,
Staggers thus the most sincere,
'Till from the gospel hope they move,
Holiness as error fear,
And start at perfect love.

4. Lord, thy real work revive,
The counterfeit to end
That we lawfully may strive,
And truly apprehend,
Humbly still thy servant trace,
Who least of saints himself did call,
'Till we gain the height of grace,
And into nothing fall.

(SH 2:317, Hymn 620)

The Book of Hebrews exhorts the faithful, "Let us go on unto perfection" (6:1). There is a road to perfection. It requires a journey, and it leads by way of the cross of Christ. Any other path to perfection is futile. There is a note of sarcasm in the first two lines of a poem based on this passage in Hebrews.

"Go on? But how? from step to step?
"No: let *us* to perfection *leap*!"
'Tis thus our hasty nature cries,
Leaps o'er the cross, to snatch the prize,
Like Jonah's gourd, displays its bower,
And blooms, and withers, in an hour.

(SH 2:354, Hymn 690)

The following poem on the same passage further rejects all dissenting voices in Wesley's day which claimed instantaneous perfection as a real possibility. He thrust the argument upon Scripture in the first line.

Which of the *old* apostles taught
Perfection in an instant caught,

Shew'd *our* compendious manner how,
"Believe, and ye are perfect *now*;
"This moment wake, and seize the prize;
"Reeds, into sudden pillars rise;"
Believe delusion's ranting sons,
And all the work is done at once!
(SH 2:354, Hymn 691)

The hope of the gospel is holiness, which is purity and perfect love.

2\. This hope of holiness,
Still may I hold it fast,
And toward the prize unwearied press,
'Till all my deaths are past!
. . .
5\. The holiness compleat,
The spotless purity,
The perfect love, which makes me meet
To share a throne with thee.
(SH 2:318, Hymn 622, based on Colossians 1:23)

Paul's words to the church at Thessalonica, "This is the will of God, even your sanctification" (1 Thessalonians 4:3), accentuate for Wesley the longing for holiness and love.

He wills, that I should holy be:
That holiness I long to feel,
That full divine conformity
To all my Saviour's righteous will:
See, Lord, the travail of thy soul
Accomplish'd in the change of mine,
And plunge me, every whit made whole,
In all the depths of love divine.
(SH 2:324, Hymn 631)

While Wesley speaks of holiness and perfect love as gradually acquired and fulfilled in union with God in death and beyond death, he also aknowledges what might be called the "impossible ideal" of their fulfillment on earth as the prelude to union with God in heaven.

Faithful I account thee, Lord,
To thy sanctifying word;
I shall soon be as thou art,
Holy both in life and heart,
Perfect holiness attain,
All thine image *here* regain,
Love my God entirely *here*,
Blameless then in heaven appear.
(SH 2:326, Hymn 638, based on 1 Thessalonians 5:24)

A poem based on Matthew 5:48 ("Be ye perfect") is an eloquent perception of a model of Christian living.

2. "*Ye shall be perfect*" here below
He spake it, and it must be so;
But first he said, "Be poor;
"Hunger, and thirst, repent, and grieve,
"In humble, meek obedience live,
"And labour, and endure."

3. Thus, thus may I the prize pursue,
And all th'appointed paths pass thro'
To perfect poverty:
Thus let me, Lord, thyself attain,
And give thee up thine own again,
Forever lost in thee.

(SH 2:140, Hymn 54)

Here the idea of "perfect poverty" being equated with the goal of perfection is quite unique in Charles Wesley. To this author's knowledge, this concept does not occur in John Wesley's writings. In the light of other writings of Charles, there is no question that he is thinking of "Be poor" not only in a spiritualized sense but also in the sense of self-divestment. For him, there is an equation which is not often drawn as one examines the goals toward perfection; namely, "be perfect" = "be poor." While there is no fully developed idea of "perfect poverty" in Charles Wesley's writings, and it is unquestionably an enigmatic concept, his integration of it into the concept of perfection is indeed extremely important and allows for no merely spiritualized concept of "poverty."

The goal of holiness and perfection does not form the norm of Christian behavior. It is not an end in itself. It does not justify behavior; rather, when Christians empty themselves and give themselves fully in love, they move toward the goal without seeking it per se, or even knowing it.

While Wesley's passion for holiness is all-consuming, it is always tempered by humility.

Not as a formal task to thee
My tale of words I pay,
But feeling my own poverty,
I every hour would pray;
Would always pray, and never faint,
'Till wholly sanctified,
Thou take me up, a sinless saint,
And seat me by thy side.

(SH 1:262, Hymn 820, based on Psalm 55:18)

Love

Perhaps the most dominant aspect of the theology of Charles Wesley is love. It is the *denouement*, that toward which everything in life moves. It is the focus of his theology, through which he understands life, discipleship, and Christian doctrine. Furthermore, the love of God encountered throughout the Old and New Testaments is one and the same.

His power I in weakness shall prove,
Confiding in Jesus's name,
The God of unchangeable love,
Forever and ever the same.
(SH 1:265, Hymn 832, based on Psalm 71:8)

Wesley draws no dichotomy between an Old Testament theology of law and a New Testament theology of love and grace. Indeed, the law is fulfilled in love. It is the end of the law.

Father, thy merciful design
We see, and joyfully approve,
Thou kindly dost thy laws injoin,
To make us happy in thy love:

With joy we own the gracious end
For which thy laws were all bestow'd,
Thou dost by each command intend
Our present and eternal good.
(SH 1:91, Hymn 285, based on Deuteronomy 5:29)

Two verses, Deuteronomy 7:7–8 ("The Lord did not set his love upon you because ye were no more in number than any people, but because the Lord loved you"), are the occasion for a powerful poem on the mystery of love. While Wesley understood the love of God revealed in the Old Testament to have been personified in the Christ of the New Testament, he still stood awestruck before the incomprehensibility of such love.

What angel can explain
The love of God to man,
The secret cause assign
Of charity divine?
Nothing in us could move,
Deserve, or claim his love:
'Tis all a mystery,
And must for ever be!
(SH 1:93, Hymn 293)

Yet Wesley is untiring in his passion to grasp the mystery.

I wait thy mind to comprehend,
I long to answer all the end

Of thy mysterious love.
(SH 1:233, Hymn 734, based on Job 13:24)

He responds to Matthew 9:13 ("Go ye, and learn what that meaneth, I will have mercy, and not sacrifice") with a poem ending with the following couplet:

The grace to all doth freely move,
The favourite attribute is love.
(SH 2:154, Hymn 114)

Love alone is the key to understanding God, others, the world, creation; and God's love has been active in every age for the healing and wholeness of all creation.

Thou goest about in every age,
Dark, sin-sick souls to teach and heal;
The published word, the written page
Conveys the balm infallible,
We now thy Spirit of love receive,
Of power, and of a vig'rous mind,
And still thou in thyself wou'dst give
Life, health, and heaven, to all mankind.
(SH 2:155, Hymn 117, based on Matthew 9:35)

Love is the fulcrum of behavior, the source of personal and social holiness, the end of all living, and most fully perceived in God's revelation in Christ. It is the unifying element of scripture, theology, and human experience. Perhaps Wesley often oversimplifies issues through the use of the word "love," but he knows love is the one means of human transformation. Lives of individuals can be changed when the love of God dwells in the heart. Indeed, the love of God in the heart is the realization of heaven.

O Saviour of all, Thy word we believe,
And come at thy call, Thy grace to receive;
The blessing is given, wherever thou art:
The earnest of heaven is love in the heart.
(SH 2:250, Hymn 432, based on Psalm 19:11)

One of the finest summaries of Wesleyan theology is found in the poem based on Matthew 9:28, "Believe ye, that I am able to do this?" Its central focus is to be made perfect in love.

I do believe thou canst, thou wilt
Mine unbelief remove,
And purge out all my nature's guilt,
And perfect me in love:
Begin thy work, restore my sight
By justifying grace,

And bid me walk with thee in white,
To see my Father's face.
(SH 2:155, Hymn 116)

God is the source of "causeless, unexhausted love, unmerited and free."

Thy causeless, unexhausted love,
Unmerited and free,
Delights our evil to remove,
And help our misery;
Thou waitest to be gracious still,
Thou dost with sinners bear,
That sav'd, we may thy goodness feel,
And all thy grace declare.
(SH 1:53, Hymn 169, based on Exodus 34:6)

Love by no means has only a vertical dimension, God to humankind; rather, it is horizontal as well, person to person. One proves the truth of purity and love by loving others; that is, giving one's life, one's all for them. The poem on James 1:27 ("Pure religion, and undefiled before God and the Father, is this. To visit the fatherless and widows in their affliction, and to keep himself unspotted from the world") states his posture succinctly.

1. Father, on me the grace bestow
Unblamable before thy sight,
Whence all the streams of goodness flow;
Mercy, thine own supreme delight,
To me, for Jesu's sake, impart,
And plant thy nature in my heart.

2. Thy mind throughout my life be shewn,
While listening to the wretch's cry,
The widow's and the orphan's groan,
On mercy's wings I swiftly fly,
The poor and helpless to relieve,
My life, my all, for them to give.

3. Thus may I shew thy Spirit within
Which purges me from every stain,
Unspotted from the world and sin
My faith's integrity maintain,
The truth of my religion prove
By perfect purity and love.
(SH 2:380, Hymn 738)

Conclusion

Certainly the hymns and poems of *Short Hymns* are theologically full of hills and valleys. Charles Wesley set out not to write a systematic theology in verse but rather to respond to the content of scripture, its message, and contemporary life through poetry. Sometimes his turn of a phrase makes a somewhat illusive idea cogent. At other times, he quotes a passage and writes a poem unrelated to the specific text. Often such poems, however, are theologically and biblically sound and have their origin in scripture, but at some other juncture than the verses cited.

Wesley's biblical and theological ideas in *Short Hymns* are made intimate and personal. He sees himself on every page, in every person, in every place of the Bible. Moses's experience at Pisgah becomes his own, and he assumes the role of innumerable biblical characters. Hence, the texts of *Short Hymns* are filled with the spiritual application of biblical passages. Characteristic of his theological interpretation of scripture is a spiritualized view. The promised land is seen as Jesus's love. The oak tree of Isaiah 6:13 is viewed as the nation of England, and the fall of Jericho is likened to the completion of the Christian life.

On the whole, one finds in *Short Hymns* a serious wrestling with the meaning of the biblical texts in terms of language, message, and the application of same to life. All this is cast in the perceptive poetical language of Charles Wesley's verse.

If one examines the over 500 Charles Wesley hymn texts in *A Collection of Hymns for the Use of the People Called Methodists*, a volume which changed the direction of English-language hymnody and set it on a new course for the succeeding centuries, published by John Wesley in 1780, especially the critical edition which is volume 7 in *The Works of John Wesley*, one will discover that almost every line of each hymn is rooted in Holy Scripture. Numerous scriptural references are noted in the margins. Hence, one of the ways that the early Methodist societies learned the message of the Bible was through the hymns they sang. Thus Methodists, a hymn-singing people, became in large measure a Bible-singing people through Charles Wesley's hymns. Charles Wesley's theological formation of the language of scripture into the language of poetry, often intended for singing by the faith community, was oriented to the daily and worship life of Christians. These poems or hymns became the nucleus and heartbeat of the spiritual formation of the acts of piety and acts of mercy which became, and still are, hallmarks of Wesleyan spirituality.

While it has not been the purpose of this chapter to explore the implications of this study for concurrent scriptural interpretation among the Early Church Fathers and contemporary Orthodoxy, hopefully this research will prove fruitful for such exploration in the future.

Endnotes

[1] 2 vols. (Bristol: Farley, 1762), henceforth cited as *Short Hymns* in the body of the text and as SH in the footnotes, followed by the volume, page, and poem or hymn number; e.g., SH 2:86, Hymn 368. See the brief discussion of SH by Thomas Jackson, *The Life of the Rev. Charles Wesley, M.A.* (London: John Mason, 1841), 2:199–210.

[2]This author's italics.

[3]See *Short Hymns* 2:232–34.

[4]See the poems in *Hymns and Sacred Poems* (1742) based on Ro. 6 (182–183), Is. 4 (184–186), Is. 12 (186–87).

[5]The total number of poems in both volumes, according to the printed number of poems, is 2,348, but in volume 2 on p. 293, there are two poems with the number 556. Hence, the total number is 2,349.

[6]The influence of the language of the *Book of Common Prayer* often surfaces in Wesley's poetry. For example,

Jesus, Lord, assume thy right,
    And Israel's Ruler be,
God of God, and Light of Light,
    From all eternity. (SH 2:82, Hymn 368)

The third line comes from the Nicene Creed.

[7]Frank Baker, *Charles Wesley's Verse* (London: Epworth, 1988; first published 1964), 7.

[8](Bristol: Felix Farley, 1762), 1: first part of "Preface."

[9]*The Life of the Rev. Charles Wesley, M.A.*, 2:200.

[10]See SH 1:199, Hymn 637.

[11]This author's italics.

[12]Henry Bett, *The Hymns of Methodism* (London: Epworth, 1913), 82. See George Osborn, *The Poetical Works of John and Charles Wesley*, 13 vols. (London: Methodist Conference, 1868–72), 2:365.

[13]This author's italics.

[14]This author's italics.

[15]This author's italics.

[16]This author's italics.

[17]This author's italics for "trouble" and "care."

[18]SH 2:306.

[19]"The upright ones" is Wesley's translation of Jeshurun. See the hymn "None is like Jeshurun's God" in *The Works of John Wesley*, Oxford Edition, ed. by Franz Hildebrandt, Oliver A. Beckerlegge [*A Collection of Hymns for the Use of the People Called Methodists*, 1780] (Oxford: Clarendon, 1983), 7:570.

[20]The poem is based on Dt. 34:7, "His eye was not dim, nor his natural force abated."

[21]See SH 1:104, Hymn 326.

[22]See SH 1:104, Hymn 331. See also 1 Co. 10:4, "that Rock was Christ."

[23]This author's italics.

[24]His own copy of the two volumes is found at his house at Wesley Road Chapel in London.

[25]See Thomas Jackson's discussion on the differing views of Charles and John on perfection, *The Life of the Rev. Charles Wesley, M.A.*, 2:207–10.

[26]This poem is based on Mk. 4:28, "The earth bringeth forth first the blade; then the ear; then the full corn in the ear." The last two lines are a paraphrase of John Wesley's comments on the passage in *Explanatory Notes upon the New Testament*, which Charles cites in a footnote to the last line.

[27]See John R. Tyson's discussion in *Charles Wesley on Sanctification* (Grand Rapids, MI: Francis Asbury, 1986), particularly chapter 7, "A Brotherly Debate." Tyson's summary of the Wesleys' ideas on sanctification is of great value; however, he unfortunately concludes that SH consists of some 5,000 compositions; see 197–98. There are only 2,349 hymns and poems in SH. Tyson has taken the number 5,000 from Osborn's *The Poetry of John and Charles Wesley*, who adds more than double the material to SH from unpublished sources. However, Osborn gives no indication of the sources, nor does he indicate that a poem which he has added does not appear in the original two volumes.

12

The Visitation of the Word

Kenneth Carveley

As one who has been fascinated by the interweaving of the seamless, though sometimes frayed, robe of the Christian tradition, I found myself intrigued by something I had read in St. Bernard, something I had glimpsed in an icon, and something I experience from my own Methodist tradition.

The Scent of Truth

Exploring these avenues in a different order, I begin where most practicing Methodists might begin, and that is in a service of the Word on Sunday. As I recall it particularly from the church in London in which I was raised, this means listening to scripture read, then sung interpretation—"scripture sense by Scripture phrase," as Wesley puts it—often in the lines of Charles Wesley, and then expounded by the preacher. In this event in my home congregation, those internally engaged would do some theological reflection of their own. For me, it meant that just occasionally my heart and mind would perceive something which resonated with a sense of authenticity. Whatever the psychological mechanism of this, such moments were rare, but when they arrived, they often came with a scent of truth like some Orthodox saint's invisible imprimatur, yet in my case it was the distinct waft of a kind of nonconformist church-dust, pitch-pine kind which is hard to describe. If this seems far-fetched to Methodist rationality, let me remind you of the conversation between the pilgrim and Seraphim of Sarov when both were transfigured in the Spirit. Seraphim says:

> "When the Holy Spirit descends and fills the soul with the plenitude of his presence, then we experience the joy which Christ described, the joy which the world cannot take away. Do you feel anything else my friend?"
>
> "I'm amazingly warm."
>
> "Warm? What are you saying, my friend? We are in the depths of the forest, in mid-winter, the snow lies under our feet and is settling on our clothes. How can you be warm?"
>
> "It's the warmth one feels in a hot bath."
>
> "Does it smell like that?"
>
> "Oh no, nothing on earth can be compared to this! There's no scent in all the world like this one!"

> "I know," said Father Seraphim smiling. "It's the same with me. It is indeed true, friend of God, that no scent on earth can be compared with this fragrance because it comes from the Holy Spirit. This kingdom is just the grace of the Holy Spirit, living in us, warming us, enlightening us, filling the air with his scent, delighting us with his fragrance and rejoicing our hearts with an ineffable gladness."[1]

I can only say that one sensed and scented truth in a kind of holistic way, beyond hearing and rationale, the kind of hearing with the heart to which Orthodoxy is no stranger. These moments of revelation and insight I do not think were mine alone and certainly had something to do with belonging to the holy common People of God.

A Heart Strangely Warmed

St. Bernard, a debtor to Origen, Cassian, and other streams of the monastic tradition, writes about a similar kind of visitation. For him, the visitation of the Word occurs mediated by scripture in *lectio divina*, and here it is clearly the dynamic *Logos*, Christ the living word. It echoes a sacramental sense. It is about presence, with something of the Emmaus Road encounter to it in both its revelation and heart-burning recognition. *Lectio divina* becomes a pathway to such a meeting, as if the tangible, visible scripture text were the outward form of Christ's mediated unseen presence (to which I hope to return later.)

> I want to tell you of my own experience, as I promised. Not that it is of any importance. . . . I admit that the Word has also come to me—I speak as a fool—and has come many times. But although he has come to me, I have never been conscious of the moment of his coming. I perceived his presence, I remembered afterwards that he had been with me, sometimes I had a presentiment that he would come, but I was never conscious of his coming or his going And where he comes from when he visits my soul, and where he goes, and by what means he enters and goes out, I admit that I do not know even now; as John says: "You do not know where he comes from or where he goes." There is nothing strange in this, for of him was it said, "Your footsteps will not be known." The coming of the Word was not perceptible to my eyes, for he has not color; nor to the ears, for there was no sound; nor yet to my nostrils, for he mingles with the mind, not the air; he has not acted upon the air, but created it. His coming was not tasted by the mouth, for there was not eating or drinking, nor could he be known by the sense of touch, for he is not tangible. How then did he enter? Perhaps he did not enter because he does not come from outside? He is not one of the things which exist outside us. Yet he does not come from within me, for he is good, and I know there is no good in me. I have ascended to the highest in me, and look! the Word is towering above that. In my curiosity I have descended to explore my lowest depths, yet I found him even deeper. If I look outside myself, I saw him stretching beyond the furthest I could see; and if I looked within, he was yet further within. Then I knew the truth of what I had read, "In him we live and move and have our being." And blessed is the man in whom he has his being, who lives for him and is moved by him.

6. You ask then how I knew he was present, when his ways can in no way be traced? He is life and power, and as soon as he enters in, he awakens my slumbering soul; he stirs and soothes and pierces my heart, for before it was hard as stone, and diseased. So he has begun to pluck out and destroy, to build up and to plant, to water dry places and illuminate dark ones; to open what was closed and to warm what was cold; to make the crooked straight and the rough places smooth, so that my soul may bless the Lord, and all that is within me may praise his holy name. So when the Bridegroom, the Word, came to me, he never made known his coming by any signs, not by sight, not by sound, not by touch. It was not by any movement of his that I recognized his coming; it was not by any *of* my senses that I perceived he had penetrated to the depth of my being. Only by the movement of my heart, as I have told, did I perceive his presence; and I knew the power of his might because my faults were put to flight and my human yearnings brought into subjection. I have marvelled at the depth of his wisdom when my secret faults have been revealed and made visible. At the very slightest amendment of my way of life I have experienced his goodness and mercy; in the renewal and remaking of the spirit of my mind, that is of my inmost being, I have perceived the excellence of his glorious beauty, and when I contemplate all these things I am filled with awe and wonder at his manifold greatness.

7. But when the Word has left me, all these spiritual powers become weak and faint and begin to grow cold, as though you had removed the fire under the boiling pot, and this is a sign of his going. Then my soul must needs be sorrowful until he returns, and my heart again kindles within me the sign of his returning.[2]

"Only by the warmth of my heart did I know he was there," says Bernard. To which Seraphim and Wesley may also say, "Amen."

On a Wing and a Prayer

The third in my experiential trilogy is my encounter with Mary's encounter with the angel. In some icons of the Annunciation, Gabriel appears to descend at speed, to the startled shock of Mary, either at the well or as she is at home spinning the twine for the temple curtain.

I suspect this is about encountering presence, but dogmatically, as at her *fiat* the *shekina* of God leaves the temple to dwell in the womb of the Virgin, it is about much more. In many icons of the Annunciation, the angel is depicted as if his flight was still not quite completed; although he stands on the ground, one wing is raised, which too is a symbol of his being a messenger.

This symbol is also transmitted in the service, says Ouspensky, when the deacon, who according to the interpretation of John Chrysostom, represents the angel, symbolically repeats this gesture by lifting his stole with his right hand every time he calls the faithful to prayer. But while at the Annunication the flight of the angel is from heaven down to earth, in the Divine Service the deacon invokes the faithful to lift themselves up with him in prayer.[3]

There are two iconographic types of the Annunciation in the Protoevangelium of St. James. In one called the pre-Annunciation,[4] the angel calls out to Mary as she fills her pitcher at the well. Mary, startled, drops her pitcher and flees into the house. She sets down her pitcher of water and begins spinning for the temple veil (thus forging a link between the two dwelling places of God). The angel then appears to her a second time.[5]

This, then, concerns divine communication in an incarnational way. It is about how God speaks to us, but also, as Mr. Wesley might say, it is about "the best of all, God is with us."

As Breck expounds it:

> In the image of the Mother of God we receive that eternal Word into ourselves precisely through the grace and power of the Spirit. We read it, we meditate upon it, and interiorize it so that it comes to fruition within us for our own spiritual growth. We take the words of Scripture and "ponder them in our heart" as the very source of knowledge, wisdom and life. And, like the Holy Virgin, we offer the Word to the world, "for the life of the world and its salvation."
>
> For *lectio* is fulfilled, it achieves its true purpose, insofar as it issues in loving service as well as in contemplation, in *diakonia* as well as in personal communion with God.[6]

In the reading of the scriptures and in preaching, Methodists experience the dynamic sense of the icon, an encounter with the Word.

Thou who did so greatly stoop
    To a poor virgin's womb,
Here thy mean abode take up,
    To me my Saviour come![7]

A Methodist *Lectio Divina*

There is a real sense in which Methodists experience *lectio divina.* Charles Wesley expresses this in a hymn which is infused with a sense of the Emmaus Road and Thomas in the Upper Room encounters, yet with a sense too of Breck's consequent *diakonia,* a hymn which also manages to relate this to morning and evening prayer. What is clear here is that reading the Word brings with it a sense of the Lord's presence.

1. When quiet in my house I sit,
    Thy Book be my companion still,
My joy thy sayings to repeat,
    Talk o'er the records of thy will,
And search the oracles divine,
Till every heartfelt word be mine.

2. O may the gracious words divine
    Subject of all my converse be!
So will the Lord his follower join,
    And walk and talk himself with me;
So shall my heart his presence prove,
And burn with everlasting love.

3. Oft as I lay me down to rest,
O may the reconciling word
Sweetly compose my weary breast!
While on the bosom of my Lord,
I sink in blissful dreams away,
And visions of eternal day.

4. Rising to sing my Saviour's praise,
Thee may I publish all day long;
And let thy precious word of grace
Flow from my heart, and fill my tongue;
Fill all my life with purest love,
And join me to the Church above.[8]

An experience from the Methodist preaching service, a word from St. Bernard, and the presence of the icon—these remind me that the tradition is one, but the icon in particular evokes a sense of the visibilty of tradition, *traditio* which includes the written word from Israel and the Christian oral traditions committed to writing, the visual text of iconography in the living visibility of the community of the faithful. As this has been described, *traditio* is the reality of Christ made known, made visible.

Many writers see a bond between the interior and exterior—between the scriptural canon, iconography, and ecclesiology and Christology. Were this not true, visible unity and *communio* might be of little concern. I become convinced that where the visibility of the tradition is ignored or neglected, it will find its own alternative forms. Hitherto for Methodists, we appear to have paid little attention to the visual place of the Bible/New Testament codex itself within our worship and practice. This for a tradition in which the incoming president of the Methodist Conference is inducted by passing to him or her the Field Bible of John Wesley, the nearest, I suspect, that Methodism gets to the *instrumenta* of Latin ordinations.[9]

As one might expect of a Protestant tradition, our churches are replete with pulpit Bibles, and in past days, scriptural texts emblazoned apses, where in the Orthodox tradition we might expect the enthroned Christ *Pantocrator* or the *Theotokos* to be. Within our traditions, the volume of scripture assumes a place liturgically but always bound up with the living assembly of the people of God.

Text, Context, and Presence

I want therefore to consider the symbolic or iconographic use of the text of scripture. Within the Orthodox tradition, the codex, particularly the Gospel book, has a particular liturgical context in which it symbolizes Christ's presence. This is true of many of the Western Christian traditions. But there is a particular use of the Gospel codex in a conciliar context. In explaining the gospel traditions, Irenaeus seems to prefigure this when he writes, "Now the Gospel in which Christ is enthroned are like these."[10] This is true not only in the context of the Eucharist, during which the gospel is processed and read. The Gospel book was also enthroned at councils of the Church, particularly from Ephesus 431 onwards. We are indebted to Romeo de Maio for his perceptive explanation of their significance: "In the middle of the throne was placed the holy Gospel, which showed us that Christ himself was present."[11]

Cyril of Alexandria, who presided over council meetings, writing to Emperor Theodosius says:

> Certainly, not without difficulty the holy Synod was assembled in the holy church known as the church of Mary, and appointed as a member, or rather as its head, Christ; in fact on the holy throne was placed the venerable Gospel, which seemed almost to cry to the holy bishops: judge according to justice, decide between the holy evangelists and the clamours of Nestorius.[12]

Tarasius of Constantinople tells Pope Hadrian concerning Nicaea II (787):

> Having seated ourselves we appointed Christ as our president. In fact on the sacred chair was placed the Holy Gospel, which said to all of us, holy men, there assembled: Judge according to justice, decide between the Church of God and the present novelty (iconoclasm).[13]

At the Council of Constantinople 869, the Gospels were enthroned in St. Sophia and alongside them a relic of the true cross. This tradition later appeared to the surprise of all, pope, patriarch, German emperor, and cardinals, in 1438 at Ferrara, where the Gospels on their *etoimasia* presided. This liturgical conciliar enthronement is marked in an early Christian mosaic in St. Maria Maggiore and post-431 in the Arian Baptistery and in the Orthodox Baptistery at Ravenna.[14] De Lubac describes this:

> For the Fathers through the arches of the years of the first eight Councils, the Scriptures were the Logos, were Christ himself, their enthronement was meant as recognition of the fact that he was invested with the authority and majesty of divine judgement.[15]

A codex of the homilies of Gregory of Nazianzen shows the Gospels and the emperor adjacent to the throne.[16] From Nicaea II 787, in its decrees after iconoclasm, we read of the attention which the codex of the Gospel demands:

> Like the holy cross, the gospels, and the relics of the saints, to these images offerings of lights and incense may be made as was the pious custom of our ancestors.

This custom of enthroning the Gospel was used as recently as the opening of the holy door in Rome for the millennium. The rite for this occasion prescribes:

> When the procession arrives at the altar, the Orthodox deacon places the Book of the Gospels on the special seat before the Altar. Afterwards the Holy Father fills the incensory and the two deacons, Orthodox and Latin, incense the Book of the Gospels.

Such liturgical use of the *etoimasia*, the enthronement of the Gospel book as symbolic of Christ's presence and presidency, may seem light years away from post-Reformation Anglican-derived Methodism. We might cite the Reformed tradition adopted in many of our churches whereby the Bible is placed on the holy table and occasionally processed in and out to symbolize the church under the Word. Yet Methodists do have a sense of the presence of Christ in the assembly. In reflecting upon these descriptions of the visual image of the presence of Christ in the Gospels enthroned among the council fathers, we might consider Charles Wesley's words:

Thee we expect our faithful Lord
Who in thy name are joined;
We wait, according to thy word,
Thee in the midst to find.

With us thou art assembled here
But O thyself reveal,
Son of the living God appear,
Let us thy presence feel.

Cause us the record to receive,
Speak and the tokens show;
O be not faithless but believe
In me who died for you.[17]

Scripture Sense and Scripture Phrase

If there is one passage from John Wesley's Journal which most Methodists might be able to quote as their title deed, it would doubtless be the passage from May 24, 1738. Hearing this read in monastic choir, on the day we commemorate the Wesleys, I was struck by how much scripture it contains:

> I think it was about five this morning that I opened my Testament on those words "There are given unto us exceeding great and precious promises, even that ye should be partakers of the divine nature." 2 Peter 1.4
>
> Just as I went out I opened it again on those words "Thou art not far from the kingdom of God."
>
> In the afternoon I was asked to go to St Paul's. The anthem was "Out of the deep have I called unto thee O Lord; Lord hear my voice. O let thine ears consider well the voice of my complaint. If thou, Lord, wilt be extreme to mark what is done amiss, O Lord, who may abide it? For there is mercy with thee; therefore shalt thou be feared. O Israel trust in the Lord: For with the Lord there is mercy and with him is plenteous redemption. And he shall redeem Israel from all his sins.
>
> In the evening I went very unwillingly to a society in Aldersgate Street where one was reading Luther's preface to the Romans. About a quarter before nine, while he was describing the change which God works in the heart through faith in Christ, I felt my heart strangely warmed. I felt I did trust in Christ, Christ alone for salvation. And an assurance was given me that he had taken away my sins, even mine, and saved me from the law of sin and death.[18]

Its use of the text from 2 Peter coincidentally unites both eastern deification (*theosis*) theology with Pietist religion of the heart. Wesley's use of scripture and of the actual text itself is worth noting. The act of opening the Bible, often to find a word from the Lord to meet an immediate circumstance, is something which he does frequently. As he explains:

> At some rare times when I have been in great distress of soul, or in utter uncertainty how to act in an important case which required a speedy determination, after using all other means that occurred I have cast lots or opened the Bible. And by this means I have been relieved from distress, or directed in that uncertainty.

Wesley explains that the use of lots is a Moravian Church practice, so possibly he may have learned this from them.[19]

> Tuesday 6th June 1738
>
> Begging God to direct me I opened my testament on 1 Cor. 3.1 where Paul speaks of those who are babes in Christ who were "not able to bear strong meat."[20]
>
> Saturday 14th October 1738
>
> After crying to God I took up my Bible which opened with these words (1 Chron. IV.10). This however, with a sentence in the evening lesson, put me upon considering my own state more deeply.[21]
>
> Monday June 22nd 1741
>
> The words on which my book opened at the society in the evening were these . . . (Mal. 3.7, 13, 14.)[22]

This may suggest that Wesley held a high doctrine of biblical inspiration, but occasionally such a view could be unnerving and possibly bibliomantic, and he clearly held to a more rational exegesis and indeed a more inward sense than the letter might reveal.

Such a practice appears eventually to have ceased, maybe as a result of the entries for March 1739, when he was urged to go to Bristol:

> Saturday 10th March 1739
>
> This I was not forward to do and perhaps a little less inclined to it, because of the remarkable scriptures which offered as often as we inquired, touching the consequence of this removal.
>
> Wed 28th March 1739
>
> By this it was determined I should go. Several afterwards desiring we might open the Bible concerning the issue of this, we do so on the several portions of scripture which I shall set down without any reflection upon them. 2 Sam. 3.1, 4.11, 2 Chron. 28.27.[23]

I suspect that the latter text, "And Ahaz slept with his fathers and they buried him in the city, even Jerusalem," made not only the prospect of Bristol but also the practice of using scripture as a kind of *Urtext* for British Rail less and less inviting.

Such occurrences do less than justice to the sense that Wesley has of Christ's speaking to us through the scriptures. Writing to the Bishop of Gloucester, he quotes from the Anglican Homilies, in particular *The Homily on Reading the Scripture Part II*:

> Human and worldly reason is not needful to understanding the Scripture; but the "revelation of the Holy Ghost" who inspireth the true meaning unto them who, with humility and diligence, search for it.[24]

Within scripture there speaks a living voice, for the Holy Spirit who inspires it supernaturally assists in its interpretation.[25]

> The soul transforming word
> In us, even us fulfil,
> Join to thyself our common Lord,
> And all thy servants seal.
> Confer the grace unknown
> The mystic charity.[26]

The reading and preaching of the Word works its effects in us by the grace of the Spirit, issuing in living *diakonia* in the life of the world. Charles Wesley expounds the necessity for faith, which makes the experiential difference between the dead letter and the living truth:

> Whether the word be preached or read
> No benefit I gain
> From empty sounds or letters dead,
> Unprofitable all and vain;
> Unless by faith Thy word I hear,
> And see its heavenly character.
>
> Unmixed with faith, the Scripture gives
> No comfort, life, or light to see,
> But me in darker darkness leaves,
> Implunged in deeper misery,
> O'erwhelmed with nature's sorest ills.
> The Spirit saves; the letter kills.
>
> If God enlighten through His word
> I shall my kind Enlightener bless;
> But void and naked of my Lord
> What are all verbal promises?
> Nothing to me; till faith divine
> Inspire, inspeak, and make them mine.
>
> Jesus, the appropriating grace
> 'Tis Thine on sinners to bestow.
> Open mine eyes to see Thy face
> Open my heart Thyself to know.
> And then I through Thy word obtain
> Sure, present and eternal gain.[27]

The Spirit and the Letter

Without falling into Gnostic dualism, we may glimpse here a reflection of the patristic writing on the spirit and the letter. Breck describes how in *lectio divina* the Spirit inspires and guides the reader, granting knowledge in the sense of participation and communion, so that God is known through the text of the scripture as he is known through the text and action of the liturgy.

> By the grace of the Holy Spirit a prolonged quiet and meditative reading of Scripture can lead beyond the original literal sense of the passage to a moral or mystical sense which pertains to our own faith and life. And from there also in the power of the Spirit we can journey onward to what the tradition calls the anagogical sense. This is the higher spiritual sense that enables us, in the most sublime moments, to perceive through the Spirit "what God has prepared for those who love him" (1 Cor. 2.9).[28]

This occurs in Origen's sense of the letter and the spirit. Daniélou says of him:

> The only one who can interpret scripture is the one who inspired it. Christ is the inner principle dispensing the spiritual understanding of scripture.[29]

This is echoed in Symeon the New Theologian:

> Think of the Chest as the Gospel of Christ and the other divine scriptures. In them are enclosed and sealed up eternal life together with unutterable and eternal blessings. Even he who . . . has learned all the divine Scriptures by heart will never be able to know and perceive the mystical and divine glory and power hidden in them without going through all God's commandments and taking the Paraclete with him. The Paraclete will open to him the words like a book and mystically show him the glory they contain.[30]

Origen himself says:

> The aim of the Holy Spirit was chiefly to preserve the connexion of the spiritual meaning, both in the things that are yet to be done and in those things which have already been accomplished, whenever he found those which had been done in history could be harmonised with the spiritual meaning, he composed in a single narrative a texture comprising both kinds of meaning, always however concealing the secret sense more deeply.[31]

This leads some to see in Origen an undermining of incarnational theology and a reduction of the significance of the acts of God in history.[32] There is however a vital connection between the flesh of Christ and the text of scripture and the Church and the continuing visible *traditio*.[33]

For Origen the literal sense of the gospel has the humanity of Christ for its subject matter. The Incarnation of the *logos* defines the movement of exegesis in the New Testament, but in the reverse direction, from the humanity of Christ to the revelation of his divinity. It is always necessary to read from the humanity of Christ to his divinity, just as it is necessary to pass beyond the literal sense to the spiritual.

There is a living sense in Origen of Christ inseparably united with the Church which is now his dwelling place and visible presence.[34]

Daniélou indicates how in Origen the spiritual and philosophical meaning can tend to dissolve incarnational realities. He does, however, give a succinct summary of the relation of outward form to inner meaning in all of the senses in which I have sought to describe their interrelationship.

> In the Old Covenant the presence of God was in the temple in Jerusalem, but from the Incarnation dwelling in the human nature of Christ and his members, the Christian community, not the stone-bound church. Against Celsus's charge that Christians form a secret society which is a danger to civilization, Origen points to the visible presence of the Church as a city within a city. In the presence of truth, type and shadow cease and when the temple was built in the Virgin's womb by the Holy Spirit, the stone-built temple was destroyed. The temple of lifeless stones gives way to that of living stones (1 Peter 2.5), the earthly altar giving place to the heavenly altar at which Christ celebrated the true liturgy. The position is the same whether the issue is the material side of worship, the literal meaning of scripture or the visible humanity of Christ. It affects the reality of all three, for Origen regards them only as starting points."[35]

I have sought here to explore how the scriptures relate to the common visible doxological tradition. I began with three images: a warmed heart, an experience of *lectio divina* and worship, and an encounter. I conclude with three more:

(a) John Wesley on the scripture and the religion of the heart:

> living faith is, not only to believe the Holy Scriptures and the articles of faith are true, but also to have a sure trust and confidence to be saved from everlasting damnation by Christ, whereof doth follow a loving heart to obey his commandments.[36]

(b) Nicholas Cabasilas on *lectio divina* and worship:

> Because the holy scriptures contain divinely inspired words and praises of God, and because they incite to virtue, they sanctify those who read or chant them.[37]

(c) Anthony Bloom on an encounter:

> When I was reading the beginning of Mark's Gospel, before I reached the third chapter, I suddenly became aware that on the other side of my desk there was a presence. And the certainty was so strong that it was Christ standing there that it has never left me. That was the real turning point. Because Christ was alive and I had been in his presence I could say with certainty that what the gospel said about the crucifixion of the prophet of Galilee was true and the centurion was right when he said "Truly he is the Son of God."
>
> It was in the light of the Resurrection that I could read with certainty the story of the Gospel, knowing that everything was true in it because the impossible event of the resurrection was to me more certain than any event of history.
>
> I did not discover, as you see, the Gospel beginning with the first message of the Annunciation, and it did not unfold for me as a story which one can believe or disbelieve.[38]

Endnotes

[1]V. Zander, *Seraphim of Sarov* (London: SPCK, 1975), 91–92.

[2]Bernard of Clairvaux, sermon 74, in Harvery Egan, S.J., ed., *An Anthology of Christian Mysticism* (Collegeville: Liturgical Press, 1991), 166–79. Bernard of Clairvaux, trans. by G. R. Evans, *Selected Works* (Mahwah, NJ: Paulist, 1987), 252–258.

[3]Leonid Ouspensky and Vladimir Lossky, *The Meaning of Icons* (Crestwood, NY: St. Vladimir's Seminary Press, 1952), 173n. 3.

[4]Ibid., 173.

[5]H. Maguire, *Art and Eloquence in Byzantium* (Princeton: Princeton Univ. Press, 1981), 47.

[6]John Breck, *Scripture in Tradition: The Bible and Its Interpretation in the Orthodox Church* (Crestwood, NY: St. Vladimir's Seminary Press, 2001), 86.

[7]Hymn by Charles Wesley, in John Wesley, ed., *A Collection of Hymns for the Use of the People Called Methodists* (London: John Mason, n.d.), hymn 413, stanza 2.

[8]*Methodist Hymn-Book* (London: Methodist Conference Office, 1933), hymn 310.

[9]In *The Methodist Worship Book*, the Bible is presented to local preachers at their service of admission and to presbyters and deacons at their ordination, as a sign of the authority given to them to fulfill their office in the church. I seem to recall that at the consecration of a patriarch in the Orthodox tradition, the Gospel book is laid upon the shoulders of the new patriarch. Cf. *Methodist Worship Book* (Peterborough: Methodist Publishing House, 1999), 307, 322, 334.

[10]Irenaeus, "*Adversus Haereses*," 3.11.8, in R. M. Grant, *Irenaeus of Lyon* (London: Routledge, 1997), 131.

[11]Romeo de Maio, *The Book of the Gospels at the Oecumenical Councils* (Rome: Biblioteca Apostolcia Vaticana, 1963), 10.

[12]Ibid.

[13]Ibid.

[14]Ibid., 9, 10, 13.

[15]Ibid., 21.

[16]Ibid., 22, 25.

[17]Charles Wesley, in *Methodist Hymn-Book* (1933), hymn 719.

[18]Thomas Jackson, ed., *The Journal of John Wesley*, in *The Works of John Wesley*, 14 vols. (London: Wesleyan Conference Office, 1872), 1:103, paragraphs 13–14, entry for May 24, 1738. The Jackson edition is henceforth cited as *Works*, followed by volume and page numbers.

[19]"Principles of a Methodist Farther Explained," *Works*, 8:449, paragraphs 3–4.

[20]*Works*, 1:106.

[21]*Works*, 1:160–61.

[22]*Works*, 1:316.

[23]*Works*, 1:176.

[24]John Wesley, "Letter to the Bishop of Gloucester Occasioned by His Tract On the Office and Operations of the Holy Spirit," *Works*, 9:169.

[25]Scott J. Jones, *John Wesley's Conception and Use of Scripture* (Nashville: Kingswood/Abingdon, 1995), 105–106.

[26]Charles Wesley, in *A Collection of Hymns for theUse of the People Called Methodists* (1780), hymn 448, stanza 3–4b.

[27]Charles Wesley, in J. Alan Kay, ed., *Wesley's Prayers and Praises* (London: Epworth, 1958), 46.

[28]John Breck, *Scripture in Tradition*, 81, 85.

[29]J. Daniélou, *Origen*, trans. by W. Mitchell (London: Sheed and Ward, 1955), 24, 16.

[30]*Simeon the New Theologian*, trans. by C. J. de Catanzaro, "On Spiritual Knowledge XXIV," *The Discourses* (London: SPCK, 1980), 261–263.

[31]Origen, *On First Principles*, trans. by G. W. Butterworth, book 4, chapter 2 (Gloucester, MA: Peter Smith, 1973), 286.

[32]John Meyendorff, *Catholicity and the Church* (Crestwood, NY: St. Vladimir's Seminary Press, 1983), 35, 41. For Origen, "history did not matter by itself, but only as a pointer toward the eternal world of the Spirit." Origen's difficulty comes from squaring the biblical given in time with theological speculation.

[33]H. E. W. Turner, *The Pattern of Christian Truth* (London: Mowbray, 1954), 284–285.

"Origen recognized the existence of a literal or historical sense which he normally takes as his starting point. He was sufficiently alive to the dangers of Docetism in thelogy not to fall willingly into a similar error in the field of exegesis. As in the Incarnation the divine Logos was born of Mary and proceeded into the world veiled in the flesh, so that whilst the flesh was perceived by all, the revelation of the Godhead was vouchsafed only to a few, so in the Old Testament the same Logos came to mankind . . . through the veil of the letter which both shrouds and contains the spiritual sense. The veil of the flesh in the Incarnation corresponds exactly to the veil of the letter in scriptural exegesis. It is arguable that in both fields Origen displayed a defective sense of history and that despite his disclaimer of Docetism, he cannot easily be acquitted in either field of a strong tendency towards Apollinarianism."

[34]V. D. Verbrugge, "Origen's Ecclesiology and the Biblical Metaphor of the Church as the Body of Christ," in C. Kannengeisser and W. L. Petersen, eds., *Origen of Alexandria, His World and His Legacy* (Notre Dame: Notre Dame Univ. Press, 1989), 280, 282, 292.

[35]J. Daniélou, *Origen*, 36, 115–6, 149, 154, 265.

[36]"Principles of a Methodist," *Works*, 8:363, paragraph 9.

[37]Nicholas Cabasilas, *A Commentary on the Divine Liturgy*, trans. by J. M. Hussey and P. A. McNulty (London: SPCK, 1966), 27.

[38]Anthony Bloom, *School for Prayer* (London: Darton, Longman and Todd, 1970), xii.

13

The Impact of the Psalms on Worship within Methodism

George Mulrain

Introduction

The singing or chanting of Psalms is an integral aspect of Methodist liturgical heritage. It is a practice that predates Christianity. Psalms go back to the time of the Davidic dynasty (c. 1000–586 BCE), where they had their origins within the worship life of the Temple and synagogue. The worshippers used to recite or sing psalms to the accompaniment of vocal or instrumental music. In fact, the name "psalm" is derived from the Greek word *psalmos*, which is a translation of the Hebrew *mizmor*, one of those hymns that were sung during worship to the accompaniment of a stringed instrument. In the Hebrew Bible, some of the psalms carry the word *selah* perhaps to indicate a musical interlude, where not only stringed instruments, but also wind instruments (e.g., flute) and percussion instruments (e.g., cymbals) might have been used.

The singing of psalms was a practice with which Jesus was familiar. In Matthew's Gospel, it is recorded that after the singing of a "hymn," he and his disciples went out to the Mount of Olives.[1] Tradition has it that they actually sang the words contained in Psalms 113–118. Christian worship in the early days certainly involved the psalms. The *Venite, Exultemus Domino*, or Psalm 95, is known to be one of the earliest of psalms that was employed in worship, dating back to its use in Constantinople by Athanasius, the fourth-century Christian theologian.

Psalmody and the Wesleys

The founders of Methodism, John and Charles Wesley, had their liturgical home in the Church of England, where, in the eighteenth century, the chanting of psalms was a regular feature. But back in the fifteenth and early sixteenth centuries, when the Western Church took its instructions from Rome, only the constituted choirs were allowed to sing, in Latin. However, following the Reformation instituted by King Henry VIII (1509–1547), which led to the breach with Rome, a number of changes came about that affected the worship life of the Church of England. Shortly after the accession to the throne of the Tudor Queen Elizabeth I (1558–1603), permission to sing hymns in public worship was granted by royal injunction.[2] This was in June 1559. The *Book of Common Prayer*, which became the official prayer book of the Church of England, did include psalms. As psalm singing gained in popularity, the use of Latin hymns in the Church of England was dying out. "Psalm-singing soon came to be regarded as the most divine part of public worship. When a psalm was read the heads of the worshippers were covered, but all men sat bare-headed when the psalm was sung."[3]

Tribute must be paid to Thomas Sternhold, who served in the court of King Henry VIII, for his contribution to psalmody. Sternhold set musically created metrical versions of the psalms and hoped that they would be preferred to some of the love songs as well as the obscene songs that many of the courtiers used to sing. As they became known in Scotland and in Geneva, versions of his psalms spread beyond England. Sternhold was undoubtedly the father of English metrical psalmody. He died ten years before the injunction regarding hymn singing was issued.

Just as in the eighteenth century the Psalter occupied an important place in Anglican worship, so too the practice continues today. The Book of Common Prayer remains the norm for public worship within the Anglican Church. When, for example, *The Alternative Service Book* was published in 1980, it was made clear in its preface that "it is intended to supplement the Book of Common Prayer, not to supersede it."[4] In keeping with the pattern as set in the Book of Common Prayer, in the various services there were readings from the psalms. Indeed, for the convenience of worshippers, in the *Alternative Service Book* publication, the *Liturgical Psalter*, complete with one hundred and fifty psalms, was included under the same cover.

Liturgical practice within the Church of England did have some effect on John Wesley's interest in the Psalms. However, it is worth mentioning the comment of one scholar: "While Wesley clearly respected Anglican worship, it would be unfair to view him as just another eighteenth-century Anglican priest who followed the worship prescribed by the Common Prayer. He was innovative both in his use and understanding of Anglican worship and in his introduction of new forms of worship."[5] Indeed, "Besides introducing extemporaneous preaching and prayer, and hymn singing into the Anglican liturgical worship, Wesley also introduced testimonies in non-liturgical worship settings."[6] According to another scholar, Wesley made detailed alterations to the Book of Common Prayer: "He omits a third of the Psalter (882 verses out of 2507) on grounds of brevity and unsuitable sentiments, and substitutes whole phrases and verses with the text of the Authorized Version."[7]

Whatever the motivation, John Wesley was very much interested in singing psalms. In 1737, while he was in Georgia, "Lewis Timothy printed for him at Charlestown *A Collection of Psalms and Hymns*, which marks the birth of Methodist hymnody."[8] In 1738, when John Wesley returned to England, he published the collection. There was also in 1743 another London publication, titled *A Collection of Hymns and Psalms*. Wesley made daily use of the psalms in public worship as well as in his personal devotions. For example, he used to spend time after Sunday evening services with a few of the communicants in singing, reading, and conversation. His journal entry for Thursday 10 June 1736 describes how "after a psalm and a little conversation," he "read Mr. Law's *Christian Perfection*, and concluded another psalm."[9] An entry for Saturday 15 October 1737 states, "We began the service (both at Highgate and

Hampstead) with singing a psalm. Then I read and explained a chapter in the French or German testament, and concluded with prayers and another psalm."[10]

An account of happenings on Sunday 26 March 1738 tells how Wesley "went in the evening to a society in Oxford, where (as my manner then was at all societies), after using a collect or two and the Lord's Prayer, I expounded a chapter in the New Testament, and concluded with three or four more collects and a psalm."[11] So great a value did Wesley attach to the psalms that he was quite disturbed whenever they were not used in worship. A Journal entry for Saturday 11 November 1738 states that he had "spent the evening with a little company at Oxford" when he "was grieved to find prudence had made them leave off singing psalms."[12]

It was obvious that the singing of the psalms gave much satisfaction to John Wesley. According to his Journal entry of Friday 9 May 1740, "Part of Sunday my brother and I then used to spending walking in the meadows and singing psalms."[13] This incidentally was in reference to a practice that was followed in the 1730s. We may safely conclude that singing psalms helped these two Wesley brothers to relax; it added to their enjoyment of nature.

The psalms were valuable in private pursuits as well as in public ventures. John Wesley often used them to secure people's attention when he was about to launch his open-air preaching. A Journal entry for Sunday 30 May 1742 describes a visit to Newcastle-upon-Tyne:

> At seven I walked down to Sandgate, the poorest and most contemptible part of the town, and, standing at the end of the street with John Taylor, began to sing the hundredth Psalm. Three or four people came out to see what was the matter; who soon increased to four or five hundred. I suppose there might be twelve or fifteen hundred, before I had done preaching; to whom I applied those solemn words, "He was wounded for our transgressions, He was bruised for our iniquities; the chastisement of our peace was upon Him; and by His stripes we are healed."[14]

John Wesley himself testified to the psalms' meaningfulness in worship. His journal entry of Sunday October 1 1749 states, "I preached at the Gins about eight, to the usual congregation; and surely God was in the midst of them, breaking the hearts of stone. I was greatly comforted at church, not only from the Lessons, both morning and afternoon, and in the Lord's Supper, but even in the Psalms which were sung both at morning and evening service."[15]

Charles Wesley, the great poet and hymn writer, also made use of the psalms. Several of his hymns were inspired by verses from the Psalms. The example of Psalm 2 will substantiate the point. Verse 6 of this psalm ("I have set my King on Zion, my holy hill") must have been in Wesley's thoughts when he penned the lines:

> Our souls are in his mighty hand,
> And he shall keep them still;
> And you and I shall surely stand
> With him on Zion's hill.[16]

Psalm 2:8, "Ask of me, and I will make the nations your heritage, and the ends of the earth your possession," must have been responsible for the following:

O for thy truth and mercy's sake
The purchase of thy passion claim;
Thine heritage, the nations, take,
And cause the world to know thy name![17]

Psalm 2:11, "Serve the Lord with fear, with trembling," must have influenced him to write:

Be it my only wisdom here
To serve the Lord with filial fear,
With loving gratitude;
Superior sense may I display,
By shunning every evil way,
And walking in the good.[18]

Finally, Psalm 2:12, "kiss his feet, or he will be angry, and you will perish in the way; for his wrath is quickly kindled," must have inspired:

Extol his kingly power,
Kiss the exalted Son,
Who died; and lives, to die no more,
High on his Father's throne:
Our Advocate with God,
He undertakes our cause,
And spreads through all the earth abroad
The vict'ry of his cross.[19]

The results would be astounding if we were to go through the entire Psalter and cross-reference verses with stanzas from Wesley's hymns.

Charles Wesley, like his brother John, had a high regard for the Psalms and for their usefulness as a liturgical tool. Charles also produced several paraphrases of psalms, an activity in which he was involved especially during the latter years of his life. It was Henry Fish who made a collection of these and had them published in a volume in 1854.[20] Apart from Fish's collection, the legacy that Charles Wesley left behind following his death was "a poetic version of a considerable part of the Psalms, which appeared in the *Arminian Magazine*."[21]

Methodism and Psalmody

For over two centuries Methodists have had the example of both John and Charles Wesley to follow for the use of psalms. Whenever they met for worship, they, like Anglicans, not only sang hymns but chanted psalms. The December 1933 publication in London of the *Methodist Hymn-Book* included several ancient hymns, canticles, and psalms which, according to the Methodist Book of Offices, were to be sung during the Order of Morning Prayer: the *Venite, Exultemus Domino* (Psalm 95), the *Te Deum Laudamus* ("We Praise Thee, O God"), the *Jubilate Deo* (Psalm 100). In addition, there were fifty-two other psalms, all of which were set to music. British

Methodists, as well as Methodists from West Africa, the Caribbean, and other "overseas districts," made full use of the 1933 publication. However, over the years, there has been a decline in the practice of singing psalms. Most congregations seem quite contented to read them.

In 1983, the British Methodist Church changed its hymnal and launched a new publication titled *Hymns and Psalms.* Although it included the ancient hymns, canticles, and fifty-six psalms, all set to music, it is significant that in the "Introduction to the Canticles and Psalms" it is stated, "The canticles and psalms are set out for congregational reading . . ." This was in recognition, surely, of the fact that the majority of British Methodists no longer sang the psalms as their first option. A subsequent paragraph in the introduction noted, "If the canticles and psalms are sung, the following indications may be noted . . ."

The influence of the Wesleys on psalmody within the United Methodist Church was somewhat different from that exerted upon the British. American Methodists are grateful to John and Charles Wesley for the encouragement to pray and sing the Psalms. However, they did not embrace the Psalter that had been prepared by the Wesleys, but developed their own. Today, the United Methodist Liturgical Psalter, published in the current hymnal,[22] "links Methodism to this rich heritage and to our own renewal of interest in the psalms as central to prayer, celebration, singing, and vital worship." According to the preface to the hymnal:

> Seventeen canticles from traditional and contemporary sources with sung or spoken responses are also included. Service music appropriate for the congregation is found within the services and among the hymns.
>
> The psalms, with spoken or sung responses, occupy a more prominent position than in previous editions. One hundred psalms prescribed by the lectionary of the Consultation on Common Texts as well as psalms for special occasions are included.
>
> The keyboard edition of the United Methodist Hymnal contains harmonic settings of the congregational responses for the psalms, the canticles and services of Holy Communion and Baptism.

Psalmody within Caribbean Methodism owes much to the 1933 edition of the British *Methodist Hymn Book* and to the widespread use of the Methodist Book of Offices. The latter stipulated in the Order for Morning Prayer the singing of the *Venite, Exultemus Domino* (Psalm 95), the *Te Deum Laudamus* ("We Praise Thee, O God") and the *Jubilate Deo* (Psalm 100). When the Book of Offices gave way to the Prayer Book of the MCCA, the Morning Liturgy left open the options for reading or chanting. According to the directive that followed the reading of the Old Testament:

> Here shall be sung the Canticle/Psalm appointed for the Day, otherwise it shall be read responsively, the congregation standing and the reader of the Epistle leading, at the end of which the "Glory be to the Father" shall be sung and the congregation shall sit.[23]

Caribbean Methodism used to boast that as part of the Wesleyan tradition, hymns are sung and psalms are chanted. What we find today is that the psalms are losing their popularity insofar as chanting is concerned. Praise in Worship sessions rely on choruses, many of which are verses of psalms. For example:

Psalm 20:7, Some take pride in chariots, and some in horses, but our pride is in the name of the Lord our God.

Psalm 23:6, Surely goodness and mercy shall follow me all the days of my life, and I shall dwell in the house of the Lord my whole life long.

Psalm 46:10, Be still and know that I am God.

As one who grew up aware of and involved in both Anglican and Methodist worship traditions (my father was an Anglican, my mother a Methodist), I can affirm that the chanting of psalms adds significantly to the experience of worship. I have always enjoyed singing hymns and have, of late, come to appreciate choruses. However, there is something special about chants. Their style and character are markedly unique. They add to the variety of musical offerings in worship; this is most welcome. But for chants to be effective, they must be well rehearsed. This is why congregations with choirs fare much better than those without. Choirs have a duty to practice beforehand the music to be used in any worship event so that they can give a lead to the congregations. I must add, though, that I do know of congregations across the Caribbean that can chant the psalms beautifully, and in harmony, despite the fact that they have neither instrument nor instrumentalist among their members.

My personal conviction is that we should always strive to give of our best in the worship of God. Music is of such vital importance that every leader of worship ought to invest careful thought in the musical offerings that he or she plans to utilize in any act of worship. As one selects appropriate hymns, songs, and choruses, one must also consider the use of complete psalms, to be chanted. No church should be satisfied with the choruses that contain just the few selected verses from the Psalter. Unfortunately, this is what many worshipping communities today continue to do in their Praise and Worship sessions. They focus on those verses that offer praises and thanks to God. However, there is more to the Psalter than just praise. The Psalter suggests that God can be angry at times. Dare we refuse to sing about that? The Psalter admits that as a people, we are often full of hatred for our enemies and sometimes are even angry with God. Are we fearful in the house of God to sing the truth about human nature? The psalms are honest insofar as they express some of our deepest feelings about God and about life. For this very reason, they should be retained, in their entirety, for use in worship. What is also worthy of note is that those psalms which seem to express anger with God in the earlier parts, do, in the closing verses, offer hope in and reconciliation with God. Chanting the complete psalm is to be preferred to singing individual verses, because in so doing, we are more likely to receive the total picture of our relationship with God.

Reclaiming Psalmody for the Caribbean Methodist Heritage

The Methodist Church in the Caribbean and in the Americas is actively pursuing the idea of replacing the 1933 publication of the *Methodist Hymn-Book* with a more modern hymnal. This edition will include hymns and songs from other Christian traditions, from the World Church, as well as compositions from Caribbean hymn writers.

Concrete plans still need to be made insofar as the psalms are concerned. Based on what was mentioned earlier about their contribution to a worship experience, it is imperative that the psalms not be left out of the new publication. There is the danger that unless Caribbean Methodists are intentional about actually including a liturgical psalter under the same cover as their hymnal, the ability to chant will be lost.

One hundred Jamaican Methodists were surveyed with a view to determining the extent of the threat to psalm use in worship. The results showed that there is no need for alarm insofar as familiarity with the Psalter is concerned. Thirteen percent said that psalms were used in their congregation every Sunday. Thirty-nine percent stated that psalms were used on "most Sundays" and 48 percent said that psalms were used "on a few Sundays." It is therefore true that every Methodist congregation in Jamaica at some time or other will make use of the Psalter.

Usage of the psalms in worship is not the problem. The real concern is psalm singing. According to the survey, a mere 9 percent said that in their congregation psalms are chanted. The remaining 91 percent stated that psalms are read, mostly responsively (87 percent) and in unison (4 percent). The conclusion to be drawn is that Jamaican Methodists are not singing psalms as before. I am reliably informed that if a similar survey were to be carried out in other parts of the Caribbean, the pattern that emerged would be the same. The present generation of Methodists is slowly but surely losing the ability to chant psalms. John Wesley would certainly be displeased, just as he was in November 1738 when he had visited that little company at Oxford and learned that they had left off psalm singing.

The survey also addressed the question of psalms that mention vengeance upon enemies. Those who took part in the survey were presented with the following sample verses:

> Psalm 35:8, Let ruin come on them unawares. And let the net that they hid ensnare them; let them fall in it—to their ruin.
>
> Psalm 56:5–7, All day long they seek to injure my cause; all their thoughts are against me for evil. They stir up strife, they lurk, they watch my steps. As they hoped to have my life, so repay them for their crime; in wrath cast down the peoples, O God.
>
> Psalm 5:10, Make them bear their guilt, O God; let them fall by their own counsels; because of their many transgressions cast them out, for they have rebelled against you.
>
> Psalm 63:9, 10, But those who seek to destroy my life shall go down into the depths of the earth; they shall be given over to the power of the sword, they shall be prey for jackals.
>
> Psalm 109:8–10, May his days be few; may another seize his position. May his children be orphans, and his wife a widow. May his children wander about and beg; may they be driven out of the ruins they inhabit.

As stated earlier, my personal conviction is that the psalms are so honest in the expression of deep-seated human emotions that they ought to be retained for use in worship. However, only 40 percent shared sentiments similar to mine. Thirty-seven percent said that psalms mentioning vengeance upon enemies do not have a part to play in worship. The remaining 23 percent said that they did not know. One of the main reasons advanced against the inclusion of such psalms was that in worship one ought to focus on forgiveness rather than revenge. There was some sympathy, though, with the idea that one ought not to simply discard the psalms that present difficulties but that these should be treated in other church contexts besides worship. Seventy-five percent suggested Bible study as the place where this can be achieved.

In spite of the negative reaction to the idea of using in worship those psalms that ask for revenge upon enemies, 63 percent of the persons surveyed admitted that sometimes these psalms do reflect the personal feelings that men and women actually have when they are wronged.

Caribbean people are accustomed to hearing psalms sung on radio. Psalms 23, 91, 137, and 150 are a few that have been arranged and sung by local artistes and have caught the fancy of listeners. Their popularity is due to the fact that the message contained in them is considered relevant to the Caribbean context. If the man and woman in the street are singing psalms as they go about their daily routine, then all the more reason why Christian people ought not to desist from singing psalms when they meet with other Christians to worship God!

The oral recitation of psalms is not enough. When Caribbean people want to celebrate, they sing. Hence, if the psalms do indeed constitute a cause for rejoicing, given their relevance to the context, then care must be exercised so as not to lose the habit (or the ability) of singing them. Methodists will have to be intentional about ensuring that such a great tradition as chanting is not lost to present and future generations. The proposed replacement hymnal will certainly enrich the worship of Methodists in the Caribbean. But more benefit is likely to be derived from the presence, under the same cover, of ancient hymns, canticles, and psalms, with the necessary arrangements for spoken and sung responses.

Endnotes

[1]Matthew 26:30.

[2]John Telford, *The Methodist Hymn-Book Illustrated* (London: Epworth, 1924), 25.

[3]Ibid., 26.

[4]*The Alternative Service Book* (1980), together with the *Liturgical Psalter* (Clowes: SPCK / Cambridge Univ. Press, 1980).

[5]Kenneth Bedell, *Worship in the Methodist Tradition* (Nashville: Tidings, 1976), 25.

[6]Ibid., 18.

[7]C. Norman R. Wallwork, "Wesley's Legacy in Worship," in John Stacey, ed., *Wesley: Contemporary Perspectives* (London: Epworth, 1988), 85.

[8]John Telford, *The Methodist Hymn-Book Illustrated*, 1.

[9]*John Wesley's Journal*, Abridged Edition (London: Charles Kelly, 1903), 15.

[10]Ibid., 30.

[11]Ibid., 43.

[12]Ibid., 62.

[13]Ibid., 98.

[14]Ibid., 128.

[15]Ibid., 238.

[16]*Hymns and Psalms* (London: Methodist Publishing House, 1983), Hymn 820, stanza 4.

[17]Ibid., Hymn 316, stanza 5.

[18]Ibid., Hymn 786, stanza 1.

[19]Ibid., Hymn 262, verse 2.

[20]Henry Fish, *A Poetical Version of Nearly the Whole of the Psalms of David* (London: Nichols for Mason, 1854).

[21]John Telford, op. cit., 8.

[22]*The United Methodist Hymnal* (Nashville: United Methodist Publishing House, 1989); *The United Methodist Book of Worship* (Nashville: United Methodist Publishing House, 1992).

[23]*The Prayer Book of the Methodist Church*, published on behalf of the Methodist Church in the Caribbean and the Americas (Peterborough: Methodist Publishing House, 1999), 70.

14

At Home in the Body of Scripture

Maxine Walker

What characterizes "being at home" is joy that comes from a place where one is nourished by love and where one flourishes in hope. Home is not necessarily a rational place but rather is a place discovered and recovered over the whole of life by persons who are bound together by the same potent and authoritative stories that provide direction and norm one's identity.

What might this metaphor of "at home" mean for two women, Frederica Mathews-Green, twentieth-century convert to Orthodoxy, and Susanna Wesley, eighteenth-century mother of John and Charles Wesley and called "the mother of Methodism" in their respective traditions' use of scripture? What might this metaphor of "at home" mean for us who want to construct ecumenical discussions emerging from corresponding and differing narratives? I chose these two women, nearly three centuries apart, because both are neither trained theologians nor clergy; they live "at home," are married to clergy, and have significant responsibilities in running their homes and raising their children.

Frederica Mathewes-Green in her spiritual autobiographies has introduced many Americans, Protestants and otherwise, to the Orthodox tradition; Susanna Wesley in her letters and journals introduces us to the influences that shaped her famous sons and that guided her spiritual instruction. These are women without the power of academic or ecclesial position, but they are women who live a kind of spiritual correspondence to each other, at home.

A major hazard in using the metaphor of home especially in connection with women is that a lingering nineteenth-century view of women as the ornament and comfort of home is an insufficient reading of the metaphor in our time, as well as being inadequate to deal with historical realities of both Christian men and women over the centuries. On the other hand, the use of home can suggest some kind of "pure space" that is free of a particular time and ambient culture.[1] In this supposedly "free" place, home can be equivalent to a fortress waging a defensive battle against the winds of cultural influences and social change.

At the outset, the value of the home metaphor lies in its symbolic power to draw us together and to recover a way of breaking the triumph of the partial and the fragmentary. The semiotic language and non-semiotic signs of home are part of a shared system of meaning as discovered in these women's respective stories. (I use the term "semiotics" here as the study of signs and the production of meaning from them.)

Being at home in the body of scripture is, as the metaphor suggests, life lived at the following address:

1. Home is the incarnate God in whom we live and move and have our being.

2. Home is a lens for reading and interpreting.

3. Home is being in communion.

Home Is the Incarnate God

First and last, home is the Word of God, the incarnate God. This is the Christian's address. Frederica Mathewes-Green and Susanna Wesley, in their respective traditions, provide two ways of looking at this central home address. Frederica Mathewes-Green, Orthodox, preserves the closed metaphor, and Susanna Wesley, the early Methodist woman, opens the metaphor. That is to say, Mathewes-Green lifts up Christ as both divine and human, whose Incarnation is *the* single subject, both synchronically and diachronically, of the church. Frederica Mathewes-Green's emphasis is always on the physical body and the mysteries of an incarnate God. There is the incomprehensive mystery of God's enfleshment in Christ; there is the ordinary body as we know it. This is the divine-human metaphor whose meaning and significance is the Word, and Mathewes-Green orients all of her Orthodox life within that metaphor. This is a totalizing act of closure in which reality is indeed changed; the metaphor becomes a transubstantiating act.

Susanna Wesley opens the metaphor in the sense that she explores Christ's work in the created order, primarily in the way her journals and letters are punctuated with notions of how revelation and natural law are different and yet complementary. Wesley maps out the signs of divine presence in her reading and reflections. By the "open metaphor" I am suggesting that Susanna Wesley intentionally launches into the questions and even tensions posed in Anglican "comprehensiveness" (agreement on fundamentals while tolerating differences without the necessity of breaking communion) even as she acknowledges her belief in the redeeming work of God in Christ.

First, the closed metaphor in Mathewes-Green's work. The Incarnation, God enfleshed in a body, the weight of divine mystery, is evident throughout all of ecclesial life. Frederica Mathewes-Green describes the divine liturgy as a "full body event," an immediate reference to the deep bows in the *metania*.[2] The body permeates her Orthodox life. She describes the meal following Pascha, the fabulously rich foods, the plate of paska, the beef, pork, lamb, fried chicken, champagne, red hard-boiled eggs, ice cream, cheese. It is the physical response to the reading of the prologue to the Gospel of John and the sermon of St. John Chrysostom, who exuberantly proclaims the "triumphal feast" and exhorts his listeners to partake and "enjoy the feast of faith," to come, for "the table is fully laden; feast sumptuously," for "it took a body, and met God face to face. . . . It took that which was seen, and fell upon the unseen."[3] In the spirit of American poet Emily Dickinson, Frederica Mathewes-Green says of her church, "A little church on Sunday morning is a neglible thing," but it is the spot where a divine lighting will strike (Isaiah 6:1).[4] It comes to the body.

As Mathewes-Green watches the communicants step forward to receive the body and blood of Christ, eighty-nine-year-old Lillian leads the way as the first communicant. Lillian, as a very young girl, had a vision similar to Jacob's ladder.[5] Mathewes-Green does not find this vision odd but sees it as a part of a mosaic of mysteries. These mysteries draw this "holy family" together as the communicants chant verses from John 6. These verses witness to the "body of Christ and tasting the fountain of immortality, the mystery of mysteries." Then, Mathewes-Green remembers the lives of Christian martyrs tortured and killed by persecutors who thought Christians were flesh-eating cannibals. As Frederica Mathewes-Green points out, these early Christians literally were eating flesh—"this is the hard saying"[6]—that Jesus spoke of the necessity of eating his flesh and blood.

Mathewes-Green describes this "feast": the communion line trickles forward, and the icons and relics are in sight. Suddenly she notices a stuffed red crab on the floor that belongs to a small child. There it is—another kind of suffering, a sea creature boiled red. The crab is red, the flicker of the candles is red, and the cloth under her chin is red as she is given the sacramental bread and wine.[7] Orthodoxy's "earthiness and groundedness in body reality"[8] are echoed in the Advent hymn: "The virgin cometh today to the cave to give birth; who shall appear, by His own will, as a young child: He who is from eternity God."[9]

Frederica Mathewes-Green's description and explanation of the meaning of icons in the life of the church also notes that the material world is a revelation of the invisible world.[10] The icons—the "is" between the tenor, the incarnate God and the "vehicle," the ecclesial life of the church. Since the incarnate God is the scriptural paradigm for icons, the metaphorical impulse in icons suggests the nature of metaphor itself (i.e., the sacred metaphor). The concrete, which alone is idolatrous, is reconciled in and transformed by the sacred.[11]

Frederica Mathewes-Green notes that it is characteristically Orthodox to be unconcerned with getting the full text into the icon.[12] Anton Vrame in *The Educating Icon* states it this way: the high value of both the visual and the verbal in Orthodox views allows the icon to be equally important as the medium of God's revelation. Thus, the art can focus on the most important point of the scriptural narrative; for example, in the icon of the Annunication, Mary is startled by Gabriel's appearance; she raises her hand in surprise and awe, and her left hand has pulled away from her spinning. Literal reading, yes. Literal reading, no. Spiritual reading, yes. Mary has encountered a being from God's world, although the iconography has said both more and less than the scriptural narrative. What visual grace says best, "Hail, O favoured one, the Lord is with you, blessed are you among women" (Luke 1:26–28). The Seventh Ecumenical Council describes the icons as being "of equal benefit to us as the Gospel narrative."[13] Vrame comments that both the icon and the Word help us know that the Incarnation of God the *logos* has a body that can be viewed.[14]

Now to turn to Susanna Wesley. Susanna Wesley, throughout her life, offers herself absolutely and entirely to Jesus Christ, the incarnate God, only Savior of the world. "He is our way, our truth, our life" (*Journals*, Nov. 27, 1727). Susanna Wesley "opens" this metaphor of Incarnation, of the totalizing Word; she does this by rejecting self-warranting metaphors and by her analyses of our human metonymic landscape.

In letters and journal entries destined for immediate family members, Wesley educates her family on "what it means to have faith in Christ." To her daughter Susanna, "Suky," Susanna Wesley writes from her home in Epworth, January 13, 1708, " 'the sacred treasure of knowledge' contained in the books of the Old and New Testament reveal to us knowledge of the Saviour. This is a treasure infinitely more valuable than the whole world because . . . therein we [find] all things necessary for our salvation."[15]

In Wesley's comments to Suky, as a part of a mother's explication on phrases of the Apostles' Creed, Susanna makes it quite clear that faith in Christ is first "to be understood as assent to whatever is recorded of him in Holy Scripture or is said to be delivered by him, either immediately by himself or mediately [sic] by his prophets and apostles or whatsoever may by just inferences or natural consequences be collected from their writings."[16] This is not a woman who reads and interprets *sola scriptura.*

Susanna Wesley's certainty of God incarnate is as Frederica Mathewes-Green's, in the sense that scripture writings from the prophets and apostles, reveal this mystery. Wesley's primary concern, as was other thinkers' in the eighteenth century, is the question of how a person's *reason* does or should respond to this mystery. Her concern is that reason, to phrase it in our literary terms, becomes the metonym for how the paths to eternal life and to God are found. Reason can lead us. Reason can misdirect us.

Thus, it must be said, Susanna Wesley always underscores that revelation is how we have any just and true ideas of Christ. Christ is not merely a more virtuous or nobler man among men. To know him only as a reasonable creature can "administer nothing but horror and amazement to the soul, since, obscure as natural reason is, it is clear enough to show us [what] we have done, and daily do, many things contrary to the purity of the Divine nature and according to the dictates of our own reason."[17] The Godhead dwells in Christ bodily as one sees by faith, not by reason, that "infinite, all-glorious Being assuming the character of a Savior, a repairer of the lapse, and healer of the diseases and miseries of mankind . . . the heart feels and labours under, but the tongue cannot express."[18]

On the other hand, one of Susanna Wesley's major emphases in her letters and catechetical writings to her children are the right uses of reason and the "reasonableness" of Christianity.[19] To her oldest son, Samuel Wesley Jr., she writes that (11 March 1704) the law of reason, the law of nature, are the foundation of morality and this law teaches us the care of life, to sustain and preserve the body. The law of nature also teaches us our duty to ourselves and to our neighbors.[20] Wesley exalts the virtues of reason to her brood as a way "to preserve the government of reason [over our] passions [so they] do not get the ascendant over us"—worthy advice to sons away at University![21] Nonetheless, she quickly qualifies this advice to assert that it is faith or God at work in the heart that will establish the body and soul:

> 'Tis true God did at first bestow on reasonable beings sense, perception, and reason, but sin hath so weakened these powers that, *unless divine grace restore them and renew the mind,* they are in a manner perfectly useless, or at least will not serve to the end for which they were given.[22]

In this vista, one is looking outward away from the mirror world of self-enclosure. Susanna Wesley's windows are wide open as she struggles with a range of readings in ancient and modern philosophy, ethics, natural religion, poetry—read by seventeenth and eighteenth century intellectuals—to inform her theological perspectives given to her family. She wants to "discern" God's scripture-revelation in these multiple contexts. She believes that the mind, as well as the body, is in captivity to habits of sin, and that the Holy Spirit, grace given by God to us, is the principal agent in breaking these chains. Thus, what the mind can grasp can be illuminated by light to discern spiritual things.[23] She is unwilling to ground her understanding of God or the life of faith in reason alone, or experience alone, or assent alone.[24] Upon hearing the report of son Charles's assurance of faith, she says:

> I think you are fallen into an odd way of thinking. You say that till within a few months you had no spiritual life nor any justifying faith. Now this is as if a man should affirm he was not alive in his infancy, because when an infant he did not know he was alive. A strange way of arguing, this![25]

Susanna Wesley makes the analogy that spiritual life is like bodily life. Growth is continual, and her inferences are that much wide reading under the direction of the Holy Spirit is a part of that development.[26] A prominent figurative way for her to explain the dynamic work of the Holy Spirit is such: the natural life is like the spiritual life. The Christian goes through many degrees of grace: first, we are infants, or babes in Christ, as St. Paul calls them, before they become strong Christians. "For spiritual strength is the work of time, as well of God's Holy Spirit."[27] Holiness is not the observance of a rigid set of rules but a work begun and perfected throughout all of life. She continues in another letter to son John (four years before Aldersgate), "the work of regeneration is not performed at once, but proceeds by slow and often imperceptible degrees . . . a single grain of mustard seed will take root and bring forth fruit with patience."[28] Grace works metonymically in that there is continuous association between "degrees" of grace, grace that "grows" and matures or else "withers" away. Orthodox see this as *theosis*, participation in the divine life.

Home Is a Lens for Reading and Interpreting

Home is a particularly apt metaphor to describe the way we read ourselves, our immediate surroundings, and the larger world. Two particular aspects of interpretation seem valuable at this point: one is our view from the inside looking out, and the other is from the outside looking in. For postliberal theologians or for poststructuralist literary critics, this is the complex interrelation between the text and the world. How do we understand our location? "What is the nature of the world [we] inhabit?"[29]

Helpful ways to think about reading and interpreting home are basic questions that inform our stories and our relationships; that is, questions that control the interpretation and reading. The questions become paths on which we create metaphors, much as the question, What is the kingdom of God like?

For Frederica Mathewes-Green, the questions are: How did I come to Orthodoxy, and how is the incarnate God worshipped in twentieth-century Baltimore, Maryland, in the continuation of the ancient faith? For Susanna Wesley, Stephen Gunter helps identify the questions that emerge from her writings:

1. What is the role of reason in matters of faith? If we compare the understanding of the world as perfect creation, then perfectly are revealed truths congruous with reason if pursued faithfully and patiently?[30]

2. How can we differentiate between assertions that are generically religious and those that are distinctively Christian?[31]

3. Can reason both define and confine the definition of faith?

4. What is saving faith? It is not just any assent from testimony and reason.[32]

These theological questions for both Frederica Mathewes-Green and Susanna Wesley indeed are "home questions." These women might recast some of these questions in this way:

1. How will I teach my children, given who they are and where they are?

2. What practices and symbols characterize the Christian life?

3. How do we participate in the divine life?

Toward the conclusion of *At the Corner of East and Now*, Mathewes-Green's daughter, Megan, decides to get a nose ring, much to her parents' dismay. This account set in the context of the Nativity and the week of Zacccheus Sunday is a hurtling forward of promises that bodies do indeed have meaning. In *Facing East*, Megan (now without nose ring after her college demanded that she remove it!) announces that she is getting business cards made. On one side is the 6th century icon of the Christ of the Sinai; on the other is the address of the church and a bold statement, "You should be Orthodox."[33] Frederica Mathewes-Green remembers others whose lives have been transformed by looking at this Christ of the Sinai holding a jeweled Bible, his right hand raised in blessing. A college professor once said of this icon, "I think [Christ] is looking into my soul."[34] Icons do the evangelizing—mother and daughter agree.

Most of her life as a mother, Susanna Wesley struggled to keep enough food on the table for her large family, and wrote about her anguish at not having enough tea. As her sons left for university, she frequently reminded them about the right uses of food and drink: "'Twill be very necessary to think often upon the true end of eating and drinking, which is to repair the decays of nature and thereby to strengthen and refresh the body, that it may be serviceable to the mind, as both must be to God.[35] Her teaching method for each child was to spend one day with each one in lessons, for each to say the Lord's Prayer from their earliest days as a child, as soon as they could speak. As early as five years of age, the Wesley children began reading the first chapter of Genesis.

After the rectory fire, the children were sent temporarily to "foster" homes, and Susanna Wesley had to retrain them in the things of God after they returned home. In the morning, they read psalms and the Old Testament. In the evening, they read psalms and the New Testament.[36] As Susanna Wesley's firstborn son leaves for

Westminster School in London, her concern continues for his moral and religious education. She urges Sammy to be obedient to the commandments of the glorious Creator; it is possible to obey that law only by praying for the assistance of the Holy Spirit. "Besides the promise of his Holy Spirit he has already given us the Holy Scripture which is a perfect rule of faith and manners. This read and study constantly . . . where you want direction, have recourse to the law and to the testimony." Also if there is anything he cannot understand, "[seek] out [your] father or schoolmaster."[37]

External performances do not determine one's spiritual state, but it is the manner more than the matter that is to be regarded. "Be sure you never forget Jesus Christ, but always acknowledge that you receive any influences of the spirit or any other blessing, either spiritual or temporal, only for his sake and upon his account."[38] "God's presence fills heaven and earth and all imaginary spaces . . ."[39]

For Frederica Mathewes-Green, icons are the means whereby "the believer maintains visual contact with the embodied, incarnate, historical Jesus."[40] For Susanna Wesley, a disciplined ordered life mortifies pride and the appetites of the body and can be done "without ensnaring [y]ourselves by obliging [us] to a multitude of external performances."[41] "Controlling irregular passions allows us to continue steadfast in the spirit and disposition of Jesus Christ."[42] Both women's home teachings are guided by Christ as the way to participation in divine life. As Anton Vrame notes in iconic catechesis, "teachers are icons, bearing the Tradition in themselves, with the models of iconic living and knowing."[43]

Susanna Wesley concludes a letter to her son John this way:

> That you may continue steadfast in the faith and increase more and more in the knowledge and love of God, and of his son, Jesus Christ! That holiness, simplicity, and purity . . . may recommend you to the favour of God Incarnate! That his Spirit may dwell in you, and keep you still (as now) under a sense of God's blissful presence, is the hearty prayer of, dear son, your affectionate mother, and most faithful friend, S[usanna] W[esley].[44]

This letter was written four years before Aldersgate. *Theosis* is the goal of home education.[45]

Home Is Being in Communion

What stories—whose stories—matter at home? Who gets to select and preserve the stories that are passed down to the generations? Are the stories embellished or understated? Do some stories go out of fashion for one generation and then surface in the next? How do these stories—whether from women, or from a particular ethnic region, or from a particular historical period—help us discover what it means to be one in the Eucharist and as members of the catholic church of Christ?[46]

Visiting an Orthodox church, one is struck by the "master stories" of the ancient and local community depicted in the icons. Visiting a Methodist church in the years following John Wesley's death, one would have been struck by the fervent testimonies of the faithful. My grandmother in the American Holiness movement taught her children and grandchildren early to sing, "I love to tell the story of Jesus and his love." Are these all the same stories with changes in persons and places?

Based on Frederica Mathewes-Green and Susanna Wesley's views of home, Christian stories are about assisting us toward *theosis*—human participation in the divine way of being—"life as a free, concrete person, loving and being loved in the communion of persons."[47] This is holy living for Wesleyans. Moreover, the primary truth of the Christian story consists in the Holy Spirit's illuminating the "performance" of Jesus Christ—his life, ministry, passion, death, and resurrection.[48]

These two women have shown us that narrative—the visual and the verbal—are essential to talk about conversion and growth in Christian faith.[49] The creeds, the "solemn confession of our most holy faith," as Susanna Wesley puts it, must be "attested whether the heart join with the tongue."[50] Christian narrative that unfolds over the whole of life is that confession. The symbols and practices of the Christian life are anchored in the story of God. This is our semiotic system—the grammar of faith.[51]

There is another dimension to this language system that helps us tell and participate in the story of the incarnate God. Miroslav Volf calls this the "non-semiotic dimension"; that is, the "experiential" aspect in the transmission of Christian faith. Volf uses the analogy that we become human not only through a mother's language but also through how she touches the child, how she smiles or frowns, how she stands at the kitchen counter and cuts bread, her posture in prayer. The taste of the wine and bread spilling off of the spoon into the communicant's mouth, the slight smile on Mary's face as she touches Jesus's chest in the icon ("Mourn not for me, Mother"), the smell of freshly crushed bay leaves and then walking on them—these are the non-semiotic signs of the resurrection. Watching his mother prepare for the Sunday evening services in the rectory, opening a letter from home written on precious paper, watching her shut her door for morning and evening devotions—non-semiotic signs of the influence of the Holy Spirit for Christ's account.

Through the Holy Spirit's work, persons in specific times and places are connected to the word and power of Christ through semiotic and non-semiotic dimensions. We can tell this full story only because Christ came to suffer and to redeem and transform the world. This is "the history of God with the world,"[52] and our stories intersect with and enter into God's story through persons.[53]

In the life of Susanna Wesley, the Holy Spirit assists in "family devotions, in the disposition and ability to speak of [Christ], in the instruction of the children, in the performance of domestic duties, in the preservation of [your] health from all ill accidents, terrors and dangers. . . ." She continues, "[T]rust in and rely on Jesus Christ . . . Glory be to thee, O Lord!"[54] The Word of God through the Holy Spirit begins with her individual conscience in the privacy of her devotional discipline and then reaches out to family and parish.[55]

Susanna Wesley and Frederica Mathewes-Green's stories emerge in their own time and place and intersect with the confessions, practices, gestures, and silences of the those in scripture, the saints in the icons, the seventeenth- and eighteenth-century writers and thinkers who struggled with moral virtue and goodness, the children who are watching and listening and learning about transformation in the image of Christ.

Even so, it is the story of incarnate God, the risen Christ—the Closed Metaphor—that opens the possibilities for communion and faithful witness along a postmodern metonymic horizon.

As Frederica Mathewes-Green attends the Orthodox *Litia* service, five loaves, with cruets of oil and wine and a small bowl of wheat berries, are blessed to be multiplied throughout the city, in the houses of those who celebrate this feast, and in all world. The words are pronounced: "sanctify the faithful who partake of them . . . rich men have turned poor and gone hungry; but they that seek the Lord shall not be deprived of any good thing." As the service progresses, Frederica Mathewes-Green notices a footnote in the service book that mentions "*omophorion* and *epitrachelion*" and thinks silently, "I have no idea what these terms mean." Her memories turn to a persistent dream she used to have: "I was exploring an old house with winding stairs and funny rooms leading to more hallways and other rooms. I never got to the end, but I had a wonderful time. I know I'll never get to the end of Orthodoxy. It will always be Grandma's attic to me."[56]

Ah, the mysteries of home!

Susanna's son, Charles Wesley, puts it this way:

> Incomprehensible thou art;
> Yet we still by faith conceive
> And bear thee in our heart.[57]

Endnotes

[1]Miroslav Volf, critiquing George Lindbeck's well-known position on the biblical text's absorbing the world, notes the following: "the notion of inhabiting the biblical story is hermeneutically naïve because it presupposes that those who are faced with the biblical story can be completely 'dislodged' from their extra-textual dwelling places and 'resettled' into intratextual homes. . . . We continue to inhabit our cultures even after the encounter with the biblical story. . . . *There is no pure space on which to stand even for the community of faith*" ("Theology, Meaning and Power," in *The Nature of Confession*, ed. Timothy R. Phillips and Dennis L. Okholm [Downers Grove, IL: InterVarsity], 51, italics in original). The work on "closed metaphor" as the Incarnation which stands in bold contrast to the Romantics' use of the metaphor and the organic imagination is best stated in Murray Kreiger, *A Reopening of the Closure: Organicism against Itself* (New York: Columbia Univ. Press, 1989).

[2]*Facing East*, 19. (All citations for Frederica Mathewes-Green are from *At the Corner of East and Now: A Modern Life in Ancient Christian Orthodoxy* [New York: Jeremy P. Tarcher/Putnam, 1999], and *Facing East: A Pilgrim's Journey into the Mysteries of Orthodoxy* [San Francisco: HarperSanFrancisco, 1997].)

A. M. Allchin in *A Taste of Liberty* (Fairacres: SLG Press, 1982) notes that although the richness of visual imagery in Orthodoxy is lacking in the West, Anglican (and Wesleyan) worship makes up for that loss in some measure by the beauty and richness of the music. What also is telling is that Allchin calls us back to Richard Hooker's recognition that "worship must express the whole of our being, the outward part is essential to its fullness as well. Therefore he [Hooker] defends the use of outward gesture in worship and has much to say in defence of church music" (19).

[3]*Facing East*, 88.

[4]*At the Corner*, 3.

[5]Ibid., 239.

[6]Ibid., 244.

[7]Ibid., 248.

[8]*Facing East*, 198.

[9]Ibid., 161–162.

[10]As Patrick Miller suggests, the "*imagination* is a central locus of *revelation* as well as the ground of *preaching and proclamation.*" See, for example, Walter Brueggemann, *Texts under Negotiation: The Bible and the Postmodern Imagination* (Minneapolis: Fortress, 1993).

[11]Kallistos Ware points out that "through icons the Orthodox Christian receives a vision of the spiritual world" (*The Orthodox Church* [Middlesex: Penguin, 1975], 214). Icons are the doorway between heaven and earth—the place of reconciliation, the place where inner spirit and body touch (Linda Proud, *Icons: A Sacred Art*, with comments on quotations and text by Brother Aidan and Professor Andrew Louth [London: Jarrold Publishing, 2000], 20).

[12]*Facing East*, 174.

[13]D. Sahas, *Icons and Logos, Icon and Logos: Sources in Eighth-Century Iconoclasm* (Toronto: Univ. of Toronto Press, 1986), 69, quoted in Anton Vrame, *The Educating Icon: Teaching Wisdom and Holiness in the Orthodox Way* (Brookline, MA: Holy Cross Orthodox Press, 1999), 62.

[14]Vrame, 52.

[15]All citations for Susanna Wesley are from Charles Wallace Jr., ed., *Susanna Wesley: The Complete Writings* (New York: Oxford Univ. Press, 1997), 381. Present in Susanna Wesley's gloss are distinct similarities to Article VI in the Book of Common Prayer: "The Sufficiency of the Holy Scriptures for Salvation."

[16]Susanna Wesley's view on the plenary inspiration of scripture is evident in that, although the books of the Old and New Testaments contain all things necessary for salvation, there are other truths to be learned: "There also we learn many truths which though we cannot say 'tis absolutely that we should know them, since 'tis possible to be saved without that knowledge, yet 'tis highly convenient that we should, because they give us great light unto those things which are necessary to be known and solve many doubts which could not otherwise be cleared" (Wallace, 381). She discusses angels "or spirits" to illustrate her point.

[17]*Notebook*, "Morning," entry 246 (Wallace, 352).

[18]Ibid.

[19]"Educational, Catechetical, and Controversial Writings," (Wallace, 448).

[20]Letter to Samuel Wesley Jr., 11 March 1704, (Wallace, 41–42).

[21]Susanna Wesley advises, "Do nothing unworthy of the reason God has given you" (*Journals*, entry 21, "Noon" [Wallace, 219]).

[22]*Journals*, entry 44, "Noon" (Wallace, 234, italics mine). Moreover, Susanna Wesley defines sin as that which "weakens reason, impairs the tenderness of your conscience, obscures your sense of God . . . in short whatever increases the strength and authority of your body over your mind; that thing is sin to you" (Letter to John Wesley, 8 June 8 1725 [Wallace, 109]).

The following is a response to Susanna Wesley about her deliberations on the nature of faith: "Faith is a species of belief, and belief is defined as 'an assent to a proposition upon rational grounds.' Without rational grounds there is therefore no belief and consequently not faith . . . I call faith an assent upon rational grounds because I hold divine testimony to be the most reasonable of all evidence whatever. Faith must necessarily at length be resolved into reason" (Letter to Susanna Wesley, 29 July 1725, quoted in Kenneth Collins, *The Scripture Way of Salvation: The Heart of John Wesley's Theology* [Nashville: Abingdon, 1997], 74).

[23]*Journals*, entry 116, "Morning" (Wallace, 276). Susanna Wesley defines "understanding" as not just the "simple power or . . . an act of perception, though the first is in order, but include judgment and reason with the verge of that power" (*Journals*, entry 33, "Evening" [Wallace, 224]).

[24]Note the passage above in which Susanna Wesley explicates the Apostles' Creed for daughter Susanna, "Suky."

[25]Letter to Charles Wesley, 6 December 1738 (Wallace, 176).

[26]Geoffrey Wainwright notes that "both Orthodox and Methodists will affirm, as the Fathers and John and Charles Wesley likewise did, that authentic Tradition is found only where the Spirit of faith is present" (*Dialog*, 178). Susanna Wesley seems to anticipate this in her own struggles to see how God fills "heaven and earth and all the imaginary spaces beyond this universal system of beings," and in particular the events and evidences in her own time (*Journals*, entry 104, "Morning" [Wallace, 272]).

[27]Letter to Charles Wesley, 6 December 1738 (Wallace, 176).

[28]Letter to John Wesley, 30 March 1734 (Wallace, 164).

[29]Volf, "Theology, Meaning and Power," in *The Nature of Confession*, 49.

[30]Stephen W. Gunter, "Susanna Annesley Wesley: A Woman of Spirit and Spirituality," paper presented

at the Wesleyan Center for 21st Century Studies Conference, "Work Done, Work Begun: Women Creating Sacred Spaces" (Point Loma Nazarene University, October 4–6, 1999), 8–9.

[31]Ibid., 10.

[32]Ibid., 11.

[33]*At the Corner*, 261.

[34]Ibid., 264. Frederica Mathewes-Green begins with the mystery at the heart of faith, with the fourth-century nun Egeria, who wrote back to her Spanish convent. Egeria says that catechumens in their years of instruction, among a wealth of knowledge, had been given instruction in the whole of scripture and learned as much as one is allowed to know of the meaning of the creed (148). What catechumens cannot be told is about God's secret mysteries.

[35]Letter to Samuel Wesley Jr., 27 November 1701 (Wallace, 60–61). Also see Charles Wallace Jr., unpublished paper, "A Regular Method of Living: Sacred Space at Susanna Wesley's Table."

[36]*Educational, Catechetical, and Controversial Writings*, Letter to John Wesley, 24, 1732 (Wallace, 371–72). Susanna Wesley insisted that it is necessary to observe "some method in instructing and writing for your ch[ildren]": "Go through your brief exposition on the Ten Commandments, which are a summary of the moral law. Then briefly explain the principles of revealed religion, which will make up the second letter. Subjoin by way of essay a short discourse on the being and attributes of God (*Journals*, entry 52, 24 May 1711 [Wallace, 236]).

[37]Letter to Samuel Wesley Jr., 11 March 1704 (Wallace, 48).

[38]*Journals*, entry 102, "Noon" (Wallace, 271).

[39]Ibid., entry 104, "Morning" (Wallace, 272).

[40]Vrame, 53.

[41]*Journals*, entry 249, "Morning" (Wallace, 353).

[42]Letter to John Wesley, 21 February 1731 (Wallace, 148).

[43]Vrame, 129; the use of icons in the home form the art of sacred living (Proud, 26).

[44]Letter to John Wesley, 14 February 1734 (Wallace, 164).

[45]Father John Breck notes, "then indeed one can interpret the Scriptures faithfully when one lives in accordance with them" (*Scripture in Tradition: The Bible and Its Interpretation in the Orthodox Church* [Crestwood, NY: St. Vladimir's Seminary Press, 2001], 31).

[46]Much work has been done on the role of women in the Wesleyan tradition. Stephen Gunter, Charles Wallace Jr., Paul Chilcote, Rebecca Laird Christensen, Susie Stanley, and Patricia Crawford are a few in a growing number of writers exploring women's stories in the long and varied trajectories of Methodism. Kyriaki Karidoyanes Fitzgerald's work *Women Deacons in the Orthodox Church: Called to Holiness and Ministry* contributes to our knowledge about the responsibilities and witness of women deacon saints. Following the Damascus Consultation, Orthodox women gathered in Istanbul, Turkey, for a conference on women in the Orthodox Church, "Discerning the Signs of the Times." The additional concerns and recommendations posed at the conference are pertinent to "home as communion" ([Brookline, MA: Holy Cross Orthodox Press, 1998], 218–26). In the re-emergence of the order of deaconesses, Fitzgerald does not diminish other lay ministries but hopes that this vocation may be experienced "as another response to the Holy Spirit who fills and guides the church (Eph. 4:11–13)" (221).

[47]Vrame, 92.

[48]"Theology, Meaning and Power," 59.

[49]Ibid., 56.

[50]"Educational, Catechetical, and Controversial Writings," The Apostles' Creed (Wallace, 384).

[51]The notion of language as performance always suggests the possibility for faulty or "pluralistic" performances and practices, which, as John Meyendorff points out, can threaten church unity when those practices have doctrinal implications (*The Byzantine Legacy in the Orthodox Church* [Crestwood, NY: St. Vladimir's Seminary Press, 1982], 120).

Susanna Wesley herself cautions against judging one's spiritual state by the multitude of "external performances. Neither concludes because you are constant in private and family devotions that therefore you do certainly love God above all things and are in a state of grace" (*Journals*, entry 101, "Evening" [Wallace, 271]).

[52]"Theology, Meaning and Power," 55.

[53]"The power of the Christian semiotic system is the power of the third person of the Trinity, a semi-

otically mediated power that is *more* than the power created by the semiotic impact of the system of symbols and practices" (Volf, 57, italics this author's). Allchin recounts what D. J. Williams said about his father: "His greatest gift was the gift of prayer. It was a joy to *listen* to him when he knelt" (italics this author's). Allchin says of this gift that when he knelt, he "grew taller and entered into the fullness of human dignity" (23).

[54]*Journals*, entry 105, "Noon" (Wallace, 272). Some changes were made in the quotation for readable sentence structure. Cf. the Wesley hymn and the open path ahead of the delivered: "Long my imprisoned spirit lay, / fast bound in sin and nature's night; / Thine eye diffused a quickening ray; . . . / I rose went forth and followed thee." The work of Christ is the work of the Holy Spirit, along the road. Wallace also points out that the Trinity functions for Susanna Wesley as spirituality and God's goodness in the world ("Methodist Matrix," 19).

[55]"Methodist Matrix," 19.

[56]*Facing East*, 96.

[57]*Short Hymns on Select Passages of the Holy Scriptures* (1762).

15

The Use of Scripture in the Lives of Early Methodist Preachers

Timothy L. Bryan

Introduction

About three months after the Anglican priest and Methodist apologist John William Fletcher died, John Wesley led a memorial service for him in London. He preached on the text "Mark the perfect man and behold the upright! For the end of that man is peace" (Psalm 37:37).[1] He concluded his remarks by noting, "Many exemplary men have I known, holy in heart and life, within fourscore years. But one equal to him I have not known—one so inwardly and outwardly devoted to God. So unblameable character in every respect I have not found either in Europe or America. As it is possible we all may be such as he was, let us endeavour to follow him as he followed Christ."[2]

Later, in the only biography Wesley would write, he recounted his sermon thoughts about Fletcher and included, "Nor do I expect to find another such this side of eternity."[3] In that same biography Wesley, although still frustrated that Fletcher had opted for a settled pastorate at Madeley instead of Methodist itinerancy and leadership, favorably compared him to George Whitefield.

> He had a more striking person, equal good-breeding, and equally winning address: together with a richer flow of fancy, a stronger understanding: a far greater treasure of learning, both in languages, Philosophy, Philology, and Divinity: and above all (which I can speak with fuller assurance, because I had a thorough knowledge both of one and the other), a more deeper and constant communion with the Father and with the Son, Jesus Christ.[4]

In January 1773, the elder Wesley wrote to his younger colleague about the need for a successor to lead Methodism after Wesley's death. Clearly, thought Wesley, Fletcher was the one to assume that responsibility. He wrote, "But has God provided one so qualified? Who is he? Thou art the man! God has given you a measure of loving faith and a single eye to His glory. He has given you some knowledge of men and things, particularly of the whole plan of Methodism."[5] Charles Wesley concurred in a previous letter, "There is reason to hope J. F. [John Fletcher] will succeed J. W. [John Wesley]."[6] However, the then forty-four-year-old Fletcher declined the invitation. He died twelve years later, before the Wesleys.

John and Charles Wesley were not the only ones impressed by Fletcher. Henry Moore recalled, "We went to look at him, for heaven seemed to beam from his Countenance."[7] An *Encyclopedia Britannica* article on Fletcher suggested that Voltaire named him a person as perfect as Christ.[8] For decades after his death, his works were required reading for Methodist preachers.[9] His *Last Check to Antinomianism* (also published separately as *Treatise on Christian Perfection*) was second only to John Wesley's *Plain Account* among the "Textbooks of Methodism" in America.[10] In 1827, the Illinois Conference recommended his five *Checks to Antinomianism.*[11] It has also been suggested that his writings had an impact on the nineteenth-century Holiness movement and twentieth-century Pentecostalism.[12]

Yet Fletcher is seldom remembered. His work and name are unknown among most Methodists themselves. Lack of theological interest, poor understanding of the historical circumstances that gave rise to his polemical writings, and little exposure to his works may explain much of the neglect.[13] A renewed reading of his writings, however, can give us clues to John Wesley's enthusiasm about his insights.

> It seems God has raised him up for this very thing—
> "to vindicate eternal Providence
> And justify the ways of God to man."[14]

Trying to mediate divisive theological factions, Fletcher developed a methodology that included "opposites" to understand the "whole." He became convinced that truth and beauty unfold out of the contrasts and dichotomies of life, a mysterious confluence of point and counterpoint, light and shadow. Trying to understand holy living and perfection, he composed an amalgam of grace and will, sin and moral effort, and, ultimately, the sanctifying power of the Holy Spirit. His great model for perfection was St. Paul, and near the end of his life, he created a portrait of the saint that was infused with gospel evidence, his own personal struggles and experiences, and the conviction that all are called to be as holy as Christ's apostle.

This chapter will investigate Fletcher's view of perfection, with his *Portrait of St. Paul* as a touchstone to interpreting that doctrine. A brief survey of his life and controversies will conclude with some general remarks on his notion of holiness and perfection. A description of the *Portrait of St. Paul* will then provide a practical model of the integrated, perfected holy life. It will also reflect Fletcher's ongoing concerns about the integrity of scripture, the reconciliation of conflicting theologies and opinions, and the "wholeness" of truth. In the end, Fletcher's *Portrait* will emerge as a metaphor for God's recreative effort to paint the image of perfection on the canvas of human life.

Background

At the age of thirty-one, Fletcher was appointed vicar of Madeley. He served that parish the rest of his life. When he began his ministry, he wrote to the Countess of Huntington that he hoped that after ten years of pastoral work, he would be able to say, "I am nothing—I have nothing—I can do nothing."[15] Similar thoughts about his relationship to God were expressed in letters to John and Charles Wesley, using the Pauline language of "dying to oneself."[16] These were not the reflections of vocational crisis nor mystical annihilation, but the natural inclinations of a person whose pious propensities were determined early on. When he was seven, he underwent his first spiritual crisis and experienced the love of God.[17] According to a letter from his wife to his brother, it set him on a path that culminated in a deathbed encounter with the fullness of that love.

> [H]e told me, he had received such a manifestation of the full Meaning of that Word, "God is Love," as he could never be able to tell. "It fills me," said he, "it fills me every Moment. O Mary, my Dear Mary! God is Love! Shout, shout aloud—Oh! It so fills me, I want a Gust of Praise to go to the Ends of the Earth."[18]

His was not an easy path to perfection. Yet it was remarkable for its apparent consistency between his inner reflections and external activities. He abandoned the process of ordination in the Reformed Church (he was a Swiss native) because of qualms about some elements of Calvinism. His seriousness about religion and trying to live a holy life made him equally serious about his early duties as a private tutor to the Hill family in England. Personal struggles with sin and exposure to the Methodists led him into a spiritual crisis that was partially relieved by a conversion experience. His conversion and sense of new birth in Christ stimulated a renewed sense of courage and strength to wage the moral battle. At twenty-five, he wrote a "covenant" with God detailing his duties before God and surrendering himself to God's grace through Christ.[19] It was a charter for holy living that echoed his youthful struggles and set a course from which he would never deviate. At first, eschatological concerns inspired moral effort; later, his desire for full sanctification did the same. He could be harsh with both young and old, female and male, as demonstrated in his *An Appeal to Matter of Fact and Common Sense.*

> How excessively foolish are the plays of children! How full of mischief and cruelty the sports of boys! How vain, foppish, and frothy the joys of young people! And how much below the dignity of upright, pure creatures, the snares that persons of different sexes perpetually lay for each other? . . .
>
> Here a circle of idle women, supping a decoction of Indian herbs, talk or laugh all together like so many chirping birds or chattering monkeys, and, scandal excepted, every way to as good purpose. And there a club of graver men blow, by the hour, clouds of stinking smoke out of their mouth, or wash it down their throat with repeated draughts of intoxicating liquors. The strong fumes have already reached their heads; and while some stagger home, others triumphantly keep the field of excess; though one is already stamped with the heaviness of the ox, another worked up to the fierceness and roar of the lion, and the third brought down to the filthiness of the vomiting dog.[20]

Nor would he hesitate to criticize himself. In a letter to John Wesley, his "spiritual guide," he confessed, "I so plainly see my want of gifts, and especially that soul of all the labours of a minister."[21] Yet his critiques were engendered by the optimistic belief that God's grace is available to all, and, because of that, everyone, including himself, had the potential to live a sanctified life worthy before God, despite the persisting effects of the Fall.

Bible reading, contemplation, and prayer could consume a whole night. Most of the time, he was a vegetarian. Sometimes he would subsist on little more than bread, milk, and water. His ordination as a priest did not lead him into uncharted territory. It only reinforced his conviction that true ministry is sustained and empowered by the pastor's internal commitments and external disciplines, and it opened up an arena in which his deepest interests and concerns could be enfleshed and put to the test.

In 1770, he entered his severest theological test. He was caught in the two streams of Methodism: those who emphasized in a Calvinistic way the importance of grace and election, and those who championed the freeing of the will by grace and the working out of one's salvation. John Wesley sparked a controversy when the Methodist Conference Minutes of that year reported him as saying that "We have leaned too much toward Calvinism."[22] Fletcher had friends in both streams, including the Countess of Huntington and the Wesleys, and wanted to demonstrate to all Methodists that Wesley's remarks had been misinterpreted.[23] But more importantly, he believed that neither a Calvinistic extreme (which he would call Antinomianism) nor a free-will–good-works extreme (which he would call Pharisaism) were faithful to the truth of scripture. His five *Checks* were an extended argument for inclusiveness and theological moderation. He wrote in a sixth *Check*, titled *An Equal Check to Antinomianism and Pharisaism,* that there were two gospel axioms, "two pillars of Gospel truth."

> These two Gospel axioms may thus be expressed: (1.) Our salvation is of God: or there is free grace in God, which, through Christ, freely places all men in a state of temporary redemption, justification, or salvation . . . and crowns those who are faithful unto death with an eternal redemption, justification, or salvation. (2.) Our damnation is of ourselves: or, there is free will in man, by which he may, through the grace freely imparted to him in the day of temporary salvation, work out his own eternal salvation.[24]

Grace and free will were not antithetical principles, but two vital elements of faith witnessed to by scripture. On the front page of his *Equal Checks*, he titled his method of arriving at true biblical understanding *Scripture Scales* and described it with the rhetorical call "O weigh the gold of Gospel truth, to balance a multitude of opposite scriptures, to prove the Gospel marriage of free grace and free will, and restore primitive harmony to the Gospel of the day."[25] He lined up contrasting texts, not to demolish one or the other, but to include and integrate them into the whole body of revelation. His polemics, couched in a barrage of scripture texts that appealed to both sides, pleaded with both sides to come together. The results were mixed. His *Checks* were seen by Wesley as a strong support for his emphasis on free will and holy living;[26] however, they did little to reconcile the Calvinistic stream.

A seventh and final *Check* (*The Last Check to Antinomianism: A Polemical Essay on the Twin Doctrines of Christian Imperfection and a Death Purgatory*) quoted from scripture on the title page:

> Be ye perfect. Every one that is perfect shall be as his Master. If thou wilt be perfect, go and sell that thou hast, and give to the poor. —Jesus Christ. If any man teaches

> otherwise, and consent not to wholesome words, even the words of our Lord Jesus Christ, and the doctrine which is according to godliness, he is proud. —St. Paul.[27]

Pride had been Fletcher's introspective demon. It resisted his fundamental drive for complete sincerity and humility.[28] By the time he wrote his *Last Check*, perfection had become his obsession, while the link to previous spiritual concerns remained. As Howard Slaatte observed, according to Fletcher, "Before men can be 'perfect Christians' they must receive the teaching and Spirit of Christ by faith so as to receive the love of God into their hearts by the Holy Spirit and receive the 'meek mind of Christ' and be emptied of self."[29] The *Last Check* is a scriptural and theological reflection on his desire to live a holy, perfect life in Christ, the culmination of years of moral effort, biblical study, prayer, preaching, contemplation, and theological controversy in which he tried to place the doctrine of Christian perfection in a "scriptural light," presented Paul as a "striking picture of a perfect Christian," and, as the subtitle hints, described a perfection that could be realized in this life, not in a purgation following death.

Sanctification and Christian perfection were not new concepts to Fletcher. His early "covenant" with God stressed the role of the Holy Spirit as an active power in the life of the believer. The earliest published writing that we have from him is a 1759 sermon *Necessity of Regeneration*, in which he commented on John 3:3 and suggested that sanctification is the renewal of the our whole being through the recovery of the image of God; without which, he added, we cannot be saved.[30] Throughout his life, he continued to aim high. In a 1771 letter to Charles Wesley, he acknowledged, "I still want a fountain of power, call it what you please. Baptism of fire, perfect love, sealing. I contend not for the name . . . In short, I want to be established."[31] Could any less be expected of a person who defined Christian perfection in the *Last Check* as "a spiritual constellation made up of these gracious stars, perfect repentance, perfect faith, perfect humility, perfect meekness, perfect self denial, perfect resignation, perfect hope, perfect charity for our visible enemies, as well as for our earthly relations; and, above all, perfect love for our invisible God, through the explicit knowledge of our Mediator Jesus Christ"?[32]

For Fletcher, perfection is the "great pearl." To those who were in quest of the pearl and had already experienced the love of God in their lives, Fletcher made the following points:

1. It is possible to lose Christian perfection and fall from grace.
2. Everyone who is perfect shall be as the Master.
3. Perfect love is not perfect knowledge, but perfect humility and teachability.
4. Perfection is not persistent ecstasy, rapture or extreme enthusiasm.
5. Suffering like Christ may accompany the ascent of the heights of perfection, so the focus should be more on seeking God's highest gift of love.
6. Love is humble.
7. The more love we have the more we see the need to confess our sins.
8. Assist the weak.
9. Remove prejudice and bigotry.
10. Desire nothing less than the supreme good of God.
11. Expect opposition.

12. Although love is modest, one should always be prepared to witness to their hope.
13. In prayer, any glory of achievement should be given to God.
14. And, remember that perfection is an active growing in grace and the knowledge of Christ; it is never static.[33]

He would return to these in his *Portrait of Paul.*

Fletcher believed that perfection is relative according to the state of the believer and the dispensation of God's grace. Some were children in the faith; others, young people; and others, the ones perfected in love, parents. Because he believed that sin is a known transgression of the moral law of God, both the child and the young person in the faith could be "perfect" in their relationship with God. His reading of the early church's Pentecostal experience asserted that the apostles were given perfect love and the other three thousand a new birth and the beginnings of sanctification that would build on their discovery and lamentation of indwelling sin.[34] When Fletcher argued for repeated baptisms in the Holy Spirit and a progressive spiritual growth to final immersion in the Spirit's gift of perfect love, John Wesley was concerned that he was slighting the true gift of the Holy Spirit at the time of justification.[35] Fletcher concluded that for some people it took years to achieve perfect love, while for others it may occur in a moment. It is a matter of grace, a grace that Fletcher sought to the end of his life, a grace that he invited all to seek, like his students at the college at Trevecca, where he would conclude his morning sermon with an invitation to all who were "athirst for the fullness of the Spirit" to join him in his room, where they would sometimes wrestle "like Jacob for the blessing."[36]

Slaatte summarized Fletcher's idea of perfection:

> Christian perfection does not imply faultlessness and perfect capability but the perfect spirit of love and humility. Included is a sensitivity to sin and error together with the ambition to help the needy and avoid all superficiality. It was always the desire "to press toward the mark." While it can begin with justification it moves on from there in sanctification. But sinless perfection, as Fletcher dared speak of it, is the Zenith of spirituality and is possible only as one is willfully Christ-centered in faith and life and yearns to be dead to sin, because by the Holy Spirit he has a new heart and mind with new and higher affections. This is full salvation. It does not contribute to a form of self-righteousness or pride, because it is in every sense grounded in Christ and his work.[37]

It was a concept, or, more properly, a way of life, that Fletcher believed is grounded in the witness of scripture and the experiences of the faithful. He criticized those who deny its reality by pointing out that the word "perfection" "occurs, with all its derivatives, as frequently as most words in the scriptures, and not seldom in the very same sense in which we take it." He contrasted it with the words "predestinate" (which he claimed is found only four times in the Bible), "predestination" (which is not found), and even the "unscriptural" word "trinity."[38] His exhaustive use of scripture in the *Checks* as well as personal comments like his remark "I seldom look into any book but my Bible" in a letter to Mr. Melville Horne[39] would belie any other possible foundation for his understanding of perfection than scripture confirmed by the power of the Holy Spirit on the human mind and heart.[40] It was not that he was unreasonable. He had a high regard for reason. Likewise, he utilized the insights of experience and tradition.[41] But he was only fully convinced by scripture, and what he clearly saw there was a call to holiness and perfect love—and the voice that often spoke to him of such things was that of Paul.

Portrait of St. Paul

The seeds for Fletcher's *Portrait of St. Paul* appeared in the ninth section of the *Last Check*, in which he states that the

> apostle sits for his own picture before the glass of evangelical sincerity; and that, turning spiritual self painter, with the pencil of a good conscience, and with colours mixed by the Spirit of truth, [he] draws this admirable portrait from the life—
>
> "Be followers of me. This one thing I do; leaving the things that are behind, I press toward the mark for the prize of the heavenly calling [a crown of glory]. Charity is the bond of perfection. Love is the fulfilling of the law. If I have not charity, I am nothing."[42]

The seeds would sprout into an extensive treatise that occupied the last years of his life. He did not live long enough to see it published. It was written in French, and then it was translated into English and published in 1790. The *Portrait* makes a number of allusions, especially in the last section, "An Essay on the Connection of Doctrines with Morality," to the relationship between the Enlightenment and religious life and thought on the Continent. Nevertheless, its graphic portrait of Paul and the evangelical character of the faithful minister quickly established it as a favorite among Methodist preachers. However, like the rest of Fletcher's writings, and maybe even more so, it has been relegated to obscurity.

The work has three main parts. The first includes "A Portrait of St. Paul" contrasted with "The Portrait of Lukewarm Ministers and False Apostles." The second part is titled "The Portrait of St. Paul," but is essentially a description of the attributes and doctrines of a true evangelical pastor. The third and final part is "An Essay on the Connection of Doctrines with Morality" and is an extended response to the natural religion and philosophy of the European Enlightenment.

In the preface, Fletcher notes, "An example is more powerful than precept."[43] Paul, for Fletcher, is the preeminent example of the true Christian, and the diversity of primary materials—the Acts of the Apostles and fourteen letters—composed in varying circumstances make the details of his life even more vivid. Fletcher observes that Paul's pastoral situations were able to unveil his true character and provide substance for the biographer's sketch: "It is on such occasions that a man is most likely to discover what he really is; and it is on such occasions that the moral painter may take an author in the most interesting positions, in order to delineate, with accuracy, his sentiments, his circumstances, and his conduct."[44] Fletcher stakes the validity of his *Portrait* on the Holy Scriptures (virtually every paragraph in the text is highlighted by one or more quotes or allusions to scripture), the "testimony of reason," and the "confessions of faith adopted by the purest Churches." He hopes that its evidence is convincing enough to bring back "bigoted divines to evangelical moderation" and "either reconcile, or bring near to one another, the orthodox professor, the imperfect Christian, and the sincere deist."[45] But, ultimately, the work is grounded in the conviction that Paul's example is a challenge to all Christians, in their different states, to be "filled with the piety of that apostle," to be perfect as he was perfect.

In the first part of the treatise, Fletcher identifies, with some redundancy, forty traits of Paul. His first trait is "piety." Fletcher calls this the parent of all virtues and defines it as "that knowledge of God and his various relations to man, which leads us to adore, to love, and obey him in public and in private."[46] The last element of the definition is crucial. Fletcher believed that personal morality is vital to effective preaching. Amid the plethora of scripture, he even referred to Quintillian's claim that it is impossible to be a good orator without being a good man. But, continues Fletcher, the young Paul's piety was not enough. He had to become acquainted with his own heart. He needed the gift of repentance and faith in Christ. He needed to experience the "first evangelical principle": "Blessed are the poor in spirit, for theirs is the kingdom of heaven."[47]

Paul's second trait, therefore, is "extreme sorrow for having offended God." Even though Paul was cast to the ground on the way to Damascus, says Fletcher, it is not necessary to hear voices, see light, or behold a vision to be convicted of sin. It is necessary, however, to hear the Word of God; and, adds Fletcher, those ministers who do not strive for this "convicting" Christian experience will never be able to comprehend the gospel.[48]

Repentance is followed by the third trait: "union with Christ by faith." Fletcher quotes Paul's declaration of faith in Galatians 2:20 and identifies "living faith" as "the source from whence all sanctity of the Christian is derived, and all the power of the true minister."[49] It was out of this faith that he lived his "extraordinary vocation to the holy ministry" (the fourth trait). But note, says Fletcher, his was a call that was the same as every other minister's call and must be seen neither as unique to the apostle nor essentially characterized by some of the daily activities of ministry.

> As for taking the ecclesiastical habit, reading over some pages of a liturgy, solemnizing marriages, baptizing infants, keeping registers, and receiving stipends, these things are merely accidental; and every minister should be able to say, with St. Paul, "Christ sent me, not [principally] to baptize, but to preach the Gospel," 1 Cor. 1, 17.[50]

After a brief discussion of how ministers discern their call to ministry, Fletcher describes two more traits of Paul that are essential to effective ministry: "entire devotion to Jesus Christ" (trait 5) and "strength in the Scripture and Christ" (trait 6). Of the latter, he says, "The ministers of the present age . . . are continually seeking after the beauty of metaphors, the brilliance of antithesis, the delicacy of description, the just arrangement of words, the aptness of gesture, the modulation of voice, and every other studied ornament of artificial eloquence. While the true minister, effectively convinced of the excellence of the Gospel, relies alone for the effect of his public ministry upon the force of truth, and the assistance of the Divine Master."[51]

Throughout part 1 of the *Portrait*, the litany of Pauline traits continues: trait 7, "the power to bind, loose and to bless in the name of God"; every Christian's sword is the Word of God, says Fletcher, and all experienced Christians can bless and exhort, but the pastor can also bind and loose. Trait 8, "earnest and diligent." Trait 9, "balancing time between prayer and preaching." Trait 10, "able to discern when to threaten and when to console." Trait 11, "humility." Trait 12, "acknowledging one's errors"; here Fletcher criticizes those who paint portraits of the saints without including the shadows as well as light. (Paul, he believes, was ready to confess his errors.) Trait 13, "detested party spirit and divisions." Trait 14, "rejects praise"; Fletcher encouraged the pastors to affirm their calling with zeal, but do it carefully, observing that Paul sometimes spoke in the third person to distance himself from praise. Trait 15, "universal love." Trait 16, "particular love for the faithful," recognizing that our principal life comes from Christ, but our accessory life is derived from the faithful through the medium of brotherly love. Trait 17, "love for those whose faith waivers." Trait 18, "love for countrymen and enemies." Trait 19, "love (and prayer) for those who only had been reported to him." Trait 20, "charity for the poor." Trait 21, "readiness to offer spiritual assistance—balancing social service with care for the immortal soul." Trait 22, "charity that avoids all appearance of haughtiness and relates to the needs and abilities of the receiver." Trait 23, "courage in the defense of truth." Trait 24, "prudence." Trait 25, "tenderness towards others and severity towards oneself." Trait 26, "boldly reproves and consoles"; Fletcher is quite harsh toward those ministers who are unwilling to reprove and remarks that the true pastor "after having manifested the courage of a lion he puts on the gentleness of the lamb."[52] Trait 27, "perfect disinterestedness," to do things without any special interest in gain. Trait 28, "the ability to labor with one's own hands," so that the minister might preach industry through his own example of working without shame among the poor. Trait 29, "respect for matrimony while called to celibacy." Trait 30, "more fear for his flock than his own safety." Trait 32, "glory only in the Cross of Christ and his sufferings and labors." Trait 33, "patience and fortitude." Trait 34, "modest firmness before magistrates." Trait 35, "courageous consoler of persecuted brethren." Trait 36, "labors confidently to produce fruit"; however, Fletcher concedes that some congregations have an "invincible hatred" of gospel truths and sometimes have to be refused ministry. Trait 37, "willingness to be a martyr." Trait 38, "endures with joy his separation from Christ because of his service." Trait 39, "constantly zealous and diligent to the end." Trait 40, "triumphs over the evils of life and the terrors of joy." Fletcher says that "the true Christian, prepared for all events, sees and submits to the order of Providence. He receives the mortal blow, either with humble resignation, or with holy joy."[53]

The second section of part 1 responds to the criticisms of using Paul as a model for Christian life. Fletcher carries on his artistic metaphor:

> The essence of painting consists in a happy mixture of light and shade, from the contrast of which an admirable effect is produced, and the animated figure made to rise from the canvas. Upon this principle we shall oppose to the Portrait of Paul, that of the lukewarm ministers and false apostles, whose gloomy traits will form a background peculiarly adapted to set off the character of an evangelical pastor.[54]

What emerges on the canvas is a man who was very human, exposed to the dangers which beset every Christian generally, a resident pastor of three years in Ephesus, shut up in a house in Rome, and yet was able to maintain his pastoral zeal through his love for Christ. To object that he is too exalted a model and complain that the contemporary Christian is "not endued with the miraculous gifts of Paul" is to misrepresent him. If Christ had been portrayed as the "model," the excuse might have some weight. Paul, however, is not a model of a "large description of miraculous gifts, but a faithful representation of those Christian virtues, which are found in every believer, according to his vocation."[55]

Fletcher readily dismisses a second criticism that it is presumptuous to pretend to be a successor to Paul. Paul exhorted others to follow in his steps, he says. A third criticism, that contemporary ministry cannot be proven by miracles, is, likewise, rejected as irrelevant and unscriptural. Some real apostles did not perform miracles; some false ones did. The real miracle is a transformed heart and the opening of sinful eyes. The pure test of apostleship is charity. To the fourth objection that Paul's ministry to the Jews and idolatrous heathens is different from contemporary ministry, Fletcher responds using Pauline language, that the key is "a new creature," not a profession of faith. He observes, "The most painful part of his duty is still before him, when he attempts to convert those sinners who are baptized, and those infidels who are communicants."[56] And finally, to the seemingly weak complaint that it is too difficult to prepare a sermon that people accept and honor, Fletcher, with great humor, reconstructs an imaginary epistle from Paul to Timothy.

> O Timothy, my son! I have frequently commanded thee to labour in the work of the Lord, according to my example. But as thou art not an apostle, properly so called, and hast not received the gift of languages, I advise thee to write over thy sermons as correctly as possible. And after this, do not fail to rehearse them before a mirror, till thou art able to repeat them with freedom and grace: so that when thou art called upon public duty, thou mayest effectually secure the approbation of thine auditors. Furthermore, when thou art about to visit any distant Churches, lay up in thy portmanteau the choicest of thy sermons. And wherever thou art, take care to have, at least, one discourse about thee, that thou mayest be prepared for any sudden emergence, and never appear unfurnished in the eyes of the people.[57]

Satire then gives way to exhortation as Fletcher asserts that it is meditation and study that prepare one to speak, that desire and zeal generate natural eloquence, that ardent love for God and humanity animates each sentence, that sincerity and vigilance must not be replaced by indolence and artifice, nor generous sympathy succumb to "study and affection." He sums up the duties of the true pastor in one sentence: "he should cause the light that is in him to shine out in every possible direction, before the ignorant and the learned, the rich and the poor; making the salvation of mankind his principle pursuit, and the glory of God his ultimate aim."[58]

Part 2 of the *Portrait* is a discussion of the four main points of true preaching—repentance, faith, hope, and charity—while contrasting the superficial message of the contemporary minister with the doctrine of the evangelical pastor. He criticizes ministers for fearing true repentance because they think that it is a dangerous psychological disorder. He has harsh words for pastors who respond to parishioners' sincere questions about faith with the "comforting" advice that they need not concern themselves with such things. He lists the products of hope (such as consolation, charity, holy joy, purification, and salvation) and marks charity as "the crown of every grace." As he introduces his considerations on charity, he draws a summary sketch of the true, evangelical pastor:

> In preaching repentance, he lays the axe to the root of every corrupt tree. In publishing evangelical faith, he plants the tree of life. When he proclaims the hope of the Gospel, he causes the tree to put forth a beautiful blossom. But when he preaches Christian charity, he calls forth the rich fruit from every vigorous branch.[59]

In all of his thoughts, Fletcher never seemed to stray far from the fullness of God's love and the call for all to receive and live it.

His discussion of charity essentially completes his portrait of Paul. The remainder of the second part is given to a description of the three dispensations of God's grace: the promise of the Father to manifest the Son, the promise of the Son to manifest the Holy Spirit, and the promise of the Holy Spirit about Christ's second coming. The third part is basically an argument for the Christian foundation of true morality.

Conclusion

So what did Fletcher accomplish with his *Portrait of St. Paul*? Explicitly, he had tried to draw upon the power of example to enhance the precept of holy living. He wanted to bring flesh to the notion of perfection. He wanted to reveal holy living and the fullness of love, as exemplified by Paul, as a daily event, accessible to every person, grounded in the grace of God and a human will conformed to the will of God through Jesus Christ. It was love not in the abstract, but in the everyday efforts to pray, read, and understand scripture, be patient, remain sincere, manifest true humility, and embrace those and a world that were not always so kind.

What emerged, however, was not an image of perfection that was infused in light, but a portrait of contrasts and shades and lights that made the picture more beautiful and true. To the modern reader, Fletcher's earlier *Scripture Scales* may appear to be proof-texting. Knickerbocker described his method like this:

> The method of the *Scales* is to quote in one column certain passages of Scripture which support the doctrines of free grace, mercy, and faith and to quote in a second, parallel column certain passages which support the doctrines of free will, justice, and good works. In these *Scales*, no distinction is made between the Old Testament and the New Testament, between the various books of either Testament, or between the words of Jesus in the Gospels and the words of other biblical figures. The passages he quotes are short, usually not more that one verse, and sometimes only a part of a verse.[60]

Nevertheless, Fletcher, said Knickerbocker,

> Regarded the *Scales* as a harmonious whole, the meaning of which would be lost if it were separated into individual parts. He compared the various Scripture passages in the *Scales* to "the lights and shades of a picture [which] help to set off each other." In this way the *Scales* are illustrations of a type of rational argument which he calls "opposition" or "contrast."[61]

It is important to note that this "contrast" was not dialectical opposition. Nor was it a synthesis of antithetical elements. It was the whole simply described; its truth evident in the inclusion of all of the elements. To draw together apparently disparate passages and conflicting doctrines was both an act of piety and a revelation of the whole truth. Theologically, for Fletcher the mediator, something of the whole truth was lost when the Calvinistic and Arminian Methodists could not reconcile. Philosophically, the enlightened thinker remained incomplete without the foundation of Christian doctrine. And spiritually, thc light of God's perfecting love did not absorb the shadows of life but highlighted them as part of God's full revelation.

Much of *The Portrait of Paul* echoed the same methodology. The perfect love of Paul was all the more evident because he was so human. Fletcher wanted to paint an image of struggle and triumph, full in weakness, humble in strength. He contrasted his portrait with previous images of the saints:

> They who give the portraits of legendary saints generally paint them without a single failing. But they who wish faithfully to imitate the sacred authors are obliged to employ shades as well as lights, even in their most celebrated pieces. If this part of the portrait of St. Paul [concerning Paul's acknowledgement of error] should not appear brilliant, it will serve, at least, to manifest the reality of the original, the liberality of the apostle, and the fidelity of the painter.[62]

Later, in an attempt to encourage the contemporary pastor, Fletcher observed that Paul's extraordinary labors were not always sufficient to answer the design of his sacred ministry.[63]

For Fletcher it was the wholeness of the rainbow that manifested its beauty and truth. How ridiculous it would be, he said, for naturalists to confine their observations to only one line of its color.[64] It is all the colors and all the light and shadows that make the perfect picture. Although he once wrote, "Humanity is not as a cloud to the sun of the Godhead but as a crystal that reflects its beauty,"[65] his tendency was to accent the possibility of perfection just as we are. Only God, he said, is absolutely perfect.[66] Christ in his manhood was not. Both Christ and Adam needed mortification and watchfulness; so we also need to be diligent and observant of our weaknesses as we move toward perfection. And we can do so in faith through the guidance of the revelation of God. But about this, Fletcher warns, "To desire a revelation without any obscurity is to desire a day without a night, a summer without winter, a sky without a cloud . . . The faith which is unaccompanied with anything mysterious no more merits the name of faith than the tranquility of a man who has never been in danger deserves the name of bravery."[67] For Fletcher, convincing truth was displayed in the opposites, the contrasting, the blending of shadow and light, where the strokes of God's grace on the canvas of the human will brought into focus the image of perfect love.

Endnotes

[1]Patrick Streiff, *Reluctant Saint? A Theological Biography of Fletcher of Madeley*, trans. from the German by G. W. S. Knowles (Peterborough: Epworth, 2001), 298.

[2]John Wesley, "Sermon 114," in *The Works of John Wesley*, Bicentennial Edition (Oxford, 1975 / Nashville, 1984), 3:619.

[3]John Wesley, *The Works of the Rev. John Wesley, A.M.*, 3rd ed., 14 vols. (London: John Mason, 1830), 11:365.

[4]Ibid., 11:302.

[5]John Wesley, *The Letters of the Rev. John Wesley*, ed. John Telford, 8 vols. (London: Epworth, 1931), 6:11.

[6]Quoted in Frank Baker, *John Wesley and the Church of England* (London: Epworth, 1970), 208.

[7]Quoted in Peter Forsaith, "Portraits of John Fletcher of Madeley and Their Artists," *Proceedings of the Wesley Historical Society* 47 (1990): 187–201; see 194, 199.

[8]"John Fletcher," in *Encyclopedia Britannica*, 14th ed., rev. (Chicago: Encyclopedia Britannica, 1960), 9:373. This is probably an apocryphal story.

[9]Streiff, 187.

[10]John Knight, "John Fletcher's Influence on the Development of Wesleyan Theology in America," *Wesleyan Theological Journal* 13 (1978): 13–23; see 23.

[11]George Allen Turner, "The Baptism of the Holy Spirit in the Wesleyan Tradition," Wesleyan Theological Journal 14 (1979): 60–76; see 72.

[12]Streiff, 187.

[13]Robert Mattke, "John Fletcher's Methodology in the Antinomian Controversy of 1770–1776," *Wesleyan Theological Journal* 3 (1968): 38–47; see 39.

[14]Wesley, *Letters*, 6:146.

[15]Quoted in Streiff, 116.

[16]Streiff, 117.

[17]Ibid., 3–4.

[18]Quoted in Streiff, 298.

[19]Streiff, 35–37, reproduces the covenant.

[20]John Fletcher, *The Works of the Reverend John Fletcher, Late Vicar of Madeley*, 4 vols. (Salem, OH: Schmul, 1974), 3:295.

[21]Ibid., 4:369.

[22]Ibid., 1:8.

[23]Knight, "Fletcher's Influence," 15.

[24]Fletcher, *Works*, 2:269.

[25]Ibid., 2:3.

[26]John Knight, "Aspects of Wesley's Theology after 1770," *Methodist History* 6 (1968): 33–42; see 42.

[27]Fletcher, *Works*, 2:483.

[28]Streiff, 57.

[29]Howard Slaatte, *The Arminian Arm of Theology: The Theologies of John Fletcher, First Methodist Theologian, and His Precursor, James Arminius* (Washington, D.C.: University Press of America, 1979), 104.

[30]Fletcher, *Works*, 4:139–147.

[31]Quoted in Turner, 76.

[32]Fletcher, *Works*, 2:492–493.

[33]As summarized by Slaatte, 111–112.

[34]Timothy Smith, "How John Fletcher Became the Theologian of Wesleyan Perfectionism 1770–1776," *Wesleyan Theological Journal* 15 (1980): 68–87; see 79–81.

[35]David Cubie, "Perfection in Wesley and Fletcher: Inaugural or Teleological?" *Wesleyan Theological Journal* 11 (1976): 22–37; see 25.

[36]Smith, 70.

[37]Slaatte, 114.

[38]Fletcher, *Works*, 2:492.

[39]Ibid., 4:367.

[40]W. E. Knickerbocker Jr., "Doctrinal Sources and Guidelines in Early Methodism: Fletcher of Madeley as a Case Study," *Methodist History* 14 (1976): 186–202; see 191.

[41]Ibid., 187–201.

[42]Fletcher, *Works*, 2:547.

[43]Ibid., 3:8.

[44]Ibid., 3:8–9.

[45]Ibid., 3:10.

[46]Ibid., 3:12.

[47]Ibid., 3:14.

[48]Ibid., 3:17.

[49]Ibid., 3:19.

[50]Ibid., 3:20.

[51]Ibid., 3:24.

[52]Ibid., 3:55.

[53]Ibid., 3:78.

[54]Ibid., 3:80.

[55]Ibid., 3:87.

[56]Ibid., 3:94–95.

[57]Ibid., 3:103–4.

[58]Ibid., 3:107.

[59]Ibid., 3:154.

[60]Knickerbocker, 192.

[61]Ibid.

[62]Fletcher, *Works*, 3:36.

[63]Ibid., 3:98.

[64]Ibid., 3:174.

[65]Quoted in Streiff, 284.

[66]Fletcher, *Works*, 2:522.

[67]Ibid., 3:229.

PART 4

Liturgy and Scriptural Interpretation

16

The Poet as Expositor in the Golden Age of Byzantine Hymnography and in the Experience of the Church

Elizabeth Theokritoff

A well-known point of contact between the Orthodox and Methodist traditions is the important role played by liturgical poetry, and a readiness to draw on such poetry as a source of theology. This point of contact has been explored at previous consultations, as have some of the detailed parallels between examples of Orthodox and Wesleyan hymns.[1]

What I want to look at today is the approach to scriptural interpretation found in Orthodox hymnography. To illustrate the role of the liturgical poet as expositor, we will look at examples of the work of three of the greatest hymnographers: St. Romanos the Melodist (†ca. 560), St. John of Damascus (ca. 665–749), and St. Kosmas of Maiouma (ca. 675–752). They were, respectively, a deacon in Constantinople, a lay- or possibly a priest-monk in Palestine, and a bishop in Gaza; all three seem to have been hellenized Syrians. In taking examples from the "golden age" of Byzantine hymnography, we are looking at poetry of the highest quality and also the most intensely scriptural; later hymns are more inclined to go off into flights of decorative rhetoric. But at the same time, we are looking at samples from the texts most widely known even today (with the exception of Romanos's hymns, which, sadly, are never now heard in their entirety). Hymns for Sundays in the eight tones and for great feasts were composed early on; later poets filled in the gaps on other days.

The Poet as Expositor and the Experience of the Church

It should be made clear that we shall be concerned less with the particular approaches of individual poets and more with their work as an example of the Church's interpretation of scripture. It will quickly become apparent that the hymnographers are rarely original in their exegesis. Like icon painters, who are also interpreters of scripture, they are bearers of a tradition, using their artistic skill to convey that tradition to the fullness of the Church in a form that is memorable and compelling.

Indeed, it can be said that hymnography is the primary way in which the tradition of scriptural interpretation is passed on, since it is readily accessible to every churchgoer in a way that systematic commentaries are not. And since the "steel-like objectivity"[2] attributed to Orthodox festal hymns applies no less to their interpretation of scripture, they are introducing the worshipper to primary meanings of the scriptural text. It should also perhaps be underlined at this point that when we speak of Orthodox hymnography, we are talking not about a body of available material which might or might not be chosen for liturgical use but, almost exclusively, about the material prescribed in the service books. The hymnography makes up the greater part of the evening and morning services as they are celebrated today.

Systematic exegetical sermons were once a feature of the services, as we see from the works of earlier Fathers such as St. John Chrysostom and St. Basil the Great. Then came the proliferation of hymnography. The profusion of hymnographic texts, which throw light on the scriptures, by no means precludes further exposition in sermons, as we see both in later patristic times and today. What it does is provide a framework for such exposition. We might compare the wealth of exegetical hymnography with the traditional manner of reading liturgical texts: the precise style of reading varies between traditions, but reading is always formalized is such a way that the reader is not superimposing his emotions and subjective reactions on the text. In a somewhat similar way, an Orthodox who is preaching, or simply reflecting on the scriptures heard in church, has ready-made guidelines for interpreting them according to the mind of the Church.

In presenting examples of Orthodox liturgical poetry, I have attempted some comparison with Charles Wesley's treatment of the same themes. I am very well aware that there is much more to be said about Wesley as a theologian and an interpreter of scripture, and I hope that some of it will be said in the ensuing discussion. The necessarily rather cursory comparisons here make no pretense of doing Wesley justice; for one thing, it is rarely possible to compare like with like. Setting some of Wesley's festal hymns alongside those of Orthodox hymnographers would undoubtedly reveal more similarities, but I wonder whether it would give a true picture of the impact of the poets as exegetes on their respective communities, if one is comparing what a Methodist might hear at Easter, Ascension, Pentecost, or Christmas with what an Orthodox hears most of the year. I hope that the approach I am taking may help us appreciate not only the commonalities but also the significant differences between the Orthodox and Wesleyan experience of poetry as a vehicle for scriptural exposition.

St. Romanos the Melodist

The emphasis of the present consultation on the "formative period" of the tradition seemed sufficient excuse to include St. Romanos; for Romanos with his *kontakia* was a pioneer in the expansion of liturgical poetry which gave our services their present shape. The *kontakion* is a metrical sermon, usually about twenty stanzas long, full of drama and color, and, in Romanos's case at least, written in a distinctly popular idiom. One of the most memorable, *On the Victory of the Cross*, involves an animated and acrimonious exchange of recriminations between hades and the devil, with bylines from the serpent, over whom was responsible for the dreadful mistake (from the infernal point of view) of the crucifixion.[3] Late in the seventh century, however, the *kontakion* falls into disuse, probably because daily preaching (in prose) was reintroduced.[4] What we know today as the *kontakion* and sing at matins and in the Liturgy is simply the prelude to the *kontakion* proper; the first *oikos* (stanza) may also be read at matins. This usually means that we miss all the dramatic development. One exception, however, is the *oikos* for Holy Friday. Looking on as "her own Lamb is dragged to the slaughter," Mary questions Him in anguish: "Why such haste? Is there another wedding in Cana? And are you hurrying there now to make water into wine for them?"[5] The irony is poignant and engages us deeply on the human level, and it is also profoundly theological and scriptural. Yes, He is going to a wedding at which He is the bridegroom. Yes, He is going to pour out wine for all those present at the feast. And Romanos seems confident that his audience will pick up the allusions without needing them spelled out.

Probably the closest parallels to the *kontakion* in Wesley, albeit not very close, would be some of the extended poems on a scriptural passage. But we are immediately aware of a very different use of scripture. Wesley interprets the stories in intensely personal terms.[6] The paralytic by the pool of Bethesda becomes an image of my own spiritual state, "sick of anger, pride and lust, and unbelief";[7] Wesley's masterpiece "Wrestling Jacob"[8] takes Jacob's encounter with the angel as a powerful and profound allegory of the struggle to know God. For Wesley, scripture undoubtedly speaks to the universal human condition, but the experience of the individual usually seems to be the primary point of reference.

Romanos's *kontakia* are typically "topped and tailed" by verses relating the story to our own spiritual state and relationship to God:

> Christ God, who called the harlot "daughter,"
> declare me also a son of repentance
> and deliver me, I implore,
> from the filth of my deeds.[9]

Or on the Samaritan woman:

> Grant me the water of faith
> and I shall receive the streams of the font
> Joy and redemption.[10]

Straightaway, we see that our appropriation of the scriptural story has two aspects: the individual and the ecclesial. My sinfulness is my own, although it reflects a condition shared with the rest of mankind (including most of the protagonists in a scriptural story), but my relationship with God is inextricably linked to my relationship with His body, which is the Church.

The bulk of the *kontakion* is concerned with retelling the scriptural story. It is an interpretative retelling, enhanced with dramatic details, plenty of added dialogue, and imaginative commentary on what was probably going through the minds of various characters. We are immediately engaged with the characters in the story, seeing ourselves vividly in their human frailties, through which God is working out salvation. In *kontakia* on the Old Testament, the connection to our ecclesial experience is often made by spelling out a typological reference explicitly. Rebekkah is a type of the Church;[11] Elijah is "a type of things to come," and his mantle an image of "the Comforter and Holy One which we have all received, we who are baptized, and through whom we are being sanctified."[12]

Romanos's very human characterizations sometimes trick us into recognizing unwelcome truths about where we stand in the story. The Prodigal's brother seems to make a persuasive case, until the father points out where his argument leads: "You, the prosecutor, I appoint as judge. Sentence me, my child, as you blame me, and become my arbitrator."[13] There are notable instances where Romanos focuses not on the obvious sinner but on the character who does not think himself a sinner. In the *kontakion* on the Harlot, Christ carefully explains the parable of the debtors to Simon (who is a Pharisee, as in Luke):

> I will indicate to you his debtors—you are one of them . . .
> Simon, you have lived according to the Law, but you are in debt.
> Come then to my grace, that you may pay me back.
> Look at this harlot in front of you as, like the Church, she cries out:
> "I renounce and blow upon the filth of my deeds."[14]

The "blowing" refers to the baptismal rite, in which the candidate is invited to confirm his renunciation of satan by "blowing and spitting upon him."[15] Here, as is frequently the case in Romanos, sacramental allusions are an important key to relating the story to our own experience, and there is more to this particular allusion than meets the eye. Earlier in the poem, Romanos has depicted Christ's making the Pharisee's dining table into an altar on which he himself lies, granting forgiveness, "so that every debtor, taking courage *draws near*";[16] the verb recalls the words of invitation to Communion ("With fear of God and in faith [and love] draw near"). The sinful woman sees this and makes straight for the bread, ignoring the crumbs; Romanos's train of thought leads him to make a parallel with the Canaanite woman. In contrast, Simon seems to be guilty of the very failure that he attributed to Christ; he does not realize what sort of person he has under his roof. That is why Christ has to tell him to come to His grace in order to pay back the debt he owes. Even though the verbal parallel is not precise, we may well suspect that Romanos has in mind the "repayment" spoken for by the Psalmist: "What shall I give back [*antapodoso*; cf. *apodoses moi* in the *kontakion*] to the Lord for all that He has given me? *I will receive the cup of salvation* . . ."(Ps. 115:3–4/116:12–13).

With the eclipse of the *kontakion*, the dramatic development of scriptural stories was largely lost to liturgical experience, along with the particular opportunities it gave for perceiving one's own place in the story. What is not lost is a strong awareness of the sacramental dimension of scriptural stories. Also well preserved, as we shall see, is a compact style of "commentary" in which the briefest of verbal echoes of another scriptural passage can give a whole new dimension of meaning to the primary passage under discussion. This may be a translator's nightmare, but it should be a homilist's paradise.

Kanon on the Baptism of Christ

From the works of Kosmas and John, we will look at a few *stikhera*—short stanzas inserted into psalm verses—but principally at some *kanons.* The *kanon* is a long hymn of nine odes, each based on a scriptural ode.[17] *Troparia* of the same ode often share a refrain, but usually they are loosely connected. We almost never find systematic treatment of a theme or the sequential unfolding of a story, as in the full *kontakion*; the *troparia* of a *kanon* are better regarded as a series of verses grouped around a theme.[18]

For the first example, we have taken Kosmas's *kanon* and *stikhera* on the baptism of Christ from the feast of Epiphany, or Theophany (6 January).[19] The story of Christ's baptism is a complex one, particularly by the time one has taken into consideration all four Gospel accounts, and several details clearly invite explanation from the commentator.

Comparing Kosmas's hymns with Wesley's hymns on the relevant Gospel passages, we find a measure of agreement on which details require comment. The reference to undoing the latchet of Christ's shoes, and the Baptist's other protestations of unworthiness, are taken by Wesley as just that, an indication of human abasement and inadequacy before the Lord. "If the chief of saints confess / In the presence of their Lord / all their own unworthiness," how much more should we (XI. 127, no. 1199 [Lk.])? This is in marked contrast to the *kanon,* where the "latchet" is given, unusually, an interpretation that is pure allegory: "as the Forerunner teaches, it is not possible to loose the bond that joins the Word to our nature" (1 *Kanon* 6.1).[20] The allegory is at first sight somewhat strained, but in the wider context, it actually explains quite precisely in what sense Christ is "mightier" than the Forerunner. Furthermore, this christological affirmation is the key to harmonizing John's (quite correct) objection that "I have need to be baptised of Thee" with Christ's insistence that His baptism "fulfills all righteousness," as we see in the first ode: "The Lord who purges away the filth of men was cleansed in Jordan for their sake, *having of His own will made Himself like unto them,* while remaining that which He was . . ." (1 *Kanon* 1.3). It is the "unloosable latchet" that makes Jesus's baptism into a baptism also for the Forerunner and the rest of humanity.

Here we see a very characteristic difference in interpretation, or, more precisely, in the level of meaning that interests the hymn writers: the christological and soteriological emphasis in Kosmas, the moral in Wesley. "Fulfillment of righteousness" for Wesley simply shows Christ as paradigm of obedience: the Saviour "answers all God's will / and we shall do the same" (X. 148, no. 23 [Mt.]). And John's need to be baptized by Christ prompts reflection on our constant sinfulness: "Plunge, replunge me in Thy blood" (X. 148, no. 22 [Mt.]).

Wesley's hymns inspired by the fourth Gospel show special emphasis on atonement through the cross, prompted by the Baptist's recognition of Christ as the Lamb. When hymns on this passage speak of sins "carried down that purple stream" (XI. 325, no. 1625 [Jn.]) or of washing "in the fountain of Thy blood" (XI. 325, no. 1626 [Jn.]), there may be an implicit analogy with the baptism of Christ as a washing of sin, but Wesley does not take the opportunity to explore the connection between the baptism of Christ and His death, into which we are baptized. This must in part be a consequence of the nature of these hymns, as meditations on discrete verses; the Orthodox hymnographer's interpretations belong in a liturgical matrix which provides the broader context for interpretation. Thus, we find that Kosmas does explore the baptism-passion connection, in the way characteristic of Orthodox hymnography, through his choice of scriptural allusions. Indeed, he begins his *kanon* by speaking of the Lord forming Adam anew in the streams of Jordan and "breaking in pieces the heads of the dragons that were hidden there" (1 *Kanon* 1.1). The psalm verse (73/74:13) casts the Lord's descent into the waters in the image of a triumph over the infernal powers (once in the Red Sea, now in the Jordan), which in turn is inextricable from His "working salvation in the midst of the earth" (i.e., on the cross). In the same vein, the fifth ode depicts Christ's acceptance of baptism in terms that clearly parallel His acceptance of death: "As God He needs no cleansing, yet for the sake of fallen man He is cleansed in the Jordan"; and it continues, "*in its streams He slew the enmity*" (1 *Kanon* 5.e), precisely the work attributed in Ephesians 2:16 to the cross.

The opening of heaven is taken up by Kosmas as a sign for mankind, brought up from the water with Christ; it reveals the event as marking a key stage in the restoration of our relationship with God.

> [Christ] comes up out of the waters, and with Him He carries up the world. He sees the heavens opened that Adam closed for himself and his posterity. (Lity 4)

Here Wesley's interpretation is in sharp contrast. He connects the opened heavens and the descent of the Spirit with the sacrament of baptism.[21] Restoration in our relationship with God also features, but it is associated with the voice from heaven, which Wesley links to Christ's humanity[22] as firmly as Kosmas, with the rest of the Orthodox tradition, links it with His divine nature.[23]

Kosmas's treatment of Christ's baptism is clearly dependent on the understanding that a whole range of scriptures is being fulfilled at the same time. One aspect of the event being celebrated is set out in the Gospel accounts of Christ's baptism, read at various points in the feast. But all sorts of other things are happening as well, as we learn from other scriptural texts appointed for the feast: "In the exodus of Israel out of Egypt . . . the sea looked and fled, Jordan turned back" (Ps. 113/114:1–3; Ninth Hour, Matins, Liturgy); "Thou didst break the heads of the dragons on the waters" (Ps. 73/74:13, Sixth Hour); "The voice of the Lord is upon the waters . . ." (Ps. 28/29:3; First and Third Hours, Blessing of the Waters, Liturgy); and, very significantly, "The grace of God has appeared [*epepháne*, cognate with the name of the feast] for the salvation of all men . . . He saved us . . . by the washing of regeneration and renewal in the Holy Spirit" (Ti. 2:11, 3:5; Ninth Hour, Liturgy). When these and similar texts are interwoven with the Gospel accounts, it is not in the first instance a matter of interpreting one scriptural text by another. It is primarily a matter of understanding not the written word but the actions of the incarnate Word,[24] different aspects and levels of which are signified in various ways by Gospels, Epistles, Old Testament events and prophecies. This then has the *effect* that the Gospel account is interpreted in the light of other scriptural texts.

Let us take one example of what happens when the event in the Gospel is seen as fulfilling several scriptures. We have in the Gospel accounts a definite contrast between baptism in water (as administered by John), and the baptism in the Holy Spirit to be given by Christ; Matthew and Luke further associate the baptism in the Spirit with fire. Wesley, in hymns inspired by these Gospels, connects the fire, the "pure baptismal flame" with our baptism (XI. 127–8, no. 1200 [Lk.]; cf. X. 146–7, no. 20 [Mt.], where he makes the connection with Pentecost). Kosmas, on the other hand, mentions "fire and the Spirit" once, glossing it as the fire of the last day for the disobedient, and the "new birth through the Spirit and the grace that comes through water" for those who believe (1 *Kanon* 6.2). For the most part, the opposition of water on the one hand and fire and the Spirit on the other is replaced in the Epiphany hymns by images of water and the Spirit working together, as in most other relevant scriptures: "The cloud and the sea in which the people of Israel were once baptized by Moses . . . prefigured the wonder of divine baptism. The sea was an image of the water and the cloud of the Spirit . . ." (1 *Kanon* 7.2). Then there are the references to the blessing of water at Christ's baptism, even to the Spirit descending "to hallow the waters" (Lity 3).[25] Such statements are clearly not inspired by Gospel accounts of events surrounding Christ's baptism.[26] What they are doing is establishing the link with the many other New Testament texts, notably in the fourth Gospel, in which water is a vehicle and an image of the Spirit. The presence of the Spirit when Christ is baptized in the waters of Jordan shows that baptism in mere water is a thing of the past. Kosmas further points out that the waters have now received in their streams the immaterial fire, prefigured, according to the eighth ode, by the Babylonian furnace.

Kosmas's treatment of the dialogue between Jesus and John gives a very clear picture of the scriptural framework within which the incident is understood. He elaborates John's objections over an entire ode, of which the concluding stanza reads:

> Endowed with an understanding soul and honoured with the power of reason, I yet respect the things that have no soul. For if I baptise Thee, I shall have as my accusers the mountain that smoked with fire (Ex. 19.18), the sea which fled on either side, and this same Jordan which turned back (Ps. 113/114.5). (1 *Kanon* 4.3)

Using a degree of poetic license that would not be available if he were writing a straightforward commentary, the melodist elucidates John's reluctance by setting out the precedents for it. We know from the psalm why the sea flees and the Jordan turns back: it is on account of "the presence of the Lord" as He leads His people to salvation through the waters, which will drown their adversaries, and turns the flint into a spring of water (Ps. 113/114:7–8). This sums up precisely what the Fathers see as happening when Jesus comes to John. It should be noted that the titles "epiphany" and "theophany" for the celebration of this event refer in the first instance not to the manifestation of the Trinity but to the manifestation of Christ as God: the presence of the "one standing among you," as the Baptist says (Jn. 1:26), is revealed as the "presence of the Lord." In this light, the Baptist's hesitancy is seen not primarily as an expression of human unworthiness but as a reflection of cosmic awe: it shows humanity in accord with the rest of creation in its reaction to the coming of the Lord. Just to drive the point home, some hymns depict the phenomena described in the psalm as repeating themselves at Jesus's baptism: "The Jordan, seeing Thee, crouched in fear and stopped" (Lity 3).[27]

As Jordan effectively speaks for John in answer to the Psalmist's rhetorical question, so John might speak equally for the waters when he objects, "I have need to be baptized of Thee."[28] It is in the last two odes of the *kanon* that Kosmas treats Christ's response ("It is fitting for us[29] to fulfil all righteousness") and shows implicitly how He responds to the waters' need as well. He shows Christ commanding the Baptist, "Cast aside all fear and, obedient to my command, *come unto me* as *I am good* . . ." (1 *Kanon* 8.1); John then performs his ministry, crying out, "Sanctify me" (1 *Kanon* 8.2). What may not be immediately apparent (especially in the *Festal Menaion* translation, which I have amended here) is that the words in which Jesus tells John to baptize Him are precisely an answer to the latter's objection: John is told to "come unto Him" (sc. "*and be enlightened*"), since He (the Lord) is "good" (as you will "taste and see"), the language is that of Psalm 33/34. In baptizing Christ, John himself is indeed baptized, because thereby he cooperates in making baptism available to the human race. The next ode confirms that Kosmas has Psalm 33 in mind:

> O David, come in spirit to those who are about to be enlightened, and sing: "Come now unto God in faith and be enlightened. Fallen Adam, the poor man, cried and the Lord heard him; He has come and in the streams of Jordan He has made him new again, who was sunk in corruption" (Cf. Ps. 33/34:5, 7). (1 *Kanon* 9.1)

It is the baptism of Adam in Christ that makes His baptism the "fulfillment of righteousness"; accordingly, the remaining *troparia* elaborate on our baptism. The "grace and seal of baptism" is equivalent to the blood of the paschal lamb on the lintel, and the "laver of regeneration" is our Exodus. And the water too has been "baptized" in the baptism of Christ, so as to become the vehicle for the grace of the Spirit. Kosmas does not speak explicitly here of the water being blessed at the baptism of Christ, but he indicates as much obliquely, by showing how the insight of Isaiah is fused with that of John the Evangelist:

> "Wash you, make you clean," says Isaiah. "Put away the evil of your doings from before the Lord (Is. 1:16). Ho, everyone that thirsteth, come ye *to the living water*" (Is. 55:1, Jn 7:38). (1 *Kanon* 9.2)

Kanons on the Transfiguration

Let us turn now to the Transfiguration. We shall look at the two *kanons*, the first by Kosmas and the second by John of Damascus, and some vespers *stikhera* also by Kosmas.[30] Again, there are points of interpretation shared by Wesley's hymns on the relevant Gospel passages. Most notable is the eschatological emphasis: "Thy Kingdom, Lord, I fain would see," as Wesley writes (XI. 183, no. 1327 [Lk.]); he also interprets "after six days," not mentioned in the Orthodox hymns, as referring to eternal rest (XI. 20, no. 957 [Mk.]). It is a vision deliberately given "Before the Crucifixion" (*Stikhera* 1 and 2)[31]—Orthodox usage places it forty days before the feast of the cross—in order to "take off the scandal of His Cross" (Mk. XI. 20, no. 956).

While looking forward to Christ's coming in glory, the vision also reveals Him as He is. John Damascene especially is very explicit about the revelation of Christ *in two natures*, but this is implicit also in Wesley, where he speaks of Christ seen "as on a dazzling throne" (cf. Isaiah's vision) while "He remains a man of tears" as He "speaks of death alone" (XI. 183, no. 1328 [Lk.]). Characteristically, however, Wesley goes on to speak of the importance for us of remembrance of death, whereas when John speaks of the Transfiguration in terms of Isaiah's vision, it is to depict "the live coal of the Godhead that consumes sins while it enlightens souls" shown to us "in a union without confusion" (2 *Kanon* 5.3).

The Transfiguration clearly has a significant anthropological aspect, indicating as it does our own potential transformation. The inward aspect of this transformation encouraged commentators from an early date to allegorize the "high mountain" in a moral sense,[32] and, unusually, this has found its way into the festal hymns: Kosmas takes the scene as showing "that those who surpass in the height of their virtues shall be counted worthy of the divine glory" (Vespers, 3). For Wesley, the moral interpretation is far from unusual,[33] but in one hymn inspired by St. Luke's Gospel, where Christ is praying when the Transfiguration takes place, he makes the connection between inward transformation through prayer and its outward manifestation: "The glory which all thought transcends / Ev'n to his outward man extends / The wisdom from above."[34]

The appearance of Moses and Elijah has traditionally been interpreted in a variety of ways, most of which appear somewhere in the *kanons*. Wesley uses them in quite a remarkable way as an image of how the Church reads the Old Testament:

> Moses and the prophets speak / And witness to our Lord:
> Him and only Him we seek / Throughout the sacred word.
> When we find the Saviour there / The figures and predictions shine:
> Seen with Christ, they all declare / The majesty divine. (X. 305, no. 431 [Mt.])

This sums up so aptly what the Orthodox hymnographers are doing all the time that one starts to wonder why it is so hard to imagine any of them writing such lines. One significant reason, I think, is that they are not concerned with reflecting on a use of scripture that is second nature to them, to their sources, and to their listeners. They give no formulations, even poetic ones. Their profound understanding of the unity of scripture is expressed in ways that appear deceptively simple because they are dramatic and pictorial; thus according to Kosmas's *kanon*, we have Moses and Elijah crying out, "Behold the Saviour . . . Lo, here is Christ whom we in ancient times proclaimed as God" (1 *Kanon* 5.2). While Wesley places a strong emphasis on Moses and the prophets preparing the way for Christ and being superseded by him,[35] the Orthodox hymnographers allow more time for the "shining figures and predictions" to tell their own story.

In both *kanons* for the feast, the primary concern is with the Transfiguration as a theophany: Christ appears in His glory and in the glory of His Father. Hence the primary significance of Moses and Elijah lies in the fact that both were parties to Old Testament theophanies, so that their presence indicates the event of Tabor as being in the same line.[36] Here at last is the vision of God that Moses was not granted in his lifetime (Ex. 33:20); we see this in the bold acrostic[37] to John's *kanon*, "Moses saw the face of God on Tabor." The Old Testament readings for the feast of the Transfiguration describe Moses's vision of God's glory from a cleft in the rock (Ex. 33:11–23; 34:4–6) and God's appearance to Elijah on Horeb in the voice of a light breeze (1/3 Kings 19:3–7, 11–13, 15–16), and also the glory of the Lord resting on Mount Sinai when Moses received the Law (Ex. 24:12–18). Moses and Elijah take us straight back to the Old Testament theophanies, which form the indispensable matrix for understanding what is happening on the mountain of the Transfiguration.

Certainly, the Old Testament theophanies invite contrasts: "The mountain that was once gloomy and veiled in smoke has now become venerable and holy, since Thy feet have stood upon it, O Lord" (Vespers, 4); for what is now revealed upon it is not the Law but "the mystery hidden before the ages" (Col. 1:26), the incarnation of God. The same comparison becomes more explicit in the second *Kanon*: "Thou hast appeared to Moses both on the mountain of the Law and on Tabor: of old in darkness, but now in the unapproachable light of the Godhead" (2 *Kanon* 1.3). There is a progression: "the shadow of the Law has grown exceeding weak, and Christ the truth is plainly come," as Moses exclaims according to Damascene (2 *Kanon* 6.2). But the presence of Moses (and to a lesser extent that of Elijah) shows us that this vision of "the face of God" has deep roots in the history of His self-revelation to His people. The Lord once hid Moses in a cleft of the rock; now Moses receives his vision of the invisible God, "protected by the deified body as by a rock" (2 *Kanon* 1.2). Here Damascene is drawing on a tradition of interpretation, going back at least to Irenaeus,[38] that sees in the rock a figure of the Incarnation. But when he speaks of the "deified body," this further suggests that he is thinking of the Incarnation in terms of "immaterial fire that does not burn the material substance of the body," as he characterizes the revelation on Tabor later on (2 *Kanon* 4.3). So again, who better than Moses to recognize in Christ's "flesh shining with divine brightness" the fulfillment of his vision in "the bush unharmed though united with fire" (2 *Kanon* 4.1)?

So Moses had been party to at least two visions long regarded as classic prefigurations of the Incarnation.[39] But he had also experienced the divine presence in a form directly related to the interpretation of the Transfiguration as a revelation of the Holy Trinity: he "prophetically saw the glory of the Lord in the cloud and the pillar of fire" (2 *Kanon* 1.1). So John writes in the first ode, the theme of which is the Red Sea crossing, and further on, he elaborates: "The pillar of fire showed to Moses Christ transfigured, and *the cloud pointed to the grace of the Spirit that overshadowed Mt Tabor*" (2 *Kanon* 6.3). The cloud at the Transfiguration—like the cloud or divine overshadowing in the Old Testament, for that matter—can be interpreted on several levels. In a verse for vespers, for instance, Kosmas describes it as "spreading out to form a tabernacle" ("Oh Lord, I Have Cried," 1), by implication showing Peter and the others what is the tabernacle proper to Christ. But Kosmas's *kanon* again suggests a connection with the Holy Spirit. He probably has in mind Luke's narrative, which connects the disciples' fear with the vision *in the cloud*, when he describes them as falling on their faces "and with their minds enlightened, they sang a hymn of praise to Him and to the Father and the Spirit" (1 *Kanon* 8.5).[40]

If John's main interest in his *kanon* is the vision of God promised to Moses, Kosmas's is more specifically the vision of God *as light* (which is by no means to deny that there is a large measure of overlap). It is an ancient tradition of interpretation that

Matthew's description of Christ shining "as the sun" is in no way meant to indicate parity[41] and can properly be glossed "more brightly than the brilliance of the sun" (1 *Kanon* 6.1). Indeed, the comparison often becomes a starting point for emphasis on the *disparity* between created light and the uncreated. "The visible sun was eclipsed by rays of [Christ's] divinity," as John writes (2 *Kanon* 4.2), for, as he says further on, the Sun of Righteousness now shines from the earth (2 *Kanon* 6.1). Clearly, the key to interpreting the light of Tabor is less the evangelists' attempts to describe the vision than their reference immediately before to the Son of Man in the glory of His Father (Mt. 16:27 and parallels). This directs the interpreter to a wealth of scriptural texts which speak of God in terms of light. Even more to the point, it encourages him to explore the notion of light as a revelation of the relationship between the Father and the Son.

Kosmas begins his *kanon* by connecting the light of the Transfiguration with both the vision of the Kingdom (cf. Mt. 16:28, etc.) and the relationship between the Father and the Son, and he does so with the help of the evangelist who says nothing whatsoever about the Transfiguration of Jesus on the mountain:

> Delivering to His friends words of life concerning the Kingdom of God, Christ said to them: "When I shall shine forth with unapproachable light, ye shall know that the Father is in me" (1 *Kanon* 1.1).

This is not, of course, an exact quotation from John. It echoes two passages, the more obvious being John 14:10 ("I am in the Father and the Father in me"), Jesus's answer to Philip's request "Show us the Father." But the characterization "words of life concerning the Kingdom" clearly suggest that Kosmas connects the Transfiguration, not unreasonably, with Christ's final discourse, in which He prays, "Now, Father, glorify Thou Me in Thine own presence with the glory which I had with Thee before the world was made" (Jn. 17:5), and says, "this is eternal life, *that they know Thee the only true God and Jesus Christ whom Thou hast sent*" (Jn. 17:3).[42]

For Kosmas, then, the Transfiguration is a revelation of the Kingdom above all because it conveys knowledge of God. This is confirmed two troparia later: "Today, as He promised, Christ . . . disclosed to His disciples the image and reflection of the divine brightness . . . " (1 *Kanon* 1.3). The "promise" seems to be the statement that some will see the Kingdom; the content of its fulfillment clearly echoes Hebrews 1:3, which is one of Kosmas's favorite expressions of how Christ is manifested on Tabor as the divine Son (cf. 1 *Kanon* 8.2–3). It is also one of a number of passages that make the point that Christ is not, strictly speaking, altered at all but is briefly perceived *as He actually is*, for He is not the receiver of the light but its source. Kosmas points out the contrast with the "transfiguration" of Moses through his contact with God:

> The face of Moses once shone with glory because of the divine voice he heard in the darkness (Ex. 34.29), but *Christ covers Himself with light and glory as with a garment* (Ps. 103/4.2). For He . . . is by nature Himself the Author of light . . . (1 *Kanon* 8.4)

Directly related to Kosmas's emphasis on the light as a vision of God Himself is another feature of his interpretation: the Apostles' reaction of falling to the ground is interpreted not simply as fear but as worship (cf. 1 *Kanon* 9.1). Recognizing Christ as God, they "bend the knee before Him" (1 *Kanon* 6.3).

The glory in which Christ appears, several times identified with the "unapproachable light" in which God dwells (e.g., 1 *Kanon* 7.3, cf. 1 *Kanon* 7.1, 1 *Kanon* 8.2), is not only the glory of His Father; it may equally be spoken of as the glory proper to Him, "glory as of the Only-begotten of the Father," as we hear in a vespers verse attributed variously to Kosmas and John.[43] Thus the light becomes a trinitarian revelation: as the Lity verse goes on, "in light let us receive light (cf. Ps. 35/36.10), and, uplifted in spirit [or "in the Spirit"], let us ever sing the praises of the consubstantial Trinity." We should note that in echoing Psalm 35:10, the melodist is invoking a passage long understood as referring to the Son as a revelation of the Father.[44] It is an idea that John takes to its logical trinitarian conclusion when he speaks in the *kanon* of "the immaterial Godhead of the Father and the Spirit shining forth in the Only-begotten Son" (2 *Kanon* 9.2).

We can see that John, too, identifies the experience of the Kingdom with the knowledge of God conveyed by the Transfiguration, but he places less emphasis on the divine light, more on the understanding of the Incarnation. Either side of a *troparion* describing the Apostles as awestruck "before the beauty of the divine Kingdom" (2 *Kanon* 7.2), he relates events on the mountain to the things that "God has prepared for those that love Him," which "no eye has seen nor ear heard" but are now revealed through the Spirit (1 Cor. 2:9–10): "Now what has not been seen becomes visible to the Apostles . . . the Godhead has shone forth before them in the flesh" (2 *Kanon* 7.1); "Now what has not been heard is heard. For the Son who came forth without father from the Virgin receives glorious testimony from His Father's voice, that He is both God and man for ever more" (cf. Heb. 13:8) (2 *Kanon* 7.3). Consistently with his emphasis on the vision of Christ *in two natures*,[45] in the next *troparion* Damascene stresses for good measure that Christ is Son of the Most High "not by adoption, but in essence" (2 *Kanon* 7.4).

What actually happens when "the appearance of Jesus's face is altered"? It is a question that perennially occupies commentators, and we have seen some of the answers reflected in the hymns. It reveals Christ in the glory of His Father, Christ Himself as a reflection of that glory. It is related to the promised vision of the Kingdom, not only as a revelation of God but also as a revelation of man as he is destined to be. We find this theme taken up by Wesley too: "The image of the heavenly man / Our bodies, spiritual as His, / In that sabbatic day shall gain" (XI.21, no. 958 [Mk.]). Kosmas and John go into more anthropological detail, as we shall see.

The vision of Jesus in glory reminds us that as man, too, He is the "image of the glory of God" (cf. 1 Cor. 11:7). This is the connection that leads both melodists, seeing Jesus transfigured, to recall the act of creation. John sets before us a remarkable (if complex) vision of the archetype shining through the image:

> Thou who in the beginning with invisible hands hast fashioned man in Thine image hast now displayed thine original [or "archetypal"] beauty [*kallos*: the substantive form of the word used where "God saw that it was *good*"] in this same human body formed by Thee, revealing it, not as in an image, but as Thou art in Thine own essence, being both God and man. (2 *Kanon* 5.2)[46]

There might be a temptation to conclude that humanity, the image, is getting rather short shrift here—that it is wholly eclipsed by the divine archetype. But any such conclusion ignores the force of the reference to the act of creation. We were fashioned by divine hands with an original beauty which is that of the Archetype, even Christ; we are thus bearers of a nature, which, as Fr. John Breck aptly puts it, "is 'truly itself,' it realizes its full potential, only by its *participation in divine nature* rendered accessible in and through the divine energies."[47] This is precisely the anthropology that Damascene sees revealed to us in the light of the Transfiguration.

Kosmas is in accord with John, although he speaks explicitly in terms of deification:

> Having put on Adam entire, O Christ, and changing the nature grown dark in past times, Thou hast filled it with glory and deified it by the alteration of Thy form. (1 *Kanon* 3.1)

This, too, is an aspect of the Transfiguration as a glimpse of the Kingdom: it looks forward to our own future glory, to the fulfillment of the potential for which we were created. John takes up the explicitly eschatological theme in the last ode of his *kanon*, where he also prays to be found worthy to "take my fill of delight in Thee, that dancing with joy I may magnify both Thy comings" (2 *Kanon* 9.3),[48] for when Christ shines upon the Apostles and upon Moses and Elijah, it is "to show plainly how, at Thy mysterious second coming, Thou wilt appear as the Most High God standing in the midst of gods" (cf. Ps. 81/82:1) (2 *Kanon* 9.1).

Type, Image, and Truth in the Easter *Kanon*

For the final part of this chapter, I want to refer briefly to the crown of John Damascene's poetic work, the Easter *kanon*. I would like to address an important principle of scriptural interpretation so strikingly exemplified in this *kanon*, the notion of a double fulfillment of scriptural types. In this, as in so much of this *kanon*, John is drawing directly on St. Gregory the Theologian. Gregory, in his homily on the feast, speaks of our partaking in a Passover that is still typological, though less veiled (*gymnoteron*) than the old Passover.[49] This notion had been set out in more detail in the *Symposium* of Methodius of Olympus, who says (in connection with the pattern for the tabernacle shown to Moses, Ex. 25:40) that the Jews saw the shadow of the image, the "third from reality," while we clearly see the image of the heavenly order, and the truth is to be made manifest after the resurrection.[50] John is likely to have Methodius in mind as well as Gregory, because his main concern is precisely to present the life of the Church as the clear image of the heavenly order; the "holy people of God" now sees the "outcome of symbols," as he writes in connection with the paschal lamb of Exodus (*Kanon* 4.3).

The gap between "image" and "truth" becomes apparent only in the last two odes: after inviting us to "commune in the new fruit of the vine, in divine gladness, on the high day of the Resurrection and the Kingdom of Christ" (*Kanon* 8.1), the melodist concludes with a prayer to "commune in Thee more perfectly [perhaps literally, "more untypically," *ektypoteron*] in the day of Thy Kingdom which knows no evening" (*Kanon* 9.2). Now, it is not unexpected that a vision of the Church as Eucharistic gathering should look forward to an eschatological fulfillment. We find the same in some of Wesley's Hymns on the Lord's Supper, which present striking parallels to John

Damascene's Easter *Kanon.*[51] Wesley agrees in seeing the Supper as "type of the heavenly marriage feast" (cvii). And he certainly recognizes an element of realized eschatology: "By faith and hope already there / Even now the marriage feast we share" (xciii); but his main emphasis seems to fall on the fulfillment yet to come. The hymn most devoted to imagery from the Book of Revelation (cvi), imagery that pervades the Easter *Kanon*, makes no explicit reference to our participation *among* those whom "the Lamb shall always feed." The striking feature of the Easter *Kanon*, on the other hand, is that the note of fulfillment *predominates.* It begins with the Passover in which Christ *has brought us across* from earth to heaven as we "sing the triumphal song"—in the image, surely, of the victors over the beast who sing the song of Moses (the theme of the first ode of the *kanon*) and of the Lamb (Rev. 15:2–3). We might expect that the notion of our experience in the Church as an image (let alone St. Gregory's "still typological") gives rather a weak sense in which Old Testament types are already fulfilled. But what we see in fact is that the notion of double fulfillment allows the biblical interpreter to assert a very strong sense in which the Church experiences the fulfillment of types and prophecies, without doing violence to our commonsense awareness that the "truth" is still to come.

Conclusion

We have suggested that liturgical poetry, such as the examples we have examined, is the primary way in which the Orthodox Christian "taps into" the Church's tradition of scriptural interpretation. Let us now try to summarize the approach to scripture that it conveys.

1. Most obviously, we learn that interpretation of scripture is a function—a "liturgy"—of the life of the Church. It is within the celebration of the incarnate Word through the week and through the year, and within our sacramental participation in Him, that our nourishment with the written word most naturally takes place.

2. Because most of our hymnography comes out of the liturgical celebration of incidents in scripture, it leads us to think in terms of interpreting *events* rather than *texts.* This entails a rather sophisticated understanding of the Gospel account as itself an interpretation, presenting the event in such a way as to bring out particular aspects of what is really happening; other aspects will be indicated by other New Testament and Old Testament passages.

3. The hymns are focused on an event, but in order to discern the full dimensions of the event, they pay minute attention to the details of the way in which it is depicted, the mold in which it is cast—in short, the text. It may be the structure of the story, the choice of a word, or even a grammatical form that alerts us to how this event relates to other events in God's work of salvation. If there is one thing the hymns teach us about reading scripture, it is to be alert to the resonances of every word.

4. Liturgical poetry directs us to the objective meaning of scripture, the story of the Word active in human history. The christological emphasis in interpretation, such as

we have seen in the *kanons*, keeps us very much aware of the scriptural roots of dogmatic formulations. And conversely, by presenting Christology in a pictorial way through images from the Old and New Testaments, the hymns intimate mysteries which cannot be contained in formulae.

5. The liturgical texts are always urging us to join in the event celebrated. At first sight, this might seem to be calling for an effort of pious imagination. But the texts also keep reminding us that through sacramental experience, our baptism and participation in the Eucharist, the scriptures are being fulfilled in us; the hymnographers never let us forget that sacramental life forms part of the background to the New Testament, not *vice versa*. I would want to suggest that the sacramental dimension of scriptural interpretation forms the bridge between the "steel-like objectivity" of the hymns and what Geoffrey Wainwright has called the "existential intention of human life towards the divine Kingdom which is also human salvation."[52]

There are many ways in which the Church brings us face to face with scripture as a record of, and a challenge to, our own sinfulness, failure, and faithlessness; scriptural readings, daily psalms and prayers are obvious examples. With some important exceptions in penitential seasons,[53] this is not the role of hymnography. The hymnographic masterpieces which still shape it affirm that the symbols of scripture have been fulfilled in Christ, but as we celebrate that interpretation liturgically, the fulfillment becomes something we taste and see.

Our Sunday and feast-day services keep us in mind of another reality, one that we would scarcely dare to claim for ourselves as individuals: that we are no longer living among shadows but experience the image of the Kingdom. In accepting the Church's interpretation of scripture, we affirm that the symbols of scripture have been fulfilled in Christ, but as we celebrate that interpretation liturgically, the fulfillment becomes something we taste and see.

Endnotes

[1]Notably Karen B. Westerfield Tucker, "The Liturgical Functioning of Orthodox Troparia and Wesleyan Hymns," chapter 18 in this volume; S T Kimbrough, Jr., "Kenosis in the Nativity Hymns of Ephrem the Syrian and Charles Wesley," in S T Kimbrough, Jr., ed., *Orthodox and Wesleyan Spirituality* (Crestwood, NY: St. Vladimir's Seminary Press, 2002), 265–283.

[2]C. Northcott, *Hymns in Christian Worship* (London: Lutterworth, 1964), 19, quoted in Geoffrey Wainwright, *Doxology: The Praise of God in Worship, Doctrine and Life: A Systematic Theology* (New York: Oxford Univ. Press, 1980), 202.

[3]Paul Maas and C. Trypanis, *Sancti Romani Melodi Cantica—Cantica Genuina* (Oxford: Clarendon, 1963), no. 22, 164–171; English translation in *St. Romanos the Melodist: On the Life of Christ: Kontakia*, ed. and tr. Archim. Ephrem Lash (San Francisco: Harper Collins, 1995), 155–163.

[4]Egon Wellesz, *Byzantine Music and Hymnography*, 2nd ed. (Oxford: Clarendon, 1961), 203.

[5]Maas and Trypanis no. 19, 142; *On the Life of Christ*, 143; *The Lenten Triodion*, tr. Mother Mary and Kallistos Ware (London: Faber and Faber, 1978), 594. The free translation given here is this author's.

[6]Cf. S T Kimbrough, Jr., "Charles Wesley as a Biblical Interpreter," *Methodist History* 26:3 (April 1988): 139–153, especially 145ff.

[7]*The Poetical Works of John and Charles Wesley*, collected and arranged by G. Osborn, D.D., 13 vols. (London: Wesleyan-Methodist Conference Office, 1869–1872), 2:153. Unless otherwise indicated, all refer-

ences to Wesley's works refer to volumes of this collection, henceforth cited as *Poetical Works* followed by volume and page numbers.

[8]Poetical Works, 2:173–176.

[9]*On the Harlot*: Maas and Trypanis, no. 10, 73–80; Archim. Ephrem, 77–84, translation adapted.

[10]Maas and Trypanis, no. 9, 64–72; Archim. Ephrem, 63–72.

[11]Maas and Trypanis, no. 42, *On Jacob and Esau*, 338.

[12]Maas and Trypanis, no. 45, *On Elijah*, 379–380.

[13]Maas and Trypanis, no. 49, *On the Prodigal Son*, 428; Archim. Ephrem, 110.

[14]Maas and Trypanis, 80; Archim. Ephrem, 84.

[15]See I. F. Hapgood, tr., *Service Book of the Holy Orthodox-Catholic Apostolic Church*, 4th ed. (Brooklyn: Syrian Antiochian Orthodox Archdiocese, 1965), 274.

[16]Archim. Ephrem, 78.

[17]Scriptural odes:

1. Ex. 15:1–19
2. Deut. 32:1–43 (normally omitted)
3. 1 Sam. 2:1–10
4. Hab. 3:1–19
5. Isa. 26:9–19
6. Jonah 2:3–10
7. Song of the Three Children 2–21, 28–33
8. Song of the Three Children 34–65
9. Lk. 1:46–55; 68–79

[18]A partial exception is the *kanon* for the Annunciation, ascribed in some editions to "John the Monk" (of Damascus?); this *kanon* takes the form of a dialogue between the Angel and the Virgin. See Mother Mary and Kallistos Ware, tr., *The Festal Menaion* (London: Faber and Faber, 1969), 448–458.

[19]First *kanon* for the feast; English translation in *Festal Menaion*, 367–80. *Stikhera* for the Lity (Vespers/Compline), ibid., 360–61. I have modified the translation on occasion to clarify the scriptural allusions.

[20]*Troparia* of the *kanons* are indicated as follows: first or second *kanon* for the feast, number of ode, number of *troparion* within the ode. The "e" stands for *eirmos*, i.e., the first verse of the ode, which makes the connection between the scriptural ode and the subject of the *kanon* and sets the meter for the other *troparia* of that ode.

[21]"Where'er the pure baptismal rite / Is duly ministered below, / The heavens are opened in our sight / And God His Spirit doth bestow" (X. 446, no. 785 [Mk.]; cf. XI. 326, no. 1627 [Jn.]), but his main concern is to remind us that we lose this grace through sin.

[22]"In Jesus Thy beloved Son / Thou art well pleased with me" (X. 148, no. 24 [Mt.]); "But did He not our nature take, / Thy grace and favour for His sake, / That every soul might find?" (ibid., 150, no. 26; cf. no. 25).

[23]Thus the above *stikheron* continues, "The Spirit bears witness to His divinity, for He hastens towards His like; and a voice sounds from heaven, for it is from heaven that He has come down . . ." (*Festal Menaion*, 361).

[24]Cf. Fr. John Breck's pertinent remark that "the Word of God" is in the first instance "the eternal Logos" (*Scripture in Tradition: The Bible and Its Interpretation in the Orthodox Church* [Crestwood, NY: St. Vladimir's Seminary Press, 2002], 38).

[25]*Festal Menaion*, 361.

[26]The problem of the relationship between the Gospel accounts of Christ's baptism and the rite of the blessing of the waters at the feast of Theophany is discussed by Bishop Cassien, "*La Bénédiction de l'eau de l'Épiphanie à la lumière du Nouveau Testament*," *Irénikon* 31 (1958): 5–18, esp. 8–9.

[27]Cf. Lity 5: "The river Jordan turned back, not daring to minister to thee."

[28]In some hymns, he does so: "O Saviour, who takest away the sin of the world, sanctify me and the waters" (First Hour, *Festal Menaion*, 317).

[29]A verse at the Lity, perhaps by John of Damascus, gives a profound explanation of the plural here: "O Lord, wishing to fulfil that which Thou hast appointed from eternity, Thou hast received from all creation ministers at this Thy mystery: Gabriel from among the angels, the Virgin from among men, the star

from among the heavens, and Jordan from among the waters: and in its stream Thou hast washed away the transgression of the world" (Lity 6, *Festal Menaion*, 361–62). In undergoing the baptism proper to sinful man, Christ fulfills a vital element in the economy of salvation, in which He does not act without the cooperation of His creatures.

We should not overemphasise the contrast with Wesley's hymn on this verse (X. 148, no. 23 [Mt.]), quoted above, in which "us" simply means "us"—sinful humanity. Many other Orthodox hymns reflect the understanding that in saying, "It is fitting for us," Christ is speaking for all humanity.

[30]*Festal Menaion*, 482–494, 470–471.

[31]"Oh Lord, I Have Cried," Vespers, *Festal Menaion*, 470.

[32]E.g., Cyril of Alexandria, *On Mt*, PG 72:425A; *On Lk*, PG 72:653A.

[33]Thus we find, for instance, that the scene on the mountain indicates that those who hear Moses and the prophets and receive Christ shall appear transfigured with Him (XI. 21, no. 959 [Mk]).

[34]S T Kimbrough, Jr. and Oliver A. Beckerlegge, *The Unpublished Poetry of Charles Wesley*, 3 vols. (Nashville: Abingdon/Kingswood, 1990), 2:111. The hymn continues, "The image in his face is seen, / His simple meek and modest mien, / His innocence and love"; it seems that Wesley has in mind the effect on the whole person of a prayerful soul, rather than the potential for holiness to be manifest in visible, bodily glorification.

[35]E.g., "Him, only Him, we long to hear . . . who comes in Moses's place" (XI. 186, no. 1333 [Lk.]).

[36]This is implicit also where Wesley writes, alluding to Elijah's experience, "His Spirit's small and quiet voice / Makes all our broken bones rejoice" (XI. 185, no. 1332 [Lk.]).

[37]Acrostic: a word, phrase, or sequence of letters formed from the initial letters of each *troparion* of a *kanon* (or each *oikos* of a *kontakion*).

[38]Cf. *Against Heresies* 4.20.9.

[39]The first use of the Burning Bush as a specific type of the Incarnation, Godhead united with the flesh, seems to be in St. Gregory of Nyssa (*Life of Moses* 2.21, SC 1bis, 37; cf. numbers 2 and 3).

[40]The final *troparion* of the eighth ode is frequently dedicated to the Holy Trinity.

[41]Cf. Chrysostom, *On the Capture of Eutropios* 10–11, PG 52:404–5. As Basil of Seleucia remarks, "it is not right to compare what is created with the Creator" (Hom. 40, *On the Transfiguration*, 1, PG 85:453A).

[42]It is notable that St. Gregory Palamas, some centuries later, will cite Jn. 17:24 and 17:5 as showing Christ's intention to bestow the vision of divine light; cf. *The Triads* D16, tr. N. Gendle (Mahwah: Paulist, 1983), 60.

[43]Lity 4, on "Glory," *Festal Menaion*, 475–76. The *stikheron* is anonymous in the printed service books. It has been attributed to Kosmas by Th. Detorakis, *Kosmas o Melodos: Vios kai Ergo* (*Analecta Vlatadon* 28) (Thessaloniki: Patriarchal Institute for Patristic Studies, 1979), 216, and to John by Bishop Sophronios Evstratiades, "*O agios Ioannes o Damaskenos kai ta poietika avtou erga*," *Nea Sion* 27 (1932): 332–333.

[44]Cf. Origen, "Thy Word and Thy Wisdom, which is Thy Son, in Him we see Thee, the Father" (*On First Principles* 1.1.1, *Griechische christlichen Schriftsteller der ersten drei Jahrhundert* [Leipzig: Hinrich, 1897–], 22, 17).

[45]Cf. 2 Kg 3.3: "Being complete God, Thou hast become complete man, bringing together manhood and the complete Godhead in Thy person, which Moses and Elijah saw on Tabor in two natures."

[46]The idea is expressed more succinctly in Damascene's homily on the feast: "The archetype is mingled with the image, and today shows its own proper beauty in that image" (*On Transfiguration*, 4, PG 96:552C).

[47]Op. cit., 188.

[48]This *troparion* of the *kanon* is used, in some traditions at least, as a prayer in preparation for Communion.

[49]Hom. 45, *Second Homily on Easter*, 23; PG 36:653C–56A.

[50]*Symposium of the Ten Virgins* V.7; PG 18:109BC. Cf. Maximus the Confessor: "The things of the old covenant are the shadow. Those of the new covenant are the image. The truth is the state of things to come" (*Scholia* on Dionysius, *On the Church Hierarchy*, PG 4:137).

[51]*Poetical Works*, 3:283–95, especially nos. xciii, xcvi, cvi, cvii.

[52]*Doxology*, 204.

[53]Most notably the *Great Kanon* of St. Andrew of Crete. See discussion in chapter 4 above: "Praying the Scriptures in Orthodox Worship."

17

The Recovery of the Great Eucharistic Prayer in the Wesleyan Tradition

Grant Sperry White

Please allow me to begin with an anecdote which I think may point to the future. This past semester, I taught a course on the history of Christian worship. Naturally we spent a significant amount of time on the development of the liturgy of Eucharist, and on the development of theologies of Eucharistic consecration and their liturgical expressions. One day, after I had lectured on the *epiklesis* in Orthodox *anaphoras* and revised Western Christian Eucharistic prayers, one of my students (in his mid-twenties) came up to me and said enthusiastically, "Grant, the *epiklesis* rocks!" For those unfamiliar with American slang, my student had expressed his great appreciation of and consonance with a theology of Eucharist in which the role of the Holy Spirit in the Eucharistic action was primary. I was extremely happy to hear my student's affirmation. It represents, I think, one small sign that the great Eucharistic prayer is beginning to be recovered in United Methodism.

Having glimpsed what I hope is the future, let us first begin this discussion of the recovery of the great Eucharistic prayer in Wesleyan traditions by defining what this paper means by "great Eucharistic prayer." It is the great prayer of thanksgiving in the liturgy of the Eucharist, in which over bread and wine the Christian assembly thanks God for creation and redemption, makes memorial of the saving work of God in Christ, and asks God to fulfill God's purposes for the cosmos through the action of the Holy Spirit. I recognize that this brief definition of the great Eucharistic prayer does not say everything one might wish to say about it, but I think that at the very least, this definition has the virtue of indicating the thanksgiving-petition structure of this prayer in both the Byzantine rite and in contemporary Methodist churches.

Second, a brief word about the meaning of the word "recovery." It seems to me that we can take it to describe two separate but related things. On the one hand, recovery indicates the reclaiming, if you will, of a specific tradition—a structure—of praying at the Lord's table. Thus recovery in this sense involves the process of various Methodist churches coming to adopt this structure and texts based on it in their revised service books over the course of the past thirty or so years. On the other hand, recovery also implies something much deeper and more wide-ranging than simply the acquisition of texts. In this sense, recovery means giving flesh and blood to the great Eucharistic prayer by living out the profound spiritualities which underlie it. I shall discuss both of these dimensions of this phenomenon of recovery, and shall attempt to relate my discussion to the context of Methodist-Orthodox conversation about worship and spirituality.

The Recovery of Texts

Worldwide Methodism has been influenced, at least with respect to liturgical texts, by the liturgical movement of the twentieth century. The liturgical movement gave birth from the late 1960s to the early 1990s to a wave of liturgical revision in Protestant churches based on ecumenical, biblical, and patristic scholarship. To be sure, there had been revisions of service books prior to this time. But those revisions had been aimed almost exclusively at restoration of older or earlier texts and practices from the Reformation period onwards. There was little if any attempt to seek models in early Christian practices. Thus, for example, the services in the 1936 British Methodist *Book of Offices* reflected the needs of a reunited British Methodism and the liturgical traditions represented in it. Likewise, the 1944 *Book of Worship* of The Methodist Church (United States) contained liturgical texts from the Methodist Episcopal, Methodist Episcopal Church, South, and Methodist Protestant traditions. These services in turn bore the marks of more than a century and a half of Methodist liturgical revision of the Anglican Book of Common Prayer tradition bequeathed to the American Methodists by John Wesley in his 1784 abridgement and light revision of the Book of Common Prayer titled *The Sunday Service.*

It is a commonplace, but worth repeating, that if there is such a thing as a Methodist liturgical tradition, it is a tradition combining both "fixed" and "free" liturgical prayer. I prefer to view the elements of Methodist liturgical practices in terms of ecclesiology; thus, I suggest that it is possible to view the Methodist liturgical tradition as the fruit of a tension between the practices of the *ecclesia* (i.e., Eucharist, baptism, ordination) and those of the famous or infamous Pietist *ecclesiola in ecclesia* (class meetings, preaching services, Love Feast, Watch Night service, and others). When viewed from the perspective of ecclesiology, the vicissitudes of Methodist liturgical practice can be interpreted as reflections of a fundamental ecclesiological ambivalence in at least some Methodist churches. In other words, the question, "Are we *ecclesia* or *ecclesiola*?" has not yet been decisively answered by Methodists, although I will argue later on in this paper that at least some of the liturgical signs are pointing toward an embracing of an identity as *ecclesia.*

This ambivalence about official liturgical texts is highlighted, I think, when we realize that for the majority of its history (at least in the United States), the primary liturgical text for Methodists has been the hymnal, not a prayer book of worship. Thus the famous hymnal of 1780 contained no liturgical texts, true to its identity as a book for an *ecclesiola.* In fact, through the entire nineteenth century in the United States (and never, to the best of my knowledge, in British Methodism), Methodist hymnals did not contain prayers for the Eucharist or baptism. For American Methodists, those services were found in the portion of the Anglican liturgical heritage to survive Wesley's death, the Ritual. The Ritual (first titled "Sacramental Services, etc." in 1792) was to be found in the Book of Discipline, the other indispensable text in American Methodism. Thus the content of normal Sunday worship was conditioned by practices in origin rooted in the Pietist small groups, not in the churchly practice of the Sunday celebration of the Eucharist. The central liturgical text, in other words, had and has much more to do with the *ecclesiola* than the *ecclesia.* Only comparatively late in its history did American Methodism come to include liturgies for the Lord's Supper, baptism, weddings, and funerals in its hymnals, and such additions often seem awkward appendages rather than integral elements.

The post-Vatican II era ushered in a period of Methodist liturgical revision. To date, the chief study of this revision in the United States is the unpublished 1992 Notre Dame dissertation by Robert B. Peiffer, "How Contemporary Liturgies Evolve: The Revision of United Methodist Liturgical Texts." A summary of developments in the United Kingdom during this time appears as chapter 9 of John Fenwick and Bryan Spinks's *Worship in Transition: The Twentieth-Century Liturgical Movement.* James F. White wrote an early account of the institutional dimensions of liturgical revision in his 1976 *Worship in Transition,* in a chapter titled "Behind the Liturgical Establishment." Karen Westerfield Tucker's history of American Methodist worship has also been a long-anticipated volume.

The first United Methodist experimental liturgy of the Eucharist appeared in 1972 under the title *The Liturgy of the Lord's Supper: An Alternative Text.* It set forth the main principle followed by all subsequent United Methodist revisions of the Eucharist in containing a great Eucharistic prayer based on early Christian models rather than the Anglican-Cranmerian tradition which had until then been the textual standard, if not the standard in practice. The influence on the United Methodist services of Roman Catholic and other Protestant efforts at liturgical revision is undeniable. Indeed, this was perhaps the greatest era of liturgical ecumenism ever seen, at least in Western Christianity. The influence of Orthodox liturgical texts and practices is less clear. Fenwick and Spinks suggest, "It must be acknowledged . . . that the process [of Eastern Christian influence on Western liturgical revisions] has been one of [the Western churches'] looking back rather than simply looking East. Many of the Eastern practices have been adopted because they were recognized as early Church forms preserved by Orthodoxy."[1] I think Fenwick and Spinks are correct as far as prayer texts are concerned. However, with regard to liturgical and sacramental theology, it seems to me that Orthodox theologians (such as Alexander Schmemann, Vladimir Lossky, and John Zizioulas) have influenced and continue to influence Methodist thought.

The 1972 liturgy was a greater success than anyone had anticipated, and it sold more than one million copies. Further revisions followed, culminating in the texts found in the 1989 *United Methodist Hymnal* and the 1992 *United Methodist Book of Worship.* These later revisions addressed the theology of Eucharistic offering as well as inclusive language. Some have suggested that the post-1972 revisions moved too quickly and made it impossible for congregations to live into any one version of the liturgy of the Eucharist. The Order of St. Luke, a United Methodist order devoted to promoting the sacraments, in turn published its own series of great thanksgivings based on the United Methodist prayers but keyed to each Sunday of the liturgical year.

In the United States, it is the African American Methodist churches which have most faithfully retained the Anglican-Cranmerian texts and practices bequeathed by John Wesley, and as far as I can determine, there has not been liturgical revision as there has been in the United Methodist Church. However, the latest edition of the African Methodist Episcopal Church Hymnal includes an alternative great thanksgiving very similar to the 1989 United Methodist great thanksgiving.

In 1975, the British Methodist Church published the *Methodist Service Book*, which contained a great Eucharistic prayer briefer than its American Methodist counterpart, but sharing with it a structure based on early Christian *anaphorae*. The process of revision continued and culminated in 1999 with the publication of the *United Methodist Worship Book*.

Other Wesleyan churches in the world have not followed to the same extent the United Methodist and British Methodist adoption of a great Eucharistic prayer. Liturgical revision is in process in the Korean Methodist Church, and it is possible that some form of the great prayer will be adopted. Australian Methodists live with other Australian Protestants in the Uniting Church of Australia, and there the service book published in 1988 contains, among others, a great thanksgiving similar to the United Methodist. As in other parts of the Methodist-Wesleyan world, Australian Methodists were heir to the Anglican-Cranmerian liturgical tradition.

It is difficult to speak with certainty about the revision of Eucharistic rites in other Wesleyan churches. The churches of the Holiness tradition tend not to use printed service books, and so I cannot speak to the extent to which any have attempted to restore or reclaim a great Eucharistic theology in some segments of the Church of the Nazarene, including the institution of more frequent celebration in some congregations and interest in the so-called blended type of worship advocated by the Episcopal theologian Robert Webber, in which patristic-liturgical movement texts and practices are combined with musical and stylistic elements from Charismatic worship traditions. Nazarene theologian Rob Staples has published a widely used textbook on sacramental theology. It remains to be seen how much the current Pentecostal interest in patristic and Byzantine theologians affects Pentecostal Eucharistic practice and theology, if at all.

Salient Features of the Great Eucharistic Prayer in Methodism

Let me summarize the most noteworthy features of the great Eucharistic prayer as its has come to be in worldwide churches of the Wesleyan tradition:

1. *Structure.* Methodists have chosen the ecumenically popular West Syrian tradition of Eucharistic prayer. The prayer contains an extended narrative of thanksgiving centered on the history of salvation, culminating in Christ and the gift of the Holy Spirit after the Resurrection. In addition, the prayer has an *epiklesis* after the *anamnesis* and oblation following the verba. As Fenwick and Spinks note, "no really sound argument has been advanced as to why West Syrian fifth-century prayers should be the basis for twentieth-century prayers."[2] This strikes me as an overstatement, because it seems to me that at least two theological goals born of Methodist participation in

the ecumenical movement are met by such a structure: (a) the need for an *anaphora* embracing a broader narrative of salvation than only the Last Supper and Cross (as was the case in most of the Reformation-era communion prayers); and (b) the need for such a prayer not simply to be a Methodist creation, but to stem from an older, more widely held tradition, thus establishing Methodist Eucharistic prayer in text as well as in theology with recovered and reclaimed patristic models. Finally, in view of the discussions of this volume, one might also say that the choice of the West Syrian model is fortunate because it establishes a point of contact between Methodists and members of the Byzantine rite. I will return to the question of exactly what we mean when we say that some members of the Wesleyan tradition have embraced Eucharistic prayers of a West Syrian structure.

As an appendix to this paper, I provide the full text of the Great Thanksgiving from "Service of Word and Table I" in *The United Methodist Hymnal* (9–10).

2. *Invocation of the Spirit.* Historians and theologians alike have noted the distinctly pneumatological dimension of Wesleyan Christianity, especially with regard to the Eucharist and the journey of sanctification. For the Wesleys, the Holy Spirit works in the heart to re-create it in the image and likeness of God. As well, some of the 1745 *Hymns on the Lord's Supper* explicitly invoke the Spirit. However, Wesley's abridgement of the Book of Common Prayer did not itself restore an *epiklesis* (unlike the Scottish Episcopalians and their American cousins), and so it was left to the aforementioned Wesleyan hymnody to supply an invocation of the Holy Spirit in the Eucharist. Thus the inclusion of an *epiklesis* in the most recent Methodist Eucharistic prayers can indeed be seen simply as a making liturgically explicit something that has always been a part of Wesleyan tradition. At the same time, this explicit *epiklesis*, coupled with Wesleyan insistence on sanctification and the fundamental role of the Holy Spirit in it, opens the door to a more thoroughgoing exploration of the relationship between Eucharist, sanctification, and *askesis* than has to date taken place.

The *epiklesis* in the American United Methodist rite prays:

> Pour out your Holy Spirit on us gathered here,
>   and on these gifts of bread and wine.
> Make them be for us the body and blood of Christ,
> that we may be for the world the body of Christ,
>   redeemed by his blood.
> By your Spirit make us one with Christ,
>   one with each other,
> and one in ministry to all the world,
>   until Christ comes in final victory
> and we feast at his heavenly banquet.

The 1975 British Methodist *epiklesis* focuses more on the congregation, but also expresses the eschatological dimension of the Eucharist:

> Grant that by the power of the Holy Spirit
> we who receive your gifts of bread and wine
> may share in the body and blood of Christ.

> Make us one body with him.
> Accept us as we offer ourselves to be a living sacrifice,
> and bring us with the whole creation to your heavenly kingdom.[3]

Intercessions and memorial of the saints are not typically part of the *epiklesis* in any Methodist Eucharistic prayer, although they are a possibility in the United Methodist Church in the Great Thanksgiving for All Saints and Memorial Occasions. It prays, "Renew our communion with all your saints, especially those whom we name before you."[4] The earlier collections *At the Lord's Table* and *Holy Communion* also included "A Common Eucharistic Prayer," which is based on a version of the *anaphora* of St. Basil and was recommended for use in a spectrum of North American denominations, including The United Methodist Church. This prayer also contains the possibility of intercessions and explicit naming of the saints at the *epiklesis*. Curiously, neither the hymnal nor the book of worship of the United Methodist Church contains it.

3. *Structure of the Sunday Service.* In the revised Methodist liturgies, the Sunday service follows the ancient *ordo* attested from the time of St. Justin Martyr of a liturgy of the word followed by a liturgy of the Eucharistic table. As so much of the twentieth-century liturgical movement has presupposed this basic "deep structure" for the Sunday liturgy, it may well be worth pointing out here that adoption of the word-Eucharist pattern was not inevitable! For example, in the congregations which eventually became the denomination known as the Disciples of Christ and the Church of Christ, the Eucharist was fitted to what James White has named a frontier pattern of worship in which the sermon served as the culmination of the service. Thus the table preceded the preaching of the word. To this day, in many Methodist congregations in the world, the Eucharist is viewed as a special, occasional addition to a service normally consisting of praying, singing, and preaching (of either a Morning Prayer or frontier model). For such congregations, the deep structure of word followed by table remains a mystery, and one not infrequently hears questions about what is perceived as a decentering of the sermon on communion Sundays.

If I understand correctly, by adopting or recovering a word-table structure, those Methodists who have done so are arguing (implicitly, in most cases) that form as well as content matters in worship. There is something significant about retaining this ancient pattern, something which goes missing when the main Sunday service is ordered according to another pattern. Ultimately, of course, this question has to do with the value one places on the liturgical tradition as an expression of Tradition. I think it is fair to say that Methodists tend to look for a logical "meaning" to the order of the Sunday service. In other words, somehow it has to "make sense" that the various prayers, hymns, readings, and actions of the service follow as they do. I know of no study of this question, but I suspect it has something to do with the liturgical pragmatism of American revivalism coupled with an inherent mistrust of the broader Christian liturgical tradition, if I may be allowed to speak of such a thing. In such a context (not limited to American Methodists), for table to follow word is inexplicable, whereas it makes sense for a sermon to follow the reading of at least a small portion of scripture. This view of the Eucharistic liturgy is, of course, very different from what I understand to be the more ikonic understanding of the Orthodox tradition. In this view, the meaning of the Divine Liturgy can be discovered not by appeal to one supposedly rational criterion or another, but by the participation of the worshiper in the liturgy, which itself is an ikon of the liturgy around the throne of God. Of course, I am not claiming that an Orthodox approach to liturgical meaning is irrational! Perhaps instead it is noetic, deeply requiring the active participation of the heart rather than only the intellective faculty of the human person. Of course, what else are the Wesleyan hymns but songs of the noetic life?

Recovery of Spirituality

I suggested at the beginning of this paper that the recovery of the great Eucharistic prayer had to do not only with regaining certain texts, but also with recovery of the spirituality or spiritualities undergirding them. The work of the future lies in this second dimension of recovery. At least some in the Wesleyan tradition have the texts. Will they now, so to speak, live into them? Will they give them life by their faithful lives in Christ, lived in the power of the Holy Spirit?

Before I raise a few questions regarding this recovery of spirituality rooted in the great Eucharistic prayer, let me make two preliminary observations. First, I agree with those theologians today and in the past who recognize that Wesleyan Christianity in many ways stands closer in theory, in its deep wellsprings, to Orthodox Christianity than any other Protestant communion. As many authors have noted, the Wesleyan emphases on the work of the Holy Spirit in the heart (indeed, what seems in some places to be Wesley's insistence on an *aisthesis* of the Spirit in the heart) and the centrality of sanctification and perfection (amounting in fact, if not in word, to a utilization of the idea of *theosis*) have deep roots in patristic Christian thought and practice. Thus, there is in Wesleyan tradition itself a deep consonance with the view of God and salvation one finds in the recovered great Eucharistic prayer. If Wesleyan Christians choose to drink again from those wells, then the recovery of spirituality linked with the Great Thanksgiving may indeed be possible.

Second, a Wesleyan recovery of this spirituality rooted in the Eucharist does not happen in isolation. For Orthodox Christians as well are in the midst of a recovery of sorts, a reawakening to the depths of the full tradition that is already theirs. As Orthodox statements during the past twenty years have made clear, there is a movement among Orthodox to make more clearly manifest in today's world the riches of a common life of witness, service, and hope which springs from the Eucharist.[5] Thus, I suggest that Wesleyan and Orthodox Christians are fellow-pilgrims on this difficult road. Perhaps each can support the other on the way, and perhaps even learn from each other.

What follows are questions concerning how Wesleyan Christians might more fully recover a biblical and patristic spirituality by living out what they pray in the renewed great prayers of thanksgiving which are theirs. Of course, this list is not exhaustive. I offer it in the hope of stimulating conversation between Wesleyan and Orthodox on this most important subject.

1. *Is common structure enough?* We have seen that some Methodist great thanksgivings have a West Syrian structure (as does the *anaphora* of the Liturgy of St. John

Chrysostom). Indeed, The United Methodist Church has opted almost exclusively for this model of praying at the Eucharistic table. In theory, this consonance of structure between some Methodist and Orthodox Eucharistic prayers ought to make possible some fruitful conversation about the spirituality or spiritualities flowing from it. I want to be clear here that I do not have in mind any discussion of Eucharistic fellowship, which is not possible without the sharing of a common faith. But surely there is a vast realm of spirituality or the ascetic life which Wesleyans and Orthodox can at least discuss together.

However, is a common or very similar structure of the Great Eucharistic Prayer in itself enough to form the foundation of such a discussion? Common structure, as important as it is, does not necessarily imply common content. Two areas immediately come to mind: the *epiclesis* and the intercessions in the *anaphora.* Jasper and Cuming's English translation of the *epiclesis* of the Liturgy of St. John Chrysostom reads:

> We offer you also this reasonable and bloodless service, and we beseech and pray and entreat you, send down your Holy Spirit on us and on these gifts set forth; and make this bread the precious body of your Christ, [changing it by your Holy Spirit, Amen; and that which is in this cup the precious blood of your Christ, changing it by your Holy Spirit,] Amen; so that they may become to those who partake for vigilance of soul, for forgiveness of sins, for fellowship with the Holy Spirit, for the fullness of the kingdom [of heaven], for boldness towards you; not for judgement or for condemnation.[6]

I do not wish to open here a detailed discussion of *epikletic* verbs in Orthodox *anaphorae* or of the history of the term *metousiosis* in Orthodox theology. My question is more modest. Although Orthodox and Methodist Eucharistic *epikleses* are not identical, is there at least enough in the very fact that both acknowledge the central role of the Holy Spirit in the Eucharistic action, and pray for the Spirit's descent and operation, for there to be the beginning of a conversation about what that acknowledgment and prayer might mean for living as members of the body of Christ today?[7]

Related to the form of the *epiclesis* is the presence of intercessory prayers in the Great Thanksgiving. Such prayers exist in the *epikletic* section of the *anaphorae* of St. John Chrysostom and St. Basil the Great. They do not in the Methodist prayers. I noted above that the United Methodist Great Thanksgiving for All Saints' and Memorial Occasions allows for the possibility of naming (aloud or silently) the names of persons to be commemorated. But this prayer is unique in the *Book of Worship*, and such prayers are not a typical Methodist practice. The revised Sunday services of the United Methodist and British Methodist churches place intercessory prayer after the sermon, presumably following the witness of St. Justin Martyr.

Here I see two issues related to intercessions in the body of the great Eucharistic prayer. Both have to do with *koinonia.* First is the expression of *koinonia* with the saints and with those who have died in the hope of the resurrection. The *anaphora* of St. John Chrysostom continues from where we left off above:

> We offer you also this reasonable service for those who rest in faith, (forefathers), fathers, patriarchs, prophets, apostles, preachers, evangelists, martyrs, confessors,

> ascetics, and all the righteous (spirits) perfected in faith; (*aloud*) especially all-holy, immaculate, highly glorious, blessed Lady, Mother of God and ever-virgin Mary; Saint John the (prophet) forerunner and Baptist, and the holy (glorious) and honoured apostles; and this saint whose memorial we are keeping, and all your saints: at their entreaties look upon us, O God.
>
> And remember all those who have fallen asleep in hope of resurrection to eternal life, and grant them rest where the light of your own countenance looks upon them.[8]

I do not wish to repeat material which is discussed in another section of this volume, but one or two brief observations should be made here. It will be remembered that John Wesley in his 1784 revision of the Book of Common Prayer actually removed all of the "saints' days, so called" from the Church of England's calendar. In his view, "at present [they serve] no valuable purpose." Wesley's followers have continued until very recently in his footsteps and, even when revising the liturgical calendar in the twentieth century, were reluctant to include even the commemoration of figures named in the New Testament writings. Perhaps at least part of this reticence can be attributed to reaction to Anglo-Catholicism (at least in England). In part also it stems, I think, from a Wesleyan insistence upon the sole mediatorship of Christ and a desire not to do anything liturgically which could even potentially compromise Christ's unique role.

And yet, we hear in another place in this volume that there is in John and Charles Wesley's theology a strong sense of the communion of the church on earth with the church in heaven. A hymn from 1759 by Charles Wesley sings:

> Come, let us join our friends above
> Who have obtained the prize,
> And on the eagle wings of love
> To joys celestial rise.
> Let saints on earth unite to sing
> With those to glory gone,
> For all the servants of our King
> In earth and heaven are one.
>
> One family we dwell in him,
> One church above, beneath,
> Though now divided by the stream,
> The narrow stream of death;
> One army of the living God,
> To his command we bow;
> Part of his host have crossed the flood,
> And part are crossing now.[9]

You can hear in these two stanzas the deeply liturgical and doxological character of this reflection on the *koinonia* of the saints. Such a perspective also appears in the 1992 United Methodist Great Thanksgiving and in the 1975 British Methodist Thanksgiving when immediately before the *sanctus* they evoke the transspatial, transtemporal character of the worshiping communion by specifically joining the congregation's praise with that of "all the company of heaven." It is perhaps also worth noting that John Wesley's journals make clear his particular love for the feast of All Saints. This strand of Wesleyan Christianity is beginning to be embraced by some Methodists. I have already mentioned the Great Thanksgiving for All Saints and Memorial Occasions. In 1996, an unofficial United Methodist sanctoral was published in the United States by the Order of Saint Luke. Titled *For All the Saints*, it contains an extensive list of commemorations of women and men from the Wesleyan traditions (including the United Brethren and the Evangelical Association), as well as from the wider Christian communion.[10] Included are one-page biographies of each person, and propers, as well as commons of saints, in a variety of categories. My experience has been that students are extremely happy to discover this resource and to use it catechetically and occasionally liturgically in their congregations. One criticism I would make of the book is that it does not include enough figures from the Methodist and Wesleyan churches from outside of North America and the British Isles. Thus, there is a lack of persons, for example, from the Korean Methodist Church and other Methodist churches of Asia, or from the Methodist churches of Africa and continental Europe. I hope that subsequent editions will rectify this shortcoming. In addition, the Methodists in Australia, who have entered into the Uniting Church of Australia, also have a sanctoral for their use.

Even given these developments in some churches of the Wesleyan tradition, it still must be asked what place the commemoration of the saints has in the life of the church. Some Methodist theologians (David Carter comes to mind here) have raised the significance of Mary for Wesleyan theology. Here again, I wonder if there might be some fruitful exchange between Methodists and Orthodox, particularly around the question of how Methodists and Orthodox express this *koinonia* and the relation of this expression to Christology and to the church's witness and diaconal service in the world.

2. *Eucharist and askesis.* There is an ascetic dimension to the Methodist tradition, and it is this ascetic theology and practice which may well be the most immediate point of contact between Wesleyan Christians and Orthodox. Other Protestant traditions have ascetic strains as well, but the difference, I think, lies in the Wesleyan tradition's insistence that the ascetic life be lived in the context of the ongoing work of sanctification in the human heart. Both traditions view the human person as (in the traditional Wesleyan terminology) "going on to perfection." Although John Wesley never uses the term *theosis*, it has been argued that the idea itself is prominent in Wesley's thought. That is (to use the words of 2 Peter), we are being made "partakers of the divine nature." Thus fasting, prayer, scripture reading, meditation, and the frequent receiving of the Eucharist are all means of grace, of receiving the life-giving, life-renewing, re-creating power of the Holy Spirit so that the image of God in us might be healed and renewed, that we might be made perfect in love.

Well into the nineteenth century, the Methodist people were keen to foster and nurture that "new birth," which meant a dying to the things of this world. By now, it is well known outside of Wesleyan circles how the Methodist class meetings nourished and supported this ascetic struggle, and how at times the class leader also had to call backsliding members to the more perfect way. Not only was this (and is it to this day in African American and Korean American Methodism) a means of collective spiritual counsel, but it seems to me that the class leader can be seen as a kind of *geron* or *gerontissa.* It is interesting that at the same time the Wesleyan movement was raging in the British Isles, there was a revival and renewal of hesychasm, led by the labors of St. Paisius Velichkovsky and prompting in its turn the compilation of the *Philokalia,* a work generating great interest today, and not only among Orthodox. It might be worthwhile to compare these two eighteenth-century movements, both of which revived the ascetic struggle not only for a select few, but for ordinary Christians. The vitality and influence of the Optino community and the nineteenth-century work *The Way of a Pilgrim* attest to this revival, as does the growth and spread of Wesleyan Christianity in the nineteenth century.

Be that as it may, the more direct question here has to do with the relation of the Eucharist to this ascetic contest to which all Christians are called. The ascetic traditions in Wesleyanism and Orthodoxy tend to stress the role of the Eucharist in the ascetic life in terms of the individual's receiving in it the very life of God for the individual's perfection. Does the narrative of salvation in the great Eucharistic prayer hint to a broader context for understanding the role of the Eucharist in the journey of sanctification? As Orthodox theology stresses, we are never made perfect alone. Our salvation is but a part of the salvation of the entire cosmos, a salvation of which the Eucharist is an experience here and now. How might our individual ascetic struggle appear in the light of God's loving purposes for the entire creation? The Wesleyan tradition has insisted from the very beginning that sanctification of the individual demands the works of love and mercy in the world. What then does the Eucharist say to us about the relationship between *theosis* or perfection and the renewal of the structures of society? Perhaps we can even say that both traditions know that the Eucharist has much to do with *martyria,* as well as *diakonia.*[11]

3. *Eucharist and ecclesiology.* As I understand it, for Orthodoxy, the Eucharist constitutes the church. That is, the church is fully manifest when gathered around the Eucharistic altar with bishop, presbyters, deacons, and the faithful people. This Eucharistic ecclesiology, as explicated by Afanasiev, Florensky, Kern, Schmemann, Lossky, Meyendorff, Zizioulas, and others, views the Eucharist not simply as another of the things the church does. It is, rather, what the church *is.* The responses of the Orthodox to BEM, and to their own intra-Orthodox statements in the past twenty years, frequently allude to this understanding of church.

Such a view is implicit, I think, in the very great Eucharistic prayer itself. As Orthodox theologians themselves have recognized, however, the church must constantly renew the Eucharistic sources of its life so that Eucharistic ecclesiology does not degenerate into liturgical formalism or a vague reliance on mystery. With their recovery of the great Eucharistic prayer, Wesleyan Christians have the opportunity to live into Eucharistic ecclesiology. Such an opportunity implies that Wesleyan Christians will come to see themselves as *ecclesia* rather than *ecclesiola.* It also suggests that Wesleyan Christians must state clearly their theology of the Eucharist. This is happening now in The United Methodist Church, where a statement of Eucharistic theology, parallel to that of the baptismal theology approved by the General Conference in 1996, was presented to the General Conference of 2004. In addition, the ongoing reception of BEM and the Faith and Order labors toward a common expression of the apostolic faith for our time will also, it is to be hoped, bear fruit in Wesleyan churches.

However, this goal of living into a Eucharistic ecclesiology will be no easy task. The responses of some Methodist churches to BEM make clear the unease of some Methodists with the emphasis it places on Eucharist. Not surprisingly, many Orthodox responses to BEM are quite positive toward what it says about Eucharist. I suspect that this is an area in which Wesleyan Christians could learn from Orthodox theologians.

Yet such an ecclesiology will not be imposed on Methodists. It will emerge, I suspect (if it emerges at all), from a deep, lived experience of the Eucharist as, in the words of BEM, "the central act of Christian worship." Most congregations of the Wesleyan tradition have not yet begun to celebrate a service of word and Eucharist as the main Sunday liturgy. Sometimes, as the British Methodist response to BEM indicates, this is because there is a lack of ordained clergy to preside in all congregations every Sunday. In other instances, again, as the British Methodist response notes, the Methodist people have gotten used to a weekly liturgical diet centered on preaching and are loath to give the Eucharist a more prominent place in weekly worship. In the United States, the nineteenth-century frontier experience did much to prevent the Methodist people from celebrating the Eucharist as the main service each Sunday as John Wesley clearly wished them to do.[12]

And yet a twenty-first century Eucharistic ecclesiology is different from an eighteenth-century insistence on the value of frequent, even constant, communion. At times, I think Methodists interested in the renewal of the sacraments have overemphasized the Eucharistic nature of the Wesleyan revival, for in that situation, there was no ecclesial dimension to the Eucharist to speak of. Although not absent from eighteenth-century Anglican Eucharistic theology, it was not prominent. The Wesleys were interested (and rightly so) in renewing the frequent receiving of the Eucharist as a means of grace. Their insistence on the central place of the Eucharist in sanctification is critical and might well provide another talking point between Wesleyans and Orthodox.

What might a Wesleyan living-out of the ecclesial dimensions of the Eucharist look like? I began this discussion with an anecdote; allow me to conclude with another. Since the late 1970s, a small United Methodist congregation in South Bend, Indiana—Broadway Christian Parish United Methodist Church—has celebrated the Eucharist as its main service every Sunday. It is viewed as an odd, a suspicious, and even an un-Methodist congregation by not a few United Methodists in northern Indiana. Since the congregation began celebrating a weekly Eucharist at its main service, it has prayed regularly the great Eucharistic prayer. Through a combination of congregational reflection, pastoral teaching, and encouragement, and hard work, this congregation has begun to live out the theology behind the great Eucharistic prayer. I had the privilege of being a member of that congregation for eight years, and of serving as the chairperson of its worship committee for three of those years.

What strikes me about Broadway's common life is not its perfection (for it is quite imperfect, as is any congregation or parish) or its harmony (because it is often quite an unharmonious place). Instead, what has stayed with me from those years is the deeply incarnational nature of their life together in that place. They were and are there giving flesh and blood to the gospel. For example, shortly after beginning the weekly Eucharist, the congregation, which exists in an economically impoverished neighborhood, came to the conclusion that they could not share the feast of the Lord's body and blood every week while neglecting the hunger of the people around them. And so began a meal, prepared by the congregation members, served every Sunday immediately after the liturgy. Intended as another occasion of *koinonia* (in this instance between the congregation members and members of the neighborhood), it flowed directly from the experience and practice of the Eucharistic *koinonia.* The congregation rightly saw the one as flowing from the other, as do their other ministries in and beyond the neighborhood.

I have no wish to romanticize Broadway Christian Parish or to claim that its practice of love is somehow *teleios*, perfect. But at the very least, I think that it, along with the anecdote with which I began this discussion, provides another hopeful sign that the great Eucharistic prayer is being recovered in some places in the Wesleyan tradition, not only in text, but in lives.[13]

Appendix

The Great Thanksgiving, A Service of Word and Table[14]

The Lord be with you.

And also with you.

Lift up your hearts.

We lift them up to the Lord.

Let us give thanks to the Lord our God.

It is right to give our thanks and praise.

It is right, and a good and joyful thing,
   always and everywhere to give thanks to you,
   Father Almighty, creator of heaven and earth.
You formed us in your image
   and breathed into us the breath of life.
When we turned away, and our love failed,
   your love remained steadfast.
You delivered us from captivity,
   made covenant to be our sovereign God,
   and spoke to us through your prophets.

And so,
with your people on earth
and all the company of heaven
we praise your name and join their unending hymn:

Holy, holy, holy Lord, God of power and might,
heaven and earth are full of your glory.
Hosanna in the highest.
Blessed is he who comes in the name of the Lord.
Hosanna in the highest.

Holy are you, and blessed is your Son Jesus Christ.
Your Spirit anointed him
to preach good news to the poor,
to proclaim release to the captives
and recovering of sight to the blind,
to set at liberty those who are oppressed,
and to announce that the time had come
when you would save your people.
He healed the sick, fed the hungry, and ate with sinners.
By the baptism of his suffering, death, and resurrection
you gave birth to your church,
delivered us from slavery to sin and death,
and made with us a new covenant
by water and the Spirit.
When the Lord Jesus ascended,
he promised to be with us always,
in the power of your Word and Holy Spirit.
On the night in which he gave himself up for us,
he took bread, gave thanks to you, broke the bread,
gave it to his disciples, and said:
"Take, eat; this is my body which is given for you.
Do this in remembrance of me."
When the supper was over, he took the cup,
gave thanks to you, gave it to his disciples, and said:
"Drink from this, all of you;
this is my blood of the new covenant,
poured out for you and for many
for the forgiveness of sins.
Do this, as often as you drink it,
in remembrance of me."
And so,
in remembrance of these your mighty acts in Jesus Christ,

we offer ourselves in praise and thanksgiving
as a holy and living sacrifice,
in union with Christ's offering for us,
as we proclaim the mystery of faith.

Christ has died; Christ is risen; Christ will come again.

Pour out your Holy Spirit on us gathered here,
and on these gifts of bread and wine.
Make them be for us the body and blood of Christ,
that we may be for the world the body of Christ,
redeemed by his blood.
By your Spirit make us one with Christ,
one with each other,
and one in ministry to all the world,
until Christ comes in final victory
and we feast at his heavenly banquet.
Through your Son Jesus Christ,
with the Holy Spirit in your holy church,
all honor and glory is yours, almighty Father,
now and for ever.

Amen.

Endnotes

[1]John Fenwick and Bryan Spinks, *Worship in Transition: The Twentieth-Century Liturgical Movement* (Edinburgh: T. and T. Clark, 1995), 98.

[2]Ibid., 131.

[3]Max Thurian and Geoffrey Wainwright, eds., *Baptism and Eucharist: Ecumenical Convergence in Celebration*, Faith and Order Paper 117 (Geneva: World Council of Churches / Grand Rapids: Eerdmans, 1983), 170.

[4]*The United Methodist Book of Worship* (Nashville: United Methodist Publishing House, 1992), 75.

[5]See, for instance, the 1991 Bucharest Report concerning an inter-Orthodox consultation on "Renewal in Orthodox Worship," and Ion Bria, "The Liturgy after the Liturgy," in Gennadios Limouris, ed., *Orthodox Visions of Ecumenism: Statements, Messages and Reports on the Ecumenical Movement 1902–1992* (Geneva: WCC Publications, 1994), 180–185, 216–220.

[6]Thuirian and Wainwright, *Baptism and Eucharist*, 118.

[7]As an aside, it will be noticed that I have not chosen to address the subject of Eucharistic offering, which is also closely related to the *epiclesis*. As I read the Orthodox responses to the Faith and Order document, *Baptism, Eucharist and Ministry*, it seemed to me that Eucharistic offering remains a *leitmotif* of Western Christian debate over Eucharistic theology, and that it continues to be a secondary, if not unimportant, issue in Orthodoxy. Thus, I think raising the question of Eucharistic offering would be more of a distraction than a help in the context of the discussions of this volume.

[8]Thurian and Wainwright, *Baptism and Eucharist*, 118.

[9]*The United Methodist Hymnal* (Nashville: United Methodist Publishing House, 1989), no. 709.

[10]Clifton Guthrie, ed., *For All the Saints* (Akron, OH: OSL Publications, 1995).

[11]One might also note that several of the Orthodox responses to BEM stress the need for proper preparation before receiving communion (including confession of sins and reception of absolution). This issue is related to the correspondence between the Eucharistic celebration and the moral and ethical life of the community, and is of concern for theologians in the Wesleyan tradition as well, even as the particular ascetic practices deemed necessary for participation in the Eucharist might differ in churches of the Wesleyan tradition. Here it might well be worthwhile to raise the question of the contemporary Methodist interpretation of the Eucharist as a means of converting grace.

[12]Here it is important to distinguish the weekly celebration of the Eucharist from its weekly Sunday celebration as the main liturgy. At least in the United States a growing number of congregations is celebrating the Eucharist at some point during the week, often at a second or third Sunday morning service apart from the main congregational service (which remains centered on preaching). Yet such celebrations, while to be welcomed, still ignore the centrality of the Eucharist for the life of the entire church. It seems to me they are rooted in a theology of the Eucharist as a means of grace as opposed to the wellspring of ecclesial life. Methodists will not develop a Eucharistic ecclesiology until the Eucharist is celebrated at the main Sunday service each week.

[13]I express my thanks to Bishop Hans Växby of the Northern Europe Area of the United Methodist Church, and to his staff in Helsinki, Finland, for their gracious willingness to lend me copies of *The United Methodist Hymnal* and *The United Methodist Book of Worship* for use in preparing this paper.

[14]*The United Methodist Hymnal*, 9–10.

18

The Liturgical Functioning of Orthodox Troparia and Wesleyan Hymns

Karen B. Westerfield Tucker

In the early 1990s, a Preparatory Commission of Orthodox and Methodist members convened three times to discuss the possibility of a worldwide bilateral dialogue. A product of those meetings was the publication of a short booklet that included observations from each side about the other. The Orthodox were clearly struck by Methodist congregational hymn singing:

> These hymns—the singing of which so impresses an Orthodox who attends Methodist worship—are at the same time profoundly theological; they do not appeal only or primarily to the emotions but constitute a *confession of faith*. Here is another all-important point of convergence, for in Orthodoxy likewise the hymns are full of theology. Orthodox can see exemplified in Methodism an interconnection that is very dear to their own heart: the integral unity between faith and prayer, between doctrine and doxology, between proclamation and praise.[1]

For Methodism as with Orthodoxy, worship (*lex orandi*) is understood to stand in an intrinsic relationship with doctrine (*lex credendi*) in keeping with St. Paul's recognition of the essential correspondence between what is "confessed with the lips" and what is "believed in the heart" (Rom. 10:9). To these may be joined the formulation of Christian song (*lex canendi*), for singing has the capacity to bring words and convictions together in an exercise of body and soul.[2] If Methodists and Orthodox share such conceptual similarities, it is appropriate to ask whether connections may also be found in the cantillated texts, liturgical practices, or worship performance even though the liturgies and songs themselves and the contexts for their celebration are vastly different. Given the preference of both bodies to sing the faith, the focus will be on the musical and literary traditions and the function of song in the liturgy, with emphasis on *troparia* on the Orthodox side and the Wesley hymns on the Methodist.

Connections with Ancient Musical Models

The founders of Methodism, John Wesley (the theologian and organizer) and his younger brother Charles (the principal hymn writer), judged the Bible to be the primary standard and norm for Christians. But the Wesleys also ascribed authority to the doctrine and practices of the church's first three centuries—and certain regional churches and figures from the fourth century—as best representing true, uncorrupted, scriptural Christianity. From reading the Fathers (including the writings of John Chrysostom, Basil, and Ephrem Cyrus) and studies of the early church by William Cave, William Beveridge, and others, the brothers observed that liturgical music in antiquity consisted of biblical psalms, scriptural canticles, and hymns of human authorship (on the latter category: "it was usual then for any Persons to compose Divine Songs, to the Honour of Christ, and to sing them in the Publick Assemblies").[3] Lord Chancellor Peter King's *Enquiry* informed them that primitive singing was done with "all the People bearing a part in it," whether "all together or Antiphonally," but without instrumental embellishment. The people were "to offer up unto God the Praises of their Voices, Lips, and Mouths" as if one, though King does not suggest this meant monophonic singing.[4] Music in this fashion enabled doxology and, according to Claude Fleury's paraphrase of St. Basil's first homily on the psalms, "help'd to convey the Religion of the Hymn into the minds of the People with more advantage."[5] In 1768, John Wesley apparently was surprised to learn from reading the second edition of Charles Avison's Essay on Musical Expression that "the music of the ancients was as simple as that of the Methodists," for "their music wholly consisted of *melody*, or the arrangement of single notes"; and that "what is now called *harmony*, singing in parts, the whole of *counterpoint* and *fugues*, is quite novel."[6]

Hymn singing during Methodist public worship in the Wesleys' lifetimes stood in sharp contrast to the Church of England's singing of psalms only and its use of "screaming [choir] boys, who bawl out what they neither feel nor understand."[7] John Wesley preferred congregational singing in unison "with the spirit and with the understanding," neither interrupted by organ accompaniment nor replaced by a choir. Participation of young and old singing lustily had the practical benefit of "raising or quickening the spirit of devotion, confirming faith, enlivening hope, and kindling or increasing love to God and man."[8] The Wesleys encouraged singers to unite their voices to make "one clear melodious sound" and to have "an eye to God" in every word that was sung.[9] All this, the brothers felt, conformed to primitive Christian praxis, though evidently the Methodists did not engage in antiphonal singing, unless one counts the congregational response to the lining out of hymns by a song leader. To ensure that their method of simple performance practice was perpetuated, the Methodist legislative "Minutes" (and later, for some Methodists, the *Discipline*) included a section devoted entirely to the regulation of music in worship.

At their earliest stages, Orthodox and Methodist principles of liturgical music are similar: unaccompanied congregational singing in unison as an expression of spiritual harmony and unity in Christ (cf. Rom. 15:5–6).[10] As both ecclesial communities matured, their song became more elaborate, most likely reflecting an accommodation to the preferences of the ambient musical culture. Rich, homophonic singing supplanted or stood alongside monophony. Choirs offered a portion of the liturgical song, though their employment in Methodist worship came with protests until roughly the end of the nineteenth century. While polyphonic settings were not unknown to Methodists once choirs became fashionable, the use of polyphony has been far more circumscribed among the Orthodox since a distorted hearing of the all-important text is eschewed. Methodists eventually sang with instruments, and evidence exists that organs have sounded on occasion in the worship of the Eastern churches.[11] In their respective musical developments from simplicity to complexity, the two groups exhibit common trends.

Differences and Similarities in Hymnic Vocabularies

The form of sung text taken up by Orthodox and Methodists in their respective liturgies is as much a consequence of the historical period of their decisive shaping as their geographical location. The basic unit of Orthodox hymnody is the antiphon sung with a psalm. At first the antiphon was a verse taken from the psalm (*responsorium*), but later it could be an ecclesiastical composition of various lengths and complexities that continued to be sung in the liturgy oftentimes long after the psalm to which it had been originally attached disappeared or was truncated.[12] The earliest and simplest of these compositions was the short, prayer-like prose *troparion* that was constructed in accordance with many of the principles for accented Greek prose. By the fifth century, *troparia* had grown in length and were composed in strophic form; they were typically a single stanza of one to a dozen lines and, musically, appear to have been set one syllable per note. *Troparia* could be rendered in numerous ways, but they commonly were sung between the verses of a psalm cantillated by one or two soloists. The people, divided into two choirs, responded alternately with the same *troparion* or, in some cases, each offered a different refrain. Lengthy *troparia* might be sung in their entirety at the beginning and end of the psalm, with only the final phrase (*akroteleution*) interjected after each verse.[13] As the *troparia* evolved and multiplied, they were written as commentaries or summaries of the liturgical action and the emphasis of the day (especially festivals and saints' days), and collected together in books called *tropologia*. The form especially flourished in the daily office and became the foundation for more complex and lengthy compositions of liturgical poetry, namely the *kontakion* (which exhibits features of Syriac poetry) and the *kanon*.

Wesleyan hymnody similarly developed from a connection with psalmody, but in this case, as an expansion of the repertoire of Christian song beyond King David's odes to include other parts of the biblical canon and reflection on the great themes of the Christian faith. Yet the Wesley hymn as strophic, regularly metered poetry is a direct descendent of English metrical psalmody as well as the English evangelical hymn developed by Particular Baptist Benjamin Keach, the Independent (Congregationalist) Isaac Watts, and others. The collection of Wesley hymns, like that of the *troparia*, is vast and rich. In his recent study of English hymnody, J. R. Watson explains that "the truth of Jesus Christ as saviour is to Charles Wesley so compelling that he has to go on writing and writing about it."[14] Charles preferred to have more than four lines in a stanza; Frank Baker estimated the average length at six lines.[15] Most hymns had multiple stanzas—the Methodist favorite "O For a Thousand Tongues to Sing" has eighteen—but many were single stanza, including numerous representatives from the two-volume versified scripture collection *Short Hymns on Select Passages of the Holy Scriptures*

(1762). Hymns on similar themes were oftentimes published in discreet collections. *Hymns for our Lord's Resurrection*, *Hymns for Ascension-Day*, and *Hymns of Petition and Thanksgiving for the Promise of the Father*, each published separately in 1746, could, if taken together, constitute a near equivalent to the Orthodox *Pentekostarion*.

It is not known how familiar Charles Wesley was with the Orthodox liturgy as it had developed by the eighteenth century, though of course he was acquainted with descriptions of the Eastern liturgy in early church orders such as the *Apostolic Constitutions* and may have known parts of the liturgy as conveyed through the works of Lancelot Andrewes (*Preces Privatae*) and others. A few Wesley hymns show textual parallels or similarities with some of the *troparia*, most likely because of their common dependence on and basis in scripture, the early councils of the church, the patristic writings, and the shape (and content) of the liturgical year. Certain turns of phrase and imagery in several of the original ten stanzas of the "Hymn for Christmas Day," first published in *Hymns and Sacred Poems* (1739), correspond with those in one of the *troparia* for the Nativity of Christ:

> Thy Nativity, O Christ our God, hath revealed to the world the Light of wisdom: for in it those who worshipped the stars were taught by a star to adore thee, the Sun of Righteousness, and to know thee, the Dayspring from on high. Glory be to thee, O Lord.

Hark how all the Welkin rings[16]
"Glory to the King of Kings,
Peace on earth, and mercy mild,
God and sinners reconcil'd!"
. . .
Hail the Heav'nly Prince of Peace!
Hail the Sun of Righeousness!
Light and life to all he brings,
Ris'n with healing in his wings.

Perhaps coincidentally, the first stanza of the morning hymn "Christ, Whose Glory Fills the Skies" (originally in *Hymns and Sacred Poems* [1740]) uses analogous language in addressing the birth of lively faith at the dawn of a new day:

Christ, whose glory fills the skies,
    Christ, the true, the only Light,
Sun of Righteousness, arise,
    Triumph o'er the shades of night:
Day-spring from on high, be near:
Day-star, in my heart appear.

Common theological emphases, veiled in the retelling of the birth narrative, are shown in another *troparion*, this one for the Eve of the Nativity, and in the third stanza of the hymn "Glory Be to God on High" out of the *Hymns for the Nativity of Our Lord* (1745). Both texts accentuate the kenotic aspect of the Incarnation in the language of doxology:

See th' Eternal Son of God,
A Mortal Son of Man,
Dwelling in an earthly clod,
Whom heaven cannot contain!
Stand amaz'd ye heavens at this!
See the Lord of earth and skies,
Humbled to the dust He is,
And in a manger lies!

> This is our God, none other can be compared unto Him; it is He who was born of the Virgin and dwelt among men. The Only-begotten Son is laid in a poor manger, and the Lord of glory is wrapped in swaddling clothes.

Although the second stanza of the Wesleyan hymn does not directly tie to the *troparion*, it does echo the christological doctrine of the Council of Ephesus when it affirmed Mary to be the *Theotokos*:

Him the angels all ador'd
Their Maker and their King:
Tidings of their Humbled Lord
They now to mortals bring:
Emptied of his majesty,
Of His dazzling glories shorn,
Being's source *begins to Be*,
And God himself is born!

Comparable parallels can be seen in other hymns on the subject of the Christian year. A *troparion* for the Thursday of the Ascension of our Lord Jesus Christ reads:

> Thou hast ascended in glory, Christ our God, thou hast made glad the disciples by the promise of the Holy Spirit: through this blessing thou hast verily assured them that thou art the Son of God, the Redeemer of the world.

These themes of ascension, the outpouring of the Spirit, and recognition of the salvific work by the second Person of the Godhead find a counterpart, though in more priestly terms, in one of the texts collected in *Hymns for Ascension-Day* (1746):

Hail, Jesus, hail, our Great High-Priest,
Enter'd into thy glorious rest,
That holy happy place above!
Thou hast the conquest more than gain'd,
The everlasting bliss obtain'd
For all who trust thy dying Love.

. . .

That we the promise might receive,
Might soon with Thee in glory live,
Thou stand'st before thy Father now!

For us Thou dost in heaven appear,
Our Surety, Head, and Harbinger,
Our Saviour to the utmost Thou.

Not without blood—Thou pray'st above:
The marks of thy expiring love
God on thy hands ingraven sees!
He hears thy blood for mercy cry,
And sends his Spirit from the sky,
And seals our everlasting peace.

Textual affinities similarly may be found between Wesley hymns on the subject of the resurrection and the eight Sunday *troparia* of the resurrection (from the *Oktoechos*) introduced into the Byzantine liturgy after the tenth century and used as introits.[17] The *troparion* of the first tone both describes the event and offers doxology:

> When the stone had been sealed by the Jews and soldiers set to watch thine undefiled body, on the third day, O Saviour, thou didst rise and give life to the world, whereat the heavenly powers cried aloud to thee, Giver of Life, Glory, O Christ, to thine uprising! Glory to thy rule! Glory to thine ordering of all things, only Lover of mankind!

A corresponding Wesley text is the "Hymn for Easter-day" from *Hymns and Sacred Poems* (1739), in which the third stanza unites the images of the stone, the seal, and the watch ("proofs" of the resurrection since they confirmed the body to be untouched) likewise found in the *troparion*:

"Christ the Lord is ris'n to Day,"
Sons of men and angels say,
Raise your joys and triumphs high,
Sing ye heav'ns, and earth reply.

Love's redeeming work is done,
Fought the fight, the battle won,
Lo! our Sun's eclipse is o'er,
Lo! He sets in blood no more.

Vain the stone, the watch, the seal;
Christ has burst the gates of hell!
Death in vain forbids his rise:
Christ has open'd Paradise!

...

Hail, the Lord of earth and heav'n!
Praise to Thee by both be giv'n:
Thee we greet triumphant now;
Hail the Resurrection Thou!

King of Glory, Soul of Bliss,
Everlasting life is this,

Thee to know, thy pow'r to prove,
Thus to sing, and thus to love!

Another text from *Hymns for Our Lord's Resurrection* (1746) keeps the themes of the *troparion* and adds an emphasis on discipleship in response to the kerygma:

All ye that seek the Lord who died,
Your God for sinners crucified,
Prevent the earliest dawn, and come
To worship at his sacred tomb.

. . .

An Earthquake hath the cavern shook,
And burst the door, and rent the rock,
The Lord hath sent his angel down,
And he hath roll'd away the stone.

. . .

The Lord of Life is ris'n indeed,
To death deliver'd in your stead;
His rise proclaims your sins forgiven,
And shews the living way to heaven.

Haste then, ye souls that first believe,
Who dare the Gospel-Word receive,
Your faith with joyful hearts confess,
Be bold, be Jesus' witnesses.

Some Wesley hymn texts bear some likeness to *troparia* that are part of the ordinary in the Divine Liturgy. The Trisagion ("Holy God, Holy Mighty, Holy Immortal, have mercy on us") and *Ho Monogenes Huios* ("Only-begotten Son")[18] may be connected with various Wesleyan trinitarian hymns published in *Gloria Patri, &c. or Hymns to the Trinity* (1746), *Hymns on the Trinity* (1767), and scattered throughout the rest of the hymn corpus. A surprising similarity is found between a stanza in one of the Wesleyan Eucharistic hymns and the Cherubic Hymn sung as part of the Great Entrance. Although today it is not recognized as such, the *Cherubikon* in its earliest stages was a *troparion*:[19]

Let us, who mystically represent the Cherubim, and sing the thrice-holy hymn to the life-creating Trinity, now set aside all earthly cares.

That we may we welcome the King of all, invisibly escorted by angelic hosts. Alleluia, Alleluia, Alleluia.

While the fifth stanza of Hymn 98 ("Where Shall This Memorial End?") from the *Hymns on the Lord's Supper* (1745) does not identify the worshippers with the cherubim, it does associate the angelic host with the Supper in an allusion not found in scripture or in the Anglican liturgy:

Lo, He comes triumphant down,
Seated on his great white throne!
Cherubs bear it on their wings,
Shouting bear the King of Kings.

The resemblance of selected Wesley hymns to Orthodox *troparia* comes also, in part, because both forms share certain hermeneutical principles in interpreting Old Testament texts. Both read the story of the old covenant through the lens of the new, an approach which invites a typological use of Old Testament events and figures. The common hermeneutic is evident, for example, by looking at how the narrative describing Moses's call at the burning bush is appropriated: the focus for both is on the bush that burns but is unconsumed. An Orthodox interpretation, taken from a Vespers *theotokion-dogmatikon* (a *troparion* that expounds the divine maternity, here tone two), equates the bush with the ever-virgin *Theotokos*:

> At the coming of grace, the shadow that is the law passed away. Just as the bush that burned was not consumed, so hast thou, O Virgin, given birth and Virgin remained. Gone was the pillar of fire, and lo, in its stead, the Sun of Righteousness shone forth. Behold, instead of Moses, Christ, the salvation of our souls.

Charles Wesley, in his single stanza reflection on Exodus 3:2 in *Short Hymns on Select Passages of the Holy Scriptures*, sees in Moses's encounter the church created and kept safe by the eternal Son—a perspective doubtlessly consistent with Orthodox theology:

See here the miracle renew'd,
A bush that doth the fire abide,
A burning bush, bedew'd with blood,
A church, preserv'd in *Jesu's* side!

Placement in the Liturgy

Despite the considerable differences in structure, constituent actions, and ethos evident when comparing Orthodox and Methodist liturgies, there are striking similarities between the two in the musical realm. Singing, whether by the people, a choir, a soloist, or the clergy (the latter occurs only rarely in Methodist practice), constitutes a significant proportion of the liturgy and is regarded as an essential component thereof. Hymns or *troparia* are part of the ordinary; sung propers for the day are selected as prescribed or chosen. Nineteenth-century Methodists would often frame their liturgy as a "hymn sandwich" in which hymns picked to fit the occasion opened and closed the service. British Methodists during the first half of the twentieth century understood hymns to be an integral part of the ordinary, with the placement of what were typically five hymns in effect determining the shape of the entire *ordo*.[20] Although Methodists have not observed a daily office in a manner equivalent to the Orthodox, Methodist private and family worship, at least historically, included the singing of hymns.

Both *troparia* and hymns enable the dialogue that is the church's encounter with God; the dialogical aspect of prayer and praise is realized in singing: God calls and the community of faith responds with life and breath. In Orthodox practice, alternating, antiphonal, and responsorial styles actualize the dialogue. For Methodists and Orthodox, the location of the sung text in the sequence of the liturgy, along with the theological intention of the text, helps to determine the nature of the dialogue: whether it be doxology or acclamation, supplication or intercession.

Overall, Orthodox and Methodists employ similar kinds of hymns in their worship. In addition to songs articulating doxology and devotion, both ecclesial communities sing texts intended for dogmatic instruction, as well as those that recount historical events or extol the virtues of the moral life. Growth in holiness is a regular theme in the Wesley hymns; *troparia* that encourage contemplation on the mysteries are found in the Orthodox repertoire. Although Methodists employ hymns that comment on the liturgical action (particularly in regard to the sacraments), this category is more frequently found in the Orthodox liturgy, as, for example, with the previously mentioned *Cherubikon* in the Entrance rite and with the *troparion Phos hilaron* ("O Gladsome Light"), the use of which in the evening office at the lighting of the lamps is already attested by St. Basil.

A Shared Appreciation for Christian Song

Christian song is the comprehensively mental and physical counterpart to doctrine, and singing itself is a form of worship. The dynamic quality of singing helps to shape belief by instructing in the faith, inviting participation, evoking memories, and encouraging sanctification and holiness. These characteristics are not unique to singing, for they are also functions of the icon.[21] Liturgical song is thus perhaps an "auditory icon." This claim may be supported by evidence of the colorful descriptions and metaphors that decorate the *troparia* and the Wesley hymns. Sung texts can impress an image on the mind and heart as do the visual arts. The *troparion* from the *Menaion* for the feast of the great martyr Katharine readily paints a mental picture as the words are sung:

> O wise one, thou with virtues, as with rays of the sun, hast shone on them that had not faith, and, as a most bright moon, hast driven away darkness from them that walk in the night of unbelief; and thou, God-chosen Virgin, blessed Katharine, art assured of royalty and invested with martyrdom. Thou, with desire, art risen unto Christ, thy glorious Spouse, into the heavenly bridechamber, and by him art crowned with a royal crown; and with Angels thou standest before him, praying for us who keep thine honored memory.

The singing and hearing of texts such as these have an anamnestic quality: they evoke the past event into the realities of the present. Within the Wesley corpus, nowhere is the "visual" and the anamnestic better expressed than in the second stanza of the hymn "God of Unexampled Grace" in the *Hymns on the Lord's Supper*:

Endless scenes of wonder rise
　　With that mysterious tree,
Crucified before our eyes
　　Where we our Maker see:
Jesus, Lord, what hast Thou done!
　　Publish we the death divine,
Stop, and gaze, and fall, and own
　　Was never love like thine!

For Methodists and Orthodox, singing is understood to be a holistic experience. The physiological mechanisms required for singing engage the entire person and permit the embodiment of belief—a person takes in the gospel message and becomes that message. Hymns may be identified as a channel or means of grace, imparting the knowledge and love of God, but also the experience of God.

Both communities give prominent place to eschatological themes in texts that are sung while at the same time recognizing the eschatological character of singing itself. The new songs to be sung to the Lamb by the heavenly choir composed of the faithful from the East and West are anticipated in the contemporary liturgy. Singing is also regarded as a collaborative event between those on earth and those above, whereby saints from every generation join with the angels to sing. There is no competition between the singers, for the song is the same. So concludes St. John Chrysostom:

> O wonderful gifts of Christ! Above, the hosts of angels sing glory; down below in the churches, choirs of mortals imitate their doxology. Above, the seraphim shout the thrice-holy hymn; below, a multitude of mortals sends up the same thing. So there is a common solemn assembly between the denizens of heaven and earth: one thanksgiving, one exultation, one joyful choir.[22]

Charles Wesley agrees:[23]

Vyeing with that happy quire
　　Who chaunt thy praise above,
We on eagles wings aspire,
　　The wings of faith and love:
Thee they sing with glory crown'd,
　　We extol the slaughter'd Lamb,
Lower if our voices sound
　　The subject is the same.

The shared appreciation for Christian song may provide the impetus for continuing conversations between Methodists and Orthodox. Although the tonal systems of the music and the styles of musical performance may differ, the texts respectively employed demonstrate and express the "integral unity between faith and prayer, between doctrine and doxology, between proclamation and praise." Despite the mutual strangeness of their liturgies, the intention behind the employment of the Wesley hymns in Methodist worship or the *troparia* in the Orthodox rites is the same: the glorification of the triune, eternal God and the sanctification of humanity.

Father, God, thy Love we praise,
Which gave thy Son to die,
Jesus full of truth and grace
Alike we glorify,
Spirit, Comforter Divine,
Praise by all to Thee be given,
'Till we in full chorus join,
And earth is turn'd to heaven.[24]

Endnotes

1"Orthodox and Methodists" (Lake Junaluska, NC: World Methodist Council, n.d.), n.p.

2For a discussion of *lex credendi,* see Karen B. Westerfield Tucker, "*Lex credendi, lex canendi:* Noting the Faith of the Church," in *Ecumenical Theology in Worship, Doctrine, and Life: Essays Presented to Geoffrey Wainwright on His Sixtieth Birthday,* ed. David S. Cunningham, Ralph Del College, and Lucas Lamadrid (New York: Oxford University Press, 1999), 40–54.

3William Cave, *Primitive Christianity: Or, the Religion of the Ancient Christians in the First Ages of the Gospel,* 5th ed. (London: printed for R. Chiswel, 1698), part 1, cp. 9, 184–185.

4Peter King, *An Enquiry into the Constitution, Discipline, Unity, and Worship of the Primitive Church* (London: printed for J. Wyat at the Rose, and R. Robinson at the Golden-Lyon, 1713), part II.1.7–8, 10–11.

5Claude Fleury, *An Historical Account of the Manners and Behaviour of the Christians: And the Practices of Christianity throughout the Several Ages of the Church* (London: printed for Thomas Leigh, 1698), 207. John Wesley retranslated and published only the pre-Constantinian sections of Fleury's *Moeurs des Chrétiens.*

6Journal, 22 October 1768, *The Works of John Wesley,* vol. 22, eds. W. Reginald Ward and Richard P. Heitzenrater (Nashville: Abingdon, 1993), 161n. 99, 162; cf. "Thoughts on the Power of Music," *The Works of John Wesley,* vol. 7, ed. Franz Hildebrandt and Oliver A. Beckerlegge (Nashville: Abingdon, 1983), 769 (section 12).

7"Letter to a Friend," 20 September 1757, *The Works of John Wesley*, vol. 13, ed. T. Jackson (London: Wesleyan Methodist Book Room, 1872; repr. Grand Rapids: Baker, 1978), 217.

8Preface, *A Collection of Hymns for the Use of the People Called Methodists, The Works of John Wesley,* 7:75.

9"Directions for Singing, 1761," *The Works of John Wesley,* 7:765.

10On the early church's preference for the practice of *una voca dicentes,* see Johannes Quasten, *Music and Worship in Pagan and Christian Antiquity,* trans. Boniface Ramsey (Washington, D.C.: National Association of Pastoral Musicians, 1983), 66–72.

11Egon Wellesz, *A History of Byzantine Music and Hymnography* (Oxford: Clarendon, 1961), 366.

12For evidence of both cathedral and monastic antiphonal singing, see Basil, Epistola CCVII, 3, PG 32, 765, and selected passages in *Itinerarium Egeriae.*

13Juan Mateos, *La celebration de la parole dans la liturgie Byzantine,* Orientalia Christiana Analecta, 191 (Rome: Pontificum Institutum Studiorum Orientalium, 1971), 7–26.

14J. R. Watson, *The English Hymn: A Critical and Historical Study* (Oxford: Clarendon, 1997), 222. Also on the English hymn see the classical study by Louis F. Benson, *The English Hymn: Its Development and Use in Worship* (New York: George H. Doran, 1915; repr., Richmond: John Knox, 1962), 54.

15Frank Baker, *Charles Wesley's Verse* (London: Epworth, 1964), 54.

16In 1753, George Whitefield altered this line to the now more familiar "Hark! the herald angels sing."

17Dimitri Conomos, *Byzantine Hymnography and Byzantine Chant* (Brookline, MA: Hellenic College Press, 1984), 14.

18"Only-begotten Son and Word of God, who art immortal and who didst deign, for our salvation, to be incarnate of the Holy Theotokos and ever-Virgin Mary, and without change didst become man, and wast crucified for us, O Christ, our God, who by death didst vanquish death; who art one of the Holy Trinity, and art glorified together with the Father and the Holy Spirit: Save us." Authorship of this text is generally ascribed to Justinian I (527–565).

[19]Robert F. Taft, *The Great Entrance: A History of the Transfer of Gifts and Other Preanaphoral Rites of the Liturgy of St. John Chrysostom*, 2nd ed., *Orientalia Christiana Analecta*, 200 (Rome: Pontificium Institutum Studiorum Orientalium, 1978), 83–98.

[20]A. Raymond George, "From *The Sunday Service* to 'The Sunday Service': Sunday Morning Worship in British Methodism," in Karen B. Westerfield Tucker, ed., *The Sunday Service of the Methodists: Twentieth-Century Worship in Worldwide Methodism* (Nashville: Kingswood, 1996), 35–36.

[21]See Constantine Cavarnos, *Orthodox Iconography* (Belmont, MA: Institute for Byzantine and Modern Greek Studies, 1977), 30–34; and his essay "Knowing God through Icons and Hymns," *Greek Orthodox Theological Review* 23 (Fall/Winter, 1978): 282–98.

[22]John Chrysostom, Homilia 1 in *Oziam seu de Seraphinis*, 1; PG 56, 97.

[23]The third stanza of the "Preface" hymn "Meet and Right It Is to Sing," *Hymns and Sacred Poems* (London: William Strahan, 1749); the hymn is listed as number 14 in the section of "Hymns for the Watch-Night."

[24]The fourth stanza of "Meet and Right It Is to Sing."

19

The Transfiguration Liturgy in the Orthodox Church

Thomas Hopko

"The Transfiguration of our Lord and God and Savior Jesus Christ"[1] is celebrated liturgically on August 6.[2] In churches of the Byzantine tradition, the festival begins with a pre-feast celebration on August 5.[3] It concludes with a festal "leave-taking" (*apodosis*) on August 13.

Vespers inaugurates the liturgical day. On great church festivals like Transfiguration, monastery churches will sometimes serve two Vespers services, a Small Vespers before a modest meal, and a Great Vespers to begin an all-night vigil. On great feasts in parish churches, Small Vespers is generally not served. Great Vespers is served alone or (especially in the Great Russian tradition) as part of a vigil service with Matins and the First Hour.[4]

Vespers always begins with a call to worship followed by Psalm 104[5] and the Great Litany. A set of psalms (*kathisma*) is then appointed to be read, which in non-monastic churches is usually shortened or omitted.[6]

Psalm 141 is always sung at Vespers with the incensing of the entire church:

> Lord I have cried to You, hear me; hear me, O Lord . . . attend to the voice of my prayer when I call upon You. Let my prayer arise in Your sight as incense, and let the lifting up of my hands be an evening sacrifice . . ."

With this psalm (and the appended Psalm 130), special hymns or verses (*stikheroi*) are chanted for the given liturgical occasion. On August 5, in addition to verses for the martyr Eusigius, hymns for the pre-feast of Christ's transfiguration are sung. On the feast itself, these hymns are exclusively for the Transfiguration. On the seven post-feast days (which, with the feast, comprise the festal *octave*), Transfiguration hymns are sung together with other verses assigned for the day's specific liturgical commemoration.

The ancient evening hymn "Gladsome Light" (*Phos Hilaron*) is sung at every Byzantine Vespers. On festal days, like Transfiguration, it is introduced by a procession into the sanctuary with the offering of incense.[7] It is followed by psalm verses (*prokeimena*) appointed for each day of the week. On major feasts, such as Transfiguration, there are three biblical readings at this point. Except for feasts of Christ's apostles, when the readings are from New Testament epistles, these lections are from the Old Testament.

The prayer "Count us worthy, Lord, to pass this evening without sin" is always read, preceeded by a litany of supplication on festal days (which litany is placed at the end of the service on ordinary days). The usual evening litany always follows, with the giving of peace and a prayer with the bowing of heads.

On great feasts, such as Transfiguration, special hymns and intercessory prayers (*lity*) are chanted at this point. The service then goes on with more hymns and psalm verses (*apostikha*) for the given day. On August 5, these hymns (as earlier in the service) are for the martyr Eusigius and the pre-feast of Transfiguration. On August 6, they are exclusively for Transfiguration. During the seven days of the post-feast, Transfiguration hymns are combined with those appointed for each day's particular liturgical commemoration.

Following this set of hymns, the *Nunc Dimittis* is chanted with the *Trisagion Prayers.*[8] The central hymn (or hymns) of the day (*troparion* or a*polytikion*) is then solemnly sung, together with a song in honor of Christ's mother Mary (*theotokion*). On great festivals, such as Transfiguration, this major hymn (*troparion*) is sung three times with the offering of incense around the festal icon that stands in the middle of the church. The presiding bishop or presbyter then blesses five loaves of bread, with wheat, wine, and oil.[9] Vespers concludes with the appointed dismissal and benediction.[10]

Matins always begins with the Trisagion prayers, an exclamation of "glory to the holy, consubstantial and life-creating Trinity" and the angelic doxology from Luke's Gospel ("Glory to God in the highest and on earth peace, good will among men") with verse 15 from Psalm 51 ("Lord, open my lips and my mouth shall declare Your praise").[11] At every Matins, the same six morning psalms are read (3, 38, 63, 88, 103, and 143). The Great Litany follows, with the chanting of selected verses from Psalm 118:

> God is the Lord and has revealed himself to us, blessed is he who comes in the name of the Lord. Give thanks unto the Lord for he is good, his mercy endures forever.
>
> All nations compassed me round about, but in the name of the Lord I cut them off.
>
> I shall not die but live, and recount the deeds of the Lord.
>
> The stone which the builders rejected has become the head of the corner, this is the Lord's doing and it is marvelous in our eyes.[12]

Then once again comes a solemn chanting of the main hymn or hymns (*troparia*) of the given day, followed (as at Vespers) by a lengthy set of psalms (*kathisma*) that is usually shortened or altogether omitted in non-monastic churches.

On great festal days, Psalm 136 (*polyelaion*) is then solemnly sung, with appointed psalm verses, followed by a Magnification Hymn (*megalynarion*) that is sung by the clergy and people before the festal icon, with a great incensing of the entire church.

A reading from the Gospel preceded by psalm verses is then chanted, and post-Gospel hymns are sung. Psalm 51 is read, followed by a long prayer asking the intercessions of many saints who are personally named. The matinal *Canon* follows, during which on great feasts such as Transfiguration, the faithful are anointed with the blessed oil and partake of the blessed bread and wine.

The *Canon* consists of eight odes based on the Old Testament canticles and the Song of Mary, each with several *troparia* on the themes of the day.[13] The second major hymn of the day (*kontakion*) is chanted after the sixth ode, after which comes an explanatory hymn called an *oikos*, and a reading about the saints or event of the day called a *synaxarion*. The *Magnificat* is chanted every day at Matins before the ninth ode of the canon, except on great feasts, such as Transfiguration, when it is replaced by special hymns with *theotokion* themes. This also is accompanied by a great incensing of the church. The two matinal canons that are sung on the feast of Christ's transfiguration in the Byzantine liturgy were written by Cosmas the Hymnographer and John of Damascus.[14]

On some major liturgical celebrations, the odes of the canon of an upcoming feast are added to those of the given day. This is done to prepare the faithful for the approaching feast.[15] Thus, for example, on the Veneration of the Cross on the third Sunday of Great Lent, the odes from the Paschal Canon are appointed to be sung, and on the Entry of the Theotokos to the Temple on November 21, the added odes are from the Canon of Christmas. This liturgical peculiarity also exists on the feast of Transfiguration, when the added ode to each of the festal odes is from the canon of the Exaltation of the Precious Cross, which is celebrated on September 13.

Following the canon, a small litany is chanted and a morning *Hymn of Light* is sung.[16] On festal days, this hymn incorporates the saints or event being celebrated. The *Praises* (Psalms 148, 149, and 150) are then read, with more hymns for the day. The Small Doxology is read on regular days, with the Great Doxology sung on great feasts, introduced with the exclamation, "Glory to You who has shown us the light." The Trisagion is read or sung. The *troparion* of the day is repeated. Litanies are intoned, followed by the dismissal and benediction.

At Vespers and Matins, prayers accompanying different parts of the service are to be read by the celebrant. These prayers are now usually all read silently during the reading of the opening psalm of Vespers and the reading of the six psalms at the beginning of Matins. Sometimes they are not read at all. In a few churches and monasteries today, they are read, either quietly or aloud, at the proper time in the service.

The First, Third, Sixth, and Ninth Hours have the Trisagion prayers (at beginning and end), three psalms, two short prayers, and the *troparion* and *kontakion* of the day. Each concludes with the prayer "Christ our God who at all times and in every hour in heaven and on earth is worshipped and glorified." Each Hour ends with a special prayer for the given Hour.

The Byzantine Divine Liturgy[17] has particular psalm verses for the day at the synaxis of the Word, with the singing of the day's *troparion* and *kontakion* at the entrance with the Gospel Book into the sanctuary.[18] The procession with the Gospel Book is completed with the singing of the Trisagion,[19] after which come the appointed psalm verses (*prokeimenon*), epistle reading, alleluia with incensing and psalm verses, and the reading from the Gospel.

On great feasts, such as Transfiguration, the ninth ode of the matinal canon is sung in place of the usual Theotokos Hymn at the Eucharistic *anaphora*. A selected psalm verse (*koinonikon*) is chanted during Holy Communion.[20]

On Transfiguration, "according to the tradition of the holy fathers" it is the custom to bless grapes and in some places other "first fruits of the vine" at the end of the Divine Liturgy.[21]

The Pre-Feast of Transfiguration

Typical of Byzantine liturgy, the hymns for the pre-feast of Transfiguration[22] on August 5, with their accompanying psalm verses, accomplish several purposes. They announce the coming festival. They invite the faithful to partake of the feast. They call everyone and everything to make ready. And they proclaim in advance the theological content and spiritual significance of the event to be celebrated.

Thus, for example, these hymns are sung at Vespers with the psalm "Lord, I have cried":

> Come, let us go with Jesus * ascending the holy mountain * there we will hear the voice of the Living God * the Father without origin * with the Divine Spirit witnessing in the splendid cloud * to His property of ever-existing Sonship * and with illumined mind * we shall behold light in light.[23]
>
> Come let us celebrate in anticipation * and let us purify ourselves * and faithfully prepare for the divine entrance into the most high dwelling of God * that we may become ourselves eye-witnesses of that same magnificence * and receive the glory which the chosen apostles were granted to behold * mystically on mount Tabor.
>
> Come let us go up to the mountain of the Lord * and into the house of our God * and let us behold the glory of His transfiguration * the glory of the only-begotten Son from the Father * let us receive light by light * and be caught up on high in spirit * singing forever to the Consubstantial Trinity.[24]

And a *kathisma* hymn from Matins:

> Prepare now, O Tabor * for behold Christ is coming * to show on you the splendor of divinity * to his glorious disciples as much as they could bear * Elijah and Moses stand by in fear * the cloud of light overshadows them * and a voice is heard from above from the Father of lights * "This is my beloved Son, listen to him."

And the main hymns of the pre-feast (*troparion* and *kontakion*), which are chanted at all of the liturgical services of the day:

> Let us the faithful joyfully anticipate Christ's transfiguration * solemnly celebrating the pre-feast with delight, * and let us cry aloud: * The day of divine gladness draws near * the Master ascends Mount Tabor * to shine forth the beauty of his divinity.
>
> Today human nature prepares to shine divinely * with the divine transfiguration * crying aloud with gladness: * Christ is transfigured, saving us all!

The theological and spiritual vision and instruction provided in the pre-feast hymns of Transfiguration are the same as those provided in the hymns of the feast itself. In addition to the hymns sung at the festal celebration, there are biblical readings and psalm verses that are not part of the pre-festal liturgy. I will attempt to summarize the major contents and themes of these readings and hymns, beginning with a word about the biblical texts that are used in the liturgical services.

Biblical Readings of Transfiguration

The first Bible readings at the liturgy of Transfiguration are the three Old Testament lections at Great Vespers.

The first reading is the account of Moses's reception of the Ten Commandments when he ascends Mount Sinai and enters the cloud, and the sight of God's glory is like a devouring fire upon the mountain (Exodus 24:12–18).

The second reading is the passage where Moses speaks with God "face to face, as a man speaks with his friend" in the "pillar of cloud at the door of the tent," while Joshua remains in the "tabernacle." Moses receives God's promise that he will go before him, but that Moses cannot behold God's face but can see only his "backparts" from the cleft of the rock while God's glory passes. God proclaims to Moses his name, which is "the Lord [*YHWH*] . . . merciful and gracious, longsuffering and abundant in grace and truth" (Exodus 33:11–23; 34:4–6, 8).

The third reading is about "the Word of the Lord" coming to Elijah on Mount Horeb, commanding him to "stand on the mountain before the Lord." And "the Lord passed by" the prophet on the mountain, but he was not to be found in the strong mighty wind, nor in the quaking of the earth, nor in the fire, but rather in the "still small voice." And the Lord tells Elijah to anoint Elisha in his place (2 Kings 19:3–9, 11–13, 15–16).

There are two Gospel readings for the feast of Transfiguration. At Matins, the Lukan account of Christ's transfiguration is read. At the Divine Liturgy, the lection is from Matthew's Gospel. As might be expected, the epistle reading at the liturgy is the reference to Christ's transfiguration that occurs in the Second Letter of Peter (1:10–19). The author speaks of being still "in the tabernacle," of "putting off the tabernacle" in his approaching "exodus," and of having made known "the power and coming of our Lord Jesus Christ" as one of the "eyewitnesses of His majesty."

> For when he received honor and glory from God the Father and the voice was borne to him by the Majestic Glory, "This is My Beloved Son, with whom I am well pleased," we heard this voice born from heaven, for we were with him on the holy mountain.[25]

Psalm Verses for Transfiguration

Psalm verses are used throughout the Transfiguration liturgy in a variety of ways. They are chanted between the hymns. They introduce the scripture readings. They are sung antiphonally at the synaxis of the Divine Liturgy with the refrains "Through the prayers of the Theotokos, O Savior, save us!" and "O Son of God transfigured on Mount Tabor, save us who sing to You: Alleluia!" Psalm verses are also chanted at Holy Communion.[26]

Countless references to psalms occur in the festal hymnody, mostly having to do with tabernacles and temples, hills and mountains, and power, glory, and light.

Psalm 89 names the traditional location of Christ's transfiguration, and perhaps originally provides the name. It surely provides the most-used psalm verses in the liturgical services of the feast:

> The heavens are yours, the earth also is yours; the world and all that is
> in it, you have founded them.
> Tabor and Hermon joyously praise your name. (89:12–13)

In the Greek usage, these lines join the vesperal hymns on both the pre-feast and the feast itself. They introduce the Gospel reading at Matins and are chanted with the festal *troparion* at the entrance with the Gospel Book at the Divine Liturgy.

In the Slavonic tradition, these lines are not used at the pre-feast Vespers, where we find:

> Mercy and truth have met together, righteousness and peace have kissed each other. (85:10)
>
> Blessed are the people who know the festal shout, who walk, O Lord, in the light of your countenance. (89:15)

Nor are they used at the entrance with the Gospel Book at the Eucharist, where we find:

> Oh send out your light and your truth; let them lead me, let them bring me to your holy hill and to your dwelling. (43:3)

The psalm verses used for the antiphons at the Divine Liturgy differ in the Greek and Slavonic service books. In both traditions, however, similar verses are sung with the festal refrains and the festal *troparion.* They include the lines noted above, which are also used in other places during the festal services, and others such as the following:

> O Lord, who shall abide in your tabernacle, and who shall dwell on your holy mountain? (15:1)
>
> Who shall ascend into the mountain of the Lord, or who shall stand in his holy place? (24:3)
>
> Great is the Lord and greatly to be praised, in the city of our God and on his holy mountain. (48:1)
>
> And He brought them to the mountain of his sanctuary, to the mountain which his right hand had won. (78:54)
>
> His foundations are in the holy mountains. (87:1)
>
> I will sing of your mercies forever, O Lord. (89:1)
>
> The heavens praise your wonders, O Lord, your truth in the church of your saints. (89:5)
>
> The mountains shall be joyful before the face of the Lord, for He is come to judge the earth. (97:8–9)

In all service books, the scripture readings at the Divine Liturgy of Transfiguration are introduced with the *prokeimenon* from Psalm 104:

> How manifold are your works, O Lord, in wisdom You have made them all. (104:24)
>
> Bless the Lord, O my soul; O Lord my God, You are very great! (104:1)

Psalm 104 may once have been chanted in its entirety at this point, as it continues with lines that are used elsewhere in the service, such as, "You are clothed with honor and majesty, You cover yourself with light as with a garment" (104:1–2).

The communion psalm verse (*koinonikon*) at the Divine Liturgy is the same in all texts of the service. It is again taken from Psalm 89 (which may have also been chanted in its entirety at this point in the liturgy) as the people partake of the Eucharistic gifts:

> We shall walk, O Lord, in the glory [or light] of your countenance, and in your name shall we rejoice all the day. (89:15–16)

Scriptural Allusions in the Transfiguration Hymnody

Virtually all liturgical hymns for the feast of Christ's transfiguration refer to the Transfiguration accounts in the Synoptic Gospels, to scriptural passages about Moses and Elijah in the Old Testament, and to biblical teachings (often in psalms) about God's indwelling among his people and his revelation in majesty and glory in tents, tabernacles, and temples, and on hills and high mountains. The festal icon standing in the middle of the church presents to the eyes of the faithful the scriptures that are referred to, quoted, commented on, embellished, and elaborated on in the festal hymnody.

In addition to references to the evangelical accounts of the Transfiguration, the liturgical hymns refer to other New Testament scriptures seen to be particularly relevant to the Transfiguration story. Allusions to texts abound that refer to Jesus as God's unique Son, the Holy One who is Chosen and Beloved, the one in whom God is well pleased. So do references to Jesus as God's incarnate Word who is himself "God," the one by whom all things came to be, in whom are life and light for humankind and the whole of creation; the one who being "in the form of God" is found in "human likeness" in "the form of a slave," humiliating and emptying himself to the shameful death on the cross through which he is exalted and glorified with "the name above every name" at the Father's right hand; the one through whom the Holy Spirit is given to persons made in God's image to transfigure their disfigured humanity; the one who will appear in glory at the end of the ages as Lord of the universe.

So also there are countless scriptural allusions in the festal hymnody in which Jesus is referred to as God's Son, through whom God has spoken in these last times; the Son "whom God has appointed the heir of all things, through whom also He created the ages"; he who is himself personally "the radiance of [God's] glory" and "the exact image of His nature [or person, *hypostasis*]"; the Son who is "the image of the invisible God," who is "before all things," in whom we behold "God's glory, glory as of the only Son from the Father," from whose "face" or "presence" (*prosopon*) shines "the knowledge of the light of the glory of God," who "alone has immortality and dwells in unapproachable light, whom no person has ever seen or can see." And, as may be expected, virtually every biblical passage referring to light is referred to in one way or another in the festal songs about the transfigured Christ, who is himself the "light which enlightens every man that was coming into the world" and "the light of the world" itself who comes forth from the "Father of lights."[27]

God's Glory in the Face of Christ

The central theme of the Byzantine liturgy of Transfiguration is surely that of God's divine glory shining in Christ and through Christ on the "chosen of the law and of grace," Moses and Elijah, and the leading apostles Peter, James, and John, and with them on the faithful participating in the feast, who "love to see and hear things past understanding," and who heed the call to ascend "from the earth to the highest contemplation of the virtues" to "be transformed this day into a better state" and to "direct our minds to heavenly things, being formed anew in piety according to the form of Christ."[28]

> Shining forth with the light of virtues * let us set foot on the holy mountain * that we may gaze upon the divine transfiguration of the Lord.[29]

The glory which shines forth in and from Christ on his chosen ones on the mountain and on the faithful at the liturgical feast is the same "glory of the Lord" (*doxa Kyriou / kabod YHWH*) manifested in God's mighty acts and majestic theophanies proclaimed and witnessed in the Old Testament scriptures.

> The glory that once overshadowed the tabernacle * and spoke with Your servant Moses, O Master * was a figure of Your transfiguration * that ineffably shone forth as lightning on Tabor.[30]

The theme of God's glory in Christ is central to the two major hymns of the day, the *troparion* and *kontakion*, that are sung (sometimes several times) at every service.

> You were transfigured on the mount, O Christ God * showing your glory to your disciples as far as they could bear it. * Let your everlasting light shine upon us sinners also * Through the prayers of the Theotokos * O Giver of light, glory to You! (*Troparion*)

> You were transfigured on the mountain, O Christ our God * and Your disciples beheld Your glory as far as they were able. * So that when they would behold You crucified * they might know that your suffering was voluntary * and might proclaim to the world * that You are truly the Radiance of the Father.[31] (*Kontakion*)

The theme of God's glory and power and light shining in and from the transfigured Christ before his crucifixion is repeated throughout the festival in countless ways.

> O Christ our God * who was transfigured in glory on Mount Tabor * showing Your disciples the splendor of Your divinity * enlighten us also with the light of your knowledge * and guide us in the path of your commandments * for You alone are good and the lover of mankind.[32]

> Come, let us ascend into the mountain of the Lord * even to the house of our God, and behold the glory of His transfiguration * glory as of the only-begotten Son of the

Father * Let us receive light from His light * and with uplifted spirits * let us sing forever the praises of the consubstantial Trinity."[33]

Light from Light

The theme of light, as we have seen and might well have expected, always accompanies the theme of glory in the Transfiguration hymns. Since light is always a matinal theme in Byzantine liturgy, as the faithful greet the rising of the sun in worship, this image is especially emphasized on the feast of Transfiguration.

> You parted the light from the original chaos * that Your works might celebrate You in light, O Christ, as their Creator * direct our ways in Your light.
>
> The seasons [Slavonic: mountains] bowed down before Your face * for at Your feet the sun laid its light * and its bright rays which fill the heavens * when You, O Christ, deigned to change your mortal form.
>
> When they saw You, O Christ the eternal Light * shining forth in the glory of the Father * the disciples cried out: * "Direct our paths in Your light."
>
> O Light that never sets * why have You cast me from Your Face? And why has the alien darkness covered me in my wretchedness? * But I beg You * cause me to return * and direct my paths towards the light of your commandments.[34]

The matinal *Hymn of Light* is sung solemnly three times:

> Today on Tabor in the manifestation of Your light, O Word * You who are the unchanged Light from the Light of the Unbegotten Father * we have seen the Father as Light and the Spirit as Light * guiding with light the whole of creation.

Transformation of Adam and All Creation

The transfiguration of the whole of creation, particularly the restoration of Adam's "original beauty" in the "splendor of the resurrection" is a constant theme of the festal hymnody. Christ comes and is transfigured "in the flesh" in order to transfigure Adam, the whole of humanity, and all of creation with God's divine glory and light.

> You formed the first Adam * O Compassionate Christ * and now You appeared from the Virgin as Second Adam * and by Your transfiguration on Tabor * You have shown him Your divinity.
>
> David, the ancestor of God * foreseeing in spirit the sojourn with humanity of the Only-begotten Son in the flesh * called creation to rejoice together with him * and prophetically lifted up his voice to cry: * "Tabor and Hermon shall rejoice in Your name!" * For having gone to the mount with Your disciples * You were transfigured, O Christ * and have made Adam's darkened image to shine again as lightning * transforming it into the glory and splendor of Your own divinity * Therefore we cry aloud to You: * O Lord and Creator of all, glory to You![35]

> You have put on Adam entire, O Christ * changing the nature grown dark in past times * You have filled it with glory and made it godlike * by the alteration of Your form.[36]

The theme of Adam's rejoicing with "all things" in their common transfiguration in Christ's "most pure flesh" is the message of the matinal Hymn of Magnification (*megalynarion*), sung solemnly several times with psalm verses following with the psalm of "many mercies" (*polyelaion*) before the proclamation of the Gospel according to Luke introduced by the psalm verse "The heavens are yours, the earth also is yours, the world and all that is in them" (Psalm 89:11):

> We magnify You, O Christ the Giver of life, and we venerate the all-glorious Transfiguration of Your most pure flesh.

The post-Gospel song is sung three times:

> Today all things are filled with joy, Christ is transfigured before the disciples.

Jesus Christ: God and Man

The Byzantine Transfiguration liturgy, as we have already seen in the hymns quoted, stresses Christ's perfect humanity and divinity. The festal hymnody affirms the doctrine of the "two natures" of God's only-begotten Son. It teaches the union without separation or division of Christ's manhood and Godhead, which are united without confusion and without essential change in the one person (*hypostasis* or *prosopon*) of Jesus.

> Now the unheard of has been heard * for the Son who came forth without a father from the virgin * receives glorious testimony from His Father's voice * that He is both God and man forevermore.

> Not by adoption have You become the beloved Son of the Most High * but You were such by essence before the world began * and without changing You came to dwell with us who cry to You: * "Blessed are You, O Lord our God, forevermore.[37]

> The Father, acknowledging Your natural sonship * called You His Son * We praise Him in song with You and the Spirit.[38]

> Being complete God * You have become complete man * bringing together manhood and the complete Godhead in Your Person * which Moses and Elijah saw on Mount Tabor in two natures.[39]

Repeated references in the festal hymns to Christ's mother as *Theotokos* is also a liturgical affirmation of Jesus's true divinity and humanity. Mary's child is God's Son and Word in and from whom God's divine glory shines. He is not a "mere man" to whom the *Logos* is joined, who is illumined, as it were, "from outside" like Moses on Mount Sinai. This theological and exegetical conviction perhaps provides the reason for the reference to "the prayers of the Theotokos" in the festal *troparion*. It is clearly affirmed in the ninth ode of the matinal canon, which is sung as the *Theotokos Hymn* at the festal Divine Liturgy.

Your birthgiving was without corruption * God came from your body * He appeared on earth wearing flesh * and made His dwelling [tabernacle] among humans * therefore we all magnify you, O Theotokos.

This doctrine of Christ's "two natures" in the "one person" born of Mary affirms the doctrine of the Holy Trinity that is proclaimed in a variety of ways in the Transfiguration liturgy. Jesus is witnessed as God's beloved Son by the voice of the Father, with the "over-shadowing cloud" symbolizing the presence of the Spirit.[40]

O unchanged Image of the One Who Is * O Seal that cannot be removed or altered * Son and Word * Wisdom and Arm * Right Hand and Strength of the Most High * We hymn You with the Father and the Spirit.[41]

Come and listen to me, O Ye peoples * going up into the holy and heavenly mountain * let us stand in spirit in the city of the living God * and let us gaze with our minds at the spiritual Godhead of the Father and the Spirit, shining forth in the Only-begotten Son.[42]

Moses and Elijah

Moses and Elijah are continually mentioned in the hymns. Being present at Christ's transfiguration on the mountain, they first of all testify that the glory now shining in and from Christ, which envelopes them and the three apostles who are the eyewitnesses of the event, is the exact same glory of God manifested to them during their earthly lives, as well as, in so many different ways on so many different occasions, in the Old Testament.[43]

In festal hymns, Moses and Elijah also have other symbolic functions. They represent the "elect of the law"; that is, all of the chosen people of the covenants before the final covenant in Christ. They also personify "the law and the prophets" which Christ came to fulfill, with Moses standing for the law and Elijah for the prophets. They also signify "the living and the dead," for Elijah was taken up alive into heaven in a fiery chariot to appear at the end of the ages with the coming of the messianic king, and Moses died and was buried outside the promised "land of the living." In this function, the two Old Testament figures demonstrate the "truth" that follows the "shadow" and "darkness,"[44] namely (as the festal hymns also often declare) that "Christ died and lived again, that he might be Lord both of the dead and of the living" (Romans 14:9). They also stand for "heaven and earth," with Elijah coming from heaven and Moses from the dust of the earth, to show that all power in heaven and on earth has been given to Jesus.

Moses and Elijah stood at Your side * for the law and the prophets minister to You as God.[45]

Talking with Christ * Moses and Elijah showed that He is Lord of both the living and the dead * the God who spoke of old through the law and the prophets.[46]

For You who are Lord of life and Master of death * called Moses and Elijah before You on Mount Tabor * to testify to Your divinity.[47]

> Because You are Master of heaven and Lord of earth * and have dominion over the things under the earth * there stood beside You, O Christ * the apostles from the earth, and Elijah the Tishbite as if from heaven * and Moses from the dead * singing with one accord: * O ye people, exalt Christ above all forever.[48]

Transfiguration and Crucifixion

The festal hymns also sing of the fact that according to Luke's Gospel, Christ spoke with Moses and Elijah in glory on the mountain about the "exodus" that he was to accomplish at Jerusalem.[49]

> Moses who in past times foresaw You in the fire of the burning bush * and Elijah who was taken up in a chariot of fire * were present on Tabor * and made known there Your exodus upon the Cross.[50]

> Calling Moses and Elijah to be witnesses of this exceeding grace * he made them sharers in His joy * foretelling His exodus through the Cross * and His saving Resurrection.[51]

The "exodus" at Jerusalem about which Christ speaks with Moses and Elijah is, of course, his death on the cross and his ascent into heaven to be glorified at the Father's right hand. It testifies to the crucial connection between Christ's transfiguration and crucifixion that is stressed throughout the festal services. It follows the Gospels in which the Transfiguration story comes immediately after the teaching that Jesus is the Christ who must suffer and die, and that his disciples must also "take up the cross" and endure shame and suffering with him.

Some icons of the Transfiguration include images of Peter and James and John ascending the mountain with Christ and then also descending again with him to his death. This witnesses to the Christian conviction that the world is redeemed not on Tabor, but on Golgotha, and that there can be no exaltation without humiliation, no glorification without degradation, no consolation without crucifixion, no *theosis* without *kenosis.*

The Incarnation in the flesh of God's Son, Word, and Image is for the sake of the passion. Human beings are not saved by the union of divinity and humanity in Christ's person. They are saved rather by the shameful death of the God-man on the tree of the cross outside the walls of Jerusalem. Jesus in the Transfiguration icon, with Elijah and Moses, is shown in glory within a *mandorla.* This indicates that the Transfiguration was not a "historical event" in the sense that it could have been seen by anyone around. It was a special revelation to the "pillars" capable of the glory, who would yet sleep in Gethsemane and flee at the passion before beholding the risen Christ and testifying to the Majestic Glory that he shares "in the flesh" with his divine Father forever. Thus the *kontakion* of the feast:

> You were transfigured on the mount, O Christ God * revealing Your glory to Your disciples as far as they could see it * so that when they would behold You crucified, they would know that your suffering is voluntary, and would proclaim to the world * that you are truly the Radiance of the Father.

And the first words of the first hymn at Vespers:

> Before Your crucifixion, O Lord * the mountain became as heaven * and a cloud spread itself out to form a tabernacle * When You were transfigured and the Father testified to You * Peter with James and John were there * who were to be present with You also at the time of Your betrayal * that having beheld the wonders * they should not be afraid before Your suffering * Grant in Your great mercy that we too may be counted worthy * to venerate these Your sufferings in peace.[52]

The second hymn says virtually the same thing, making the point that the disciples had to see "the splendor of the Resurrection" before Christ's passion:

> Before Your crucifixion, O Lord * taking the disciples to a high mountain * You were transfigured before them * . . . * Your desire it was to show them the splendor of Your Resurrection * Grant that we too in peace may be counted worthy of this splendor, O God.[53]

Christ's transfiguration before Peter, James, and John seems to be the liturgy's explanation for Jesus's saying that "some" who heard Peter's confession that he was the Christ, and heard him say that he must be betrayed and killed, would, as Luke's Gospel puts it, "not taste death before they see the kingdom of God."[54]

A most forceful liturgical testimony to the essential connection between Christ's transfiguration and his crucifixion is the singing of the odes of the canon of the Exaltation of the Precious Cross as the *katavasia* ode at the end of each of the festal odes at Matins.[55] Some Byzantine commentators even think that the feast of Transfiguration is kept on August 6 because it is exactly forty days before the Exaltation of the Cross on September 13.[56] Be that as it may, it is noteworthy that in some Christian traditions, Transfiguration is kept during the Great Lenten season before the Pascha of Christ, and that today the Second Sunday of Great Lent in the Byzantine tradition is dedicated to the memory of St. Gregory Palamas, whose theology and witness concerning knowledge of God in the uncreated light of God's divine glory is deeply bound to Christ's transfiguration and our human participation in it by faith and grace.

Blessing of Grapes and First Fruits

A peculiar feature of the Byzantine liturgy of Transfiguration is the blessing of grapes and, in some places, other "first fruits of the vine." This "tradition of the holy fathers" may also be connected to the date of the feast, since some see Transfiguration on August 6, with its mention of tabernacles and divine indwelling and the anticipation of the coming age of God's glory, as being a Christian version of the Old Testament feast of Tabernacles (*Sukkoth*).[57] The Gospels place the event during this feast. Peter, with his famous line, "Lord, it is good for us to be here," asks to build tabernacles for Christ and Moses and Elijah. The event also apparently witnesses to the "coming of God's kingdom" for the "pillars" who would not "taste of death" before witnessing Christ's kingdom "coming in power."

To my knowledge no Byzantine commentaries on the date of Transfiguration connect the feast to the Old Testament festival of Tabernacles. The custom of blessing grapes and other fruits, however, does seem to indicate a connection. The short prayers of blessing (which differ in the Greek and Slavonic books) recall the joy of the feast and join the offering and blessing of the new fruits, with thanksgiving and prayers for the forgiveness of sins, to the "sacred and holy Body and Blood of Christ," the "true Vine," with whom God is forever blessed with his "most holy, good and life-creating Spirit."

A Summary of the Feast

Vespers of the Byzantine feast of Transfiguration includes an extraordinarily long *lity* hymn, which may be the longest *stikhiron* in all of Byzantine liturgy. It includes virtually every aspect of the festal celebration. I offer it here as an epilogue to our reflections.

> Christ the Light that shone before the sun * who in the body went about the earth * having fulfilled before His Crucifixion * as befitting His divine majesty * all things pertaining to his divine dispensation [*oikonomia*] * this day has mystically made known upon Mount Tabor * the image of the Trinity. * For taking apart the three disciples He had expressly chosen * Peter, James and John * He led them into the mountain by themselves * and for a short time He concealed the flesh He had assumed * and was transfigured before them * making manifest the excellence of the original beauty * though not in complete perfection. * For while giving them full assurance He also spared them * lest perchance they should lose their lives at the sight * yet they saw as much as their bodily eyes were able to receive. * He likewise called before Him the chief prophets Moses and Elijah * who testified to His divinity * that He is indeed the true Radiance of the Father's hypostasis[58] * the Ruler of the living and the dead. * Wherefore a cloud covered them like a tent * and out of the cloud from above loudly sounded the voice of the Father: * "This is my beloved son, whom I have begotten without change from the womb before the morning star.[59] * I have sent Him to save those who are baptized in the name of the Father, Son and Holy Spirit * and who confess with faith that One Power of the Godhead is indivisible.* Listen to Him!" * And You Yourself, O Christ our God * supreme in goodness, who loves mankind * shine upon us with the light of Your glory that no person can approach and make us worthy to inherit Your never-ending Kingdom.[60]

Endnotes

[1]The official name of the feast in the Greek *Menaion.*

[2]On the date of August 6, see Peter Chamberas, *The Transfiguration of Jesus Christ* (in Greek) (Manchester, NH, 1999) 87–90; and Keetje Rozemond, "*Les Origenes de la fête de la Transfiguration,*" *Studia Patristica* 17, 591–593. Also the Byzantine *Festal Menaion* for August 6.

[3]The Byzantine liturgical offices are used by all Eastern Orthodox churches and by the Ukrainian, Ruthenian, and Arab Melkite Catholic churches of the Byzantine rite united with Rome.

[4]The *Menaion* has both Small Vespers and Great Vespers as two distinct services for the feast.

[5]Although the psalms in Byzantine worship are from the Septuagint, I give their numbering here according to standard English versions of the Bible. At vigils this evening, Psalm 104 is often sung solemnly, with repetition of certain verses sung as refrains, and the incensing of the entire church.

[6]The Psalter is divided into twenty sections, each of which is called a *kathisma.* Each *kathisma* is subdivided into three parts, each of which is called a *stasis.* These are appointed to be read at various services,

in various ways, during the liturgical year; e.g., the twenty sections comprising the entire Psalter are normally read through once a week at Vespers and Matins, beginning at Saturday evening Vespers. During Great Lent, these sections of the Psalter are increased and rearranged, being also added to the Hours.

[7]By "sanctuary" here I mean the altar area behind the icon screen.

[8]The Trisagion prayers are used at every liturgical service, sometimes more than once. They are also used in private devotion: "Holy God, Holy Mighty, Holy Immortal, have mercy on us! (3) Glory to the Father and to the Son and to the Holy Spirit, now and ever and unto ages of ages. Amen. Most-holy Trinity, have mercy on us. Lord cleanse our sins. Master, pardon our iniquities. Holy One, visit and heal our infirmities for Your Name's sake. Lord have mercy. (3) Glory . . . amen. Our Father, who art in heaven . . ."

[9]This rite of blessing and breaking bread and distributing it to the faithful (called *artoklasion*) has come in recent times to be used in ecumenical settings when full Eucharistic sharing is not permitted.

[10]If Matins is not served immediately, forming a vigil, the blessed bread and wine are distributed at the end of Vespers, with the anointing with oil.

[11]Byzantine Matins also has what is called a "royal" or "imperial" beginning with prayers and hymns for the civil authority. This royal beginning is often not done. It is never done when Matins is part of an "all-night vigil."

[12]During Great Lent, these psalm verses are replaced by the singing of *Alleuia* with verses from the biblical canticle of Isaiah. In Byzantine practice, the singing of *Alleluia* is increased during Great Lent and Holy Week.

[13]Canon odes are numbered, 1 and then 3 to 9. A number 2 exists only during Great Lent because this second ode is patterned on the penitential canon in Deuteronomy 32. The other odes pattern the Song of Moses in Exodus, and the songs of Hannah, Isaiah, Jonah, Habakkuk, the Three Youths, and Mary in Luke's Gospel. The *Magnificat* is sung daily, but omitted on great festivals. The *Benedictus* is also sung at certain times.

[14]St. John of Damascus (+749) also wrote the Easter canon and many other liturgical hymns, such as some sung at the Byzantine funeral service. I believe that Cosmas was John's adopted brother.

[15]Each of these added odes is called a *katavasia* because in churches with two choirs singing antiphonally from each side of the church building, both choirs "come down" from their places and sing the ode together in the midst of the church.

[16]In monasteries, the services may be regulated so that this hymn coincides with the rising of the sun at dawn.

[17]The Divine Liturgy of St. Basil the Great is celebrated in Byzantine churches on the five Sundays of Great Lent, Holy Thursday, and Holy Saturday before Pascha, the eves of Christmas and Theophany, and the Feast of St. Basil on January 1. At all other times, including Transfiguration, the Divine Liturgy of St. John Chrysostom is served. The "liturgy of the Word" is the same in both these services. The difference is the Eucharistic *anaphoras*, with that of St. Basil's liturgy being much longer.

[18]The actual psalms that are sung at the Divine Liturgy, with their order and refrains, vary among churches using the Byzantine rite. Different traditions, both Orthodox and Eastern Catholic, have different practices for this part of the Eucharistic gathering.

[19]On Pascha, Pentecost, Christmas, Theophany, and Lazarus Saturday (before Palm Sunday), the Trisagion is replaced at the Eucharistic Divine Liturgy with the solemn singing of Galatians 3:27: "For as many as have been baptized into Christ have put on Christ. Alleluia!"

[20]In some churches, the psalm from which the communion verse is taken is chanted in its entirety, with the selected communion verse being sung as a refrain to all of the other verses of the psalm.

[21]For greater detail and further explanation, see Kallistos Ware's "Orthodox Services and Their Structure," in *The Festal Menaion* (London: Faber and Faber, 1969), 38–80. This volume also contains a fine glossary of liturgical terms in Greek, Slavonic, and English.

[22]To my knowledge, no English translation exists of the liturgical office of the pre-feast of Transfiguration on August 5. Translations in this paper are my own, guided when possible by existing translations such as those found in *The Festal Menaion*, translated from the Greek by Mother Mary and Kallistos Ware, *loc. cit.*, and those used in the chapel at St. Vladimir's Seminary in Crestwood, NY, and at Holy Myrrhbearers Monastery in Otego, NY.

[23]The last words of the hymn refer to a psalm verse which is also part of the Byzantine version of the Great Doxology: "For with you is the fountain of life, and in Your light we shall see light" (Psalm 36:9).

[24]This hymn is also sung as a *lity* verse at Vespers on the feast itself.

[25]2 Peter 1:17–18.

[26]Except for the order of some hymns, the only notable difference between the Greek and Slavonic services for Transfiguration is in their respective use of psalm verses; e.g., different psalm lines are used to join the hymns at Vespers of the pre-feast, and different verses are used for the antiphons at the synaxis of the Divine Liturgy.

[27]See John 1, 12, 17; Philippians 2; Hebrews 1; Colossians 1; 2 Corinthians 3–4; 1 Timothy 6; James 1; etc.

[28]Pre-feast hymns on "Lord, I have cried."

[29]Pre-feast *apostikha* hymn.

[30]Ode 3 of the second canon at Matins.

[31]Jesus's being called "the radiance of the Father" is a confused reference to Hebrews 1:3, where God's Son is actually called "the express image of his nature [or person, *kharaktir tis hypostaseos autou*]" and "the radiance of his glory [*apaugasma tis doxis autou*]." The RSV changes the nouns of the sentence (radiance / *apaugasma*, and express image / *kharaktir*) into verb forms, making it difficult to see that this line is a direct, however confused, quotation of the apostolic letter.

[32]Vespers *lity* hymn.

[33]Vespers *lity* hymn sung also on the pre-feast.

[34]These all are from Ode 5 at Matins.

[35]These two hymns are from the post-feast Vespers of August 8.

[36]Ode 3 of the first canon at Matins. Note the reference here to Luke's version of the story, in which the word "alteration" is used rather than "transfiguration."

[37]These two hymns are from Ode 7 of the second canon at Matins.

[38]From a sessional hymn at Matins.

[39]Ode 3 of the second canon at Matins. Cf. also Ode 4 of the second canon at Matins.

[40]See Ode 6, second canon at Matins. The comparison of the Trinitarian epiphany at Jesus's transfiguration on Mount Tabor to the theophany of the Trinity at Jesus's baptism in the Jordan River is evident throughout the service.

[41]Ode 9 of the first canon at Matins.

[42]Ode 9 of the second canon at Matins.

[43]Cf. Vespers *lity* hymns, and Ode 8 of the first canon at Matins.

[44]Cf. Ode 2 of the second canon and Ode 6 of the second canon at Matins.

[45]From a sessional hymn at Matins.

[46]Vespers hymn for "Lord, I have cried."

[47]Ode 5 of the second canon at Matins.

[48]Ode 8 of the second canon at Matins.

[49]See Luke 9:31, where in the RSV the word "exodus" is translated "departure." In the *Festal Menaion* of Mother Mary and Bishop Kallistos, it is translated "decease."

[50]Ode 4 of the first canon at Matins.

[51]Vespers *apostikha.*

[52]First Vespers hymn on "Lord, I have cried," sung also at the post-feast Vespers on August 10.

[53]Second Vespers hymn on "Lord, I have cried."

[54]Luke 9:27. See also Matthew 16:28, which says "[before they see] the Son of Man coming with power in his kingdom," and Mark 9:1, which says "[before they see] that the kingdom of God has come with power."

[55]See above, p. 4.

[56]See Chamberas, *op. cit.*

[57]Rozemond sees the origin of August 6 as the date for Transfiguration as certainly connected to the feast of Tabernacles, which in the early Syrian liturgical books is called the Feast of Tabernacles on Mount Tabor and fits neatly into the calendar as a harvest festival. Cf. Rozemond, *op. cit.* Also Jean Danielou's *The Bible and the Liturgy.* It seems fitting that there should be a New Testament Christian Sukkoth, as there is a Christian Pascha, Pentecost, and Festival of Lights (Theophany).

[58]The author here again confuses the lines from the Letter to the Hebrews in which the Son is called "the express image of [the Father's] hypostasis" and "the radiance of his glory."

[59]A reference to Psalm 109:3 in the Septuagint.

[60]Vespers *lity* hymn.

20

The Transfiguration of Jesus in Wesleyan Exegesis and Application

Geoffrey Wainwright

In Orthodox understanding, the Transfiguration of Jesus on Mount Tabor is an explicitly trinitarian mystery. Thus the prayer at the blessing of an icon may be the same, whether the subject is the Three Visitors to Abraham, the Baptism of Jesus or his Transfiguration, or the Sending of the Holy Spirit at Pentecost:

> And as the Old Testament tells of your coming in the image of the three angels appearing to the most glorious patriarch Abraham, so in the New Testament in a voice the Father bestows grace on the Son in the flesh in the Jordan and the Holy Spirit appears in the likeness of a dove. And, again, the Son, who in the flesh ascended to heaven and sits at the right hand of God, sent down the Spirit of the Comforter on the apostles in the appearance of fiery tongues; and on Tabor the Father in a voice, the Holy Spirit in a cloud, and the Son in radiant light were revealed to the three disciples.[1]

In a Wesleyan understanding, the trinitarian signature is rather the watermark below the surface of an account that gives to the Transfiguration a christological focus, a soteriological purpose, and an eschatological reach.[2] It is a stage on the way whereby God the Son became what we are in order that we might, in the end, become by grace what Christ is by nature. The evidence for this Wesleyan interpretation comes in John Wesley's *Explanatory Notes upon the New Testament* at Matthew 17:1–9, Mark 9:2–10, Luke 9:28–36, and 2 Peter 1:16–18, and in corresponding places in Charles Wesley's *Short Hymns on Select Passages of the Holy Scriptures* and a few other hymnic texts.[3]

John Wesley's Exegesis

John Wesley's explanatory note on Matthew 17:2 relates what happened with Jesus on Mount Tabor thus:

> *And was transfigured*—Or transformed. The indwelling Deity darted out its rays through the veil of His flesh, and that with such transcendent splendour that He no longer bore the form of a servant. His face shone with divine majesty, like the sun in

its strength; and all His body was so irradiated by it, that His clothes could not conceal its glory, but became white and glittering as the very light with which He covered Himself as with a garment.

In his note on Mark 9:2, Wesley takes the Greek word *metemorphôthê* as the clue to the event on Mount Tabor, in that it locates the Transfiguration within the narrative sweep that is described in Philippians 2:5–11:

The Greek word seems to refer to "the form of God," and "the form of a servant," mentioned by St. Paul (Phil. 2:6–7); and may intimate that the divine rays, which the indwelling God let out on this occasion, made the glorious change from one of these forms into the other.

A closer look is thereby necessitated at Wesley's commentary on the crucial and paradoxical text of what modern scholarship has detected as a pre-Pauline hymn in Philippians 2:

Who, being in the essential *form*—The incommunicable nature. *Of God*—From eternity, as He was afterward in the form of man; real God, as real man. *Counted it no act of robbery*—That is the precise meaning of the words: no invasion of another's prerogative, but His own strict and unquestionable right. *To be equal with God*—The word here translated equal occurs in the adjective form five or six times in the New Testament (Matt. 20:12; Luke 6:34; John 5:18; Acts 11:17; Rev. 21:16). In all which places it expresses not a bare resemblance, but a real and proper *equality*. It here implies both the fullness and the supreme height of the Godhead; to which are opposed, He *emptied* and He *humbled himself*.

Yet—He was so far from tenaciously insisting upon, that He willingly relinquished, His claim. He was content to forgo the glories of the Creator, and to appear in the form of a creature; nay, to be made in the likeness of the fallen creatures; and not only to share the disgrace, but to suffer the punishment, due to the meanest and vilest among them. *He emptied himself*—Of that divine fullness, which He received again at His exaltation. Though He remained *full* (John 1:14), yet He appeared as if He had been *empty*; for He veiled His fullness from the sight of men and angels. Yea, He not only veiled, but in some sense renounced, the very glory He had before the world began. *Taking*—And by that very act emptying Himself. *The form of a servant*—The *form*, the *likeness*, the *fashion*, though not exactly the same, are yet nearly related to each other. *The form* expresses something absolute; the *likeness* refers to other things of the same kind; the *fashion* respects what appears to sight and sense. *Being made in the likeness of men*—A real man, like other men. Hereby He took *the form of a servant*.

And being found in fashion as a man—A common man, without any peculiar excellence or comeliness. *He humbled Himself*—To a still greater depth. *Becoming obedient*—To God, though equal with Him. *Even unto death*—The greatest instance both of humiliation and obedience. *Yea, the death of the cross*—Inflicted on few but servants or slaves.

Wherefore—Because of His voluntary humiliation and obedience. He humbled Himself; but *God hath exalted Him*—so recompensing His humiliation. *And hath*

> *given him*—So recompensing His emptying Himself. *A name which is above every name*—Dignity and majesty superior to every creature.
>
> *That every knee*—That divine honour might be paid in every possible manner by every creature. *Might bow*—Either in love or trembling. *Of those in heaven, earth, or under the earth*—That is, through the whole universe.
>
> *And every tongue*—Even of His enemies. *Confess that Jesus Christ is Lord*—Jehovah; not now "in the form of a servant," but enthroned *in the glory of the Father.*
>
> *Wherefore*—Having proposed Christ's example, he exhorts them to secure the salvation which Christ has purchased.[4]

Returning directly to the Transfiguration, we find in Wesley's very brief notes on the Lucan account this comment:

> *They saw his glory*: The very same expression in which it is described by St. John (1:14) and by St. Peter (2 Pet. 1:16).

Wesley's commentary on John 1:14 is important because of its declaration concerning the only Son, who, for our salvation, stooped to assume manhood; because of its recognition of the manifold nature of his glory, which was not limited to the dazzling; and because of its announcement of the benefits of participation in Christ:

> And the Word was made flesh, and tabernacled among us, (and we beheld his glory, the glory as of the only begotten of the Father,) full of grace and truth.
>
> *Flesh* sometimes signifies corrupt nature; sometimes, the body; sometimes, as here, the whole man. *We beheld his glory*—We His apostles, particularly Peter, James, and John (Luke 9:32). *Grace and truth*—We are all by nature liars and children of wrath, to whom both grace and truth are unknown. But we are made partakers of them when we are "accepted through the Beloved."
>
> The whole verse might be paraphrased thus: *And* in order to raise us to this dignity and happiness, *the* eternal *Word*, by a most amazing condescension, *was made flesh*, united Himself to our miserable nature, with all its innocent infirmities. *And* He did not make a transient visit, but *tabernacled among us* on earth, displaying his glory in a more eminent manner than ever of old in the tabernacle of Moses. *And we*, who are now recording these things, *beheld his glory* with so strict an attention, that we can testify it was in every respect such a glory as became the *only begotten of the Father.* For it shone forth not only in His transfiguration, and in His continual miracles, but in all His tempers, ministrations, and conduct through the whole series of His life. In all He appeared *full of grace and truth.* He was in Himself most benevolent and upright; made those ample discoveries of pardon to sinners which the Mosaic dispensation could not do; and really exhibited the most substantial blessings; whereas that was but "a shadow of good things to come."

In his comments on John 13:31–32, Wesley recognizes that there is also a glory of Christ which "belongs to His suffering in so holy and victorious a manner"—"His glorious work of redemption"; and on John 12:16 and 23, to "His ascension," his being "with the Father, and in the sight of every creature."

Finally, we note John Wesley's comments on 2 Peter 1:16–19. That "we were eyewitnesses of his majesty" is explained as referring to what Peter, James, and John saw at the Transfiguration of Jesus, "which was a specimen of His glory at the last day." The "display of His glorious majesty" and the voice of the Father heard from heaven were a confirmation of "the words of Moses, Isaiah, and all the prophets" concerning "the power and coming of our Lord Jesus Christ" which the apostles had made known. To that "word of prophecy"—which is "one and the same word, every way consistent with itself"—the addressees should now take heed; for whereas it had been "a lamp shining in a dark place," now the day had dawned with "the full light of the gospel," and the "morning star"—Jesus Christ (Rev. 22:16)—had arisen in their hearts ("be[en] revealed in you" [cf. Gal. 1:15]). The addressees should therefore "look for" and—by their "fervent prayers"—"hasten on the coming of the day of God," when they would "go in full triumph to glory," entering "the everlasting kingdom of our Lord and Saviour Jesus Christ" (cf. 2 Peter 3:12 and 1:11, and Wesley's comments thereon). The "precious and exceeding great promises" of God were that "having escaped the corruption which is in the world through desire [*epithumia*], ye may become partakers of the divine nature" (2 Peter 1:4), which Wesley glosses as "being renewed in the image of God, and having communion with him, so as to dwell in God and God in you."[5]

Charles Wesley's Application

Charles Wesley's hymns and poetry relating to the Transfiguration characteristically locate the event in its biblical context, both by virtue of Moses and Elijah's appearing with Jesus on the mountain and also in terms of the immediately neighboring episodes and sayings which contain Jesus's prediction of his passion and death, the promise of his resurrection, and his prophecy concerning the coming of the divine kingdom in power. The spiritual purpose of the hymns is to recognize and promote the inclusion of believers into the history of salvation, which the Scriptures narrate and announce. Charles Wesley seeks by his application of themes from the Transfiguration to encourage the faithful in the journey that can also be told in the Pauline language of, say, Colossians: Redeemed "by the blood of Christ's cross" and thereby "reconciled to God" (1:20, 22), human beings can by God's grace "put sin to death" (3:5) and enter upon a new life that is "hid with Christ in God" (3:3); in this they are being secretly "renewed after the image of their Creator" (3:10) and will one day openly "appear with Christ in glory" (3:4).

Reflecting on the Matthaean account of the Transfiguration, the poet Wesley allows Mount Tabor to summon up the Mount of Olives, the Hill of Calvary, and Zion's Mount. One verse plays on the paradoxes of glory and gloom, power and pain, that mark the life and work of the incarnate Son:

> His glory He on *Tabor* shows
> To none but the distinguished few,
> Design'd His agonizing throes
> On gloomy *Olivet* to view,
> To' adore Him in His power and pain,
> Eternal God, and mortal man.[6]

Whereas that verse refers only to the favored three disciples who, as a matter of history, witnessed the Transfiguration of Jesus in anticipation of his suffering and triumph, another verse appears to include present-day believers in the "us" for whom it is "good" (Matt. 17:4) to see Tabor's glory, "better still" to join Jesus in bearing the cross of Calvary (cf. Matt. 16:24), and "best of all" to rise as new creatures to eschatological Zion with the resurrected and ascended Lord (cf. Matt. 17:9; 26:64; 27:50–54; 28:9; Heb. 12:22–24):

Good for us, Thy joy to share,
And *Tabor's* glory see;
Better still, Thy cross to bear,
And bleed on *Calvary*;
Best of all, when nature dies
Echoing back Thy final groan,
Then to *Zion's* heights we rise,
And hail Thee on Thy throne![7]

As Wesley presents it, starting from Mark 9:1, it is by way of the cross that believers will themselves attain to the glory of which the Taborite experience gives a foretaste and glimpse:

Of every promised good our Lord
To man vouchsafes an earnest here,
And *Tabor* doth a glimpse afford
Of what on *Zion* shall appear,
A glimmering of that brightest day
When Jesus shall His power assume,
His glorious majesty display,
And robed in light, to judgment come.

Jesus, before He sheds His blood,
A foretaste of His glory gives,
Appears the true eternal God,
Our faith confirms, our hope revives:
That sweet anticipated sight
Takes off the scandal of His cross,
And arms our souls with love and might
And zeal to die in Jesus' cause.[8]

The sight of Christ's glorious body (Mark 9:3) inspires Wesley to draw the contrast between our present condition and our final destiny in language that derives also from 1 Corinthians 15:42–50:

The image of the earthy now,
The death we in our bodies bear,
And daily on His cross we bow,
The kingdom of our Lord to share;

The image of the heavenly Man,
Our bodies, spiritual as His,
In that sabbatic day shall gain
With fulness of immortal bliss.[9]

For that, the general resurrection is needed, and Wesley is this time inspired by Luke 9:32 and the awakening of Peter, James, and John:

When shall the happy moment come,
Which calls our dust out of the tomb
To see Thy glories shine?
Which doth our slumbering eyes unseal,
And all the mysteries reveal,
And all the truths Divine.

The world, and all we valued here,
Shall then an empty dream appear,
And vanish from our view,
While Thee triumphant on Thy throne,
We see surrounded with Thine own,
Creating all things new.

The fulness of the Deity
Even I shall then adore in Thee,
And on Thy beauties gaze,
Enjoy the pure eternal light,
And fall transported at the sight
In ecstasy of praise.[10]

The life of the resurrection can be anticipated even now, according to an invitatory hymn "describing the pleasantness of religion" (number 21 in the 1780 *A Collection of Hymns for the Use of the People Called Methodists*), whose sixth stanza reflects the Transfiguration stories (as well as Rev. 3:4f):

And God Himself our Father is,
And Jesus is our friend.

In Him we walk in white;
We in his image shine;
Our robes are robes of glorious light,
Our righteousness divine.[11]

Lest the nature of this surprising glory be misunderstood, a recently rediscovered poem of Charles Wesley hints that, christologically conceived, it will take the form of those virtues of selfless humility for the sake of which St. Paul invoked Christ's character and career in the passage from Philippians 2 on "the mind that was in Christ Jesus," which was treated earlier:

A faithful soul that ceaseless prays

The prayer of God, and sees his face
In Jesus Christ revealed,
Doth in his heavenly image shine,
Transfigur'd by the Spirit Divine,
And with his signet seal'd.

The glory which all thought transcends
Ev'n to his outward man extends;
The wisdom from above,
The image in his face is seen,
His simple, meek, and modest mien,
His innocence and love.[12]

Verses by Charles Wesley show sanctified souls surrounded by radiance on their deathbed. Thus, "On the Death of Mrs. Mary Horton":

The grace which saved our happy friend,
Which made her faithful to the end,
And decked her head with rays,
We shall for us sufficient prove,
And strive, in humble fear and love,
To perfect holiness.[13]

In the case of Mrs. Grace Bowen, "Christ, the object of her love, with glory gilds her final scene":

The sight [of Christ] her ravished spirit fires,
Her panting, dying breast inspires,
And fills her mouth with praise;
She owns the glorious earnest given,
The hidden life breaks out, and heaven
Resplendent in her face.[14]

As those texts indicate, the Christian life at every stage is made possible only by encounter with the living Lord, and other poems of Charles Wesley develop from the accounts of the Transfiguration some of the means and modes whereby that transformative encounter occurs along its course. Thus Christ is to be met in prayer and meditation on the Scriptures, wherein the Old Testament ("Moses" and "Elijah") is fulfilled in the New:

Who tastes the truth, and Jesus sees
In all the Scripture-mysteries,
The law and prophets' End,
Delights to meditate and pray,
Would gladly on the mountain stay,
And never more descend.[15]

Or again:

Who Moses and the prophets hear,
And Christ the Sum of all receive,
Transfigured shall with Christ appear,
With Him in light and glory live,
Obtain a never-fading crown,
Enraptured on their Saviour gaze,
For ever by His side sit down,
And talk with Jesus face to face.[16]

In a longer hymn, Charles Wesley picks up "This is My beloved Son: Hear Him" (Luke 9:35) and suggests that Christ's voice is now to be heard not only through evangelical preaching but also (unless my own hearing of the poet at this point is a little too keen) in the "mysteries" of baptism, communion, forgiveness, and healing:

Him, only Him we long to hear,
Creator of the listening ear,
Who comes in Moses' place,
Spirit and life and power imparts,
And speaks into our faithful hearts
The words of truth and grace.

He doth to us His mind declare,
By every gospel messenger
His will to sinners show;
To heathens poor He speaks His praise,
He speaks by all His mysteries,
His life and death below.

He speaks by benefits bestow'd;
We hear the language of His rod,
Who kindly doth reprove:
In trouble's storm He chides our fear,
And gives our flutter'd hearts to hear
The whispering voice of love.

His Spirit's small and quiet voice
Makes all our broken bones rejoice,
Our souls to health restores;
And then the saint renew'd by grace
Abhors himself, and hides his face,
And silently adores.[17]

Certainly, Charles Wesley was ready to exploit the fact that "Jesus came and touched them, and said, Arise, and be not afraid" (Matt. 17:7):

Jesus, extend Thine hand of grace
And let me feel Thee near;

Thy only touch my soul can raise,
Can banish all my fear:
Thy only touch shall make me clean,
My nature purify,
Expel the unbelieving sin,
And raise me to the sky.[18]

Ultimately, it is, as Charles Wesley prays in song, only the return of Christ that will bring us to the condition in which "the righteous shall shine forth as the sun in the kingdom of their Father" (Matt. 13:43):

Lord, we long to see Thy glory
Made eternally our own,
Long with all Thy saints to' adore Thee,
Bright as the meridian sun:
Come, Redeemer,
Rap us to Thy Father's throne!

In Thy Father's presence own us
Faithful witnesses of Thine,
Put Thy majesty upon us,
Let us in Thy lustre shine,
Bear Thine image
All immortal, all Divine.[19]

John Wesley draws the hortatory conclusions in prose, in his Sermon 146, "The One Thing Needful":

> Let us then labour to be made perfectly whole, to burst every bond in sunder [cf. Psalms 107:14; 116:14, *Book of Common Prayer* version]; to attain the fullest conquest over this body of death [cf. Rom. 7:24], the most entire renovation of our nature; knowing this, that when the Son of man shall send forth his angels to cast the double-minded into outer darkness, then shall the single of heart receive the one thing they sought, and shine forth as the sun in the kingdom of their Father![20]

Conclusions for Today

Dogmatically, the Wesleys view the Transfiguration of Jesus as an extraordinary manifestation of the identity of the Son of God incarnate, who did not forfeit his glory in condescending to the form of a slave for the sake of our redemption but rather displayed it in a paradox of humility that culminated in "the exodus that he would accomplish at Jerusalem" (Luke 9:33), the paschal mystery of his death and resurrection. In its quality as "a specimen of his glory at the last day," the Transfiguration of Jesus was both a testimony to his divine and cosmic status and an exemplary promise of their glorious destiny to those who find their life in him. Since John Wesley's *Explanatory Notes upon the New Testament* typically figure among the "doctrinal standards" in the constitutions of Methodist churches, Methodists are thereby helped to remain—in the areas (in this case) of christology, soteriology, and eschatology—within the classic Christian Tradition, whose supreme norm is the Holy Scriptures.[21]

Hermeneutically, John Wesley's annotations in connection with the Transfiguration show him allowing various strands in the New Testament witness—Synoptic, Johannine, Pauline, Petrine—to be mutually illuminating. Moreover, the biblical accounts of the Transfiguration receive, in Charles Wesley's verse, a meditative, moral, and mystical application by way of a "spiritual reading"—even if it has to be admitted, from a literary point of view, that these poems generally rank below his best work. In respect of both the interconnectedness of the Scriptures and their multiple senses, the Wesleys offer Methodists an example for continuing homiletical and devotional practice.[22]

Liturgically, the Book of Common Prayer in the Wesleys' day did not provide for a festal keeping of the Transfiguration on August 6, the date historically common to both East and West, and Methodists have inherited that lack. Methodist churches which have adopted the current three-year ecumenical lectionary now find the accounts from Matthew, Mark, and Luke appointed as the Gospel readings for the Sunday immediately before the start of Lent, and the designation Transfiguration Sunday has come into use. Although this is a novelty, it makes good calendrical sense to place the Transfiguration at the close of the Epiphany season, with Passiontide and Easter in prospect.[23] The appointed readings and the new designation may elevate the event of the Transfiguration and its significance in the awareness of Methodists.[24]

Visually, Methodism has developed no tradition of iconography. It might at least be asked whether the Transfiguration of Jesus could provide a place from which to start. It would offer a new line of sacred artists one of the best possible bases in Scripture, aided perhaps in their work by Wesleyan interpretations of the texts.

Meanwhile, hymns may continue to do double duty, acoustically and imaginatively, for Methodists. Fortunately, there is at least one Wesleyan hymn deriving from 2 Peter 1:16–19 whose quality has ensured it a place in many hymnals, both Methodist and other:

Christ, whose glory fills the skies,
    Christ, the true, the only Light,
Sun of Righteousness, arise,
    Triumph o'er the shades of night;
Day-spring from on high, be near;
Day-star, in my heart appear.

Dark and cheerless is the morn
    Unaccompanied by Thee;
Joyless is the day's return,
    Till Thy mercy's beams I see,
Till Thou inward light impart,
Glad my eyes, and warm my heart.

Visit then this soul of mine;
    Pierce the gloom of sin and grief;

Fill me, Radiancy divine;
  Scatter all my unbelief;
More and more Thyself display,
Shining to the perfect day.[25]

Endnotes

[1]*The Blessing of Ikons*, translated by Mother Thekla (Minneapolis: Light and Life, n.d.), n.p.

[2]For the Wesleys' undoubted trinitarianism, see the following pieces of mine: "Why Wesley Was a Trinitarian," in Geoffrey Wainwright, *Methodists in Dialogue* (Nashville: Abingdon/Kingswood, 1995), 261–74; "Wesley's Trinitarian Hermeneutics," *Wesleyan Theological Journal* 36 (2001): 7–30; "Trinitarian Theology and Wesleyan Holiness," *Orthodox and Wesleyan Spirituality*, ed. S T Kimbrough, Jr. (Crestwood, NY: St. Vladimir's Seminary Press, 2002), 59–80.

[3]John Wesley's *Explanatory Notes upon the New Testament* are accessible in a reprint edition from Epworth Press (London, 1976); in what follows, I will not give page numbers, since all citations are simply *ad loc.* For ease of reference, I will cite Charles Wesley's *Short Hymns on Select Passages of the Holy Scriptures* from *The Poetical Works of John and Charles Wesley*, ed. George Osborn, 13 vols. (London: Wesleyan-Methodist Conference Office, 1868–1872), henceforth cited as *Poetical Works* followed by volume and page numbers; I have in a few cases changed punctuation for the sake of making the syntax clearer to today's readers.

[4]In his study of the patristic interpretations of the Transfiguration, John A. McGuckin found only two authors who connected the radiant *metamorphôsis* on Mount Tabor with Christ's kenotic shift between the *morphē* of God and the *morphē* of a slave in Philippians 2, "where the form of God is laid aside for the assumption of the form of a slave before a definitive resolution, at the end of the hymn, in a glorious exaltation" (*The Transfiguration of Christ in Scripture and Tradition* [Lewiston, NY: Edwin Mellen, 1987], 111). McGuckin's two authors are Origen, *Commentary on St. Matthew* 12, 37 (PG 13:1068), and Anastasius of Antioch, *Homily on the Transfiguration* 4 (PG 89:1368).

[5]In his Sermon 16, "The Means of Grace," John Wesley appealed to 2 Peter 1:16–19 in support of his advice to "search the Scriptures" given to seekers after Christ: "Let all, therefore, who desire that day to dawn in their hearts, wait for it in 'searching the Scriptures.'" See *The Works of John Wesley* (Bicentennial Edition), vol. 1, ed. Albert C. Outler (Nashville: Abingdon, 1984), 388f.

[6]*Poetical Works* 10:304 (item 429, stanza 2). McGuckin, *op. cit.*, 115–16, lists various patristic writers who see the Transfiguration as preparing the disciples in view of Christ's impending passion: Cyril of Alexandria, *Homily on the Transfiguration* (PG 77:1012); Anastasius of Antioch, *Homily on the Transfiguration* 5 (PG 89:1369); Jerome, *Commentary on Matthew* 3, ad 16:28 (*Saint Jérôme: Commentaire sur Saint Matthieu, livres III–IV, Sources chrétiennes* 259, ed. E. Bonnard [Paris: Cerf, 1979], 26); Leo the Great, *Homily* 51, 3 (PL 54:310; and as Sermon 38 in *Léo le Grand: Sermons, tome III, Sources chrétiennes* 74, ed. R. Dolle [Paris: Cerf, 1961], 17). Orthodox commentators note that the liturgy looks forward from the feast of the Transfiguration to the feast of the Holy Cross, forty days later; see *The Festal Menaion*, translated from the original Greek by Mother Mary and Archimandrite Kallistos Ware (London: Faber and Faber, 1969), 483–495, especially in light of footnote 3 on page 483 ("The *katavasia* [concluding stanza] at the end of each canticle [at matins on the Transfiguration, August 6] is taken from the feast of the Exaltation of the Cross, 14 September, for which we now begin to prepare").

[7]*Poetical Works* 10:305 (item 432). In Orthodox great vespers on the feast of the Transfiguration, a euchological link is made between the favored three disciples and subsequent generations of Christians confronted by the passion, death, and resurrection of Christ (*Festal Menaion*, 470):

"When Thou wast transfigured and the Father testified unto Thee, Peter with James and John were there, who were to be present with Thee also at the time of Thy betrayal: that, having beheld Thy wonders, they should not be afraid before Thy suffering. Grant in Thy great mercy that we too may be counted worthy to venerate these Thy sufferings in peace.

"Before Thy Crucifixion, O Lord, taking the disciples up into a high mountain, Thou wast transfigured before them, shining upon them with the bright beams of Thy power: from love of mankind and in Thy sovereign might, Thy desire it was to show them the splendour of the Resurrection. Grant that we too in peace may be counted worthy of this splendour, O God, for Thou art merciful and lovest mankind."

[8] *Poetical Works* 11:20 (item 956, stanzas 1–2). A stanza with similar themes occurs also in connection with the Matthaean account; see *Poetical Works* 10:305 (item 430).

[9] *Poetical Works* 11:21 (item 958). For Christ as the restorer of humanity to the divine image, compare again a text from the great vespers of the Transfiguration: "[He] was transfigured today upon Mount Tabor before the disciples; and in His own person He showed them the nature of man, arrayed in the original beauty of the Image.... For having gone up, O Christ, with thy disciples into Mount Tabor, Thou wast transfigured, and hast made the nature that had grown dark in Adam to shine again as lightning, transforming it into the glory and splendour of Thine own divinity" (*Festal Menaion*, 476f).

[10] *Poetical Works* 11:184 (item 1329, stanzas 1–3).

[11] *Works* (Bicentennial Edition), vol. 7, ed. Franz Hildebrandt and Oliver A. Beckerlegge (Oxford: Clarendon, 1983), 106. Included here are lines 7–8 of stanza 5 and lines 1–4 of stanza 6.

[12] *The Unpublished Poetry of Charles Wesley*, vol. 2, ed. S T Kimbrough, Jr. and Oliver A. Beckerlegge (Nashville: Abingdon, 1990), 111. With Kimbrough, I have used lowercase initials throughout for the possessive "his." Whereas in the first stanza the reference is to God ("His face," "His heavenly image," "His signet"), in the second there seems to be a deliberate ambiguity or oscillation between Christ and the believer, who now resembles Christ in bearing the image of God.

[13] Thomas Jackson, *The Journal of the Rev. Charles Wesley, M.A.* (London: Mason, 1849; reprint, Grand Rapids: Baker, 1980), 2 vols., 2:417–18.

[14] Ibid., 2:326. A radiant scene is depicted in the hagiological painting by Marshall Claxton, R.A., "The Holy Triumph of John Wesley in His Dying" (1842), which is housed at Wesley's Chapel, City Road, London.

[15] *Poetical Works* 11:184 (item 1330).

[16] *Poetical Works* 11:21 (item 959). For the Transfiguration as an anticipation of the eternal vision of Christ and conversation with him in glory, compare the hymn at Orthodox matins on the feast of the Transfiguration: "Thou wast transfigured upon Mount Tabor, showing the exchange mortal men will make with Thy glory at Thy second and fearful coming, O Saviour. Elijah and Moses talked with Thee, and Thou hast called the three disciples to be with Thee. As they gazed upon Thy glory, O Master, they were struck with wonder at Thy blinding brightness. Do Thou who then hast shone upon them with Thy light, give light now to our souls" (*Festal Menaion*, 478).

[17] *Poetical Works* 11:185f. (item 1332, stanzas 1–4).

[18] *Poetical Works* 10:306 (item 434). In the next item also (435), the Savior is prayed "Apply Thine outstretch'd hand."

[19] *Poetical Works* 10:275–6 (item 347, stanzas 1–2). At Orthodox matins on the feast of the Transfiguration, the glorious vision of Christ's *parousia* is anticipated (*Festal Menaion*, 494):

"To show plainly how, at Thy mysterious second coming, Thou wilt appear as the Most High God standing in the midst of God [Psalm 81:1, Septuagint], on Mount Tabor Thou hast shone in fashion past words upon the apostles and upon Moses and Elijah. Therefore we all magnify Thee, O Christ.

"Come and hearken unto me, O ye peoples: going up into the holy and heavenly mountain, let us stand in Spirit in the city of the living God, and let us gaze with our minds at the spiritual Godhead of the Father and the Spirit, shining forth in the Only-begotten Son."

[20] *Works* (Bicentennial Edition), vol. 4., ed. Albert C. Outler (Nashville: Abingdon, 2004), 359.

[21] The christological focus, soteriological purpose, and eschatological reach found in the Wesleys' understanding match the three principal clusters of themes that John McGuckin (*op. cit.*, 99–128) finds in patristic treatments of the Transfiguration: (1) "theophany" or "the manifestation of Christ's essential deity," "the vision of Christ's radiance ... as a glory that did not come on him from without but rather proceeded out to his disciples from within" (125); (2) "soteriology" or "a prelude to the Passion," a "kind of strengthening sacrament for the apostles who were approaching the trials of the Passion" (115); (3) "ecclesiological eschatology" or "the Kingdom and the Parousia foreshadowed," a "revelation of what the resurrection will be like both for Christ (it is thus considered as an anticipation in his ministry of his paschal victory) and for his Church in the age to come" (123). Again, "The Fathers evidently pursue three concerns: the wonder of the event as a theophany, the power of the event as a salvific act of God, and the promise of the event as

a paradigm of the resurrection of Christ's saints. . . . The power which shone out from Jesus on the nucleus of his Church should be interpreted as his promise of Easter transfiguration for that Church universally"(125).

[22]These hermeneutical procedures of the Wesleys—dependent on what these days go by the names of "intertextuality" and "polysemy"—are, of course, entirely traditional. Treatment of the Scriptures as interconnected posits the unity of the Scriptures as the work of the Word and the Spirit, and the spiritual reading of the Scriptures according to their multiple senses takes the narrative of "what happened" (the *gesta*) as the basis for "what to believe" (*quid credas*), "what to do" (*quod agas*), and "where to head" (*quo tendas*).

[23]In the *Revised Common Lectionary* (1992), the Old Testament and Epistle readings to accompany the Gospel reading from Matthew are Exodus 24:12–18 (Moses, the cloud, and the fire on Mount Sinai) and 2 Peter 1:16–21; to accompany Mark, they are 2 Kings 2:1–12 (Elijah taken up in the chariot of fire) and 2 Corinthians 4:3–6 ("the glory of God in the face of Christ Jesus"); and to accompany Luke, they are Exodus 34:29–35 (the shining face of Moses) and 2 Corinthians 3:12–4:2 ("we all, with open face beholding as in a glass the glory of the Lord, are changed into the same image from glory to glory").

[24]In United Methodism, the unofficial Order of Saint Luke ("a religious order dedicated to sacramental and liturgical scholarship, education and practice," henceforth cited as OSL) has published under the title *And Also with You* a series of "worship resources based on the *Revised Common Lectionary*" for years A, B, and C, which provide for all Sundays, including "Transfiguration Sunday," a biblical greeting, a collect, a "general prayer for the day," and a list of suggested hymns. Similarly, the OSL's *Lift Up Your Hearts* supplies Eucharistic prayers based on the lectionary. Rather bland in tone and content, the one for the Transfiguration declares in its preface that "through Moses you revealed yourself and gave us the law; through Elijah you told of your desire for us"; and the post-sanctus reads, "Holy are you, and blessed is your Son Jesus Christ. You revealed his holy nature when he was transfigured before Peter and James and John." Is there, one may ask, any chance that contemporary Methodist worshipers could be caught up in the spirit of sheer adoration that breathes through the Orthodox offices of the Transfiguration—and indeed some of the Wesleyan hymns?

[25]The text first appeared in *Hymns and Sacred Poems* published under the brothers' joint name in 1740; it is printed in *Poetical Works* 1:224f. "Christ, Whose Glory Fills the Skies" has been a staple for the past two centuries in both Anglican and mainstream Methodist hymnals in both Britain and the United States; it figures on ecumenical lists and in the current hymn books of many English-speaking denominations throughout the world. Among more recent Transfiguration hymns from various sources may be mentioned Brian Wren's "Christ, upon the Mountain Peak" (no. 260 in *The United Methodist Hymnal* [1989], and in many other books, sometimes as "Jesus, on the Mountain Peak"); Timothy Dudley-Smith's "Our Savior Christ Once Knelt in Prayer" (no. 116 in *Hymns for Today's Church*, 1982); Christopher Idle's "When Jesus Led His Chosen Three" (no. 117 in the same); Thomas H. Troeger's "Swiftly Pass the Clouds of Glory" (no. 186 in *The Book of Praise* of the Presbyterian Church in Canada, 1997); and Carl P. Daw's "We Have Come at Christ's Own Bidding" (no. 187 in the same) and "Bright the Cloud and Bright the Glory" (no. 18 in *New Psalms and Hymns and Spiritual Songs*, 1995).